SOFTWARE
SYSTEMS ENGINEERING

WILEY SERIES IN SYSTEMS ENGINEERING

Andrew P. Sage

ANDREW P. SAGE AND JAMES D. PALMER
Software Systems Engineering

SOFTWARE SYSTEMS ENGINEERING

ANDREW P. SAGE
JAMES D. PALMER
School of Information Technology and Engineering
George Mason University
Fairfax, Virginia 22030

WILEY

A Wiley-Interscience Publication
JOHN WILEY & SONS
New York / Chichester / Brisbane / Toronto / Singapore

Library of Congress Cataloging-in-Publication Data:

Sage, Andrew P.
    Software systems engineering / Andrew P. Sage and James D. Palmer.
        p.   cm.— (Wiley series in system engineering)
    "A Wiley-Interscience publication."
    Includes bibliographical references.

        1. Software engineering.   2. Systems engineering.   I. Palmer,
    James D.   II. Title.   III. Series.

QA76.758.S24   1990
005.1— dc20   89-37350
ISBN 0-471-61758-X   CIP

To: LaVerne (APS) and
Margret (JDP)

Contents

Preface

This book is written for a first course in software engineering, particularly one that emphasizes *a systems engineering and systems management for software productivity* perspective. The book is reasonably self-contained. It is not a book specifically addressing programmer productivity concerns, although these are, in part, addressed in the book for the sake of completeness. It is focused primarily on a systems approach to lifecycle management of software production. The book discusses all the lifecycle phases of systems development. There is considerable discussion of such industrially relevant material as software quality, software reliability, development environments, integration, maintenance, management, and cost analysis.

We begin our efforts with an indication of why we necessarily associate the word "engineering" with software, as contrasted with the word "science." Then we indicate why the production of trustworthy software can be best accomplished through use of the approaches of "systems engineering." Following this, we present a brief discourse concerning various topics of interest and importance in software systems engineering. Throughout our presentations in this book, we are especially concerned with ways in which software productivity may be improved through use of the methods, design methodologies, and management approaches of systems engineering. The framework and outline that we develop in Chapter 1 provides a basis for the design of trustworthy software as well as a logical organization for this text.

Software engineering generally has given attention to the development of micro-level tools to address the growing needs to increase software productivity. The major thrust of this book is to outline a systems engineering approach to increasing software productivity that encompasses these micro-level tools. We also discuss the need for such macro-productivity tools as rapid prototyping, reusability constructs, knowledge-based systems for software development, and an interactive support system environment to aid in software development. Also, we are very concerned with systems management of all aspects of the software production process.

Thus, we are concerned with *software engineering in the small*, or program and programmer productivity; and *software engineering in the large*, or software systems engineering. We are concerned, in part, with the "tools" for software engineering that enable micro-enhancement and macro-enhancement of software quality. We are also concerned with an overarching *systems design methodology* that will enable selection of an appropriate set of software engineering tools. We are, in addition, interested in software engineering as a process, and thus we devote a considerable portion of our effort to the *systems management* of software.

Our effort in Chapter 2 begins with a discussion of lifecycle approaches to the systems engineering of software. We outline several variants that lead to phased development of software systems. Then we address the very important question of identification of the user or client requirements that a software system must satisfy. User requirements specification and software requirements specification will be the first phase of effort in our development of software, and we devote Chapter 3 to this topic. Following the initial determination of user requirements, these user or client requirements are transformed into computer software oriented requirements.

Micro-enhancement tools are important for productivity enhancement throughout the software development lifecycle. So, we next study micro-enhancement approaches for the various phases of a typical lifecycle for software development. Chapters 4 and 5 present a number of these approaches. We elaborate on the most widely used micro-enhancement approaches and, through a typical software acquisition lifecycle, establish the need for a taxonomy of methods in order to make productivity tools generally available and subject to greater use.

Chapters 6 and 7 discuss the latter portions of the software lifecycle. In particular, efforts that are concerned with reliability, maintainability, and quality assurance are studied in Chapter 6. Chapter 7 presents an overview of system integration, operational implementation, and software development environments. This is followed by a discussion (in Chapter 8) of macro-enhancement approaches to software productivity including prototyping, software reusability, and the use of expert system techniques to enhance the production of software.

The next two chapters of the book treat management, maintenance, and standards procedures for software productivity. Chapter 9 is concerned with systems management-related topics. Chapter 10 is concerned mainly with the development of models estimating cost and benefit for software development. The final chapter of the book presents a very carefully selected and annotated bibliography of pertinent references.

Thus, our book on software systems engineering provides an introductory, but reasonably complete, treatment of all aspects of the development lifecycle for software production. It is, therefore, suited for an introductory course in software engineering that emphasizes systems management of software production. It is also very appropriate for those who manage these efforts and who wish to have an overview of the programmer productivity approaches that are needed for software development.

Most introductory books on software engineering concentrate on programmer productivity. While we do not ignore this, we focus more on the macrolevel and systems management approaches that many believe offer much more promise for productivity enhancement than do approaches that rely only or primarily on enhancement of the efforts of individual programmers.

Many studies indicate that a very large percentage of system costs are expended on software. Usually, it is necessary to *maintain* new systems such that they are able to be continually responsive to changing user and environmental needs. In many systems, the larger part of maintenance monies are spent for software maintenance. A large number of difficulties both cause and emanate from the current lack of trustworthy and effective software that is produced at a reasonable price. These include: inconsistent, incomplete, and otherwise imperfect system requirements specifications; system requirements that do not provide for change as user needs evolve over time, and poorly defined management structures for product design and delivery. These lead to delivered products that are difficult to use, that do not solve the intended problem, that operate in an unreliable fashion, that are unmaintainable, and that—as a result—are not used. *And, the problem appears to be getting worse.*

These same studies generally reveal that the major problems associated with the production of trustworthy software are more concerned with the *organization and management of complexity* than with direct technological concerns that affect individual programmer productivity.

Since the critical areas associated with software productivity improvement are fundamentally systems engineering areas, we intentionally use the term "software systems engineering" to describe the general area of coverage for this book.

Individual chapters are devoted to the major efforts that need to be accomplished as part of the lifecycle of software development. A number of the major design methods are described in a stepwise, easy-to-understand fashion. References to the contemporary literature that provides more detailed discussions is a feature of the book. Many current-generation *computer-aided systems engineering* (CASE) tools are discussed throughout the book.

This is a textbook. It contains about 30% more material than can be covered in a rapidly paced three-semester-hour introductory graduate-level course. Through the use of a term paper and several projects, especially of a laboratory development nature, during the course, it provides sufficient material for a full-year course.

We have generally followed the sequenced pattern in the text from Chapters 1 through 10 in our own teaching efforts. For use in software engineering curricula where there are a number of succeeding courses on specialized topics, it may be desirable to omit coverage of some of the specialized topics that are discussed later.

We have had some experience in using this material for industrial short courses where participants were already experienced programmers who were generally familiar with the programming productivity content of Chapters 4 and 5. Omitting these two chapters led to no loss in continuity, especially because of the detailed overview of the book that is presented in Chapter 1.

The book is intended for use in an introductory graduate-level course in *software systems engineering.* The course is generally taken by many master's-level students in systems engineering who do not intend to undertake detailed study in software but who wish an overview of developments in this area. The courses on which the book is based has also been taken by computer science students who intend to specialize in one of the programmer produc-tivity areas. It has also been used for short courses offered for professional development.

Although there are no officially listed prerequisites for the course for which this text is written, it is by no means an introductory course. The students taking it are expected to be familiar either with computer programming and software design, or systems engineering, and preferably with both areas.

ANDREW P. SAGE
JAMES D. PALMER

Fairfax, Virginia
December 11, 1989

Acknowledgments

Many people contribute to a book other than the authors. Almost all of this book has been classroom tested at least twice. Many students have provided helpful suggestions. Ann Fields and Charlie Smith were very helpful with respect to their detailed reading of the final version of the text. Kathleen Johnson has assisted relative to some typing chores. George Telecki was always very supportive and understanding despite being told numerous times that the book was *in the mail*. The authors wives, LaVerne and Margret, were extraordinarily understanding of many late night and weekend sessions that the authors needed to spend with a word processor. We acknowledge the assistance and support of all these special people.

A.P.S.
J.D.P.

Chapter **1**

An Introduction to Software Systems Engineering

In this chapter we provide an overview of our efforts to follow in software systems engineering. We begin with an indication of why we necessarily associate the word "engineering" with software, as contrasted with the word science. Then we indicate why the production of trustworthy software can be best accomplished through use of the approaches of "systems engineering." Following this, we present a brief discourse concerning various topics of interest and importance in software systems engineering. Throughout our presentations in this book, we are especially concerned with ways in which software productivity may be improved through use of the methods, design methodologies, and management approaches of systems engineering. The framework and outline that we develop in this chapter provide a basis for the design of trustworthy software as well as a logical organization for this text.

There are a number of reasons why software productivity improvement studies and methods are of much importance at this time. The primary one is that the annual expenditures for software development are very large and the productivity not very high.

Software engineering generally has given attention to the development of microlevel tools to address the growing needs to increase software productivity. The major thrust of this book is to outline a systems engineering approach to increasing software productivity that encompasses these microlevel tools. We also discuss the need for such macro-productivity tools as rapid prototyping, reusability constructs, and an interactive support system environment that involves the systems engineer, the user, and the software engineer. Also, we are very concerned with systems management of all aspects of the software production process.

Thus, we are concerned with software engineering in the small, or program and programmer productivity; and software engineering in the large, or software systems engineering.

We are concerned, in part, with the "tools for software engineering" that enable micro-enhancement and macro-enhancement of software quality. We are also concerned with an overarching "systems design methodology" that will enable selection of an appropriate set of software engineering tools. We are, in addition, interested in software engineering as a process, and thus we devote a considerable portion of our effort to the "systems management" of software.

Our goal is to utilize this just described three-layer approach [Sage, 1982] to software systems engineering, as shown in Figure 1.1, in order to integrate together the technology for software production within an appropriate design approach that is matched to the organization and environment in which the software must function. From this perspective, software production becomes a systems engineering activity. It, like systems engineering, is then a management technology in that it involves technology, which is the organization and delivery science for the betterment of humankind, and management, which is the art and science of enabling an organization to function in an environment in such a way as to achieve objectives. Figure 1.2*a* illustrates this view of software systems engineering. Through use of this three-level approach to software engineering, we hope to provide and describe symbiotic relationships between individual members of a programming team to enable successful completion of projects that enable better performance of organizations in operational environments. Figure 1.2*b* indicates this symbiotic embedding with respect to people, and Figure 1.2*c* illustrates the embedding of software ingredients. Successful efforts in software systems engineering must be concerned with productivity across each of these entities; we will be much concerned with a systems management approach to software development in our efforts to follow.

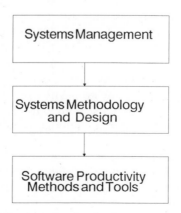

FIGURE 1.1   The three levels of software systems engineering

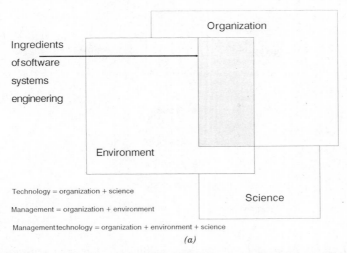

Ingredients
of software
systems
engineering

Technology = organization + science

Management = organization + environment

Management technology = organization + environment + science

(a)

FIGURE 1.2a   Software systems engineering as a management technology

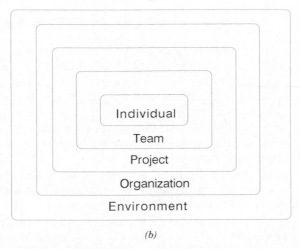

(b)

FIGURE 1.2b   Interactions addressed through software systems engineering

Our effort in Chapter 2 begins with a discussion of lifecycle approaches to the systems engineering of software. We outline several variants that lead to phased development of software systems. Then we address the very important question of identification of the user or client requirements that a software system must satisfy. Requirements specification identification will be the first phase of effort in our development of software, and we devote Chapter 3 to this topic. Following the initial determination of user requirements, these user

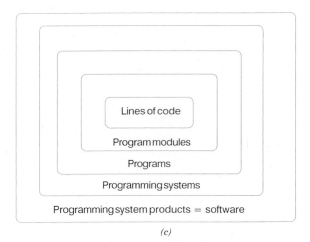

(c)

FIGURE 1.2c Programming interactions addressed through software systems engineering

or client requirements are transformed into computer software oriented requirements.

Micro-enhancement tools are important for programmer productivity enhancement throughout the software development lifecycle. So, we next study micro-enhancement approaches for the various phases of a typical lifecycle for software development. Chapters 4 and 5 present a number of these approaches. We elaborate on the most widely used micro-enhancement approaches and, through a typical software acquisition lifecycle, establish the need for a taxonomy of methods in order to make productivity tools generally available and subject to greater use.

Chapters 6 and 7 discuss the latter portions of the software lifecycle. In particular, efforts that are concerned with reliability, maintainability, and quality assurance are studied in Chapter 6. Chapter 7 presents an overview of system integration, operational implementation, and software development environments. This is followed by a chapter that presents discussions of macro-enhancement approaches to software productivity, including prototyping, software reusability, and the use of expert system techniques to enhance the production of software.

The latter chapters of the book treat management, maintenance, and standards procedures for software productivity. Chapter 9 is concerned with systems-management-related topics. Chapter 10 is concerned mainly with the development of models estimating cost and benefit for software development. The final chapter of the book presents a very carefully selected and annotated bibliography of pertinent references.

A detailed overview of our efforts in the subsequent chapters is especially helpful in establishing a perspective concerning what is to come. We present this overview in the rest of this chapter. Some of our discussions in the remainder of the chapter will need to be restated in the more detailed chapters to follow. We feel, however, that it is very helpful to have a preliminary understanding of the broad scope of software systems engineering prior to obtaining an indepth understanding of particular topics. Thus, the material to follow does provide a very important and helpful background and perspective concerning what is to come.

1.1   THE EMERGENCE OF SYSTEMS ENGINEERING

Throughout history, the development of more sophisticated tools has invariably been associated with a decrease in our dependence on human physical energy as a source of effort. Generally, this is accomplished by control of nonhuman sources of energy in an automated fashion that involves intellectual and cognitive effort. The industrial revolution of many years ago represented a major initial thrust in this direction.

In most cases, a new tool or machine makes it possible to perform a familiar task in a somewhat new and different way, typically with enhanced efficiency and effectiveness. In a smaller number of cases, a new tool has made it possible to do something entirely new and different that could not be done before.

Profound societal changes have often been associated with changes brought about by new tools. In the 1850s, about 70% of the labor force in the United States was employed in agriculture. A little more than a century later, less than 3% is so employed, and this 3% is not only able to produce sufficient food to feed an entire nation but also to generally produce large surpluses for other portions of the world. Occasionally, these tools have produced undesired side effects. Pollution due to chemical plants, and potential depletion of fossil fuel sources, are two examples of this. Occasionally, new tools have the potential for producing significantly harmful side effects, such as those that can occur as a result of human-originated operational errors in nuclear power plant operation, or software errors that potentially degrade the operation of systems used in hazardous and life-threatening situations.

Concerns associated with the design of tools such that they can be used efficiently and effectively have always been addressed, but often on an implicit and trial-and-error basis. When tool designers were also tool users, which was more often than not the case for the simple tools and machines of the past, the resulting designs were often good initially, or soon evolved into good designs.

When physical tools, machines, and systems become so complex that it is no longer possible to design them by a single individual, and a design team is necessary, then a host of new problems emerge. This is the condition today. To cope with this, a number of methodologies associated with systems design engineering have evolved that have made it possible to decompose large design issues into smaller component subsystem design issues, design the subsystems, and then build the complete system as a collection of these subsystems. Even so, problems remain. Just simply connecting together the individual subsystems often does not result in a system that performed acceptably, either from a technological efficiency perspective, or from an effectiveness perspective. This has led to the realization that systems integration engineering and systems management throughout an entire system lifecycle will be necessary. Thus, contemporary efforts in systems engineering contain a focus on tools and methods, on the system design methodology, which enables appropriate use of these tools, and on the systems management approaches, which enable the embedding of design approaches within organizations and environments, such as to support the application of the principals of the physical and material sciences for the betterment of humankind. The use of appropriate tools, as well as systems methodology and management constructs, enables system design for more efficient and effective human interaction [Sage, 1987a].

1.2   FROM COMPUTER TO INFORMATION AND KNOWLEDGE TECHNOLOGIES

Sometime around the middle of this present century, the use of a new type of machine became widespread. This new machine was fundamentally different, in many ways, from the usual combination of motors, gears, pulleys, and other physical components that assisted humans, perhaps in an automated fashion, in performing physical tasks such as pulling, or even flying. While this machine could assist in performing functions associated with physical tasks, such as computing the optimal trajectory for an aircraft to move between two locations with minimum energy consumption and cost, it could also assist humans in a number of primarily cognitive tasks such as planning, resource allocation, and decisionmaking.

It is doubtlessly correct to say that the modern stored program digital computer is a product of the physical and material sciences. The internal components of this new machine surely are products of the physical and material sciences. But it is also important to note here that the digital computer is intended, from a purposeful viewpoint, to be used to provide assistance to efforts that can be more efficiently and effectively achieved through the physical and material sciences by more appropriate use of information and knowledge.

Thus, it is appropriate and significant here to note that the purpose of the digital computer is much more cognitive and intellectual support than it is physical support. The computer is an information machine, a knowledge machine, and a cognitive support machine. It has led to the growth of a new engineering area of endeavor, which involves information and knowledge technology. This new professional area is broadly concerned with efforts whose structure, function, and purpose are associated with the acquisition, representation, storage, transmission, and use of data that is of value for typically cognitive support to humans. Often, this cognitive support results in some sort of ultimate physical effort and human supervisory control of a physical system.

Associated with this are a plethora of information technology products and services that have the potential to profoundly affect the lives of each of us. Clearly this is happening now, and the rate at which these changes will occur is surely going to accelerate. Information technology products and services based on computers and communications, such as telecommunications, command and control, automated manufacturing, electronic mail, and office automation, are common terms today. "Computer-aided everything" will surely be a common term tomorrow. The results could be truly exciting and many products of the information revolution are appearing now: electronic access to libraries and shopping services; individualized and personalized systems of interactive instruction; individualized design of aids to the disabled and handicapped; and more efficacious prediction and planning in business, agriculture, health, and education.

This has led to a fundamental change in the way in which systems design engineering is accomplished. The physical and material science basis for engineering and technology is now augmented by an information science basis. The study of each of these is very important. It is the information science basis that provides the tools that comprise systems engineering, and it is the management technology paradigms of systems engineering that enable the production of efficient and effective product designs that satisfy client needs. It is systems engineering that provides an effective basis for the production of operationally functional and reliable software.

1.3   THE NEED FOR SOFTWARE SYSTEMS ENGINEERING

The information technology revolution is having and will have major impacts on the world around us. While system designs have, in the past, relied most heavily on the mathematics of optimization and the physical and materials products that were being optimized, this can no longer be the case. Human behavioral and cognitive concerns now play a dominant role relative to the success or failure of system designs. They must be considered throughout all phases of system design. System management and integration issues are also of major importance in determining both the effectiveness and efficiency, and the overall functionality of system designs. To achieve a high measure of functionality, it must be possible for a system design to be efficiently and effectively produced, used, maintained, retrofitted, and modified throughout all phases of a lifecycle. This lifecycle begins with need conceptualization and identification, through specification of system requirements and architectural structures, to system installation and evaluation, and operational implementation.

These needs are especially critical relative to the design of trustworthy software. It may well be that the most significant change bought about by the information revolution is the need for trustworthy software. It seems not at all incorrect to say that, if we are indeed in the midst of an information revolution, it is software that is the critical armament that enables the revolution. The path that this revolution should follow is one guided by an appropriate systems engineering, and software systems engineering, process.

The reality is that there are many difficulties associated with the production of reliable, trustworthy software. The result of a very large number of studies of software productivity indicate that:

- Software is expensive.
- Software capability is less than promised and expected.
- Software deliveries are often quite late.
- Software cost over runs often occur and are generally large.
- Software maintenance is complex and error-prone.
- Software documentation is inappropriate and inadequate.
- Software is often cumbersome to use and system design for human interaction is lacking.
- Software products often cannot be integrated.
- Software often cannot be transitioned to a new environment or modified to meet evolving needs.
- Software performance is often unreliable.
- Software often does not perform according to specifications.
- System and software requirements often do not adequately capture user needs.

These studies often indicate that a very large percentage of system costs are expended on software. Usually, it is necessary to maintain new systems such that they are able to be continually responsive to changing user and environmental needs. In many systems, the larger part of maintenance monies are allocated for software maintenance.

There are a plethora of difficulties that emanate from the aforementioned central problems, including: inconsistent, incomplete, and otherwise imperfect system requirements specifications; system requirements that do not provide for change as user needs evolve over time; and poorly defined management structures for product design and delivery. These lead to delivered products that are difficult to use, that do not solve the intended problem, that operate in an unreliable fashion, that are unmaintainable, and that—as a result—are not used. And, the problem appears to be getting worse.

These same studies generally show that the major problems associated with the production of trustworthy software are more concerned with the organization and management of complexity than with direct technological concerns that affect individual programmer productivity. This does not suggest that programmer productivity improvement is unneeded or inconsequential. It does suggest that major productivity improvement possibilities are unlikely through **ONLY** better programmer productivity.

Since the critical areas associated with software productivity improvement are fundamentally systems engineering areas, including the systems management and technical direction efforts that comprise systems engineering, we intentionally use the term "software systems engineering" to describe the general area of coverage for this book.

We envision an imbedded hierarchy of programming and software performance levels, such as we have shown in Figure 1.2c. Programs (or program modules) lead to programming products. Collections of these lead to programming systems and programming system products, which might be called *software*. It is at these initial levels that the micro-enhancement efforts of software engineering can be applied. This is indeed fundamentally engineering as it involves a process whereby building, or design, is the primary objective. Learning, when it occurs, is primarily for the purpose of enabling design enhancement or construction. This should be contrasted with building or designing for the sake of learning, which is basically a scientific activity. Our efforts will be concerned, as we have noted, with software engineering. For our purposes, we may define software engineering as the design, production, and maintenance of software within cost and time constraints.

Our efforts will also be concerned with technical direction and management of programmer productivity, and the process of software design, production, and maintenance. This is systems engineering, and hence the name "software systems engineering." By adopting the management technology of systems engineering and applying it to software, we become very concerned with making sure that correct software is designed, and not just that software designs are correct. Software systems engineering is the technical direction and management of software engineering processes to ensure client needs satisfaction in an efficient, effective, and otherwise productive manner. Figure 1.3 presents an initial view of this conceptualization of software systems engineering.

Appropriate tools to enable efficient and effective error prevention and detection in the production of code will enhance the production of software designs that are correct. To ensure that correct software is designed requires that considerable emphasis be placed on the front end of the software development phases. There must be considerable emphasis on the accurate definition of a software product before one is produced and implemented. In turn, this requires emphasis on conformance to software requirements, and the development of standards to ensure compatibility and integratibility of software products. Areas such as documentation and communication are important in all of this. Thus, we see the need for the technical direction and management technology efforts that comprise systems engineering.

There is a twofold goal associated with information technology developments, including those that involve software systems engineering. Information

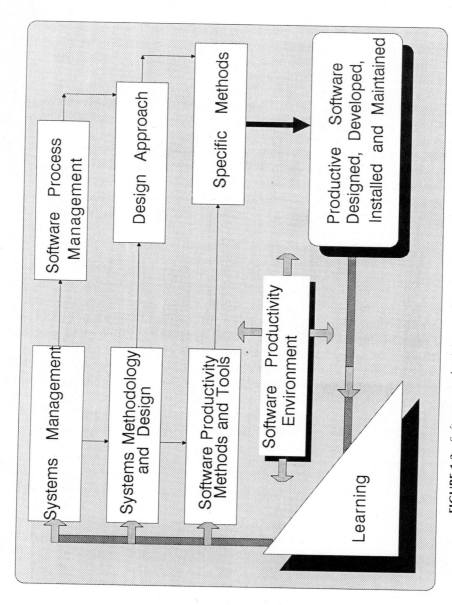

FIGURE 1.3 Software productivity as a large scale systems engineering process

10

technology has the potential for making current organizational and technological systems more effective. More importantly, information technology has the potential to facilitate creation of more effective organizational and technological designs. Major potential benefits can result from this more efficient and effective use of information and associated knowledge support. Thus, the ultimate payoffs from effective software systems engineering efforts are very significant.

1.4   A METHODOLOGY FOR SOFTWARE SYSTEMS ENGINEERING DESIGN

The primary goal of software systems engineering is the creation of a set of operational products that will enable a digital computer and peripheral components to accomplish desired tasks that fulfill identified needs of a client group. This is primarily and fundamentally an engineering task, and a design task.

1.4.1   Design

Design is the creative process through which products, processes, or systems presumed to be responsive to client needs are conceptualized or specified. Software design is, of course, the primary focus of our efforts here. There are four primary ingredients in this not uncommon definition of design, and they apply to software design just as to design of hardware and physical systems:

- Design results in specifications or architecture for a product, process, or system.
- Design is a creative process.
- Design activity is conceptual in nature.
- To be successful, a design must be responsive to client needs and requirements.

The fourth and final notion is very important and, sadly, often elusive and neglected.

Good design practice requires that the designer be responsive to each of these four ingredients for quality design effort. The latter necessary ingredient results in the mandate to obtain, from the client for a design effort, a set of needs and requirements for the product, process, or system that is to result from the design effort. This information requirement serves as the input to the design process. Design is creative, and it is a process that is conceptual in nature. The result of this creative and conceptual process is information concerning the specifications or architecture for the product, process, or service that will ultimately be manufactured, implemented, installed, or brought to fruition in some other way.

"Information" is the key word in this systems model of the design process; it is an essential feature in the input to the design process, the design process itself, and the output of the design process. The development and implementation of sound design processes is a fundamental goal of systems engineering. These are the perspectives that we will take in this text, specifically as they relate to the engineering design of software.

We first discuss systems design methodology. This is a needed element in order for design to be considered as a process. This will lead to a consideration of the nature of design. Associated with this are purposeful methodological approaches and resulting formalisms for design. These lead to theoretical and conceptual frameworks that are inherent in the nature of design as a process.

It will be clear from our discussion of the nature of design that there are a variety of knowledge frameworks or perspectives necessary for the design of software systems, as well as technological systems in general. We must be concerned with characterization and understanding of the thought process of software designers in organizing information about design; including the acquisition, representation, and use of this information. We must pay particular attention to the requirements for successful knowledge support to designers and aids that support design processes for the production of high-quality, trustworthy software. This concern naturally turns to important issues relative to the knowledge base for design, and how this knowledge base might best be employed and exercised in a support system that assists in decisionmaking and design processes. To accomplish this, both analytical and perceptual capabilities are required. Also needed is a knowledge base and model base for support that allows a purposeful interplay of these characteristics of successful design.

Clients and designers have needs and requirements that must be satisfied by the results of a successful design process. Information requirements determination is, therefore, a multifaceted need for successful systems design. In a very real sense, this is the most important need for successful design as it is highly likely that functionality of the resulting design will be noticed only by its absence, unless there exists appropriate information concerning that which is to be designed. This is not a simple task. It is especially difficult because system designers and system users often have very different perspectives relative to the issues with which they deal. They often communicate in very different ways. Each of these makes it difficult, and at the same time very important, for mutual understandings to develop.

1.4.2   Software Systems Design Methodology

There are many ways in which we can characterize design. We could describe design as an activity involving iterative hypothesis generation and test of alternatives or concepts. The hypothesis step involves primarily inductive skills, generally based on experience, that enables generation of design alternatives. These are evaluated through the primarily deductive activity of evaluation or testing. An initial hypothesis is often not acceptable. When it is rejected, generally through evaluation, iteration back through the hypothesis generation step enables modification of the identified alternative, and reevaluation such as to, hopefully, lead to a successful design alternative. When a design is evaluated as successful, then design activity—at least the particular phase of design being undertaken—ceases. Effort then turns to implementation of the acceptable design or initiation of the next phase in a design effort. Figure 1.4 illustrates this hypothesis-driven conceptualization of the design process.

More often than not, the hypothesis generation and option evaluation efforts are first conducted in a preliminary way in order to obtain several concepts that might work. Several potential option alternatives are identified, and the resulting options are subjected to at least a preliminary evaluation in order to eliminate clearly unacceptable alternatives. The surviving alternatives are then subjected to more detailed design efforts, and more complete architectures or specifications are obtained. The result of this is a system that

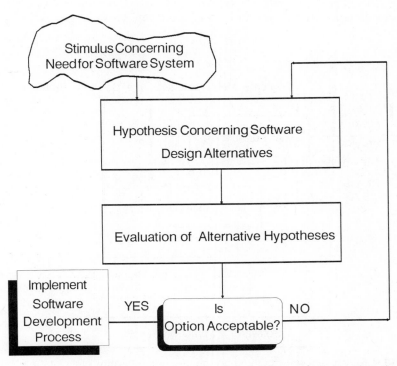

FIGURE 1.4   Classic hypothesis driven model of software design engineering

can be subject to detailed design, testing, and at least preliminary operational implementation. Once this has occurred, operational evaluation and test of the implemented system, product, or process can occur. The system design may be modified as a result of this evaluation and this will, hopefully, lead to an ultimately improved system and operational implementation. What we have then is a model of design consisting of a number of steps, such as shown in Figure 1.5, and a sequence of phases with each of the steps accomplished within each of the phases.

Figure 1.6 illustrates a typical sequence of seven phases [Sage, 1981] that we will use, almost consistently, to model the software lifecycle.

1. Requirements specifications identification
2. Preliminary conceptual design and system architecture specification
3. Logical design and system architecture implementation
4. Detailed design and testing
5. Operational implementation
6. Evaluation and modification
7. Operational deployment

These are sequenced in an iterative manner. There are many descriptions of systems design methodology and associated frameworks [Sage, 1977; Nadler,

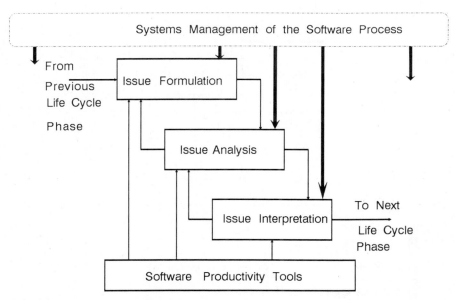

FIGURE 1.5   General steps in the fine structure of the systems process at each phase in the software systems engineering lifecycle

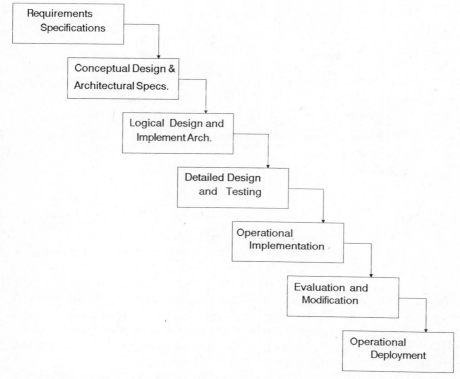

FIGURE 1.6   Typical phases in the lifecycle of software systems engineering

1985], and we outline only one of them in any detail in this chapter. The next chapter will study a number of variants of this lifecycle model of system and software evolution and development. In general, however, the overall process is structured as in Figure 1.7, which illustrates an expansion of Figure 1.5 to accommodate our identified methodological framework for systems engineering.

We will discuss, in detail, the various phases in the system and software lifecycle in the chapters to follow. Only a brief discussion is in order here.

The requirements specification phase of our system design methodology has as its goal the identification of client needs, activities, and objectives to be achieved by implementation of the resulting design as a product, process, or system. The effort in this phase should result in the identification and description of preliminary conceptual design considerations that are appropriate for the next phase. It is important to note that it is necessary to translate operational deployment needs into requirements specifications in order that these needs be addressed by the system design efforts. Thus, we see that information requirements specifications are affected by, and effect, each of the other design phases of the systemic framework for design. As is the case

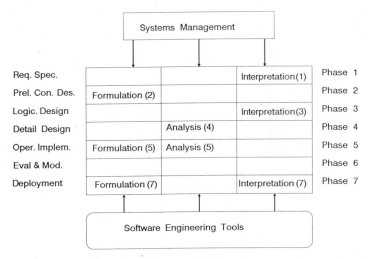

FIGURE 1.7   Methodological framework for software systems engineering

with all of the phases in the systems lifecycle, it is always possible to disaggregate a given phase into a number of subphases. The requirements specifications phase, for example, can be considered to consist of a user requirements identification, followed by the translation of user or problem specifications into technical specifications for software.

As a result of the requirements specifications phase, there should exist a clear definition of design issues such that it becomes possible to make a decision concerning whether to undertake preliminary conceptual design. If the result of the requirements specifications effort indicates that client needs can be satisfied in a functionally satisfactorily manner, then documentation is typically prepared concerning specifications for the preliminary conceptual design phase. Initial specifications for the following three phases of effort are typically also prepared and a concept design team selected to implement the next phase of the design effort. It should be noted that many, but certainly not all, of the activities in the requirements specifications phase are of a management and technical direction nature.

Preliminary conceptual design typically includes or results in a next phase effort that leads to specification of the content and associated architecture and general algorithms for the product, process, or system that should result from this effort. The primary goal of this phase is to develop conceptualization of a prototype that is responsive to the requirements identified in the previous phase. Preliminary concept design according to the requirements specifications should be obtained. Often, this conceptual design will transform the *software program plan* obtained in the requirements specification phase into a number of software project plans.

Rapid prototyping of the conceptual design, and of the requirements specifications that lead to the conceptual design, is clearly desirable for many applications. In our efforts to follow, we will illustrate how the introduction of rapid prototyping, and other macro-enhancement aids, acts to modify the phases of the system lifecycle model shown in Figures 1.6 and 1.7.

The desired product of the next phase of design activity is a detailed logical design that implements the architectural specifications of the previous phase. This logic design is implemented in the next lifecycle phase, through the process of detailed design. Detailed design amounts to coding in the case of software production; it should result in a useful product, process, or system, as a result of implementing the conceptual design. There should exist a sufficiently high degree of user confidence that a useful product will result from detailed design, or the entire design effort should be redone or possibly abandoned.

Another product of this phase is a refined set of specifications for the evaluation and operational deployment phases of the design process. In this third phase of effort, the software specifications are translated into detailed representations in logical form such that system development may occur. A product, process, or system is produced in the fourth phase of design. This is not the final design, but rather the result of implementation of the logical design that resulted from the conceptual design effort of phase number 3. User guides for the product should be produced such that realistic operational test and evaluation can be conducted. For the particular case of software, detailed design and testing will include the production of code, or a program, that will presumably accomplish the intended purpose.

Operational implementation and integration follows in phase 5. Evaluation of the design and the resulting product, process, or system is achieved in the sixth phase of the design process. Preliminary evaluation criteria are obtained as a part of requirements specifications and modified during the following two phases of the design effort. The evaluation effort must be adapted to other phases of the design effort such that it becomes an integral and functional part of the overall design process. Generally, the critical issues for evaluation are adaptations of the elements present in the requirements specifications phase of the design process. Thus, we see that there is a close linkage among the phases of the systems lifecycle, and that it is almost certain that initial errors will propagate and magnify as we proceed through this lifecycle.

It is necessary to evolve a set of specific evaluation test requirements and tests from the objectives and needs determined in requirements specifications. This is necessary to validate software systems. These test requirements should be such that each objective measure and critical evaluation issue component can be measured from at least one evaluation test instrument.

There are many possible test instruments and attributes. A nonexhaustive listing of attributes, to which it is very necessary to associate attribute measures, includes:

- Acceptable
- Accessible
- Accountable
- Accurate
- Adaptable
- Appropriate
- Assurable
- Available
- Clear
- Complete
- Consistent
- Correct
- Documentable
- Documented

- Effective
- Efficient
- Error-tolerant
- Expandable
- Flexible
- Generalizable
- Interoperable
- Maintainable
- Manageable
- Modifiable
- Modular
- Operable
- Portable
- Precise
- Reliable

- Repairable
- Reusable
- Robust
- Secure
- Self-contained
- Survivable
- Testable
- Timely
- Transferable
- Understandable
- Usable
- User-friendly
- Valid
- Verifiable

We will, in our later efforts concerning metrics for software quality and validity, attempt to develop attribute measures for performance features such as these in order to meaningfully evaluate software performance. We will structure these, and the associated attribute measures, such as to obtain a hierarchy of performance measures that enables us to determine the capability of a specific software product in terms of such operational needs as functionality, transition capability, and revisability. A key need in doing this is the identification of quantifiable attribute attainment measures. The attributes just listed are formally qualitative and not necessarily measurable without the identification of appropriate attribute measures. There are a number of scaling and other concerns that must be addressed in order to do this in a consistent and repeatable manner.

A partial hierarchy of functionality attributes is shown in Figure 1.8. Associated with each of these attributes is some degree of uncertainty, risk, and imprecision relative to the degree to which we can obtain a given value for the attribute by a specific design alternative. We will expand greatly on this concept in our later efforts.

If it is determined, perhaps through an operational evaluation, that the software product, process, or system cannot meet user needs; the systemic design process for software reverts iteratively back to an earlier phase and effort continues. An important by-product of evaluation is determination of ultimate performance limitations for an operationally realizable system and identification of those protocols and procedures for use of the result of the design effort that enable maximum user satisfaction. Often, operational evaluation is the only realistic way to establish meaningful information concerning functional effectiveness of the result of a design effort. Successful evaluation is contingent on explicit development of a plan for evaluation that is developed before initiation of the evaluation effort. In fact, validation begins with the identification of user requirements!

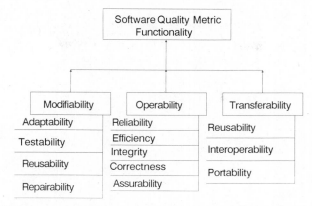

FIGURE 1.8   Partial hierarchy of quality assurance attributes

The last phase of a system design effort concerns final acceptance and operational deployment. This will generally involve a plan for integrating the new software with existing software, maintaining it when (and if) it is found to fail in one or more ways, and modifying it over time to meet evolving user needs.

This description of design methodology contains a strong process flavor. For our purposes, a process is the integration of a methodology with the behavioral concerns of human judgment in a realistic operational environment. Our description of systems design in this section has emphasized the methodological concerns and, perhaps to a lesser extent, operational environment concerns. The goal in all of this is to produce software, and systems and processes that incorporate software, that measure up to high standards. The meaning of this term is intentionally vague here. We might, for the moment, imagine that we have a software production quality yardstick such as that shown in Figure 1.9*a*. We wish to be able to measure software performance in terms of instrumentable metrics and obtain a high score on the performance indicator of Figure 1.9*a*. The need for software productivity improvement is indicated in Figure 1.9*b,* which surely illustrates that contemporary software products do not result in a very high score on the performance metric. Details of software quality assurance will be discussed in Chapter 6.

It is important to note here that the identification of seven distinct phases for a system lifecycle is somewhat arbitrary, as indeed is the naming of the phases themselves. As a minimum, it appears that the lifecycle phases of system design and development can be generally aggregated as:

Definition
Development
Maintenance

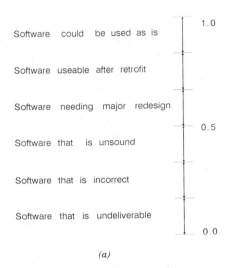

(a)

FIGURE 1.9a Ideal software functionality assurance meter

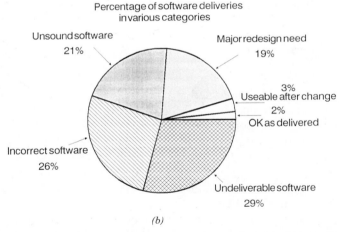

(b)

FIGURE 1.9b Software production in the six functional categories

In the particular system lifecycle discussed thus far, we have a single definition phase. As an alternate, we could have identified two definition phases.

System requirements identification
Software requirements specification

as we will do in our discussions of the waterfall lifecycle model due to Royce

[1970] in our next chapter. In either case, as a result of the definition phase or phases, system requirements and software requirements identification, we will have available.

1. Overall development project objectives that need to be satisfied by the hardware and software in order to meet client needs
2. Transformation of these system specifications to hardware and software specifications
3. A determination of development project feasibility in terms of economics, time scale, and prospects for satisfying client needs in a manner that is commensurate with allowable risks and reliability indices
4. An identified software (and hardware) systems management strategy for accomplishing program objectives and, thereby, fulfill the client's needs
5. An identification of the program development costs, available resources, and schedule

There are both technological and management implications to these. In our developments to follow, we will first deal with technological concerns. In Chapter 9, we will address management of the software systems engineering process.

It is important to note that software architectures and subsystems have not generally been identified at the end of the definition phase of the system or software lifecycle. It is the purpose of the first of the development phases, which we call the preliminary conceptual design phase, to translate the well-defined set of software requirements into a workable software architecture, structure, or preliminary design. It is in the preliminary conceptual design phase that we first define the various modules that will be used at the detail level and the control hierarchy that will need to be employed in developing a logical design for the various modules.

To accomplish this preliminary conceptual design well, we will need to.

1. Understand the structure of information flows throughout the complete software system
2. Identify the various software modules that are associated with this structure
3. Define the various control and data interfaces that will need to exist between these modules
4. Establish design constraints upon the various software modules, including such important items as storage requirements and limits and execution times
5. Provide a project management structure to enable development of the identified modules

This amounts to top-level design of the complete software subsystem. All of this must be expressed in a software design document (SDD), which is an input to the next phase, which involves detailed design and coding.

The components of the detailed design and coding phase of the software lifecycle (*SLC*) are:

1. **Design Review** This is primarily a review to ensure that each software requirement is addressed by the design obtained up to this point. Traceability to software requirements specifications, and determination of feasibility and practicality of the design, are the primary products of this review. If changes are needed, activity reverts back to the conceptual design phase and modifications are made. If no changes are needed, we proceed to the next step, module design.
2. **Module Design** This is essentially an application of the approaches used in preliminary conceptual design at the more detailed level of individual modules. Often the design of individual modules will be the responsibility of different teams. A complete set of specifications for development of these individual modules should be obtained as a result of the detailed design effort.
3. **Design Walkthrough** This enables the evaluation of each individual module by an independent evaluator. An alternative to this is a formal design inspection. When satisfaction is obtained here, we proceed to the next step, code and unit test.
4. **Code and Unit Test** This involves detailed programming and testing of the resulting program modules.

These components are illustrated in Figure 1.10, and the actual parallel flow of detailed design and coding is indicated in Figure 1.11. We note here that the latter efforts in this phase involve connection of the modules, especially for purposes of testing. As with the definition phase, the development phase could be disaggregated in several different ways. For example, we associate detailed design, code, and test with a single phase, whereas these could easily, be associated with three phases of effort. From a project management perspective, the organizational differences associated with different representations of the software lifecycle may be very significant.

It should also be noted that we are dealing with a three-level hierarchy for software systems design and development:

Software systems engineering methods
Software systems engineering methodologies
Systems management of the software engineering process

Tools can be associated with each of these three levels. Figure 1.12 illustrates a conceptual notion of how these are embedded and interrelated for the production of functionally trustworthy software.

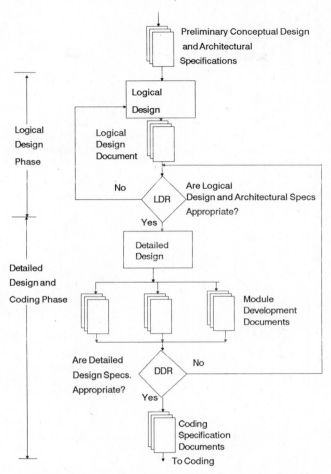

FIGURE 1.10 Transitioning to detailed design and coding

With respect to the definitional phase(s) of the software lifecycle, there are a number of tools that are used in support of systems management and methodological concerns. These enable specification of the user system-level requirements, the software technical requirements, and the software process management requirements. In the second phase of the software development lifecycle, preliminary conceptual design, the tools used assist in determination of the structure, and flows within this structure, of the modules that will ultimately comprise the software subsystems. In the detailed design and coding phase, appropriate tools* should be useful at the module level in providing

---

*Data flow diagrams, entity relationship diagrams, etc. We will discuss a number of these later.

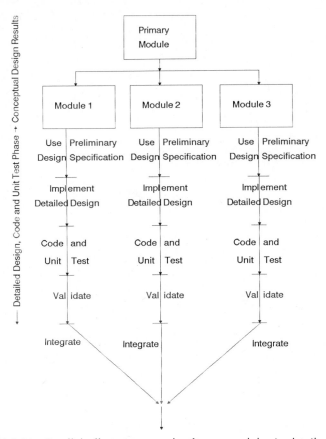

FIGURE 1.11   Parallel efforts on several software modules in detailed design

more detail structure and specifications for the individual modules. After this detailed design is accomplished, we move to the coding portion of the phase where the appropriate tools shift to those noted at the center of Figure 1.12. These are the detailed tools that enhance programmer productivity. We explicitly note here that the development and use of these tools are not a focal point for this book.

We now turn our attention to a brief discussion of some of the human and behavioral concerns in design. In later chapters, we will return to concerns in each of these phases of the design process and discuss the software design phases, and the approaches that will enable this to be effectively and efficiently accomplished, in some detail.

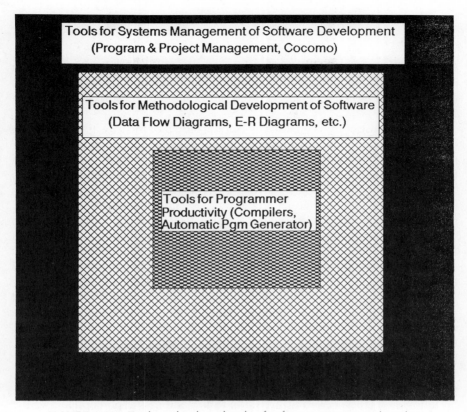

FIGURE 1.12 Tools at the three levels of software systems engineering

1.4.3 The Nature of Design

Regardless of the way in which the design process is characterized, and regardless of the type of process or system that is being designed, all characterizations will necessarily involve [Sage, 1977, 1981b, 1982]:

1. *Formulation of the design problem,* in which the needs and objectives of a client group are identified, and potentially acceptable design alternatives, or options, are identified or generated.
2. *Analysis of the alternative designs,* in which the impacts of the identified design options are evaluated.
3. *Interpretation and selection,* in which the design options are compared by means of an evaluation of the impacts of the design alternatives. The needs and objectives of the client group are used as a basis for evaluation, including validation of the software product. The most ac-

ceptable alternative is then selected for implementation or further study in a subsequent phase of design.

Our model of the steps of the fine structure of the systems process, shown in Figure 1.5, is based on this conceptualization. As we have indicated here, these three steps can be disaggregated into a number of others [Sage, 1977, 1982].

Without question, this is a formal rational model of the way in which design is accomplished. Even within this formal framework, there is the need for much iteration from one step back to an earlier step when it is discovered that improvements in the results of an earlier step are needed in order to obtain a quality result at a subsequent step of the design effort. Also, this description does not emphasize the key role of information and information requirements determination, which is concentrated in the formulation step but which exists throughout all steps of the design process [Sage, Galing, and Lagomasino, 1983].

More importantly, this morphological framework, in terms of phases of the design process and steps within these phases, does not emphasize the different types of information and different types of support that are needed within each step at the various phases. During the issue formulation step, the support that is needed tends to be of an affective, perceptive, or gestalt nature. Intuition-based experiential wisdom will play a most important role in this. During the analysis step, the need is typically for quantitative and algorithmic support, typically through use of one of the formal methods for programmer productivity enhancement that we will describe in later chapters. In the interpretation step, the needed effort shifts to a blend of the perceptive and the analytical.

Even when these realities are associated with the morphological framework, it still represents an incomplete view of the way in which people do, could, or should accomplish design, planning, or other problem solving activities. The most that can be argued is that this framework is correct in an "as if" or normative manner. It is a *morphological** box that consists of a number of phases and steps. There is also a third-dimensional variable, effort level, and this will be described later.

Within each of the phases of software systems engineering, there will generally be a number of steps. Each of the steps of the fine structure of software systems engineering is repeated at each of the phases in the software lifecycle. It is primarily the specific activities within each step, and particularly the time that is required to accomplish them, that varies across corresponding steps within the several phases of the software development lifecycle. It is also possible to disaggregate any phase of the SLC into a number of other more finely detailed phases. For example, Figure 1.13 is a modification of Figure 1.6 illustrating how this disaggregation might proceed for the logical design and implementation of system architecture phase of the software lifecycle.

*"Morphology" is just a fancy word, derived from biology, that means *study of form.*

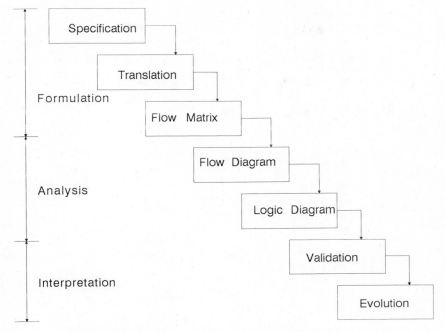

FIGURE 1.13   Activities in the logical design phase

We have identified a number of phased activities, illustrated in general terms in Figure 1.6, whose accomplishment should do much to result in the design of trustworthy software. To determine the specific activities to be accomplished within each of these boxes is one of the major methodological concerns in software systems engineering. It is important to note that there is intended to be iteration and feedback from later stages to earlier stages when deficiencies are observed. The process envisioned is not a linear sequential process, and the flow of activities is cornucopia, such as within the steps of each phase as well as within the phases themselves. There is, at least normatively, much iteration and feedback among the steps and phases of the lifecycle of software. This is shown for typical phases of the process in Figure 1.14. As we will note later, caution needs to be expressed relative to the implications of this iteration and feedback. First, there may be legal concerns involved as often different phases of the lifecycle are the responsibility of different contractors. There are also concerns with respect to when the lifecycle stops. Nevertheless, the lack of feedback and iteration will often result in the expenditures of large amounts of money to implement a system that cannot possibly solve the problem that it is supposed to solve.

We believe that a potential advantage to the systems engineering framework discussed here and illustrated in Figure 1.7 is that each of the steps of

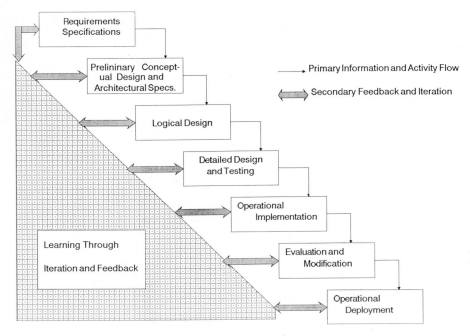

FIGURE 1.14 Software systems engineering lifecycle with iteration and feedback

the fine structure of the process, shown in Figure 1.5, has the same name across all of the phases. As we have discussed previously, the specific activities to be accomplished within each cell of this framework depend on the specific phase of effort being undertaken. This methodological framework for software systems engineering is doubtlessly extensive and exhaustive. To attempt to eliminate, or dramatically reduce, needed effort at any step within any phase is very likely to result in deficiencies in the overall software product. To follow through with all the needed effort is likely to result in such general *exhaustion* that any of several maladies may occur. Perhaps foremost among them is that the process may be so painstakingly time-consuming that continually changing system requirements may well prohibit system development from ever being completed.

This is particularly so when system integration needs are considered and when it is recognized that complete system acquisition includes hardware and software. We realize that the iterative phases of the software lifecycle must be embedded into other phases of the lifecycle of an overall system that includes hardware and other considerations. Also, there must be opportunities for a management process that assures system quality throughout all of this.

The potential advantage of the systems engineering process just described is that it allows for formal consideration of the interactions among the phases of a design effort and, in this sense, attempts to view the "whole" design problem within a contextually realistic setting. Thus efforts that may potentially enhance efficiency and/or effectiveness within a methodological approach to software productivity, in a macro-enhancement sense, are particularly enticing.

We have suggested a three-level model to accomplish this. At the first level are the specific micro-enhancement and macro-enhancement methods that potentially enhance software productivity. The methodological framework that we propose enables an open set of procedures for problem-solving to determine an appropriate mix of methods to be selected for a given software production effort. The top level of our proposed structure is the level of systems management, which represents the technical direction efforts that result in selection of a specific systems methodology and design approach, and resulting design methods to enable this. Figure 1.3 illustrates a structure for the methodology suggested here.

1.4.4   Information Requirements for Software Production

Judgments concerning design and development, at least prudent judgments, are seldom made without information. The term "information" is often defined as data of value for decisionmaking. Activities associated with acquisition, representation, storage, transmission, and use of pertinent data are generally associated with information processing. The task of information requirements determination is associated with each of these. Initially, it might appear that this would be associated only with an information acquisition effort. But since information acquisition is necessarily related to other activities associated with information processing, so also is information requirements determination. We will examine approaches to user system requirements identification in some detail in Chapter 3.

As we will discuss later, there are four fundamental methods of determining requirements, including information requirements [Davis, 1982; Sage et al., 1983]:

1. Ask people
2. Examine documents concerning plans and needs
3. Experiment with an existing system or process
4. Experiment with an evolving system or process

The cost and time required to accomplish these may be expected to vary considerably with the costs associated with approach 4 much greater than those associated with approach 1. On the other hand, the veridicality of the information obtained from approach 4 is likely to be much higher than that associated with approach 1. These approaches can be disaggregated further. For example, we can speak of actual group inquiry and nominal group inquiry as approaches to asking people. We will comment on this important subject further in Chapter 3.

There are also many ways in which we can characterize information. Among attributes that we might use are accuracy, precision, completeness, sufficiency, understandability, relevancy, reliability, redundancy, verifiability, consistency, freedom from bias, frequency of use, age, timeliness, and uncertainty. To use these attributes in a meaningful way, it will generally be necessary to define appropriate quantitative attribute measures.

It is also possible to define information at several levels. At the technical level, information and associated measures are concerned with transmission quality over a channel. At the semantic level, concern is with the meaning and efficiency of messages. At the pragmatic level, information is valued in terms of effectiveness in accomplishing an intended purpose. From the viewpoint of design, we are clearly concerned more with pragmatic and semantic issues than we are with technical level issues. At the pragmatic and semantic levels, our concerns with information for software design purposes are fivefold:

1. Information should be presented in very clear and very familiar ways, such as to enable rapid comprehension.
2. Information should be such as to improve the precision of understanding of the task situation.
3. Information that contains an advice or decision recommendation component should contain an explication facility that enables the user to determine how and why results and advice are obtained.
4. Information needs should be based upon identification of the information requirements for the particular situation.
5. Information presentations and all other associated management control aspects of the design process should be such that the designer or decisionmaker, rather than a computerized support system, guides the process of judgment and choice.

Clearly, this relates directly to the concept of value of information and indicates that this concept is very dependent on the contingency task structure. This is a term used to denote the mix of the task at hand, the environment into which the task is embedded, and the problem solver's familiarity with these as they interact to determine both the perceptions and the intentions of the problem-solver. A major failure in software systems engineering is that of producing software that does not solve the user's problem or/and is not matched to the cognitive needs and perspectives of the user. Value of information, broadly interpreted, is a very important concept relative to the important subject of user-perceived value. We will have much need, in our efforts to follow, to adopt a very broad perspective concerning the meaning of the term "value of information."

1.4.5   Objectives for Software Systems Engineering

Many goals could be stated for an appropriate software design methodology, such as:

1. The resulting methodology should encompass the entire software design process throughout all phases of the system lifecycle, including transitioning between phases.
2. The systems management process should be one that supports problem understanding and communication among all interested parties at all stages in the process.
3. The methodology adopted should enable the capture of design and resulting implementation needs early in the software system lifecycle as part of the information requirements and conceptual design phases.
4. The methodology should support both bottom-up and top-down approaches to software and code production.
5. The methodology should enable an appropriate mix of micro-enhancement and macro-enhancement approaches.
6. The methodology should support system-level quality assurance, including verification and validation procedures, throughout the design process.
7. The methodology should support system evolution over time.
8. The methodology should be supportive of appropriate standards and system integration.
9. The methodology should support the use of automated aids for software design that assist in the production of high-quality, trustworthy systems.
10. The methodology should be teachable and transferable, and should make the software design process visible and controllable at all phases of development.
11. The methodology should have appropriate procedures to enable definition and documentation of all relevant variables at each phase in the software production cycle.
12. The methodology utilized should support operational product functionality, revisability, and transitioning.
13. The methodology must support both the software development organization and the software user organization.
14. The methodology must provide a framework that allows management of all important activities associated with large-scale systems design and development.

When each of these are accomplished, much needed support will have been provided toward the production of software systems that are economical, reliable, verifiable, interoperable, integratable, portable, adaptable, evolvable, comprehensible, maintainable, and manageable, which leads to a very high degree of user satisfaction. These would seem to represent attributes for metrics, or to be potentially translatable into attributes for metrics, that can measure software quality, as we have already noted.

1.5   METHODS FOR ENHANCEMENT OF SOFTWARE PRODUCTIVITY

Much contemporary activity concerning software productivity deals with specific development of tools or processes that appear capable of producing reduction of system lifecycle costs. The process of software development is, at least normatively, a systems engineering process. In this section, we will describe salient features of this process as it now exists. As we have already noted, improvements at the level of software tools and methods take two nonexclusive generic forms. A micro-enhancement approach will leave the process little changed and will result in incremental improvements in the various stages of this existing process. A macro-enhancement approach will take a systemic and wholistic view of the process of software development and attempt improvements through the development of an integrated process. Following our description of the typical process extant, we provide the beginnings of a taxonomic description of micro-enhancement and macro-enhancement approaches to increased software productivity.

Systems engineering involves and includes a structured process to engineering that consists of a number of phases constituting the lifecycle of a process or system. This lifecycle extends from the conceptual efforts involved in planning and design on through the development and manufacture of a system and includes the evaluation of existing systems and appropriate modification to make them more responsive to client needs.

In our previous section, we identified seven phases for a lifecycle approach to system design and development. Figure 1.6 illustrated these phases. With respect to the systems engineering of software, it is possible to modify these ever so slightly, such that our seven phases of a software lifecycle are just these seven phases. Let us describe these phases as a preliminary to our more detailed descriptions in Chapter 2. Our emphasis here, and in Chapter 2, will be on the *software systems engineering lifecycle*.

In phase one, information is extracted from available sources concerning user needs and captured in some appropriate form. This is then transitioned from system requirements to *software requirements*. Important questions to be asked at this latter part of phase one are:

1. What is the system to be used for?
2. What are the resulting objectives for (hardware and) software?

After these needs have been identified, they are translated into a set of software requirements for use in phase 2 of the software systems engineering lifecycle. These requirements specifications, which are performance requirements, suggest what the resulting software system should do from an external perspective.

In phase 2, software systems managers first attempt to capture all the design requirements in some formal manner that is independent of a particular logical representation. Often, this is done by representing design structures as entity relationship models. This naturally leads to preliminary architectural specifications for the logical and detailed design to follow. Some effort at decomposition of the software design task can be accomplished at this phase, as can preliminary identification of system level data and information models. These are *not* primary objectives during this phase, however. At this stage in the design effort, the use of various methods of system level prototyping can lead to preliminary evaluation and verification of whether the resulting system can meet user requirements, at least in the most important ways.

This overall concept is translated into internal design specifications, at the level of the software projects identified in the conceptual design phase, in phase 3 of the effort. This phase also involves decomposition into subtasks that involve various modules and their interactions, and the corresponding identification of hierarchies of software subefforts. Of course, the decomposition should continue to lower and lower levels until the elemental subprojects appear feasible of accomplishment. There is an inherent trade-off in this. Smaller size subprojects may well be more easily accomplished that larger projects; however, the resulting integration efforts will be more difficult. Translation and integratability are very key concepts in this. These are really central activities that occur in the various phases of the software lifecycle. Figure 1.15 illustrates the transitioning between phases that occurs as a result of the requirements specifications phase.

A real problem in software systems engineering is that the transitioning from one phase to the other is often poorly handled. Structured tools, such as data flow diagramming tools, are of particular interest in coping with this. There are a variety of computer aided software engineering tools (CASE tools), some of them suitable for this purpose. We will describe several of these in our later efforts, especially in Chapter 7.

During the programming and code implementation phase, which corresponds to the phase 4 effort, the various modular designs of phase 3 are converted or translated or transitioned into code and the code is tested at the modular level at which it is produced. The code is assembled at the system level and system level testing is accomplished in phase 5. In phase 6, the resulting software is tested from an external perspective with respect to its efficacy in meeting client needs. To the extent possible, this is accomplished in an operational environment. Finally, the accepted software is used in an operational setting and maintained as required.

This description does not indicate the iterative nature associated with these phases. Deficiencies, when they are noted, should often be corrected through

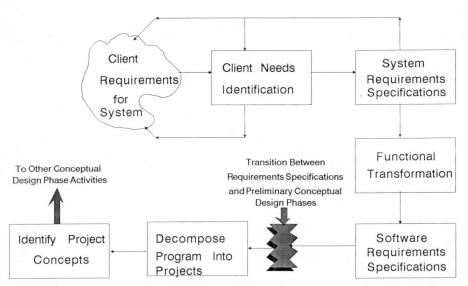

FIGURE 1.15 Functional transformation within phases and transitioning between phases

iteration back to an earlier phase in this software lifecycle model. In practice, this is seldom done for a variety of reasons; occasionally good reasons, but more often than not bad ones—bad reasons with typically bad results. A very common difficulty here is that the specific organization, or team, which existed to perform an earlier phase of the system acquisition lifecycle will have been dispersed to other projects. This is especially the case in "matrix-managed" organizations.

It is not absolutely necessary to proceed through each of these phases to develop functionally useful software. Much early software development was accomplished by initiating the process at phase 3, or even phase 4, in the lifecycle. If the development process ever reached phase 1 or 2 at all, it did so by moving backward from the developed code after the user finally rejected it! Today, it is generally recognized that this sort of ad hoc approach will be satisfactory only for the smallest of projects, in particular for programs and projects where only one programmer, or at most a very few programmers, need to be concerned with the software product throughout the lifecycle of software (or complete system) acquisition. Our earlier discussion of the emergence of systems engineering emphasized precisely these points.

For "large" software projects, a systems-engineering-based methodological approach appears potentially capable of improving software productivity. Fundamentally, as we have noted, two generic approaches can be used to enhance software productivity: *micro-enhancement approaches and macro-enhancement approaches*. Productivity improvements may be obtained through a combination of micro-and macro-enhancement approaches. A systems engineering approach may be taken to either, as we have indicated. An appropriate systems management effort will result in the identification of a suitable methodology for software production that will include a suitable mixture of these approaches.

1.6 MICRO-ENHANCEMENT AIDS

The micro-enhancement approach is based on improving the results obtained at each phase of the software acquisition lifecycle through improved programming methods and other direct productivity aids. Although many of these are available, it appears that a suitable taxonomy of micro-enhancement aids should include the following:

A. **Programmer Productivity Aids** These aids generally enhance the productivity of the individual programmer to produce functional code. They include:

A.1. **Direct Productivity Aids** These generally reduce the effort needed to produce functionally complete programs. These include very high level programming languages, automatic program generators, preprogrammed modules, and other development tools. These generally improve productivity by directly reducing the number of lines of program code that would have to be written using conventional program languages. Interactive query languages, graphics languages, report generators, data analysis and modeling tools, intelligent text editors, and other nonprocedural software aids are of value as well, especially when they are very carefully adapted to the development environment.

A.2. **Error Prevention and Removal Techniques** These generally use one or more structured approaches that enable easier visualization, especially by those who did not construct the code initially, of the logical flow of data and control within a program or of the hierarchical levels of control within a very large software system. Typical approaches include structured programming, top-down design approaches, and various hierarchical charting approaches. The use of the structured approaches generally reduces the probability of programmer error in writing code. This, in turn, reduces the amount of time required to accomplish corrective programming. Automated program testing approaches are also of potential value. Structured "walkthroughs," code inspections, and design reviews are more easily performed by others than when programming has been accomplished by unstructured, eclectic, and adhoc approaches.

There exists another general class of techniques that result in greater automation of the code production process. We denote these as

B. Nonprocedural Techniques   Nonprocedural techniques include a variety of aids that support reduction in the amount of conventional code writing necessary to produce a working program. These include a number of direct productivity aids such as report generators, automatic program generators, and very high level programming languages. A goal in most of these is to enable those knowledgeable about some particular issue to produce a solution to the problem without the direct support of a programmer.

Our efforts in Chapters 4 and 5 will be devoted to a discussion of these approaches.

1.7   MACRO-ENHANCEMENT APPROACHES

While the micro-enhancement approaches to software productivity are of much value, especially in improving individual and programming team productivity, there is potentially more to be gained from also incorporating macro-enhancement approaches. Macro-enhancement approaches generally attempt to obtain the sort of economies of scale that result from automated approaches that, at least by analogy, are more usually associated with product manufacturing. In effect, they attempt to achieve analogous results in the form of a "software factory." There are at least three related approaches that may be used, preferably in combination, to obtain a software production line: rapid prototyping, reusable software, and knowledge support systems. Clearly, these approaches are not mutually exclusive; an effective "software production line" or "software factory" should doubtlessly make use of each of them.

We will examine each of these approaches in our subsequent efforts in Chapter 8. One particular advantage of each of them is that they are very associated with overall technical direction and management of the software production process. Also, they have considerable appeal as aids to effective accomplishment of the earlier phases of software systems design.

Historically, many efforts to solve the software crisis have focused on improving the code written by applications programmers. As we have noted, this is a microenhancement approach. The process often relies on high-level programming languages, perhaps augmented by a program structuring method, as the basic development tool. The programmer productivity approach focuses on the methods of providing solutions rather than on the solution requirements. The results of these efforts (structured analysis and programming) have done little to reduce the applications development backlog even though they are a definite improvement over unstructured ad-hoc approaches. High personnel costs, extended time periods for development, and significant maintenance expenses have continued to plague software development. Wrong problem solution is an often occurring malady, as well. Our belief is that these difficulties have occurred not because applications specialists failed to use existing technology for structured approaches, *but* because they failed to use a large scale macro-enhancement approach coupled with a sound systems management perspective.

Many errors occur at the front end of the software development lifecycle, which results in the considerable need to work with users to define appropriate requirements specifications. Generally, errors introduced by inadequate requirement specifications, or inadequate conceptual software designs, cannot be corrected by the application of structured methods at the programming phase of the development effort.

The elimination of some of the error-prone steps in software development due to conventional languages and the use of new processes and technologies will result in shorter time periods required to develop and write software with concomitant lower costs, particularly when automated program construction techniques are applied. However, these improvements will not result from increasing the application of new technology to traditional structured approaches, but rather from nontraditional improvements to the software development cycle. This is, of course, important. But the improvements in productivity, while significant, may not be as significant as those obtained through the combined use of micro-enhancement techniques and systems management approaches that involve macro-enhancement approaches.

This occurs largely because the requirements specification phase is the first point at which the conceptualization of the system is translated from the user environment to the realm of the software professional, and this phase is particularly amenable to incorporation of macro-enhancement approaches. It is at this stage that we often make the fatal errors that lead to the design of correct software for an incorrect purpose. Generally, this is a very expensive error.

Software prototyping is one approach to macro-enhancement. Several potential advantages to prototyping, especially at the requirements specification phase of the system lifecycle, are easily seen. In particular, it allows the system user to experiment with versions, in terms of prototypes, of evolving systems that can be evaluated in terms of their ability to meet user needs. While prototyping may have many advantages in enhancing results that could be obtained from various micro-design enhancement approaches, and the micro-enhancement approach of automatic program generation can be regarded as an elementary form of prototyping, the advantages associated with the development and use of large-scale complete system-level prototypes are potentially very large.

While there are many ways to describe prototyping, and the lifecycle phases to use in construction of a prototype, all will necessarily involve *definition*, *construction*, and *exercise and evaluation of the prototype* as well as the ultimate conversion of the prototype into a final system, and ultimate test and evaluation of this final system. An important distinction between the phases of effort that should occur in prototyping and those that generally occur in the usual system development lifecycle is that many of the phases occur in parallel, thereby potentially reducing system development time and risks through the meta-level learning and incremental change that is encouraged. Also inherent in the prototyping process is iteration and feedback.

Figure 1.16 illustrates how this process might proceed in a typical application. The key words here, as in other approaches to software systems engineering, are *user involvement, iteration, learning, and interactive process.* The result of this, at least normatively, is software productivity and trustworthiness. We note that while this might appear to represent a change in the phases of the software lifecycle as discussed earlier, all of the essential phased activities are present, although some are aggregated together.

The software development lifecycle using prototyping differs from the conventional software development lifecycle in several very minor ways brought about through the greater interaction and feedback involved. Fundamentally, the three phases of formulation of specifications, system design, and installation and maintenance are still involved.

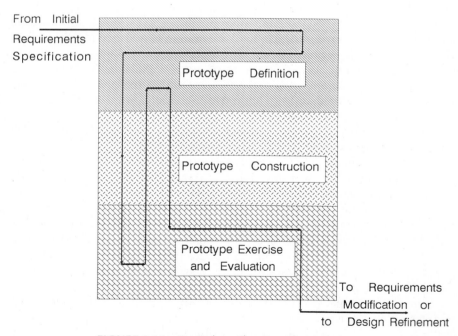

FIGURE 1.16   Typical rapid prototyping iterations

There a number of uses for rapid prototyping, including:

1. Correctness-validation prototyping
2. Performance prototyping
3. Structural prototyping
4. User interface prototyping
5. Requirements specifications prototyping

We will examine each of these in Chapter 8. Other uses for, and taxonomies of, rapidly constructed prototypes can also be identified. We indicated earlier that one method of information requirements identification, or system requirements identification, is through experimentation with an evolving system. This is not an inexpensive approach to development, but it is sometimes the only feasible approach. Conceptual prototyping can be of much use here in enabling this in an efficient and effective manner.

System evaluation is often needed. Generally, systems must be evaluated against some standards or benchmarks. To accomplish this, it is often very desirable to have some alternative system whose performance can be compared against the existing system. At the very least, this allows the determination of evaluation metrics. Thus prototyping should be useful for the evaluation of existing systems. There is no question but that prototypes could have very valuable training functions. Many other uses could be cited as well. Three perspectives may be taken in the construction and use of prototypes: *structural, functional, and purposeful.* The use for a prototype determines which type, or which combination of types, is most useful for a specific need. We will examine each of these types, and the several names by which they are known, in Chapter 8.

Software modification is another attractive macro-enhancement approach. Various *software reusability* approaches may be used to adapt existing software to new applications and potentially new operational environments. Among these, the following seem most important:

1. Modification of complete programs constructed for one purpose and modified to perform another purpose
2. Repeated use, after modification, of complete subprograms

There are also a variety of other alternatives. The two alternatives described above constitute the reuse methods that are commonly exercised, for the reason that these can be implemented using development tools (compilers, linkers, module generators) that are accepted parts of most programming environments. This does not exhaust all possibilities however. Chapter 8 may be consulted for a discussion of some of these.

Among the many needs for which reusable software is potentially applicable, the following seem especially significant:

- Linking preexisting preprogrammed modules and routines into a new program
- Incorporating the products of automatic program generators.

The success of a reusability concept depends on a number of important factors that can be posed as a series of questions:

1. Is the long-term cost of using the reusability scheme favorable as compared to traditional ad hoc programming or, more importantly, to improved programming technologies?
2. Is the long-term cost of using the reusability scheme favorable as compared to any of the nonprocedural approaches, such as automatic program generation, or parametrized applications software?
3. Is the mix of operational task requirements to be undertaken consistent with frequent modification and reuse of a limited set of high-quality modules?
4. Is the initial cost, including preparation of special modules that may be modified and used in later program developments, acceptable?
5. Has the danger of force-fitting existing software into a new application without accommodating changed user requirements been overcome?
6. Does there exist appropriate standards that supports reusability notions?

The combination of reusability and prototyping is very attractive. However, there are possible areas of conflict. Reusability and prototyping, although both addressing software development, may be addressed by different individuals or organizations and will almost certainly be addressed at different points in time, and in different phases in the system development lifecycle. This suggests the potential need for some preconditioning of software determined to be reusable, such that it can appropriately be integrated into the milieu of micro-level approaches available in a functional software systems engineering development environment.

Prototyping will most likely be exercised early in the lifecycle system development to construct customer demonstrations, to identify system requirements and possible architectural constructs based on these requirements, or to prove feasibility. Although prospects for reusability will be examined early in the system development lifecycle, it will become an active interest mainly during code development and detailed design. Whereas prototyping is likely to be carried out by a few of the brightest and most innovative software systems engineers, or system designers, reusable software concept implementation may often be accomplished by skilled programmers. Thus there are a number of systems management issues associated with the appropriate use of these two macro-enhancement concepts.

While this is certainly a correct conventional view of the reusability concept a much more useful and appropriate approach is to develop, potentially through the use of knowledge support system approaches, the equivalent of a shell that will enable software systems engineers to submit queries to a reusable software "pool" and extract pertinent components for modification. What we envision here is ultimately a developed taxonomy of reusability and an identified reuse methodology. We believe that this will involve the careful selection and integration of micro-enhancement and macro-enhancement approaches for software productivity. Through use of the reusability approach, it becomes possible to develop *reusable software parts or modules,* which we will call *softproducts.* Also, it is conceptually possible to produce *reusable parts of a software development process,* or *softprocesses.*

There are, of course, caveats in all of this. In practice, much software often remains *"almost ready"* for a great many months. An appropriate software prototyping and reuse methodology must seek to reduce the time that software remains almost ready.

To increase overall productivity, it is at least necessary for the group responsible for efforts at one phase in the development lifecycle to pass useful information to other groups involved in subsequent phases. More importantly, it suggests the strong need for iteration and interaction among the many agents responsible for different activities within the software system development lifecycle. Again, adroit systems management is a real need.

As we have noted, crucial software systems developments are dependent on good and timely decisions with regard to requirements specifications. In turn, this is strongly dependent on the quality of the information available concerning the specific problem needs of the user or client, and associated constraints and alterables. Generally the information will be imprecise and have far too many aspects for the individual systems designer to cope with without knowledge-based support. The result of this is stress and limited ability to make good decisions in a timely way. In order to handle the large amounts of information that are characteristic of large-scale complex systems and determine the degree of imprecision acceptable to make meaningful decisions, it is necessary that the software systems development team be able to develop and maintain a detailed perception of the situation to enable these perceptions to be interpreted into meaningful requirements specifications. In the development of specifications it is necessary that the requirements be assessed carefully, and that any important and likely to occur future developments that might impact the specifications be integrated into the system. Generally this is very difficult of accomplishment, especially if it is not possible to experiment with an evolving system in a realistic setting that is essentially that of the operational environment. Some of the basic issues that impact software productivity relate to the manner in which the design functions are articulated and the multiple perspectives through which users and designers understand the situation.

The problems associated with the software systems designer's understanding of the issues are not limited to information overload or incomplete or fuzzy information, but include the notion of limited attention span, failure to recognize and use information that may contradict originally held beliefs, and other uses of what amounts to improper use of the information that is available to them. The bottleneck is the natural cognitive limits of humans who are able to perceive what they are prepared to see and that which falls into the interest area of the limited attention span. Cognitive limits affect individuals differently and may cause significant discrepancies in information interpretation, dependent on the specific cognitive base of the individuals concerned.

A potential solution to these problems is the development and use of *knowledge support systems* (KSSs) for requirements specifications processes. The major need in this regard is to be able to transfer knowledge from system users to specifications in an appropriate manner. Better ideas and better problem resolution will potentially occur because individuals working inter-actively with the KSS will be working from a welldocumented knowledge base. The goal is to render knowledge accessible, intelligible, and malleable so that the KSS may be adaptable to change and to feedback for error detection, and ultimately to meta-level learning on the part of the software design team.

1.8   PERSPECTIVES ON SOFTWARE SYSTEMS ENGINEERING

A software systems engineering design issue can be viewed from the perspectives of the three principal actors involved. At one level are the users and clients who are concerned primarily with what the specific, to be developed, system can do for them. Their natural, and almost exclusive focus, is on the problem-solving tasks that they face in a particular environmental context. It is the interaction of these variables and their experiential familiarity with task and environment that determines their problem-solving needs. The perspective of the system designer, or system architect or system builder, is that of assisting the user in terms of specifying architecture to accomplish the task or evaluating an existing system to determine the extent to which it fulfills needs and is operationally functional. At the level of tools, programmers are responsible for converting these architectural specifications into working code. What we are suggesting is that a principal role of the software designer, or software systems engineer is to interact with the user to assist the user in organizing information.

This discussion also illustrates the strong relationship between the macro-enhancement tools and the micro-enhancement tools. While a macro-enhancement tool such as rapid prototyping may be most useful for developing requirements specifications for a system, or in developing a standard against which a set of metrics for evaluation of an existing system may be accomplished, it will be generally through the use of micro-enhancement tools that actual realization of major portions (if not all portions) of an operational system will be realized. This realization may be guided or controlled through the products of macro-enhancement technology.

In the software environment of today, critical application developments, invoke a number of important needs, such as:

1. Accommodating changes in external environment (the evolving enterprise needs)
2. Accommodating changes in user requirements (evolving roles and perceptions of system users) and associated internal environments
3. Use of product technologies that automate program construction
4. Use of technologies that reduce programming errors
5. Focus on information and systems management, rather than on data processing procedures

These approaches produce programs that exhibit rigid adherence to conventions for internal data and procedure names, program structure and external procedure calls, and standards for reliability and trustworthiness. Needs for the immediate future also deal with issues in the development process, such as:

6. Providing rapid turnaround for (re)development of applications
7. Coping with the structure, function, and purpose(s) of a multipurpose information system
8. Accommodating multiple users in distributed locations
9. Accommodating effective and efficient software maintenance
10. Transitioning to new environments in an efficient and effective manner

Achieving these requires a combination of appropriate software methods for micro-enhancement and macro-enhancement, software design and development methodologies, as well as systems management processes.

As with any set of methods, the approaches to software productivity are based on a variety of concepts and structures. It is unreasonable to expect them always to constructively interact. The software productivity methods of primary interest identified here and to be discussed in the sequel include:

A. Micro-enhancement based approaches
   1. Improved programming technology
      1.1 Error prevention techniques
         1.1.1 Structured programming
         1.1.2 Composite design
         1.1.3 Hierarchical design
         1.1.4 Top down design
      1.2 Error removal techniques
         1.2.1 Design code inspection
         1.2.2 Structured walkthroughs
         1.2.3 Design reviews

  1.3   Direct aids to productivity
    1.3.1   High level programming languages*
    1.3.2   On line development tools
    1.3.3   Preprogrammed Modules
 2. Nonprocedural techniques
  2.1   Query languages to update data and model bases
  2.2   Report generators to format and produce results
  2.3   Graphic languages
  2.4   Automatic program (applications) generators
  2.5   Very high level programming languages†
  2.6   Parametrized or generic application software
B. Macro-enhancement based approaches
 1. Software prototyping
 2. Reusable software
 3. Knowledge based support for software production

Generally, we do not believe that it will be possible to determine the costs and benefits, including risk elements, of particular approaches out of context. This suggests the strong need for the development of a robust set of task, functions, and methods taxonomies within meaningful operational settings. We will then be able to specify software productivity design protocols that result in the production of trustworthy operational software that is compatible with the problems desirous of solution and the cognitive perspectives of the humans who ultimately serve as user and client for the software. The developed software systems engineering methodology, which would allow the appropriate matching of functions and tasks with methods, would be of much value to both application problem-solvers and software system designers. It would enable users and clients to input problem characteristics into a *software design aid* and receive recommendations regarding appropriate software design strategies.

An initial and conceptual version of this software design aid and associated environment is presented in Figure 1.17. It involves use of the micro-enhancement-based approaches and the macro-enhancement-based approaches together with systems engineering tools for management and technological support, appropriate systems design methodologies, and systems management processes. Taken together, these result in the knowledge base for software systems engineering. This knowledge base is used for technological system design and management system design of productive and functionally useful software. We will provide much more commentary on this systems design environment in the following chapters.

We intend much more than a set of unsubstantiated personal preferences regarding the usefulness and ubiquity of selected methods for software pro-

---

*Pascal, Basic, C, and Ada are illustrations of high-level programming languages.
†The Interactive Financial Planning System (IFPS) is a very-high-level programming language.

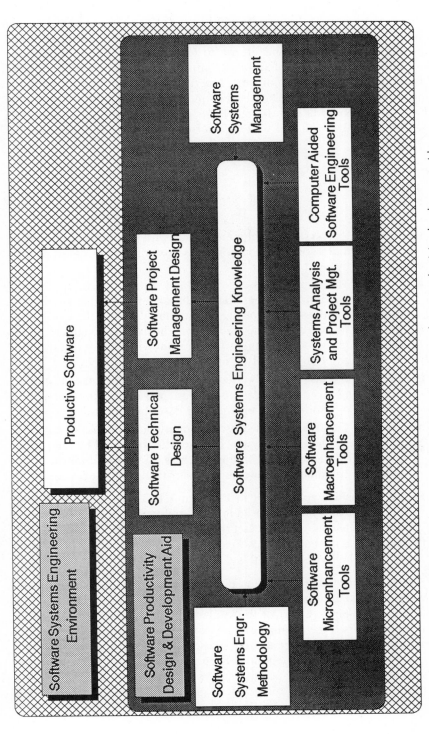

FIGURE 1.17 The conceptual ingredients in a software productivity development aid

duction. We will describe tools and methods for software productivity, design methodologies for software productivity, and systems management processes for software productivity in our efforts to follow. Nevertheless, our efforts can not be regarded as complete or definitive—for this is an evolving field that is not complete and definitive. Hopefully, they provide a substantial advance in the state of the art in this area and a basis for continued progress.

This, then, represents both the goals for and an outline of our efforts to follow. We trust that you will find the journey a pleasant and a productive one.

1.9   PROBLEMS

1.1. Please consider a system development issue with which you are familiar. One with a major software component is preferable, but not at all necessary. For this system:

   a. Consider the 12 maladies of system and software development detailed in Section 1.3. Please score the extent to which these were problems for the system you are considering. Replace the word "software" by the word "system" and rescore the extent to which problems arose. It might be convenient to use some yardstick, such as "0 = no problem at all" and "1 = major problem."

   b. Define the phases actually used to develop the system that you are considering. Contrast and compare these phases with the seven phase methodology for systems engineering described here.

   c. Consider the attributes of software quality detailed in Section 1.4.2. Please score the extent to which these were obtained for the system you are considering. Use scaling, such as "0 = not obtained at all" and "1 = obtained to the complete satisfaction of all concerned."

1.2. Please reconsider your effort in Problem 1.1. To what extent are the various scales that you have used in this problem subjective? How would you potentially cope with the fact that someone might consider precisely the same system that you have examined and come up with different scores? In what ways would this difference be significant?

1.3. Again, reconsider Problem 1.1. Please redefine the effort that actually was undertaken in the system design that you are considering according to the seven phase effort of the system lifecycle defined in Figure 1.6. If this appears to be a cumbersome set of phases for the effort that you are considering, consider a three phase effort that involves definition, development, and maintenance. Then decompose any of these phases that involved significant activity into a number of smaller phases. You have just defined your own system lifecycle. How does your system lifecycle contrast and compare with the one that we have identified in this chapter?

1.4. Please prepare a set of costs and benefits for each of the four fundamental ways of identifying information requirements that have been discussed in Section 1.4.4. Apply this set of identified costs and benefits to the system that you identified in Problem 1.1. How were information requirements identified in the actual system that you have considered? How might this have been better accomplished?

1.5. In the system that you have considered, how did the time and effort to complete the project differ across the various phases that you have identified? How did these compare with that initially contemplated?

Chapter 2

Models for the Software Development Lifecycle

2.1 INTRODUCTION

Software development lifecycles have their roots in engineering methods and more specifically in the processes and procedures of systems engineering, as we have noted in Chapter 1. Sound use of a software development lifecycle should have the most beneficial effect on the development of larger software systems, but may be used to organize and direct software development efforts of any degree of complexity.

The use of the tools of systems engineering to develop, analyze, and implement large-scale systems is embedded in the several software development lifecycles in use today. As with all large-scale systems, large-scale software systems require a considerable amount of time to develop. The purpose of a lifecycle approach to software engineering is to enhance the productivity, quality, and functionality of software through identification of a number of development phases that enable efficient and effective systems management of the software development process. One of the principal advantages to this approach is that it disaggregates a large and complex issue into a well-defined sequence of presumably simpler issues that are easier to understand, communicate with, manage, and cope with.

The lifecycle approach of systems engineering prescribes a number of phases that should be followed, generally in an interactive and iterative manner, to enable success to be realized in fielding a large-scale system that meets user requirements. There have been a number of lifecycle models proposed and used for multiphase systems engineering efforts. Each of them will start with capturing user requirements. These user requirements are then transitioned to technological system requirements and systems management requirements that will presumably, when satisfied, produce the ultimate product or service. Following the requirements phase(s), there is a detailed design phase that results in an initial working version of a system. This is evaluated and modified to enable ultimate operational deployment of the system, which is followed by maintenance-modification phase. Figure 2.1 shows a typical seven-phase systems engineering lifecycle. As we have noted in Chapter 1, feedback and iteration among these phases will often be needed.

In principal, a complex large-scale system will contain both technological system design and management system design aspects if it is to be realized in an effective and efficient manner. A system lifecycle model may be conceptualized using management or technological system design perspectives or a hybrid of the two. These are not mutually exclusive perspectives, however. In general, we believe that a management system design (and development) perspective is very much needed, as it leads naturally to an organizational structure for tasks and people. To have only one perspective is to invite, if not guarantee, failure.

Use of the systems engineering approach to systems development and management is intended to result in a tailorable software development lifecycle that addresses the specific software development needs from both technological and management perspectives. The use of a lifecycle:

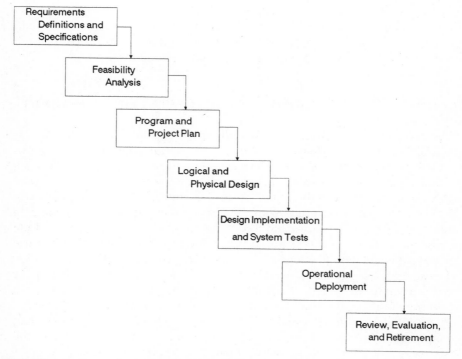

FIGURE 2.1 Typical systems engineering lifecycle showing information flow and feedback paths

1. Enhances our ability to establish requirements to be satisfied by the proposed development
2. Identifies and highlights potentially difficult problem areas
3. Permits the synthesis and evaluation of alternative solutions to difficult issues associated with each of the phases in the lifecycle
4. Enables selection of appropriate activities for each of the phases
5. Provides cost information
6. Lends itself to assignment of personnel
7. Lends itself to enforcement of standards
8. Encourages the use of support tools
9. Aids in the preparation of a quality product that is delivered on time and within budget
10. Lends itself to management control

The use of a systems lifecycle model for a software development project is essentially equivalent to placing management controls over the various functions to be performed in producing the resulting software product. As with any formal approach, the use of any specific software development lifecycle has advantages and disadvantages. However, it is safe to state that the use of an appropriate lifecycle model for software development is far better than development with no management organization or control at all. In this chapter, we will discuss some of the more popular forms of software development lifecycles, including their advantages and disadvantages.

2.2   THE "WATERFALL" SOFTWARE DEVELOPMENT LIFECYCLE MODEL

Credit for the introduction of a lifecycle for use in software development is generally attributed to Royce [1970]. The model introduced by Royce was termed the *Waterfall model* and embodied the systems engineering approach to building large-scale systems that had already been in existence for some time. Figure 2.2 presents this initial "waterfall" lifecycle model. Boehm [1976] has been especially concerned with the economic importance of regularizing the development of software and has further developed and popularized the use of the waterfall lifecycle for software development. Since its initial use by Royce, many modifications and iterations have been made to the model. The use of the conventional (waterfall) lifecycle has demonstrated that better software will result from the careful and systematic approaches that are called for through the careful use of a software development lifecycle.

The initial waterfall lifecycle model has undergone numerous refinements. Many versions of the software development lifecycle models appear in the literature, and almost all of these define five to seven-phases for systems engineering of the software development processes. One definitive presentation of the waterfall model was that of Boehm [1976]. Boehm defined the

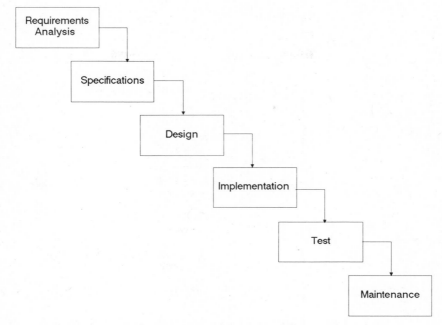

FIGURE 2.2   Waterfall model for software development due to Royce

overall set of seven-phases for the waterfall software development lifecycle shown in Figure 2.3. The similarity to the systems engineering approach is explicit. Another form of the waterfall software development lifecycle is that used by the U. S. Department of Defense, DoD STD 2167-A, which is shown in Figure 2.4. This model explicitly splits the system development process into hardware and software development efforts. We will expand considerably on this, and similar models, in Chapters 9 and 10.

In a very ideal situation, each of the above phases could be carried out individually to completion and in sequence. When all the phases have been executed, the software product is delivered and works, as intended by the original user or client, in accordance with the initial need or user requirements for the system. Actually, this rarely happens. What usually happens is that one more phases are often repeated, after deficiencies are found, until the system is correct or nearly so.

As an example, the system design commences once the initial requirements are elicited from the user. When viewing the results of system design, the user discovers that certain things have been omitted or perhaps were misunderstood when initially specifying system requirements. The development process then iterates back once again to the requirements phase. This entails additional work and further iteration with the user until the user group is again satisfied that the requirements fulfill their intentions. Then the process

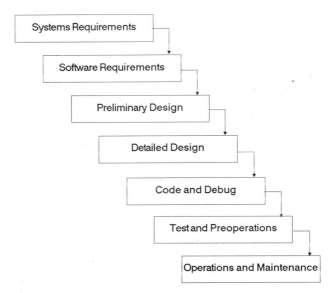

FIGURE 2.3   Waterfall software development lifecycle due to Boehm

moves on again to the development of system-level requirements. As progress is made in the evolution of the software product, we may find that some of the initially specified requirements are not able to be supported by the system due to earlier decisions that have been made. Once again, the user is involved to identify a constructive solution for the problem. This undoubtedly should call for revisiting the system requirements phase and tracking the implication of the newly resulting requirements through subsequent phases. Such multiple iterations back to the requirements phase are seldom fully accomplished. Often this is due to such legal reasons as contractual obligations, but may be infeasible because of availability of time and allocations of funds.

Iteration and interaction are the key factors to be attended to in order to produce a successful software product. A note of caution needs to be inserted here. It really is better to "do it right the first time." It is often very expensive to accomplish major iteration, reiteration, and interaction through much re-cycling through the lifecycle phases. The rapid prototyping approach, which is described in detail in Chapter 8, is very useful in achieving these goals of efficient and effective identification of requirements.

The processes to be carried out in implementation of the waterfall software development lifecycle model of Boehm [1976], shown in Figure 2.3, are as follows:

Phase 1: Systems Requirements Specification   The specification of systems

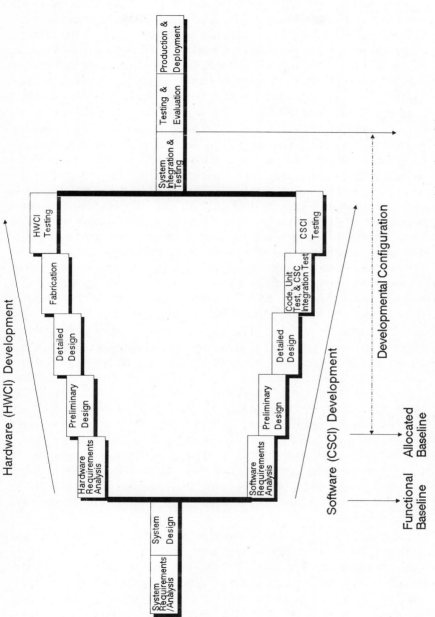

FIGURE 2.4 Department of defense standard 2167-a software lifecycle model

53

requirements is the first phase in the waterfall model of Boehm. In implementing this phase, it is assumed that the system user and the systems analyst are sufficiently informed about what the new (or modified) system is intended to achieve so as to be able to develop the system-level requirements to an acceptable level such that they can be identified in sufficiently complete detail that preliminary design can be initiated. All of this is to be done before detailed design and coding may be initiated. Some of the specific tasks that have been identified for this phase are given in Section 2.3 of this chapter, in the form of a requirements activity matrix.

Phase 2: Software Requirements   The development of the software requirements phase focuses on the outcomes of the system requirements identification carried out in phase 1 of the waterfall model of the software development lifecycle. It is concerned with the nature and style of the software to be developed, the data and information that will be required and the associated structural framework, the required functionality, performance, and various interfaces. Requirements for both the system and the software are reviewed for consistency and then reviewed by the user to be certain that the software requirements faithfully interpret and produce the system requirements. A software requirements definition document is produced in this phase. It becomes a technology and a management guideline that is used throughout all subsequent development phases, including validation and testing.

Phase 3: Preliminary Design   The software requirements developed in phase 2 are converted into a preliminary software product design in this phase, which is primarily aimed at the further interpretation of the software requirements in terms of software system-level architecture. The product of this phase is an identification and micro-level definition of the data structure, software architecture, and procedural activities that must be carried out in the next phase. Data items and structures are described in abstract terms as a guide to the detailed design phase. Instructions that describe the input, output, and processing that are to be executed within a particular module are developed. Preliminary software design involves representing the functions of each software system in a way that these may readily be converted to a detailed design in the next phase.

Phase 4: Detailed Design   The preliminary design phase resulted in insight as to how the system is intended to work at a structural level and satisfy the technological system requirements. Detailed design phase activities involve definition of the program modules and intermodular interfaces that are necessary in preparation for the writing of code. Specific reference is made to data formats. Detailed descriptions of algorithms are provided. All the inputs to and outputs from detailed design modules must be traceable back to the system and software requirements that were generated in phases 1 and 2. During this phase, the software design is fine-tuned.

Phase 5: Code and Debug   In this phase, the detailed design is translated into machine-readable form. If the design has been accomplished in a sufficiently detailed manner, it may be possible to use automated code generators to perform all, or a major portion of, this task. After writing the software design requirements as a set of program units in the appropriate high-level programming language, the resulting high-level code is compiled and executed. Generally, "bugs" are discovered, and debugging and recoding takes place to validate the integrity of the overall coding operations of this phase.

Phase 6: Testing and Preoperation   At this phase, the individual units or programs are integrated and tested as a complete system to ensure that the requirements specifications drawn up in phases 1 and 2 are met. Testing procedures center on the logical functions of the software. They assure that all statements have been tested, and that all inputs and outputs operate properly. After system testing, the software is operated under controlled conditions to verify and validate the entire package in terms of satisfying the identified system specifications and software specifications.

Phase 7: Operations and Maintenance   This phase of the waterfall lifecycle is often the longest from the perspective of the entire useful life of the software product. As noted in Chapter 1, the phases concerned with detailed design, coding, and testing are usually the most effort intensive. In phase 7, the system is installed at the user location and is tested, and then used, under actual operating conditions to the maximum extent possible. Maintenance commences immediately on detection of any errors that were not found during the earlier phase. This is usually not the intended purpose of maintenance, however. Maintenance is primarily the process of improving the system to accommodate new or different requirements as defined by the user.

These seven phases normally take place in the sequential manner described. However, there is considerable iteration and interaction intended between the several phases. Each software development firm tailors the specific software development lifecycle process to meet the particular characteristics of the personnel of the firm, the needs of users for the software to be developed, and economic, legal, and time for development concerns.

In a software development effort that is subject to extremely tight time constraints, it would not be unusual for coding to be initiated in a "fast-track" mode. In a situation such as this, once the requirements specifications are in hand, detailed design commences and coding is started as detailed design information is made available. Fast-tracking is a risky business in software design just as it is in civil engineering bridge and building construction. Should an error be made in determination of the requirements, or in detailed design, the cost of recovering from these errors late in the development lifecycle is extremely high. On the other hand, if the requirements can be easily, precisely, and completely identified, if they do not change or are modified only slightly, and if the detailed design is adequate, then the savings in time and cost that may result in an early delivery "bonus" are probably well worth the risk.

Many perceived modifications and enhancements to the initial software development lifecycle models have been made. Some of these *"improvements"* include the introduction of structured processes, the use of automated toolkits to remove manual efforts in the design process, the use of automatic code generators for the coding phase, and the automation of testing procedures. These are only a few of the *"innovations"* that have taken place. However, these are not changes to the lifecycle at all. We know from our discussions in Chapter 1 that these are just tool- or method-based changes and are in no way changes at "the methodology level." We will discuss the logical design of software and architecture and the use of various toolkits to automate certain phases of the software development lifecycle, in much greater detail, in Chapter 4, which is devoted to conceptual and logical design of software and architecture design and specification.

The major advantages from use of the classical waterfall software development lifecycle model, or one of its many modifications, are those of organizing and controlling the software development project. The introduction of new and higher-quality methods and tools into the process has also had an immediate and lasting effect on the quality and performance characteristics of software productivity efforts.

The single most important methodological need associated with use of the waterfall lifecycle model is that of effective identification of user requirements. Associated with this is the need for established processes and procedures to ensure the accuracy of the identified user requirements. In no way is this need the result of use of a software lifecycle model. It is just that in the usual lifecycle development, inadequate attention is paid to fulfilling this need. This factor is discussed in detail in Chapter 3, which concerns software requirements analysis and specifications, and elsewhere in this text.

Disadvantages associated with use of a lifecycle model include problems that occur if there is no iteration and feedback among phases. Unless there is iteration and feedback, there may be no way to improve initial imperfections in one of the phases. As noted earlier, realistic lifecycle development processes are iterative and interactive, and the software development lifecycle is one that encourages management to recognize these *facts of life* in order to be successful in guiding software development projects.

This introduces the potential concern of excessive time and expense incurred through repeated, potentially endless, iterations through the development lifecycle. Hopefully however, there is learning involved through repeated use of a system development process such that the efficiency and effectiveness in use of the process improves over time. The iterations do not, in practice, continue forever.

2.3 ITERATIVE WATERFALL SOFTWARE DEVELOPMENT LIFECYCLE MODELS

Following the introduction of the waterfall model, there have been many attempts to improve on it. Generally speaking, these attempts include one or more of the following:

1. Decrease the compartmentalization of the processes and procedures.
2. Introduce various automation toolkits.
3. Increase flexibility into the model for the development of large-scale software systems.

As we noted previously, attempt 2 is really an attempt at the tool level, not at the methodology level. The number of phases used in these models is subject to change. Seven is a very convenient number; however, it is a simple task to aggregate or disaggregate to more of less phases in the system development lifecycle. Several waterfall software development lifecycle models have been developed and some of these are included here. We make no attempt at completeness, however, as the differences between the variations is not great.

2.3.1 The Structured Project Lifecycle

The concept of the structured software development lifecycle was introduced by Yourdon and is the subject of his book [Yourdon, 1982]. The primary goal of the structured software development lifecycle is to enable incorporation of the use of structured development tools and techniques as a way of organizing and carrying out software development projects. Thus, it is much more a contribution to the use of an improved toolset for development than it is to methodological thought. Structured techniques involve the use of formal software specifications, definition of system components, the activities required to complete the design, and explication of interfaces between software modules or components. This software development lifecycle provides methods and techniques to organize, manage, and control software projects, as well as giving analysts, designers, and programmers the tools to accomplish many activities involved in software design and development.

The intent of the structured software development lifecycle process, which is the classic waterfall model augmented with structured tools, is to provide the software development team with the tools necessary to produce a quality product through the use of structured analysis, design, and programming techniques. Through the application of structured techniques, it is possible to make the analysis, design, and coding easier to manage than if unstructured techniques were used. Also it becomes easier to gauge the goodness of fit of the software requirements to the requirements of the user.

The tools suggested for use within the phases of the structured software development lifecycle include data flow diagrams, data dictionaries, structure charts, and structured English. This approach, as in the classic waterfall model, is a top-down approach to the design process. Project control is presumably enhanced because of the structured tools used.

Figure 2.5 presents the nine phases of the structured project lifecycle model of Yourdon. The nine separate phases for the activity matrix described by Yourdon are as follows:

Phase 1: The Survey   The survey phase is intended to elicit the needs of the high-level user and to determine the goals and objectives of the user for the software system development under consideration. The outcomes

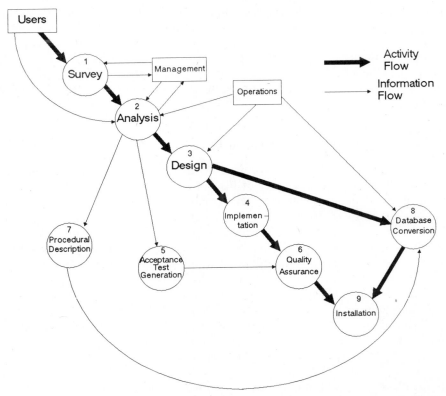

FIGURE 2.5   The Yourdan structured software development lifecycle model showing activity and information flows

of this phase are a determination of general feasibility for the project, generation of acceptable software design and development scenarios, and preparation of a "project charter" to be used as a guide for the entire development process.

Phase 2: Analysis In this phase, the survey results are transformed into structured specifications using data flow diagrams as the primary tool.

Phase 3: Design During the design phase, the proper hierarchy of modules and interfaces is identified. In this phase, the hardware constraints are introduced and integrated into the design.

Phase 4: Implementation Coding and module integration, using structured programming and top-down implementation, are completed in this phase.

Phase 5: Acceptance Test Generation Once a subsystem or module specification has been completed and this information accepted by the user, a set of acceptance test cases is prepared from the structured specification.

Phase 6: Quality Assurance Using the acceptance test data from phase 5 as input information, final testing or acceptance testing is performed to determine quality assurance specification of the product.

Phase 7: Procedure Description In this phase, the User's Manual describing the entire system is produced.

Phase 8: Database Preparation Using the current database of the customer and the design specification developed in phase 3, or starting with the design specification from phase 3 if this is a totally new program, a database for all customer needs covered by the development efforts is prepared for user access.

Phase 9: Installation Drawing from the material generated for the preparation of the User's Manual, the converted database, and the acceptance test as guidelines, the system is installed, training is conducted, and the project is terminated.

There are three essential action groups associated with design and development of a software product: (1) owners of the software product or system; (2) operational users of the actual software, specifically, those who run the executable code; and (3) software development group management.

A fourth group that could have been noted are software designers. Yourdon views the software lifecycle as a management tool. Figure 2.6 presents an activity matrix of the structured software development lifecycle involving the nine (9) separate phases interacting with the three (3) so-called external activities. It depicts the interactions between each of the groups who have a vested interest in particular phases of the structured software development lifecycle. In reality, the three groups are the parties of interest in the software development.

From this we see that the "owner of the software" is particularly interested in the survey, acceptance testing, descriptions of the operations, and instal-

groups activity	owner of the software product	development group management	operations group
survey	x	x	
analysis		x	
design		x	x
implementation		x	x
acceptance test generation	x	x	x
quality assurance		x	x
procedure description	x	x	x
database conversion		x	x
installation	x	x	x

FIGURE 2.6   Structured lifecycle activity matrix

lation of the software. The development group management has a stake in all aspects of the development project. The operations group interests begin with design activities and continue through the end of the project to installation of the software at the owner's premises.

In order to demonstrate the utilization of structured design, we will examine how a software system might be developed to assist a student in going through the process of obtaining a class assignment during the first year of college. In this case, the student applies for admission to the university, the admission office reviews the application and makes a determination as to whether to admit the applicant. Presuming successful admission, the student must be advised by a faculty member, prepare a program of study, make a selection of classes from the schedule and apply for these classes through the registration process. This process will require databases, information flows, decision points (action items), and activities.

A flowchart of a portion of a structured design diagram that describes the flow of information related to activities involving the registrar, the admissions office, and academic department is shown in Figure 2.7. Our intent here is to demonstrate the utilization of structured diagrams to depict a variety of information flow structures that will be needed during the design phase. The general problem under consideration is that of design of an integrated information system for a university for which student enrollment for the first time is a special situation. The horizontal lines represent databases; the circles,

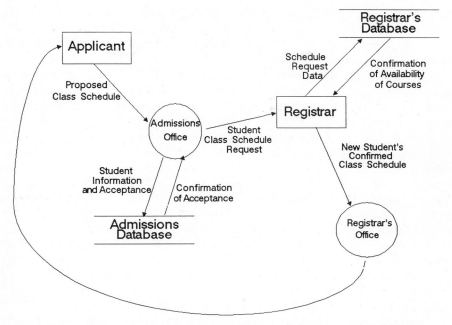

FIGURE 2.7 Level of dataflow diagram for a new student's first class schedule

activities; the directed lines, the flow of information; and the boxes, the repository for information and action items. With use of structured design the designer is able to provide feedback to the user to determine if the system meets user needs, develop detailed design information for use in generating code for the system, and give the specifications for databases. To do this successfully would seem to require that the user be able to understand and interpret potentially complicated flow diagrams.

The uses of the structured approach to software design are many and varied. In practice, the primary use has been in the area of business problems and not for real-time problems. The example we used is typical of transaction processing problems and applications for which the structured approach is found most useful. Other examples include financial systems, accounting systems, inventory systems, and personnel systems. These are similar, and each is characterized by information flows, action items, activities, and data storage that may be described in a logical structured form.

The advantages to the use of the structured software development lifecycle lie primarily in use of tools that have been provided. Their use makes completion of some of the phases of the lifecycle easier than otherwise might be the case. In a very real sense, there is nothing about this lifecycle model that is any more structured than the other models for the lifecycle that we have discussed up to this point. Nor is the lifecycle fundamentally any different.

It is some of the tools provided for implementation of the model that are structured. As shown in Figure 2.8, which contrasts the Yourdon model with the Boehm model, there is no difference in the phases specified, other than minor semantic ones.

The flow diagram tool provided for use with this software development lifecycle model depicts information flow within the user organization. We can also draw a structured model that indicates the increased feedback between activities, the iterative processes, and the interfacing between classes of users and the system development team members. This is shown by the use of the directed lines that indicate the feedback loops between the various phases. Management and resource allocation are defined to be under control of the project team at all times, thereby making it possible to track progress, by phases, against budget allocations. A structured design concept for this software development lifecycle and the interactive processes among the user organization groups are shown graphically in Figure 2.9.

The disadvantages of the structured design approach are largely those cited previously for the waterfall software development lifecycle. By regularizing the approach used to conform to the requirements of the structured modeling format, the potential for individual creativity may be reduced. The structured lifecycle development process is broken down into activities to be carried out during each phase. These activities are basically management guides for the team responsible for a given phase to use in carrying out the activities of that phase. This regularization and management of the development process, in and of itself, may lead to pressure to *get the job done within the specific phase, since performance may be measured against the outcomes of the phase.* This amounts to sublimation of the initial goal of software design for achieving the goals of the various phases. Should any of these be misdirected, the overall software product is likely to suffer.

2.3.2 Software Development Lifecycle Models with Feedback

It is relatively straightforward to obtain modification of the basic (Boehm) development lifecycle model by adding feedback from later phases to earlier occurring phases. The resulting models are virtually the same as the waterfall model in that they preserve all the phases of that model. The major departure lies in the recognition of the fact that no phase is carried on in isolation. Typical of the software development lifecycles that have embodied these feedback precepts is the one shown in Figure 2.10.

It is clear from this figure that the extensive degree of feedback and iteration made possible by considering all possible paths to connect the earlier occurring phases of the software development lifecycle may not be at all attractive. In the development of software products, it is desirable to have as much feedback and iteration as *required* to achieve the goal of a software product that meets the need of the user and one that is completed on time and within budget. Excessive feedback and iteration may be costly and may well not lead to a better product. Of course, there is nothing that says that

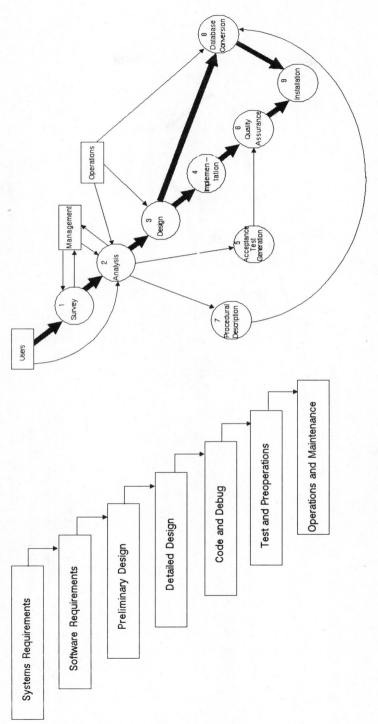

Boehm Waterfall Lifecycle Model

Yourdon Structured Lifecycle Model

FIGURE 2.8 A comparison of the Boehm waterfall software development lifecycle model with the Yourdan structured software development lifecycle

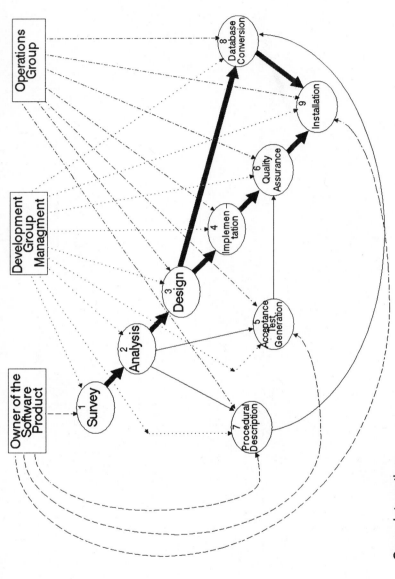

FIGURE 2.9 Interactive processes among user organization groups with activities of the structured software development lifecycle

········▶ **Owner Interactions**
– – – –▶ **Development Group Interactions**
–·–·–·–▶ **Operations Group Interactions**

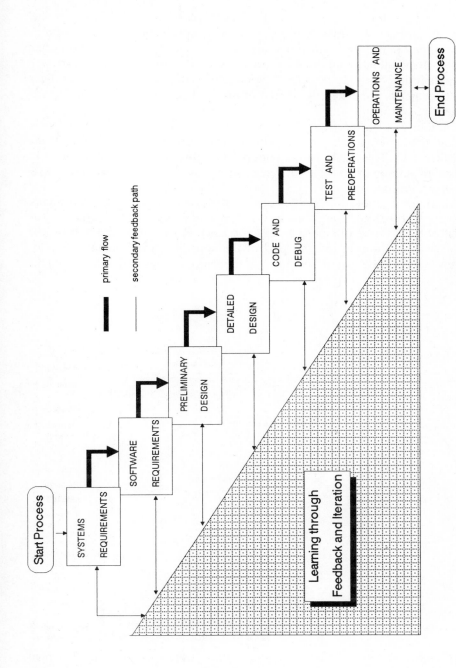

FIGURE 2.10 Software systems engineering feedback model of lifecycle phases

Start Process

SYSTEMS REQUIREMENTS

SOFTWARE REQUIREMENTS

PRELIMINARY DESIGN

DETAILED DESIGN

CODE AND DEBUG

TEST AND PREOPERATIONS

OPERATIONS AND MAINTENANCE

End Process

primary flow

secondary feedback path

Learning through
Feedback and Iteration

a path must necessarily be followed just because one is available. So excesses, if any, would be the responsibility of the developer and not the model.

Feedback needs are greatest in the early lifecycle phases, in which the software product definition and specification are prepared. This need occurs again later when these characteristics are given over to detailed design and finally when validation and testing occurs. Other phases of the software development lifecycle may require iteration and feedback between each other, but these needs are generally related to the specific way in which the development team functions.

Another way of indicating the various feedback paths in which the development team is engaged, together with the three user groups, is that depicted in Figure 2.11. This figure shows both product flow and information flow. It hints at the notion of reusable software and suggests a spiral model of iterative information flow.

Another variation on this theme is that of a feedback model that incorporates prototyping throughout the development process. In the original waterfall software development lifecycle proposal, Royce indicated that prototyping was to form an integral part of the software development lifecycle. Prototyping may be carried on at any of the major phases of the development

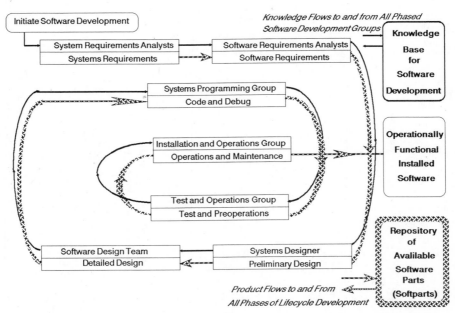

FIGURE 2.11 Multiple interactions and flows within the software development lifecycle

lifecycle. A typical software development lifecycle model for requirements definitions prototyping is shown in Figure 2.12.

In this model, the requirements specifications are identified, perhaps in a preliminary way. Then they are implemented in the form of a prototype as a part of the prototyping process, and then fed back to the user for validation that the requirements as developed will meet the needs of the user. The sequence of events is then to (1) design a prototype; (2) exercise the prototype, preferably with participation by the user; (3) submit the purposeful results of this to the user for feedback as to validity of the design; (4) refine the requirements specifications and the prototype on the basis of this; and finally (5) repeat the process until there is satisfaction with respect to the results obtained. We will return to a much more extensive discussion of prototyping in Chapter 8.

2.4   THE SPIRAL MODEL

The spiral model of the software development lifecycle developed by Boehm [1986] is intended to introduce a risk-driven approach into the development of software products. It differs from the classical waterfall model in that the

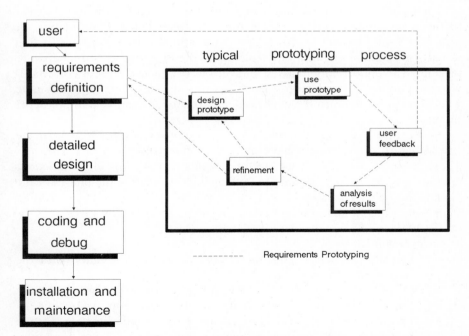

FIGURE 2.12   Software development lifecycle model with prototyping for requirements definition

waterfall model is a specifications-driven model, with prototyping perhaps incorporated. When used as proposed by Boehm, the spiral model requires the use of prototyping and calls for an assessment of the risk of process continuance during each "cycle" of a spiral. It is, however, a modification of the waterfall software development lifecycle model. It incorporates features from other software development lifecycle models as well, due to the use of feedback. The objectives leading to the spiral model are to integrate the successful waterfall model constructs and to incorporate many modifications that have been introduced to the software development lifecycle during the past 25 years, including risk analysis.

The major reasons for the departure from the conventional waterfall software development lifecycle were the disadvantages brought about by the strict application of the "top-down" approach, the "second system syndrome" of building a system twice through the use of the prototyping capability, and the need to introduce the concept of risk and risk-management into the software development process. The spiral model of the software development lifecycle is shown in Figure 2.13. This model results from aggregation of the several lifecycle models, some of which are shown in Figure 2.14.

In Figure 2.13 the radial dimension reflects the cost parameter as these costs accumulate over the several phases completed at the time of use of the model; the angular dimension represents the progress made in the development at a particular cycle.

Application of the spiral model proceeds through an iterative sequencing of the several phases of the model for each time that a different type of prototype is developed . It allows for an evaluation of risk before proceeding to each subsequent elaboration of phases in the development of a software product. The opportunity to assess the various risk factors such as cost, hardware requirements, and performance permits the developer to determine whether to continue with the development, seek an alternative path, or abort the process.

Application of the spiral model involves use of the seven (7) steps of the fine structure of systems engineering, as we have discussed in Chapter 1. These seven steps follow from the three fundamental steps of *formulation, analysis,* and *interpretation* that are implemented in each of the phases of the system lifecycle. The seven steps described by [Boehm, 1986], modified slightly to accommodate the primary three steps are as follows:

1. *Issue Formulation*
    1.1. Identify the needs, constraints, and alterables associated with the development issues at hand.
    1.2. Determine the objectives of the software product to be developed; (e.g., performance, functionality, ability to accommodate change).
    1.3. Identify alternative means of satisfying the stated objectives for the particular phase of the product development under consideration; (e.g., buy, reuse, design a, design b).

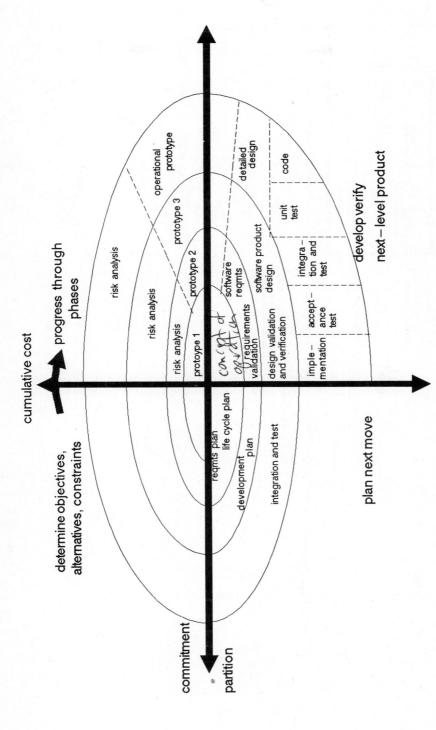

FIGURE 2.13 Spiral model of the software development lifecycle

cumulative cost

progress through phases

determine objectives, alternatives, constraints

commitment

partition

risk analysis

risk analysis

risk analysis

risk analysis

operational prototype

prototype 3

prototype 2

prototype 1

concept of operation

requirements validation

software reqmts

software product design

detailed design

code

unit test

integra- tion and test

accept- ance test

imple- mentation

design validation and verification

develop verify next–level product

reqmts plan

life cycle plan

development plan

integration and test

plan next move

69

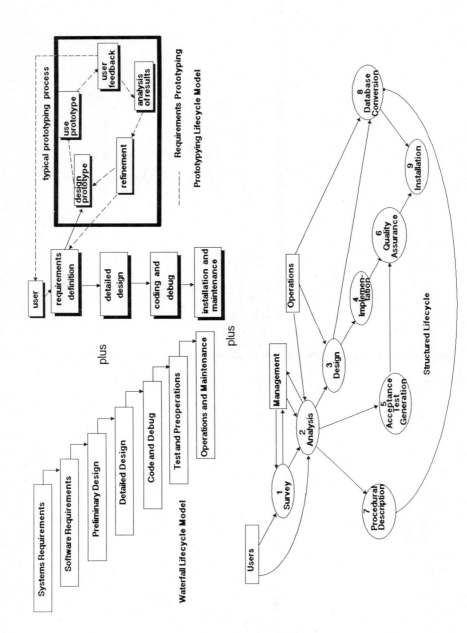

FIGURE 2.14 Other lifecycle models from which the spiral model is composed

70

2. *Analysis*
  2.1. Evaluate the alternatives in light of the objectives and the constraints. In this step, uncertainties are often identified that involve significant risk to the project.
  2.2. Evaluate the strategies to address the risk situation identified in step 2.1. This may include prototyping, simulation, user interviews, analytic modeling, or a combination of the above as well as other risk analysis techniques.
  2.3. Determine the risk remaining to complete the project.
3. *Interpretation*
  3.1. The activities of this step are dependent on the outcomes of step 2.3 that involve the type and amount of risk identified in order to complete the project. Alternative courses of action include:
    3.1.1. Use of the evolutionary model (to be discussed later in this Chapter).
    3.1.2. Use of the waterfall model.
    3.1.3. Other software development lifecycles, as appropriate.

Once the steps are completed for a given phase of the spiral model, an assessment is made as to whether to continue or abort the development process. If the risk assessment indicates the project should be continued, another application of the spiral model steps commences at a subsequent phase of effort. Otherwise, the development stops and an evaluation of the entire project is made. The plan to continue the development may include partitioning the project into smaller pieces for ease of handling and program development or continuing along the paths provided by the expanded waterfall model implied by the spiral model. The decision to proceed may be based on many factors, from an analysis of the results of an individual design walkthrough, to a major review of the overall requirements for the project.

The benefits that may accrue from application of the spiral model are essentially the ability to incorporate any one or a combination of the software development lifecycles discussed earlier, as well as any of the automated tools supporting these software development lifecycles. Software development case studies have been reported [Boehm, 1986] that provide comparisons with the conventional waterfall approach. These case studies using TRW software design and development projects to test the model, indicate that the spiral model gave a decided advantage in large complex systems design. The reasons for the advantages appear to be related to the early identification of areas of risk,* the extensive use of prototyping, and the iterative approach called for by the spiral model approach.

The spiral model has been designed to accommodate mixtures of specification models, prototyping models, simulation models, or other models as

---

*Risk indicates the degree of exposure of the software development project to the chance of failure or to an increase in time and cost to produce the software product.

the design team may choose, as appropriate to the situation involved in the software development project. In a similar way, the spiral model forces the introduction of risk-management considerations to determine the allocation of time and effort to activities such as planning, configuration management, quality assurance, formal verification, or testing. This is accomplished by requiring risk assessment before moving to another phase. Extended and enhanced systems engineering discussions of the spiral model of Boehm may be found in the work of Hall [1969] as well as several other early workers in systems engineering.

Risk elements are present at all phases in the development of software. Risk may occur during the preparation of requirements definitions because the user may not be certain of the system needs. The use of imprecise or ambiguous terms to present requirements specifications introduces risk. We will examine risk in requirements definitions and specifications in Chapter 3. Inability to estimate costs of the software development project introduces risk to the entire development effort. We look at cost models for software development projects in Chapter 9. The whole question of reliability, maintenance, and quality assurance is related to risk factors for software development projects. These concerns are covered in Chapter 6. We have introduced the need for management concern in order to ensure that the design and development process is effective and efficient in Chapter 1, and we will present management approaches in detail in Chapter 9. Risk of a different form is present during the conceptual and detailed design phases and during programming and testing. These concerns are covered in Chapters 4 and 5, respectively.

The advantages to the spiral model are the introduction of the notion of risk assessment and risk management into the software development process. As this software development lifecycle model is purported to be able to incorporate the *best* attributes of other software development lifecycle models, it represents a significant increase in capability to help ensure development of quality software products that meet the requirements specifications of the client. It addresses the concepts of *families of software products and the reuse of existing software parts*, as well as, *lifecycle evolution, growth, and changes in the software product*. It provides the user with the ability to identify the major areas of risk in a software development project. The suggested steps are:

1. Identify the project's top 10 risk items.
2. Present a plan for resolving each risk item.
3. Update list of top risk items, plan, and results monthly.
4. Highlight risk-item status in monthly project reviews.
5. Initiate appropriate corrective actions.

The spiral software development lifecycle model is well suited for iterative processes, and, in fact, it is this attribute that represents one of the major factors involved in selection of the spiral software development lifecycle over other software development lifecycle models.

The disadvantages of a spiral lifecycle are precisely the factors that make the spiral model attractive: the utilization of massive iteration and continuous assessment of the products at the end of each application of a spiral iteration. The spiral model may, if it is carelessly used, add significantly to the complexity of software development projects. This factor alone may preclude the universal acceptance proposed by the originator [Boehm, 1986]. However, models of this sort have achieved acceptance in systems engineering practice for more than 25 years and appear to be most useful for thoughtful production of functional and trustworthy software.

2.5   THE EVOLUTIONARY–PROTOTYPING MODEL

The evolutionary–prototyping model (hereafter referred to as the *evolutionary model*) was developed as a means of overcoming some of the potential shortcomings of the classical waterfall model. It is another incorporation from systems engineering and is another rather minor modification of the classical waterfall model of the software development lifecycle. This model of the software development lifecycle is based on the work of McCracken and Jackson [1982], and Gladden [1982], who suggested that the best way to resolve the "deficiencies" of the classical waterfall model would be to "scrap and replace" the prevailing (waterfall) model. It has been estimated that shortcomings in the application of the waterfall software development lifecycle model, such as, proceeding step-by-step through the design and development process without iterative feedback, have led to more than half the total life cost of a software product being expended in the "maintenance" phase. We have also seen that developer failure to validate requirements definitions with the user and poor design practices are also major contributors, although any lifecycle design approach may be defeated by these factors.

The proposed replacement lifecycle model would be the evolutionary model, a structural model approach, which incorporates prototyping as the best means of communicating with the user to obtain accurate and timely requirements specifications. This model may work exceptionally well when the user is unsure of the system requirements and benefits from an iterative process in which successive models are refined and presented as prototypes of the proposed software product. This approach, however, may prove to be a very expensive way to obtain requirements specifications, at the present stage of prototype development.

It is, of course, silly to argue that failure to validate requirements and use of poor design practices is due to a poor methodology. We are accustomed to the thought that a poor worker will often blame the tools used. This now needs to be augmented with the notion that a poor systems manager may often blame the methodology used.

Evolutionary software development lifecycle models may be depicted in several forms, and one of these models is presented in Figure 2.15. In this figure, the system-level requirements specifications have been given to the software developer by the user for prototyping. At this point in the development the system-level requirements specifications may be volatile and subject to modification as more is learned about the needs of the system. The system-level requirements specifications are evolved into software requirements specifications and detailed design through the prototyping process. These detailed designs, in turn, are evolved into the proposed final software program for consideration by the client for installation. This process may be iterated at any of the increasing levels of maturity to incorporate changing system-level requirements specifications or design modifications.

The evolutionary model is based on the premise that the user would be better able than the software designer to indicate whether the requirements specifications represented by the prototype truly correspond to those of the system that is desired. The use of prototyping becomes beneficial for situations in which the requirements may be stated vaguely or inadequately, or perhaps where the requirements call for more hardware resources than are available, or perhaps where the system developer needs to review what a potentially immature algorithm will accomplish before continuing to expend more development time, or perhaps where it is desirable to build critical portions of the system prior to making a commitment to construct a system in its entirety. Prototyping may be employed as a stand-alone process useful in viewing

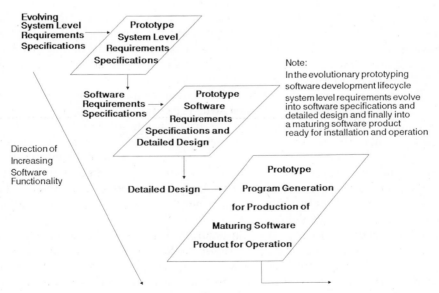

Note:
In the evolutionary prototyping software development lifecycle system level requirements evolve into software specifications and detailed design and finally into a maturing software product ready for installation and operation

FIGURE 2.15   The software lifecycle for implementing evolutionary rapid prototyping

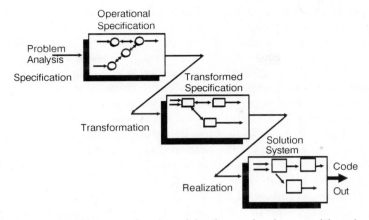

FIGURE 2.16   The operational model software development lifecycle

3. Supports an executable prototype that may be used to evaluate alternative solutions.
4. Is suitable for automation through the use of compilable code that results in a viable prototype at each stage of development.

The disadvantages of this lifecycle model arise primarily from the descriptive power advantage of the model. The descriptive nature of the model, which is intended to transform the desired external behavior of the software system to internal structures before specifying these, may result in the production of constrained and premature designs. The structure is also completely specified and rigid due to the nature of the transform process. A complete set of transformations that will enable one to proceed from an operational specification to an efficient implementation of this specification is a very difficult "reverse engineering" problem. There is little actual experience with the model to date, and little knowledge of how use of the model supports the management process.

2.7   THE KNOWLEDGE-BASED LIFECYCLE MODEL

The knowledge-based software development lifecycle model is based on the use of a combination of several models presented in this chapter, together with the application of expert systems [Bauer, 1982; Cheatham, 1984; Kant and Barstow, 1981]. Knowledge-based models have been developed primarily to assist the software designer realize a specific design through application of rule based systems. Thus the knowledge-based system becomes a partner in the system development process. It helps guide the developer through the development process. Software engineering knowledge is separated from the specific domain application knowledge, and this knowledge, along with the process paradigm, is captured in a knowledge base. Production rules, based on accepted software engineering techniques, are encoded into the expert system. The software engineering expert system is used, in conjunction with other expert systems containing application knowledge rules, to form a specific software system for an application in which a software product is desired.

This paradigm represents a goal that is being pursued by many research-and-development (R&D) organizations at this time. Three areas of the software development lifecycle that are being investigated at this time include (1) formal specifications, (2) the delivered system, and (3) the formal development record for the software development projects. A typical lifecycle model is shown in Figure 2.17.

The primary advantage of the knowledge-based lifecycle model is that it provides a design based support, in the form of a designer's assistant, in the software development process. It provides this assistance through application of rules, procedural knowledge, and domain-specific knowledge.

Disadvantages relate to the general perception that the creation of appropriate expert systems for software design is beyond the current-state-of-the-art at this time, and perhaps forever. Also, there are few truly recognized experts available to create both the software engineering and application domain knowledge bases.

Much research and development work is being conducted in the application of artificial intelligence to software development. Efforts include use of expert systems in CASE toolkits, expert systems for automation of testing, examining ways of reducing imprecision in requirements, software development environments for guiding the design effort through the entire process, and the use of expert database systems to enhance reuse of software parts. We will cover knowledge-based systems in considerably more depth in Chapter 8.

2.8 SUMMARY

Since their introduction into the software engineering literature in 1970, software development lifecycle models have significantly influenced the production of software. These models have served to organize and regularize the software development process. They provide a model of what is to be done that can be used to indicate how to proceed to accomplish the project objectives, to estimate when the project is expected to be completed, and who will implement the various phases in the development process. As we have seen, there are several lifecycle models for the development of software, and they fall generally into six categories that are all related to the waterfall model as shown in Figure 2.18.

1. Waterfall model (including the so-called structural model)
2. Spiral model

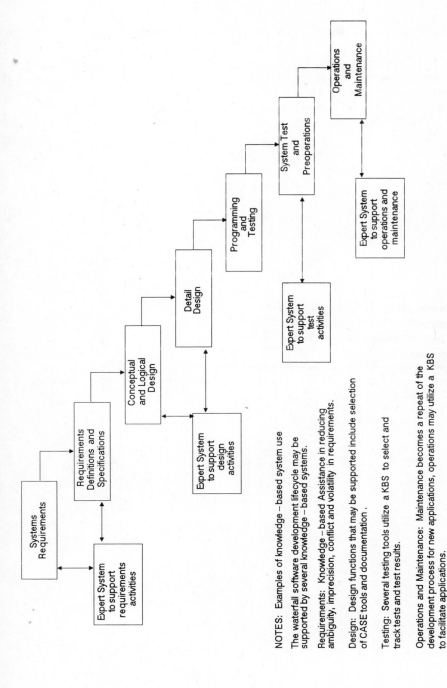

NOTES: Examples of knowledge – based system use

The waterfall software development lifecycle may be supported by several knowledge – based systems.

Requirements: Knowledge – based Assistance in reducing ambiguity, imprecision, conflict and volatility in requirements.

Design: Design functions that may be supported include selection of CASE tools and documentation .

Testing: Several testing tools utilize a KBS to select and track tests and test results.

Operations and Maintenance: Maintenance becomes a repeat of the development process for new applications, operations may utilize a KBS to facilitate applications.

FIGURE 2.17   Knowledge-based software development lifecycle

79

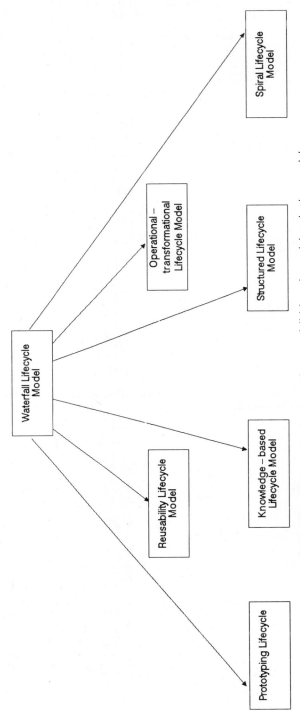

FIGURE 2.18 Relationships between the waterfall lifecycle model and other models

3. Prototyping model
4. Operational–transformational model
5. Knowledge-based model
6. Reusability model

These models are not at all independent. They each derive from systems engineering research in the 1960s. Each model type introduces the notion of phases through which sequenced progress is made in the development of the final deliverable product. The phases have been modified from their initial systems engineering origins to serve the particular needs of the software development process. The names and order of progression may change from use to use or from company to company; however, each follows a progression from requirements specifications through design, implementation, testing, installation, and maintenance.

Any of the software development lifecycle models will provide a framework that potentially allows the software to achieve the stated purposes of establishing requirements for the proposed development, identify and highlight problem areas, permit synthesis of alternative solutions to difficult issues, regularize the activities for the project, provide cost information, and assist in the role of management control. Depending on the specific nature of the project, one lifecycle may serve this purpose better than another. The determination of which one is best suited for a particular project is a function of the state of development of the software systems design group, the sophistication of the customer, the size and complexity of the project, the software development lifecycle environment available to the development process, and the management style of the organization.

Software development lifecycle models provide management and control over the processes and procedures to be accomplished in software development. Use of the lifecycle is essential to the informed assignment of personnel, enforcement of standards, use of automation tools, and development of quality products that are delivered on time and within budget. The use of one of the lifecycle models is generally better than development with no explicit lifecycle model, and experience in the application of software development lifecycles will lead the way to better software products. It is really not possible to develop software without a lifecycle model. No model at all is in reality a model—perhaps one that should be called the haphazard development model.

2.9 PROBLEMS

2.1. We have seen that software development lifecycles have common roots with systems engineering lifecycles. Examine the waterfall software development lifecycle, phase-by-phase and do the following:

     a. match each phase of the waterfall lifecycle to the corresponding phase of the systems engineering lifecycle;

     b. indicate the similarities;

     c. indicate the differences.

2.2. Explain why it took so long for software developers to recognize and incorporate the systems engineering lifecycle for software development.

2.3. Compare the ways in which management may exercise control over a software development project with and without use of a software development lifecycle. Which approach do you recommend and why?

2.4. The software development lifecycle intended for use by the U.S. Department of Defense is called DoD Standard 2167-A. Compare this lifecycle model with the systems engineering lifecycle and the traditional waterfall lifecycle and identify the differences and similarities.

2.5. Does DoD Standard 2167-A support creativity in software development?

2.6. The structured lifecycle model was introduced to bring more order into software development programs. Is this lifecycle different from the waterfall lifecycle model? If so, in what ways? If not, what are the primary similarities?

2.7. What are the reasons for the structured lifecycle model taking the seven-phase systems engineering lifecycle model and the seven-phase waterfall lifecycle model and turning the practice into nine separate phases? What is the gain (or loss) from this approach?

2.8. It is stated [Boehm, 1986] that the spiral software development lifecycle model differs from both the systems engineering lifecycle model and the waterfall software development lifecycle. Indicate the following:

     a. The similarities to the waterfall software development lifecycle

     b. The differences with the waterfall software development lifecycle.

2.9. Compare the ways in which we would break down a software development project using both the waterfall and the spiral software development lifecycles. Are there significant differences in the two decomposition approaches?

2.10. The spiral model introduces risk management into the software development process and proposes an approach to identifying and treating risk in software development. Show how risk management may be introduced into other lifecycle models covered in this chapter.

2.11. Decompose the spiral software lifecycle development model and show how it is constructed from the systems engineering lifecycle model. *Hint*: Begin with a single loop around the axis and compare the phases of the systems engineering lifecycle model to the phase of the spiral model.

2.12. The evolutionary software development lifecycle model is grounded in the approach of building successively more functional prototypes. Is this a significant departure from the systems engineering approach to software development?

2.13. Indicate how the operational software development lifecycle incorporates the seven-phases of the systems engineering lifecycle.

2.14. Operational software development lifecycles purport to have exceptional descriptive power. Assuming this feature is needed, show how this approach is more desirable for software development than either the waterfall or the spiral models.

Chapter 3

System Requirements Identification and Software Requirements Specification

3.1 INTRODUCTION

The requirements process generally follows a two-phase procedure: the identification of system requirements, followed by the development of software requirements. As we have noted in Chapter 2, most software development lifecycle models initiate the development process by calling for requirements identification, analysis, and specification. As we have also seen from the material presented in Chapter 1, the wise use of systems engineering presumes that we first determine user needs. These must realistically be based on both the objectives of the user group as well as constraints and alterables that effect potential solutions that can be implemented.

In the practice of systems engineering, it is not unreasonable to expect that major resources, in terms of time and money, will often be devoted to developing a set of requirements specifications that depict the user's needs. This should be accomplished before expenditures are committed to the development of the system itself. This need is essential in the application of systems engineering for the development of software systems as well. There exists the need to make a formal dedicated commitment to the development of requirements specifications, or the subsequent processes and procedures will suffer several possible maladies. Among these are wrong problem solutions, or type three errors, in which an elegant solution is developed for something other than the user group's problem.

Generally, there are two specific phases that concern requirements specifications in the software development lifecycle. In some lifecycle models, these are described as belonging to a single phase. Needed are system and process requirements identification and software (and hardware) requirements specification activities. The first activity, system requirements specifications, relates to the identification and development of user requirements. They must be presented in a consistent, understandable, logical, and integrated way so that both user and developer understand the problem that should and will be solved. The second activity, software requirements specification, relates to the technical document that is prepared for the internal use of the software systems development organization to provide a roadmap for the software development process. The software specifications represent, therefore, a translation of user requirements to technical specifications for the software system that will be developed. We will cover both phases, systems requirements specifications and software requirements specifications, in this chapter.

Usually, two documents are developed in the process of preparing requirements specifications. The first of these is the user system requirements, a top-level document concerned with the interpretation of the user's perceived needs that are to be served by the system. This document will cover all the alterables, constraints, and needs to be met by the system under development.

The second needed document contains the software requirements specification. It is concerned with the detailed breakdown of the software product to be developed. This document is used internally for the identification of tasks in the production of software. It is also used for the assignment of people to the various tasks that need to be accomplished in the evolution of the software product.

Two difficulties impede progress in identifying requirements:

1. **Knowledge Acquisition Difficulties** This relates to lack of definitive information concerning user needs and translation of these into software system requirements, lack of an experiential base from which to comprehend the requirements, and other cognitive factors that must be resolved to allow production of the desired software product. These are fundamentally difficulties that lie at the interface between the developer and the user in the identification of system level requirements.
2. **Technical Difficulties** These relate to hardware, algorithms, interfaces, performance, capacity, and other issues that have the potential for technical resolution. These are fundamentally technical difficulties in the development of a set of software requirements specifications from the user requirements specifications.

System-level requirements specification is difficult because of knowledge acquisition difficulties. Software requirements specification is difficult because of the technical difficulty in transitioning from system to software requirements.

System and software requirements specifications may generally be grouped in two categories: functional and nonfunctional [Yeh, 1982]. Functional requirements represent the way in which the internal system components interact with their environment. These functional requirements specifications present a precise set of properties, or operational needs, that the system must satisfy.

Nonfunctional requirements may be of a structural or purposeful nature. They may result from, for example, restrictions or constraints that are placed on the types of solutions that we may consider for the system design. Nonfunctional requirements include quality factor requirements. Formal specification of nonfunctional requirements is a difficult task, as we will discuss later. It is very necessary to consider systems management concerns as part of the purposeful activities associated with user, or system-level, requirements specifications. In general, the user or system-level requirements specifications incorporate overall system-level requirements without regard to the specific implementation approach that will be used to realize these.

The system requirements will specify *functional requirements*, and *purposeful requirements* (or performance objectives) for the system. There will also need to be systems management requirements specifications that will include:

1. Operating environment concerns
2. Overall design concept or objectives
3. Trustworthiness requirements, including quality factors
4. Maintenance concerns, including the need for software evolution over time
5. Economic resources, and time allocations, for software development

On the basis of these, we prepare *a software development plan*, or *systems management plan*, or a set of *systems management requirements* that are incorporated as an inherent part of the system requirements. The two items; *systems management requirements* and *systems technical requirements* constitute the *system requirements*.

The systems technical requirements are analyzed to produce software requirements, generally of a structured nature, as we will discuss later in this chapter. The systems management requirements are also analyzed to produce explicit management strategies for software development. Chapters 9 and 10 will discuss many aspects of systems management of software development. Of course, systems management and technology development are to be coordinated and integrated.[1]

With respect to the *systems management requirements* portion of the *system requirements*, we must:

1. Evaluate the system-level functional requirements for completeness and feasibility

---

[1]In a similar way, the system hardware is not neglected. We recall from Figure 2.4 (the DoD development cycle) that hardware decisions form a part of the overall development effort.

2. Evaluate the system-level requirements for compatibility with other systems that are to be operational in the client's environment
3. Explore relevant aspects of the client's environment, including existing systems, to determine how the new system might best be employed
4. Identify other organizations and units that need to have interfaces with the to be developed system
5. Evaluate the client stated available resources, including economic and time available resources
6. Develop a systems management strategy that incorporates these considerations and that serves, together with the *system technical requirements*, as input to the *software requirements* phase of development effort

There are four very major objectives to be fulfilled by following the requirements set forth in the *systems management plan*:

1. To further define and develop the *scope of the development effort*
2. To explicate and specify the *resources needed for development*, including people, time, hardware, software, and client cooperation

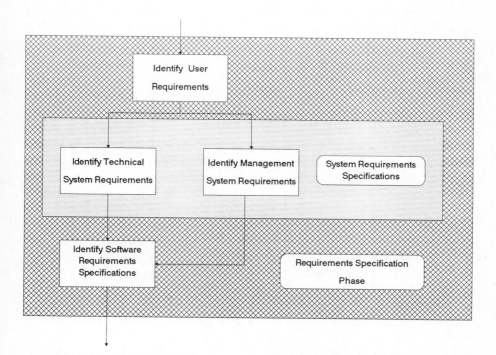

FIGURE 3.1 Important sub-phases in the systems requirements phase

3. To explicate and develop *detailed development schedules*, including important deliverables and milestones
4. To explicate and develop *cost estimates* across the phased development effort to follow

In almost all cases, this information will be used by the client for a go/no-go decision relative to continuing the development effort. This decision is made on the basis of (1) the functional and purposeful technical *system requirements*; (2) the software quality, or trustworthiness, factors; (3) the maintenance and other factors associated with evolution of the software product over time; and (4) the *systems management requirements* that have been proposed by the software development group. The first three of these are fundamentally addressed by the *technical system requirements*. As presented in this chapter, these *technical system requirements* are tempered by systems management and economic considerations that lead to the *systems management requirements*. Quality factors affecting software development are addressed primarily in Chapter 6. Systems management concerns are addressed primarily in Chapters 9 and 10. We again see that a great deal of up front information is needed for the initial phases of software development, if we are to do this wisely.

Figures 3.1 and 3.2 illustrate these concepts and provide a guide for much of the subsequent development in this chapter and in subsequent chapters.

3.2 DEFINITION OF THE USER

Prior to the examination of procedures for the development of requirements specifications, it is highly desirable to establish a common understanding of the concept of *user*. The term "user" or "client" for a software system is a complex one that requires explication.

Users of software are a diverse group. For example, the text and figures in this book were produced using two software products, a word processing package and a drawing package. In every sense of the word "user," we are users of these packages, and many others as well, to aid us in the production of this material. This is, however, a narrow perspective of the term "user" as it does take on an extended meaning for large-scale complex systems.

The narrow view of the term "user" is appropriate for those of us who utilize software packages only on personal computers (PCs) or larger systems. In this instance, the user is involved in neither any of the initial activities to generate requirements for the packages nor the maintenance of the product, except for the use of upgrades provided by the developer. In this sense, the user is the purchaser of a product much in the same way as any product is acquired and used. This view is not fundamentally different from the broader perspective of "user" for large-scale complex software systems. Any sensible user will always purchase developed software if it meets user needs.

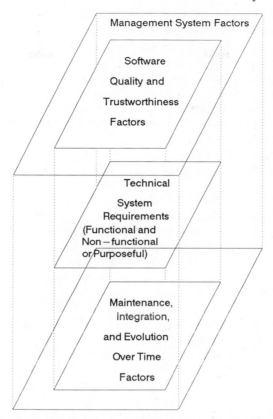

FIGURE 3.2   Interaction of management system and technological system requirements

The term "user" takes on a slightly broader meaning when applied to the individual or group responsible for system and software requirements specifications, as well as to be responsible for actual system operation, and perhaps even maintenance. In the case of the individual user of a software product, the user is normally not responsible for identifying requirements for maintenance. We could argue, of course, that a surrogate for the end user is responsible for identifying requirements; however, this is not the reason we investigate the meaning of the term.

For our purposes we will utilize the broader definition of the term "user" or "client" to be associated with the conceptualization, operation, and maintenance of large-scale complex systems. In this definition we see the user first in the role of system conceptualization, and as an associate in the development of requirements specifications. We may find the user in the role of maintenance of the software to satisfy the evolving requirements objectives as these change after installation. Hence, we will generally consider the user as the person or group with responsibilities that extend beyond only "user" as conventionally understood. Thus, we define the user as *that individual or group responsible for the articulation of the problem to be solved through implementation of the software product, for the problem definition statement, for approving the installation of the system following design, and potentially for some aspects of maintenance of the system over its useful lifetime.*

We are concerned mainly with software development rather than the utilization of developed products. The role that the "user" may wish to take may vary greatly from one product situation to another. At the one extreme, the user only "uses" a software product. At the other extreme, the user is very involved in the initial phases and later phases of the software development lifecycle.

It is clear that this definition may include many separate groups in the single name of "user." For large-scale software systems development, it is not unusual to have one group defining the goals and objectives of the system, another working with the software developer in turning these into requirements specifications, still another group may have the responsibility of working with the developer in installation, and yet another group is likely to have the responsibility, with or without support from the developer, for lifecycle maintenance.

This "user" diversity may make the job of developing and maintaining a comprehensive set of requirements specifications very difficult. The goals of one of the "user" groups may well be in conflict with another. For example, the system specifications may call for software interoperability on several operating systems, and at the same time call for the highest reliability and maintainability. The interoperability specifications may be a need of top-level user management who wish to utilize computers installed at several locations. The reliability and maintainability specification may be a need of the individual software system user who has no need at all for data or system level interoperability. These requirements form a part of the *nonfunctional requirements* and give rise to specific design problems, as they fundamentally conflict with one another. This conflict yields potential operating and maintenance difficulties when the product is fielded. For these reasons it is important to understand the utilization of the term "user" or "client" when developing requirements specifications.

As we have seen from our definition of the term user, we generally anticipate interactive involvement between the user and the software development team in the identification of system-level requirements that evolve into software requirements specifications. The relationships between the groups involved in system level identification and the activities to be carried out during this phase of the software development lifecycle are shown in Figure 3.3.

3.3   SYSTEM REQUIREMENTS SPECIFICATIONS

In the development of software products, time and money are allocated to each of the several phases of the software development lifecycle. As a rule

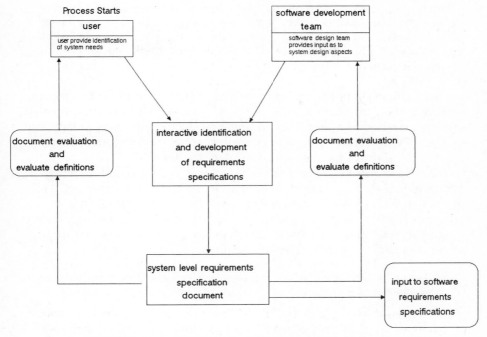

FIGURE 3.3 System level requirements specification phase

of thumb, the system-level requirements specification is generally allocated from 10 to 15% of the total cost of the project. This specification is the first thing to be accomplished in the normal phased progression of any lifecycle model.

System-level requirements specifications success depends on the skills of the user and the software systems developer team in the elicitation and explication of user system requirements. There are many difficulties in addressing knowledge acquisition issues related to the development of user requirements specifications. One of these is that not all user "needs" can be always satisfied by corresponding requirements, as the requirements may be technically or economically infeasible. This is a problem that is present in all system developments. Development constraints must be identified and recognized by user and developer. These constraints might include: the need to accommodate a particular target machine for system operation, the timing necessary for interactive response between transactions, the need for real-time interrupts, or the length of time available for software development.

Experience in user requirements elicitation may help in understanding the needs of the system user. However, this is often not the case. Insight into the problem of depending on previous experience as a guide to future wisdom is provided by Winston Churchill [1948] in his epic, *The Second World War: The Gathering Storm*, in which he states:

In the problems which the Almighty sets his humble servants things hardly ever happen the same way twice over, or if they seem to do so, there is some variant which stultifies undue generalization. The human mind, except when guided by extra-ordinary genius, cannot surmount the established conclusions amid which it has been reared.

Understanding of problems to be resolved and the acquisition of knowledge concerning these problems are difficult tasks. But, we must understand issues before we attempt to resolve them through producing software products that meet user expectations. Otherwise, we will generally produce software products that fall short of meeting user expectations and needs.

Of course, we also know that the transformation of information concerning user needs to software system requirements for design will be imperfect. Thus, we see that each of these requirements tasks is a difficult problem area.

Boehm [1976] addressed these same concerns in his survey of the software engineering field and the software development problem areas that then required immediate attention. He identified two major need areas:

1. Detailed design and coding of computer systems software by software development experts in a relatively economics-independent context

2. Requirements analysis design, test and maintenance of application systems software by software requirements applications experts in an economics-driven context

Area 1 problems have been enthusiastically addressed by computer scientists everywhere. Evidence of this activity has been expressed by the development of computer-aided software engineering (CASE) products, fourth-generation languages (4GLs) to aid in the efficient coding of user problems, automatic code generation, and automated documentation generators, to name but a few of the many advances supporting area 1.

By contrast, area 2 problems have not had the same amount of resource, human or capital, applied to lead to potential solutions. Persistent problems here have cast doubts on the ability of applications software requirements developers to keep abreast of the needs for quality software development. This becomes ever more important in the face of increasing demands for more software, for software with more complex requirements, and to take advantage of the ever increasing capability of hardware.

Software engineering incorporates the systems engineering approach for software product development. A close examination of development case histories shows that inadequate resources, both time and money, have generally been allocated to the initial phases of the software development lifecycle. What has become abundantly clear from experiences gained in the development of large-scale software systems is that: *Scrimping on the front end of a software development project will cost the user orders of magnitude more time and money during the life of the software product than would otherwise be the case. It will often result in an inferior product, or no product at all.*

3.3.1 An Activities Matrix for Preparation of System-Level Requirements Specifications

A matrix of some of the activities involved in the acquisition, development, and documentation of system-level requirements is shown in Figure 3.4. These activities, typically interactive and iterative, include most of those that take place as requirements are identified and a system-level requirements specification document is prepared. These activities, acquisition, development, and documentation of system-level requirements specifications, follow directly from the systems engineering approaches that were described in Chapter 1. These activities are described in greater detail as follows:

1. Formulate system-level requirements issues.
   a. Identify needs, constraints, and alterables, such as budget and any operational and legal requirements, through initial contact with users. Developers responsible for systems level requirements specifications interact with users to determine what the requirements should be, how the requirements should be stated, and how the requirements should be derived.

Activity \ Function	Acquisition	Development	Documentation
1. make initial contact	x		
2. prepare system parameters	x	x	
3. review ASIS* system *current system, if any	x	x	
4. examine constraints		x	x
5. develop new requirements		x	x
6. review performance characteristics		x	x
7. propose evaluation methods	x	x	x
8. compare alternatives	x	x	x
9. produce system requirements		x	x

FIGURE 3.4 User and designer group activities matrix for systems level requirements to specifications

b. The parameters or the system to be developed are derived from the interactions begun in step 1a. The purpose of this activity is to identify objectives of user groups and the ways to determine how system-level objectives can be met. This activity is applicable to the acquisition and development of system level requirements specifications.

c. Identify alternatives to the existing or "as-is" system. In this step we examine the existing system, if any, in terms of requirements specifications options. The purpose of this step is to determine whether any of the current system level specifications, and by inference the existing system, may be reused in the current application. We also look at alternative ways to determine the extent to which the requirements specifications are achieved. This step involves the acquisition and development of system level requirements specifications.

2. Analyze issues and select approach

a. Once we have completed steps 1a through 1c above, we begin the process of reviewing and analyzing any constraints or issues related to system level requirements specifications. We then select an approach(es) to meet the needs stated in the system level requirements specifications. We identify the technical, operational, and economic aspects of the new (or "as-is") system level requirements options, including preliminary estimates of limits on system-level performance characteristics such as timing, size, errors, and other operational features. In this step we are engaged in development of acquired requirements and documenting our outcomes.

b. Next we develop new system-level requirements from the information prepared and documented in step 2a. We define the criteria for evaluation and assessment of these new system-level requirements specifications. This activity involves continuing development and documentation of system-level requirements specifications.

3. Interpret the requirements.

a. At this point in our development of system-level requirements specifications, we review performance requirements stated in these documents. We accomplish this by evaluating the system-level requirements specifications in terms of user objectives. This usually involves the continuing development and documentation of system-level requirements specifications.

b. Next we propose methods of evaluating the requirements specifications to determine whether the software product as delivered will meet the system-level requirements specifications. A validation plan for requirements is necessary to ensure that we have established feasible and testable requirements. In this step we are involved with additional acquisition activities, development, and documentation of system-level requirements specifications.

c. The next step is to rank-order the system-level requirements specifications in terms of their costs and benefits or effectiveness, and select the set of requirements specifications that best satisfy user needs within allocated resources. Alternative approaches should be reviewed if there are any questions as to the system-level requirements meeting user needs. This step involves interaction with the user to ensure that the requirements so established meet user needs. Development and documentation of system level requirements specifications continues.

d. Identify the final system-level requirements and prepare system level requirements specification. This final step may involve additional resolution of any remaining problems and issues. The entire system-level requirements specifications are documented and form the input for software requirements specifications

The basic goal of these activities is to explore overall user needs for the development of the software product in terms of the technical, strategic, economic, and other aspects of the system to be designed. It is important to establish as many of the constraints and system alterables as is feasible. For example, it may be essential that the system be able to be easily modified over the life of the product as the user is aware of substantial end-user need changes that are likely to occur but have not been conceptualized. The early establishment of constraints and alterables permits the best possible set of system-level requirements specifications to be identified. The system-level requirements selected during these activities are the ones that are placed in the system-level requirements specification document and subjected to analysis later on during this phase to determine the software requirements specifications.

3.3.2   Knowledge Acquisition Approaches

The approach used to identify system-level requirements specifications from the user is one area that has changed significantly since writing of programs to satisfy user needs became a profession. This has been recognized as the first phase in the software development lifecycle since the early recognition of the need to regularize software development. There have been many studies of information requirements determination perspectives. The results of some of this work has led to the increased use of prototyping approaches for the analysis of both system and software requirements specifications. There has been an adoption of systems engineering principles for software systems development, and with this has come a substantive improvement in knowledge acquisition approaches.

The primary methods used to elicit information about user needs and systems requirements include talking with user, or reviewing existing documents, or using prototypes to explore various alternatives. The most common of the processes are [Davis, 1982; Sage et.al, 1983]:

1. Ask people. Use either:

    1.1. The traditional interview process
    1.2. Structured interview techniques
    1.3. Responses to written questionnaires
    1.4. Employ nominal group approaches when interactive approaches fail
2. Review existing plans and documents.
3. Study the existing system.
4. Study the evolving system.

These constitute the ways in which knowledge acquisition is conducted. Much of what we know about knowledge acquisition comes from management science and systems engineering literature and from cognitive psychology [Biggs et al., 1980; Boar, 1984; Sage, 1977; Agresti, 1986; Newell and Simon, 1972; Norman and Draper, 1986; Rasmussen, 1986; Schneiderman, 1980]. Few software developers are professionally trained in these fields of expertise. Systems engineers are sometimes prepared in these areas. However, they are not generally employed in the requirements definition process. This situation has seen some improvement in very recent years, as software systems have become larger, more complex, and requiring greater percentages of the resources to develop and construct major systems.

    Knowledge acquisition commences with interaction between the user or domain expert and the software developer or knowledge engineer. The software developer utilizes knowledge acquisition techniques to discover constraints, alterables, and interfaces for the proposed system. This information is then converted to system-level definitions. The process is an iterative one and continues until the user and the developer are satisfied that the system-level requirements specifications will meet user system needs. Figure 3.5 portrays a conceptual approach to knowledge acquisition techniques. The activities shown in this figure represent the interaction between the user and the developer in the elicitation strategy, determination of constraints, alterables, and interfaces that leads to system level requirements specifications. The figure intends to show the iterative nature of the information exchanges by the double-ended arrows between the user and the developer and the functions. In this figure, the domain expert (user) is interviewed to obtain knowledge concerning an identification of system-level needs. From this, a system structure is proposed and reviewed prior to forwarding this information for development of software requirements specifications.

    Both formal and informal techniques may be used to elicit requirements specifications information. The methods for requirements identification range from the submission of formal documents from the user to the software design group, to less formal interview methods to elicit information. No matter which method is used, however, the process generally begins with a preliminary statement of need. This statement may be obtained by any of the methods noted earlier. The most commonly used techniques for requirements specification identification may be based on unstructured interviews, protocol analysis, or structured interview approaches. In many cases, elicitation is

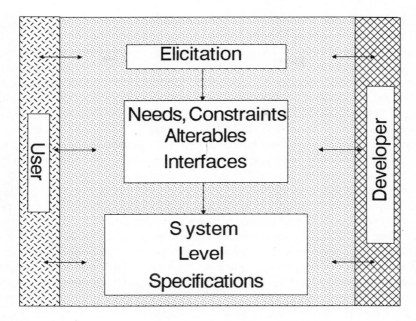

FIGURE 3.5 Interactions between the user and the developer for knowledge acquisition

accomplished by the software systems design engineers, or individuals in comparable positions, who formulate questions and pose these to the user. Often, software design specialists are not well suited for this role.

It might be expected that the system user, a domain expert for the application system, will be able to cite system design objectives or purposeful requirements. Often this is not the case, and questions will have to be posed to stimulate the user to provide responses that will lead to an adequate system definition. In actuality, the user responses to queries frequently provide some facts and values concerning the need, and perhaps some of the operational constraints that are likely to be encountered at the time of installation. These responses will likely contain perceptions that relate to financial constraints, resource allocations that the user has considered, and temporal conditions, such as schedule needs or the potential evolution of requirements over time that are viewed as essential.

If the design is relatively well formulated and many of the parameters are known, the structured interview may prove better, faster, and more economical of both time and resources than the unstructured approach. Such an interview is pre-structured by the software systems developers to reflect the experience of that group in addressing similarly structured software development problems.

As noted in the preceding, many of the techniques for eliciting domain information pertinent to user needs involve some type of interview. The two interview types used most often are the unstructured free-flowing discussion format and the more structured procedure in which limiting parameters are defined as well as possible. In both interview processes, the user is asked to review *out loud* the characteristics of the systems that are deemed most important and not subject to compromise. The results of this mental imaging of the system are later analyzed together with other relevant information to determine whether any points have been omitted during the more formal part of the procedure. These processes are usually ill-defined and involve introspection on the part of the elicitation team members.

The information thus developed, involves subjective interpretation. Therefore, considerable interaction between user and elicitation group must take place before the design characteristics are truly credible.

Among the greatest potential needs that arise, as a consequence of these techniques, are for introspection and interpretation of provided information that must then be analyzed. There is considerable evidence which suggests that humans are not always able to report reliably on the mental process used to arrive at a given solution procedure. Thus, the user may not be capable of conveying the actual requirements specification for the system to be developed in terms that are readily understood by the designers. Furthermore, it has been shown that the domain experts often are not able to provide reasons or strategies that correspond to their actual behavior under known circumstances. Both of these factors have important ramifications on the ability of the elicitation team to obtain useful, accurate, and timely information.

Much of the knowledge of the domain expert is expressed in a computer in the form of rules and heuristics that are procedural. Experience shows that it is extremely difficult for experts to convey knowledge in the form of rules, as this is simply not the way that experts conceptualize problems [Sage, 1989]. Thus, there may be a major disconnect between the way experts view issues and the way the knowledge acquisition engineers will attempt to represent this knowledge.

Still another problem arises due to the fact that much of human expertise operates on intuition, which is experientially based wisdom. Intuitive, skill-based, knowledge is most difficult to code into requirements statements, rules, or even heuristics that might lead to interpretation of the process of decisionmaking. Using intuition, an expert is frequently able to scan a situation, size up the alternatives, and propose a course of action without resorting to detailed rules. In cases such as this, the expert is able to aggregate information into clusters, review these, assess alternatives, and propose courses of action without resorting to any form of formal knowledge or rule-based knowledge.

Logic games, such as chess or checkers, are excellent representations of incorporation of formal rule- or skill-based knowledge. For the novice player, these games require memorization of sets of rules, assessment of multiple alternatives, and the need to synthesize the effect of these alternatives on possible subsequent moves by an opponent. For expert players this approach is impractical, as the expert player has gone much beyond simple rule checking to employ skill-based strategies that do not involve either formal risk analysis and inferences concerning the moves of the opponent or a set of rules. Intuition, or skill-based reasoning, is used to process enormous amounts of information rapidly without the need for conscious monitoring. Chapter 9 will address these notions in much more detail.

Finally, one of the most difficult problems to confront the software systems engineering design team in the elicitation of requirements information is characterized by the worn-out phrase: *communication*. Even if the user is fully aware of all the requirements, constraints, and needs of the system to be built, there comes the time when this information must be communicated to the software development team. In a typical situation, the software development team is not familiar with the system that is to be constructed. In addition the user lacks familiarity with the design methods to be used for software development. Thus, any attention to development of communication skills to alleviate these problem areas, is of great benefit.

It would be ideal if the developer and the user were each experts in the activities of the other and able to freely communicate with one another. More often than not, the case is one of the domain expert user trying to communicate needs in the language of the user and the software developer trying to convey the kinds of information required in the language of software design. These differing perceptions of the real world are what gives rise to the disconnects that occur between those that possess specific domain knowledge and those whose job it is to elicit this knowledge and record it.

The processes and procedures of knowledge acquisition and the methods utilized to gather this information will have a profound effect on the developed software and the ability of that product to meet the needs of the user. It is important for the user to be as aware as possible of the approach and framework used to express user requirements. It is also important for the software systems engineering design team to be aware of the potential for misinterpretation, failure to obtain all the necessary information, and the need for clear and concise communication with the user. This is a need, and there is a treachery associated with it. As we will discuss in Chapter 9, experts do not think in terms of precise rules and procedures. They use skill-based wholistic reasoning. At this time, computers typically operate upon rule-based procedures. There is an inherent danger asking people to express ideas in a (rule-based) format that they do not use.

In a large complicated software development project, it is extremely useful for the development of requirements specifications to continue until the user is satisfied that the system requirements identification and software requirements specifications have captured the actual requirements of the user.

We see that there are many ways that may be used for eliciting information from the user. Each of these is useful for some knowledge acquisition process.

In the event that both user and designer are novices at knowledge acquisition methods, it is highly likely that the resulting system requirements identification and software requirements specifications will prove to be quite unsatisfactory. This is because the user will be unable to provide proper guidance and inputs to the software designers and the software designers will not understand that they are not identifying the user requirements. Some of the possible approaches to overcome this would be to require formal training in knowledge acquisition methods, or employ expert facilitators to assist in the knowledge acquisition processes.

Plans for requirements elicitation strategies must allow for sufficient time and opportunity for the user and developer to meet and discuss the requirements specifications. All participants must be prepared to discuss and develop the requirements definition. This will serve as the baseline documentation for system development and validation.

The requirements specification process results in a deliverable, the *requirements definition document,* that serves as input to the software requirements specification document (to be described in detail in the next section). The requirements definition document will provide information on such procedures as the preliminary interface requirements specification, operational conceptualization, and how the software is to be used by the user.

Standards have been developed by the Institute of Electrical and Electronic Engineers (IEEE) that describe alternate approaches to good practice in the development of software specifications. The IEEE standard is entitled "IEEE Guide to Software Requirements Specifications" [ANSI/IEEE Std 830-1984]. The goals of the standards are to:

1. Establish a basis for agreement between customer and supplier on what the software product should do
2. Reduce the development effort
3. Provide a basis for estimating costs and schedule
4. Provide a baseline for validation and transfer
5. Facilitate transfer of the software product to new users or new machines
6. Serve as a basis for enhancement

This standard provides a prototype of the table of contents for a software requirements specifications document. Section 1 is the Introduction, Section 2 provides a general description of the software product in relation with other related products. Choice of a particular prototype outline for Section 3, Specific Requirements, depends on the application area and the nature of the software product being specified. Four prototype outlines are used to cover possible organization of the document. We have chosen to show Prototype Outline 2 (Prototype Outlines 1, 3, and 4 are given in the IEEE Standard [ANSI/IEEE Std 830-1984]), which shows the four classes of interface requirements applied to each of the functional requirements. Some of the characteristics of these interfaces are described following the Prototype Outline presentation. The selection of which prototype outline to be used for Section 3 is left to the choice of the software development team.

The Table of Contents of prototype software requirements specifications outline is as follows:

1. Introduction
   1.1   Purpose
   1.2   Scope
   1.3   Definitions, Acronyms, and Abbreviations
   1.4   References
   1.5   Overview
2. General Description
   2.1   Product Perspective
   2.2   Product Functions
   2.3   User Characteristics
   2.4   General Constraints
   2.5   Assumptions and Dependencies
3. Specific Requirements (Prototype Outline 2 is shown)
   3.1   Functional Requirements (for interface requirements)
         3.1.1   Functional Requirement 1
                 3.1.1.1   Specification
                           3.1.1.1.1   Introduction
                           3.1.1.1.2   Inputs
                           3.1.1.1.3   Processing
                           3.1.1.1.4   Outputs
                 3.1.1.2   External Interfaces
                           3.1.1.2.1   User Interfaces
                           3.1.1.2.2   Hardware Interfaces
                           3.1.1.2.3   Software Interfaces
                           3.1.1.2.4   Communication Interfaces
         3.1.2   Functional Requirement 2
                   .

                   .

                   .
         3.1.n Functional Requirement n
   3.2   Performance Requirements
   3.3   Design Constraints
   3.4   Attributes
         3.4.1   Security
         3.4.2   Maintainability
                   .

                   .

                   .
   3.5   Other Requirements
         3.5.1   Database

3.5.2 Operations

3.5.3 Site Adaption

A more detailed description of some of the activities associated with the development of the software requirements specifications outlined in the prototype document illustrated above is provided in the sections that follow. We will consider system description, hardware description, system structure models, functional requirements, and nonfunctional requirements. While the standards we reference here are for software specifications the (user) system level specifications must serve as input to these.

3.3.3 System Description

This information is derived from the system requirements specifications document. A description of the need for the system has been prepared by the user, and the applications for the system are described. In this activity the functions of the system are briefly developed and the rationale for the software system is prepared. These functions include establishing the structure for the ensuing software development project and the management controls that are to be implemented. Gantt charts, and other project management tools for work breakdown time schedules, are extremely useful and provide an overall perspective concerning the magnitude of the time, effort, and resource requirements for the project.

3.3.4 Hardware Description

The hardware intended to support the software system to be designed is introduced at this point. Any quantitative constraints that ensue, as a consequence of hardware or special hardware interfaces, must be made explicit at this time to implement these in the design efforts that follow.

Hardware design and implementation procedures follow a systems engineering approach similar to that already described for software development. A system requirements specification analysis is conducted to specify the functional, performance, and interface requirements for hardware components of the system. If there are design constraints (e.g., the power available is severely limited or the physical size of the enclosure is small), these are established. If special testing procedures are potentially needed, these are likewise now determined. At this point in the development, the separation of functions that are to be embedded in hardware from those that are to be allocated to software are confirmed, starting from earlier allocations made in the system requirements specifications, and are finally determined.

This process initiates with the system requirements specifications document that established the goals and objectives of the development project for resource allocation for both hardware and software. The systems engineer uses the user goals and constraints to prepare a system design specification, or

conceptual design, that represents hardware specific activities ana
to describe the hardware and software architectural configurations p.
for the system to be designed.

3.3.5 System Structure Model

The software system structure model represents a high-level view that comprises the major components of the system. The development of a high-level
software system structure begins with a conceptual model derived from the
software requirements specification document. Following this conceptual design, the outcomes of the software requirements specification analysis are
applied. This serves to define the information flow, the information content,
and the information structure for the software design.

Simplification of the software requirements specifications may be advisable
at this time to be able to present the system in its simplest terms to the client
in order to extract latent problems with greater ease. This simplification step
will generally lead to a cleaner and more easily understood set of software
design requirements specifications. The advantages of simplifying the design
characteristics at this time are that these changes will affect all of the remaining
design operations, and if they can be made simpler, the hardware and software
design is made easier. The disadvantages are that any errors due to this
simplification will not necessarily be discovered, and, if they are not discovered and resolved, they will propagate throughout the remainder of the design
and development effort. Much judgment must be exercised by the software
design team concerning desirability of simplification of the software
requirements.

The most important characteristics of the system structure model are information flow, content, and structure. These are used as inputs for any of
the many structured techniques that produce the design specification from
the software requirements specification analysis.

3.3.6 Functional Requirements

Functional requirements are used to indicate the directly measurable aspects
of the system design. The functional requirements specification serves to
describe the operational capabilities or services that are to be supplied to the
user. These requirements specifications are finalized to be as complete and
consistent as possible at this point in the development process. In the event
that changes are made to the system requirements specifications document
later in the development cycle, the functional requirements specifications must
be modified to reflect the current system requirements. The functional requirements specifications may be expressed in natural language, structured
languages (e.g., structured English), or in any of the formal specification
languages. The style used is strictly a function of the software design team
preferences, and the automated support tools that are in use at the design
facility.

3.3.7 Nonfunctional Requirements

Nonfunctional requirements specifications describe those constraints, alterables or limitations that relate to the structural or purposeful aspects of system requirements specifications. These include functions such as (1) product metrics, (2) process metrics, and (3) relationships with the external environment.

Typically nonfunctional requirements specifications in the form of product metrics relate to the degree of reliability, maintainability, flexibility, usability, and other quality factors specified by the user that the system must achieve. Software process metrics represent an attempt to build in quality by measuring different facets of the software engineering process to try to predict where problems might occur [Myers, 1988]. These include (1) computer resource utilization, (2) software development humanpower, (3) system requirements specification stability, (4) software progress, development and test, (5) cost–schedule deviations, and (6) use of software development tools.

3.3.8 Database Requirements

At the onset of a new project database, considerations take on one of two forms, create a new database, or support an existing one. In either instance, the procedures to be followed are quite similar. The analysis work must include the identification and description of data elements represented by the system. The primary methods are those of data flow analysis and data structure analysis.

Database requirements may be functional or nonfunctional in nature. They are either constrained to meet those in the current user environment or provided as a consequence of the design. Consideration must be given to the attributes sought in a database management system (DBMS). These are comprised of the set of tools and functions such as query languages, report generators, and data dictionaries that make it possible for users to easily and quickly utilize the database. The system used should respond to such user needs as: provision for several views of data; linkage between data elements; and database design; including hierarchical, network, or relational approaches. Relational databases use a simple table structure, hierarchical databases use a tree structure, and network databases use a network structure. The choice among these depends on the organization that is going to use the data, its experience, interface requirements with other operations, how and how often they will use the data, how data in different files relate to each other, and whether these relationships change, as well as a number of other factors.

3.3.9 Installation and Maintenance

Any of the user constraints regarding installation and maintenance should be made as explicit as possible and as early as is feasible in the program definition. If the user anticipates a hardware configuration change that will occur prior to or during the lifetime of the expected viability of the software, it would be wise to introduce these into the design specification so that migration problems may be described and reduced. If there are additional uses for which the software product may be intended, and these are either known or are under consideration, they should be given at this point in the project definition and description. Similarly, if there are extreme environmental conditions that impact routine and general maintenance, these must be considered when developing a maintenance plan. Other activities that are a part of maintenance should also be included in the plan.

3.3.10 Interfaces and Partitioning

"Module interfaces," "partitioning schemes," and "abstraction" are terms used to describe logical and physical interfaces and characteristics for the software. These aspects of the software requirements specifications are outlined at a high level and are to be explicitly defined during the detailed design phase. Identification of module interfaces, to include information flow requirements into and out of a module, are important for the software designer to provide design preferences for detailed design. "Partitioning" refers to the parallel paths that are selected along which design proceeds, and "abstractions" refer to issues such as information hiding. These topics are covered in much more detail in Chapters 4 and 5, which cover detailed design practices and programming languages and testing.

3.4 SOFTWARE REQUIREMENTS SPECIFICATION

As noted earlier, distinct but related efforts are involved in the requirements specification phase. Consequently, two documents will generally be developed: (1) system requirements specifications and (2) software requirements specifications. The system-level requirements specifications document is a top-level identification of the user's perceived needs that will ultimately be served by the software system, and a translation of these to system-level requirements. The software requirements specification document represents a translation of these user requirements specifications into software specifications to be used for the next phase for the software product to be developed.

A role of the software requirements specification team is to work with the system requirements specification document. Once the task of software requirements specification is completed, it is analyzed and detailed design documents are prepared. The system-level and software requirements specifications documents become the reference points to validate the output subsequent to these phases and ensure that the system is designed to meet user expectations.

In actual practice it is not unusual that once the system-level requirements are in hand and some of the software requirements specification analysis activities have commenced, design begins. Usually there is insufficient information to begin a complete software design at this point in time. However, victory is declared by the software design team over the requirements specifications processes, and the job of building the software product commences in earnest. While this approach may indeed appear to save both time and money, it is often counterproductive, as the system and software requirements specifications may change or may not be properly interpreted at the early stages of development. Should this occur, disaster will surely happen later in the development lifecycle. Alternatives to this approach would be to invest more resources for requirements identification and software requirements specifications. The likelihood of producing software that does not meet user needs will be less by investing in such approaches as requirements specifications prototyping, or use of knowledge-based assistants for the requirements phase.

For new system needs, the use of prototyping for this purpose is called *evolutionary development* of requirements specifications. An evolutionary rapid prototyping model for experimenting with system-level requirements specifications is shown in Figure 3.6. In this figure, system-level requirements specifications form the input for the prototyping model and are taken through a series of steps. These include writing the system-level requirements specifications into a proper format for input to the prototype, preliminary evaluation by the software developer, performing the rapid prototype, evaluation

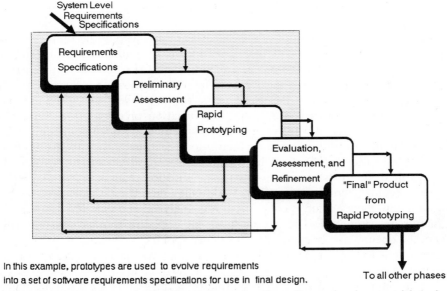

In this example, prototypes are used to evolve requirements into a set of software requirements specifications for use in final design.

To all other phases

FIGURE 3.6 Rapid prototyping for implementing the software development lifecycle

and refinement of these specifications by the software developer, and then a "final" product of software requirements specifications. The process is iterated as many times as necessary to ensure that the software requirements specifications, as developed, represent the system-level requirements specifications as provided by the user. When modifying existing systems, it is also valuable to experiment with the present system to modify or add to the current requirements specifications for a new or different application. An approach similar to that described above for a new set of system-level requirements would be applicable. Both of these approaches to prototyping have been found to be valuable. Prototyping is beginning to find widespread use for system-level requirements specifications at this time, and we see major activities involving other applications of prototyping. A more complete discussion of software development through prototyping is contained in Chapter 8.

In the preparation of software requirements specifications, it is necessary that the system-level requirements specifications be assessed carefully. Any important and likely to occur future developments that might impact the system requirements specifications should be reviewed and provisions made for them. This is very difficult to accomplish, especially if it is not possible to generate prototypes and experiment with an evolving system in a realistic setting that is essentially that of the operational environment. Some of the basic issues that impact the ability to prepare a good set of software requirements specifications are:

1. The manner in which the system function and purpose are articulated
2. The multiple perspectives through which users and designers understand the situation
3. The design philosophy of the group
4. The design environment

As we have seen in earlier sections, the knowledge acquisition process leading to system, and thence software requirements specifications, is anything but perfect. It frequently leads to a high level of uncertain, imprecise, and ambiguous information, and interpretations of the system requirements. These factors also complicate the software requirements specification process.

If inadequate information is used, it will almost always later lead to a functionally inadequate system. Particularly troublesome are:

1. Ambiguous, uncertain, and imprecise information
2. Changes in the system requirements specifications that occur during the development phases as a result of poorly derived initial specifications
3. Changes in the system requirements specifications that occur during development as a result of user modification of needs

These problem areas must be addressed as early as possible. As the possibility for change exists throughout the design process, the system and software requirements specifications must be reviewed and refined as the system requirements change. As we continue to monitor changes in system-level requirements throughout the requirements phase, we modify the software requirements to ensure that changes at the system-level are reflected at the software requirements specifications level. If the system-level requirements specifications change during the design phase, it is advantageous to modify the software requirements specifications and design as early as possible, as the cost of repair of software increases the further we are along the development process.

The need to accommodate to changes in requirements specifications must be tempered by the thought that, if things are changing too rapidly, it may be necessary to defer development of the project. In this event, the volatility of the requirements specifications is such that it is not possible to stabilize them. More investigation is then generally required to better define the system-level requirements.

On receipt of the information developed from software requirements specifications, conceptual and logical design parameters are established and software designers initiate the following:

1. Review the project scope
2. Establish the software development plan
3. Examine the design parameters for problems
4. Provide procedures for problem definition and solution

This is needed to ensure that the requirements specifications are as complete as possible. High-level information flows and structures are examined, potential system interfaces are proposed, and incorporation of any constraints and alterables that have been enumerated during the software requirements specifications process are taken into account. Following this activity, validation and verification criteria are established and metrics to determine success (or failure) of the project are defined. The following characteristics are desirable: (1) accurate representation of problem areas, (2) problem partitioning for subproblem review, and (3) logical and physical representation of the system for ease of establishing the software design. Establishing these will help ensure that an adequate software specifications document has been prepared for the next phases in the development of the software product. The deliverable for this activity is intended to provide guarantees that the software product to be produced will meet the system requirements specifications. Agreement at this time between the user and the software development team on these specifications is mandatory in order that the software specifications documents reflect the needs of the user and the design implications of the software design group.

3.4.1 Software Requirements Specification Methods

Software requirements specification methods combine systematic procedures to analyze the information from software requirements specifications. These methods enable the software designer to utilize basic analysis principles and apply well-defined techniques to develop functional requirements, from the system requirements, that serve as input to the software design process.

The information from the systems requirements specifications document must be translated to a set of attributes characterized by information flow, information content, and information structure, at least at an operational level, for the purpose of software requirements specification analysis. The outcomes of this portion of the software requirements specifications phase represent the input to the design phase and, as such, should be an accurate depiction of the actual requirements specification, as agreed to by the user.

The final software requirements specifications document must provide sufficient information for the design team to carry out the conceptual and detailed design of the software system. The features of this document include a description of characteristics such as:

1. Functional requirements
    1.1. Data requirements
    1.2. Activities the system must perform
    1.3. Measurement and test conditions
    1.4. Internal performance specifications
    1.5. Internal system processing requirements
2. Nonfunctional requirements
    2.1. Quality factor requirements
    2.2. External interface requirements
    2.3. External performance requirements
    2.4. External operating requirements
    2.5. Economic requirements
    2.6. Structural requirements
    2.7. Political requirements

Characteristics of Functional Requirements   Functional requirements, as we noted in our discussion of system level requirements specification, are those software requirements specifications that represent such user oriented operational considerations as:

1. Interactions between the system and the internal environment in which the system is to operate
2. Input/output functions
3. Data definitions
4. Processing requirements
5. Software performance provisions

Functional requirements are directly measurable or may be measured quantitatively through testing procedures that examine the input–process–output sequence.

Functional requirements may be expressed as mathematical expressions, or in structured languages (e.g., structured English) or in any of the formal specification languages. The style used is strictly a function of the software design team preferences and the support environment that is in use at the facility. Primary concerns relate to software utility, software performance characteristics and external interfaces.

Data requirements usually represent a form of functional requirements. These requirements may be measured and tested as to size, structural representation, integrity, and how they change over time. Data requirements are intended to describe what data are used and produced by the system. These requirements specifications are usually divided into two sections; data characteristics and data utilization, which describe the activities involving data. The way in which data are organized within the system is provided by the database system utilized to store the information. This is organized around three subsets of data, namely data structure, data characteristics, and data utilization.

Characteristics of Nonfunctional Requirements   Nonfunctional requirements are the result of constraints or limitations on certain descriptive requirements choices for constructing the system. These requirements, which arise from structural or purposeful considerations, directly impact the cost of system design and testing, and the overall effort required to develop and field the needed system [Roman, 1985]. The major nonfunctional requirements are associated with:

1. Quality factors such as reliability, maintainability, usability, interoperability, and portability
2. Interfaces between the system and its users that affect the way in which the system interacts with the intended users
3. Performance characteristics that affect factors such as response time, workload, information throughput, user productivity, and required storage space
4. Operating constraints that relate to the external environment such as size, weight, power needs, cooling needs, personnel training and availability, and spatial configuration
5. Economic constraints that are concerned with both immediate and long term costs of the total program
6. Political constraints that deal with political realities and legal issues and concerns

Some of these nonfunctional requirements do not lend themselves to direct measurement. They represent such parameters as quality factors, environmental constraints, economic constraints, political constraints, and development environment constraints. However, these factors are essential in describing what the user intends in the way of external performance of the system.

One of the major difficulties with nonfunctional requirements lies in the use of qualitative language constructs for a particular specification. This opens the way for problem issues such as imprecision, inconsistency, ambiguity, incompleteness, and conflict entering into the requirements specification description. Since the requirements specifications that emerge from the use of nonfunctional requirements have potential impact on the software development project, the software development team must be aware of these pitfalls.

Quality factor requirements represent a special instance of nonfunctional requirements that are commonly found in nearly all requirements specifications. They are widely used by user groups in system requirements specifications to indicate requirements pertaining to operational software trustworthiness. [Myers, 1988]. These factors are used frequently, but are not always well defined. Quality factors often have different meanings to different groups. A list of the commonly used quality factor requirements is:

1. *Efficiency*—the amount of computing resources and code required by the software to perform a function
2. *Flexibility*—the effort required to modify operational software
3. *Integrity*—the extent to which access to software or data by unauthorized persons can be controlled
4. *Interoperability*—the effort required to couple one software system with another
5. *Maintainability*—the effort required to locate and fix an error in operational software
6. *Portability*—the effort required to transfer software from one hardware configuration or software system environment to another
7. *Reliability*—the extent to which software can be expected to perform its intended function with required precision
8. *Responsiveness*—the extent to which the software provides timely results
9. *Reusability*—the extent to which software can be used in other applications
10. *Testability*—the effort required to test software to ensure that it performs its intended function
11. *Usability*—the effort required to learn, operate, prepare input, and interpret output of software

Quality factors represent a much used subset of purposeful or nonfunctional requirements. Quality factors are used in most large-scale software acquisition projects to describe features desired and/or required in the software product. We may divide quality factors into two separate groups:

1. *Effectiveness*—those quality factors that relate to how effective the software product is in accomplishing the assigned tasks
2. *Suitability*—those quality factors that relate to how suitable the software product is to perform the assigned tasks

These two groups taken together represent the adequacy of the software, in terms of quality factors, to accomplish the purpose for which it was designed. Further study by the Department of Defense [1987] has shown that these quality factors interact with one another and affect the development of the design of the software product. In a specific development situation, some of them may reinforce one another, others may have no relationship with each other, and others may each conflict with each other. The greatest concern is with those that may conflict with one another. Such conflicts lead to an increased risk that the developed software will not meet user needs and that completion of the software development on time and within the money allocated is in jeopardy. If two or more of the quality factor requirements selected for the software project are in conflict, the time and effort required to complete a specific design will increase and it is entirely possible that these conflicting goals cannot be met using the selected development approach. Suppose that, for a specific development strategy, responsiveness and interoperability conflict. If the user then demands high system responsiveness for the completed design and also requires interoperability for several target computer systems, it is unlikely that the final product will satisfy both requirements at the same time. This is due to conflicting demands that simply cannot be met unless the design and development approach is changed. A conclusion such as this could be based upon relationships between quality factor metrics shown in Figures 3.7 and 3.8.

In selecting quality factors, users often fail to provide measures of importance of these features to the final software system. This leads to an imprecise statement of the importance of these factors, which gives rise to problems in the design process. It then becomes necessary for the developer to either go back to the user for clarification or to decide internally on the relative importance of particular quality factors. Unless there is clarification from the user as to the relative importance of these quality factors, the final product is unlikely to meet with user satisfaction.

Users tend to overstate the need for quality factors in the system requirements. This may lead to the necessity for later adjustment of these when not all of them can be met, especially when factors may be in conflict. Failure to resolve these issues during the system and software requirements specifications phase places the entire software project at risk.

In Figure 3.7, the association of these nonfunctional requirements and the

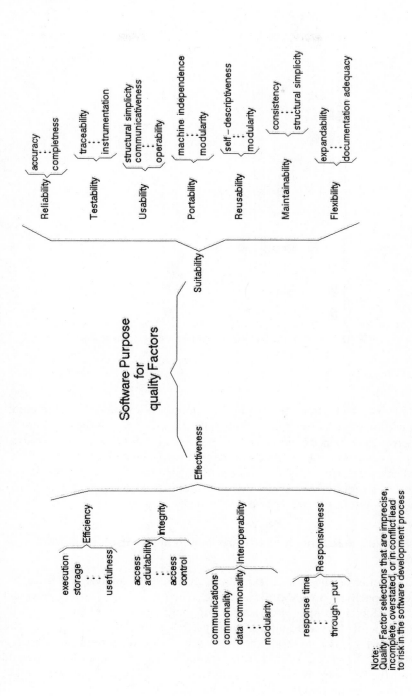

FIGURE 3.7 Quality factors for system and software requirements specifications

Note:
Quality Factor selections that are imprecise,
incomplete, overstated, or in conflict lead
to risk in the software development process

113

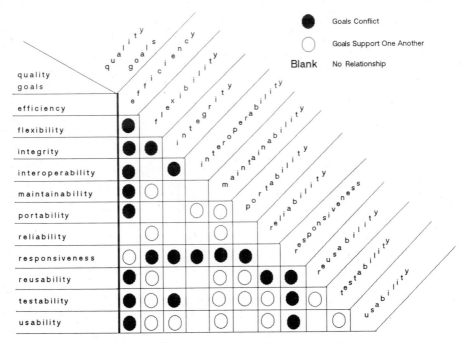

FIGURE 3.8 Conflict relationships between quality goals

associated risk elements related to imprecision, conflict, and overstatement of nonfunctional requirements is shown. In Figure 3.8, conflict is seen to occur between certain of these factors in a specific development situation. This impacts cost and risk in completion of the software development project. This indicates priorities must be assigned for the particular quality factor characteristics required, or trade-offs may occur during design that compromise the user intent for the system performance.

3.4.2 Methods and Tools for Software Requirements Specifications Analysis

There are many methods and techniques available to analyze software requirements specifications. Methods include structured design, object-oriented design, dataflow diagrams, or data structure diagrams. In this chapter we will examine some of the tools that use these methods for software requirements analysis; however, the methods themselves are covered in detail in Chapter 4. The range of approaches runs from manual to automated and includes all aspects of the software requirements specifications. The various approaches generally have common characteristics that include:

1. A means for information analysis
2. An approach for functional representation
3. An approach for nonfunctional representation
4. Definition of interfaces
5. A mechanism for partitioning
6. Support for abstraction
7. Representation of physical and logical views

Thus, these approaches address information flow, content, and structure of the software requirements specifications.

In this analysis, information flow is traced through the system from input function to output function, including any transformation operations. Interfaces are defined by the information flow requirements and are a result of information and function representations, as these are matched to the flows into and out of functions. Partitioning, which results in the parallel paths for the design development, and abstraction, which is the illustrative level at which the design is being considered, are developed through layering of the project. Layering involves looking at various design paths through decomposition of the software specification. These layers provide representation, in both information and function domains, at various levels of abstraction.

System-requirements-specifications assistance tools have become increasingly important in software engineering research. One of the major efforts sponsored by Rome Air Development Center (RADC) [Rzepka, 1988] supports a requirements engineering process that begins with system requirements specifications and ends with software requirements specifications. In the next section we will examine the RADC effort and other tools that have application to identifying and representing software requirements specifications.

3.4.3 Specific Methods and Techniques

In this section we will consider several of the automated procedures and associated tools that assist in the development of requirements specifications. We will begin with a contemporary requirements engineering approach that places a great deal of emphasis on requirements specifications and follow that by a review of some of the currently available tools to assist in this process.

A recently developed approach administered contractually by the U. S. Air Force RADC [Rzepka, 1988] proposes a requirements engineering model. The model envisions a system and software requirements specifications engineering test bed designed to incorporate engineering methods and tools within a host environment. The objectives of the host environment are to assist in the development of system and software requirements specifications analysis, documentation, and validation. The RADC approach attempts to give a detailed description of system and software requirements specifications activities, including the iterative nature of system and software requirements specifications engineering activities, and to incorporate new techniques such as dynamic analysis of requirements specifications. The process model used by RADC is depicted in Figure 3.9. System requirements specifications conceptualization is first accomplished by the user. These ideas are refined and documented. Specific software system level goals are defined, and an iterative process commences that results in final software requirements specifications and partial design.

This approach incorporates several tools. These tools include the requirements apprentice component of the *Programmers Apprentice* developed by Massachusetts Institute of Technology (MIT) [Rich and Waters, 1988], and, in addition, an object-oriented design tool and a knowledge-based requirements assistant developed by industry. The inputs are documented system-level requirements statements. These statements are analyzed for consistency between various system objectives and for conflict between requirements specifications.

As an example of the kind of operations performed by one of the tools in the test bed, we will examine an approach taken by Computer Sciences Corporation. In this approach, the requirements specifications are decomposed into a dataflow diagram using an object-oriented design, in Smalltalk 80 language. In this system, requirements are manually transformed into a structured data flow construct using DeMarco's rules [1979]. The outputs of this tool are (1) a data flow diagram for all requirements, (2) a database, and (3) a hierarchical tree structure showing the relationships between all objects. These resulting software specifications are reviewed and the process iterated until the user representative and software designer are satisfied that the software requirements specifications represent the system-level requirements. Similar operations are completed by other components of the test bed that analyze the software requirements specifications. Following this, a partial conceptual and logical design is completed and becomes the output of the model. Requirements specifications are feasible, testable, and traceable to the system level requirements statements that served as input to the model.

This approach is representative of new initiatives that have been proposed to gain control over the software requirements specifications engineering process, and to introduce formal methods, tools, and validation procedures that assist in producing software requirements specifications that reflect user needs and are correct. This approach, as with most others, provides little support for direct interactive identification of user needs. This is because the input is user-generated system-level statements that are generally accepted without challenge.

Several CASE tools have been developed in recent years that are intended to address the software requirements specifications issues. The current custom of handling software requirements specifications issues has generally been limited to provisions for software engineer support, such as through interactive graphics, program management, configuration control, consistency checking

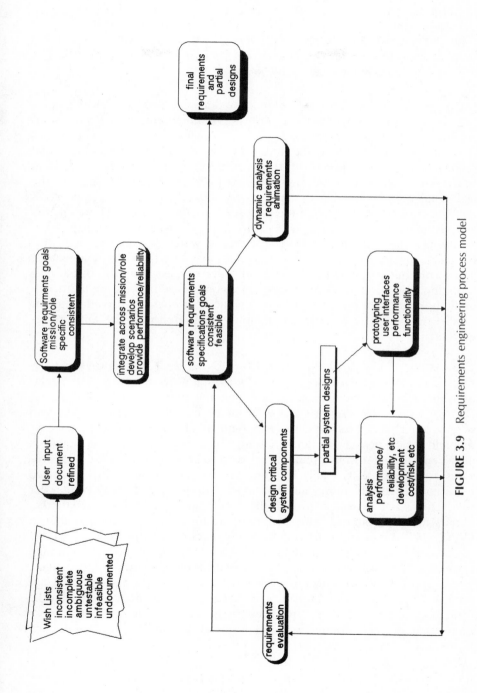

FIGURE 3.9 Requirements engineering process model

117

through database construction, and prototyping. Some of the CASE tools that have explicitly addressed the requirements area include EPOS, CASE 2000, TAGS, PSL/PSA, SADT, and SREM/SYREM. We will describe these here, as they relate to requirements. CASE tools will also be discussed as part of our environments study in Chapter 7.

EPOS EPOS, a CASE tool developed by Software Products and Services, Inc. [SPS, 1986], provides three software requirements specification languages, each with an increasing degree of formality. The first level provides the software engineer with the ability to define functional and conceptual requirements, while the more formal ones provide presentation directly in source code. Rules for analyzing program logic are developed through the use of decision tables. Factors such as redundancy, consistency, and completeness are checked through the data storage in a database. However, the checks are made for the form or structure of the software requirements specification, rather than for substance of the software requirements specifications. This means that the substance could indeed be incorrect, ambiguous, and so on, but be judged to be in good order because the form of the presentation is in good order. While this is a good move in assisting the development of software requirements specifications, it does not provide a major step in resolving risk or reducing volatility associated with the software requirements.

CASE 2000 CASE 2000, NASTEC Corp. [NASTEC, 1987], provides a variety of graphics and text supports including dataflow diagrams, entity-relationship diagrams, and state transition diagrams for use by the software engineer. CASE 2000 supports not only requirements specifications but also several other phases of software design and development, including conceptual and logical design and detail design. Program management assistance is provided through a work breakdown structure system. This CASE tool provides a database that is able to store, cross-reference, and track software requirements specifications and data models from input through system design. This is accomplished through the development of a complete data dictionary derived from the structured design techniques noted above. Input to CASE 2000 comes from the requirements specifications documents, as discussed earlier. From these documents, CASE 2000 uses the structured design approaches to transform requirements specifications statements into designs. These approaches are covered in our discussion of structured design approaches in Chapter 4. As in EPOS, however, the assistance operates on the form or structure of the software requirement specification information input rather than on the substance or content of the software requirements specifications.

TAGS TAGS, Teledyne Brown Engineering [Teledyne Brown, 1987], provides automated assistance for the definition, design documentation, simulation testing, and maintenance of a software product. In this presentation we will concentrate on that portion of the system that is directly applicable to software requirements specifications. As does CASE 2000, TAGS utilizes a structured design approach for transformation of requirements specifications statements into designs. A complete data dictionary is prepared for use in analysis of the design. For software requirements specifications, TAGS checks for completeness, correctness, and missing parts as determined from the information stored in the database related to software requirements specifications inputs. The system also includes dataflow, control flow, and timing specification in the I/O Software Requirements Specification Language. As above, the effort is concentrated on the form rather than the content of the software requirement specification information.

PSL/PSA (Problem Statement Language/Problem Statement Analysis) The PSL/PSA system was developed by the University of Michigan as part of the ISDOS project as a part of the Computer Aided Design and Specification Analysis Tool, CADSAT [Teichroew and Hershey, 1977]. With PSL/PSA, the analyst is able to describe information in a context-free manner without regard to the ultimate application; create databases that contain descriptions of the information system; add, delete, and modify descriptions; and produce formatted documentation and reports on the specifications. It is based on an entity-relationship model (covered in Chapter 4), and is a nonprocedural language that is able to describe a system from several viewpoints. PSL/PSA describe entities in terms of a set of object classes and the relationships that exist between the object classes. There are twenty (20) predefined object classes and fifty (50) available relationships. Beyond this, objects may be anything that is given a PSL name and defined by the user.

PSL is a formal language used to identify software system requirements. Once the requirements are specified in PSL, the specification is processed by the PSA. PSA produces reports about the requirements and builds a database of the requirements and system attributes, any modifications that have been made to the specification database, various reference reports, analysis reports, and summary reports that may be used to evaluate the database.

The PSL/PSA system is used in conjunction with dataflow diagrams that have been developed to describe the system. These approaches are covered in Chapter 4. Once this information is determined, the data entities are identified and specified, followed by a definition of the relationships that exist between the data elements. Then the activities of the system are defined and listed with each data element being either an input or output for a particular process.

The PSL/PSA system is used for requirements analysis and specification. It provides this support through use of the specification languages that describe the relationships between object classes. A data dictionary is provided and an entity-relationship structured approach is used to establish the design. Through the use of the data dictionary and structured design of PSL/PSA, inconsistencies and incomplete software requirements specifications may be detected and corrected; however, the system operates on the form and not the content of the software requirements specifications.

SADT (Structured Analysis Design Techniques) SADT, a product of Softech, Inc., is intended to provide assistance in the understanding of complicated structures used to accomplish system definition, requirements analysis, and software design [Ross and Shoman, 1977; 1985]. SADT was originally developed as a manual system that guides the analyst in the decomposition of software into various functions such as graphic notations, modeling principles, review procedures, and interviewing techniques. These are termed SADT actigrams and datagrams. These are the names given to graphical notations that SADT uses to provide the relationships between information and functions within the software and provides project control guides for application. The goal of this procedure is to produce models of the system that may be examined by the software development team. A typical SADT diagram is shown in Figure 3.10. This figure shows both the control functions and an example of use of the diagram.

With this tool, the analyst uses actigrams and datagrams to develop a system model that hierarchically decomposes the software project. This automated tool supports analysis procedures in an application support environment. Management tools are also provided to produce specified reviews and milestones that enable the customer to review the design development and through this review, validate customer requirements. A "development team" approach is supported which stresses analysis, design, and review.

Fundamental steps in using SADT are:

1. Develop a Level 0 Activity diagram, as depicted in Figure 3.11, consisting of input data, control data, the means by which this function or activity is to accomplish its particular operation and output data.
2. Using this same procedure, decompose the system into its component parts until the primitive levels have been determined.

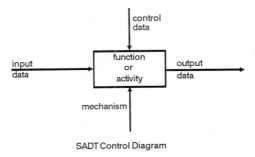

SADT Control Diagram

FIGURE 3.10 SADT (structured analysis and design technique) diagrams

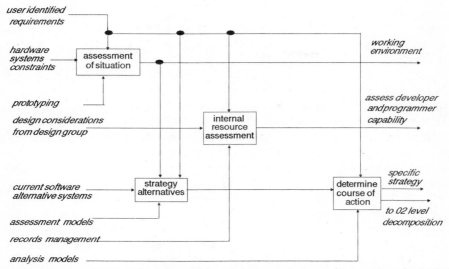

FIGURE 3.11   SADT (structured analysis and design technique) diagram (Level 0 SADT diagram for developing strategy alternatives for handling hardware constraints)

3. Next, construct a behavior diagram model showing the events that are caused by the functions determined in steps 1 and 2.

4. Circulate each of the diagrams in a kit for review by all participants to ensure that all the necessary steps have been completed and that redundancy has been eliminated.

SADT is a very robust method for accomplishing the requirements analysis phase of the software development lifecycle. It is capable of representing semantic information, possesses a good review process, but is weak in applications guidance. SADT has the same basic problems as other automated tools that are intended to address requirements specifications, namely, that it considers only the form of the requirements and not the substance.

SREM (Software Requirements Engineering Methodology)   One of the more important automated tools for requirements specifications is SREM. SREM is an automated tool that addresses the software requirements analysis phase of the software development lifecycle [Alford, 1985]. It was developed by TRW under contract with the USAF in 1976 to address deficiencies in requirements documentation. It uses a *Requirements Statement Language* (RSL), prepared explicitly for this tool, for specifying requirements. SREM also provides a set of automated evaluation techniques called the *Requirements Evaluation Validation System* (REVS). REVS is intended to interpret the computer programming language for use in a finite-state machine, perform consistency checks, do completeness and traceability analyses, develop simulators to exercise the requirements, and provide for graphic support and documentation needs. Thus, SREM is a methodology for generation of requirements using RSL and REVS.

SREM notation is used to describe elements (nouns), relationships, attributes, and structures. In this notation, elements are defined to be a set of objects and concepts that are used to develop the requirements specifications. RSL is used to define relationships between objects. Attributes are invoked to modify or qualify entities. Information flow is described by the structure relationship. RSL, and an accompanying narrative, serve to provide the necessary information for a requirements specification. The RSL primitives are :

1. Elements are defined to be RSL nouns and are used to identify a class of objects with names. These are used to provide the basis for the specification. Each element possesses a unique name, and this name is assigned to one of the classes for that element.
2. Relationships are defined to be RSL verbs and are used to provide the mathematical definition of a binary relationship or a statement of the relationship that exists between the elements of RSL. It is a noncommutative mathematical expression.
3. Attributes are defined to be RSL adjectives and are used as modifiers for the RSL elements. Attributes have value, but only one value for any one attribute.
4. Structures are defined to be the RSL representation of the flow graph. Two types of flow graph have been defined: the R-Net subnet structure, which identifies flow through functional steps and is used to specify system response; and Validation-Path, which is used to specify system performance.

SREM uses the Requirements Evaluation Validation System (REVS) to analyze the developed specifications. REVS is a combination report generator and computer graphics display used to review the flow of information, establish consistency throughout the system, and examine the dynamic relationships that exist between and among elements as we have noted.

SREM incorporates a set of steps that represent procedures to guide the user through the process. The fundamental steps include:

Translation

This transforms initial requirements from system specifications into a detailed set of data descriptions and processing steps.

Decomposition

This enables evaluation of information at the interface between software elements and provides a complete set of functional requirements.

Allocation

This enables the consideration of alternatives, trade-off studies, and sensitivity analysis.

Analytical Feasibility Demonstration

This enables the user to simulate critical processing requirements.

RSL is used in the first two procedures and REVS is used in the last two. SREM is based on a finite-state machine model specifically designed to be used in machine processing. Its primary use is for real-time design or in time critical design situations, rather than simply the static design mode of many structured design processes. As noted earlier, SREM contains automated tools to assist in the processing of information that produce reports, perform consistency checks, analyze statements for completeness, and provide a graphic interface for ease of use.

In using SREM, the designer first examines the requirements specifications documents to begin the transformation of these initial requirements into the detailed set of data descriptions and processing steps. Requirements specifications are classified into elements and relationships that call for RSL nouns and verbs. Other attributes are defined as RSL adjectives and modify the elements previously selected. Once defined and entered into the program, structures are defined in flow graph notation.

Following this, the presented system is analyzed by SREM for consistency, completeness, interface requirements, alternative approaches that provide trade-off studies, and sensitivity analysis. Through these processes, SREM provides some insight into both the form and substance of the requirements specification. It addresses the substance through consistency analysis and completeness checks; however, the system is able to confirm only the presence or absence of these characteristics. The form of the requirements specification is confirmed by consistency and completeness checks, simulation and by flow graph analysis. The same concerns that apply to the other automation tool apply equally here, namely, that it does not get to the concerns of incorrect system requirements specifications.

Other Tools for Software Requirements Sepcifications   Two automated assistance tools that do address the substance of software requirements specifications are GLITTER-S and WATSON. These knowledge based software requirements specifications assistance tools show that the content of software requirements specifications may be addressed and may be operated on by automated techniques. GLITTER-S [Fickas, 1987] incorporates nonfunctional requirements. It permits constraints and alterables, such as development resources and organizational goals, to become factors in the definition process. WATSON [Kelly, 1987] uses domain knowledge to build software requirements specifications from scenarios. It examines and corrects inconsistencies, finishes incomplete software requirements specification statements by adding rules, eliminating unreachable states, and ensuring that all pertinent data are handled in all states. While these assistance tools do address the content of the software requirement specification in addition to the form, they do not handle problem areas that relate to incomplete and imprecise information from the system requirements specifications.

Prototyping is another approach that is used for analysis of software requirements specifications. Prototyping represents one of the more important approaches to the development of software requirements specifications and is included here for completeness. Prototyping has the greatest potential of any of these approaches for reducing risk related to incomplete and imprecise information in system requirements specifications. However, prototyping generates only software requirements specifications that are provided by the designer and does not address system-level requirements unless the user is involved in the process. Prototyping does aid in analyzing software requirement specifications in terms of consistency, ascertaining the absence of key inputs, and the like. Much more information will be given on prototypes in Chapter 8.

3.4.3   Impact of Errors in System and Software Requirements Specifications

Errors will doubtlessly be introduced in the system and software requirements specifications. Errors that are a consequence of unknowns will, in all likelihood, remain with the software through implementation or until the user detects a malfunction based on an erroneous system or software requirements specification. Errors that are codified through improper interpretation of correct software requirements specifications should be caught through the various design reviews that are conducted with the user during the detailed software design phase. These approaches to error detection and correction are covered in Chapter 5, which introduces testing, validation, and verification techniques. It has been estimated that errors in the development of system and software requirements specifications account for somewhere between 35 and 75% of all the errors that will occur in the development of the software product [Charette, 1986]. These figures do not address the concerns that arise as a consequence of inadequate user-defined system requirements specifications that are picked up during the maintenance phase of the software development lifecycle.

It is important to identify and correct errors in the requirements specifications phase as early as possible. Error correction that must be accomplished following implementation of other phases of development costs considerably more in money and time than if the same errors were detected and corrected during the requirements specifications phase. It has been estimated that errors in requirements specifications that are identified and corrected during the programming phase cost more than 100 times the cost of their correction during the requirements specifications phase. Thus, it is very important that any errors be detected as early as feasible in the development lifecycle, as the later in the process that errors are detected, the higher the cost of repair.

As we have noted in the section on knowledge acquisition approaches, it is not likely that we will be able to produce software requirements specifications without the introduction of errors. This is true for any requirements elicitation techniques. However, there would be even greater problems for the delivered software product if the requirements phase were ignored and we moved directly to the design or programming.

Errors introduced at the onset of system and software requirements specifications, if not detected early, will continue to propagate throughout the entire design and development lifecycle. They will not be picked up early through the programming phase, as this activity occurs only after the errors are inserted into the detailed design. Thus, there is a need for validation of system and software requirements specifications early in the design effort.

Generally, errors introduced by inadequate system requirements specifications or software requirements specifications cannot be corrected by the application of structured methodologies during the programming phase of the development effort. These must be detected through design reviews that occur during the design process that validate the design against the user specifications system level, and the software specifications.

Errors that are the result of inadequate or poor design support, or which occur through the lack of a disciplined approach, may be minimized through the use of structured techniques. Structured approaches provide techniques that are intended to track the data entities, the logic of the program, and the relationships that are pertinent to information flow.

However, automating software requirements specifications offers little in the way of improvement of our ability to identify and correct errors in the requirements specifications unless we work on the substance of the requirements statements. Currently available tools address only the form and not the substance of the requirements specifications. We must also modify the way in which we view the life of software products, as the time spent for maintenance is generally time spent to modify the software product to do what we didn't ask it to do initially.

3.5   SYSTEM AND SOFTWARE REQUIREMENTS SPECIFICATION DOCUMENTS

The system-level requirements specifications, determined in conjunction with the user and software engineer, form the best description of the system requirements specifications for translation into the software requirements specification document. The system requirements specification document must contain a set of precisely worded statements that the software is intended to satisfy and be agreed to by the user, as the system requirements specifications needed to build the software. It is not necessary that this document be a statement of the design, and, in fact, it is useful to maintain the system requirements specification document as the meta-level specification against which progress, verification, and validation of the software design are measured. In this way it is possible to evaluate the design, determine whether the constraints, as stated, are met; and assess whether all the properties given by the user are included.

We have noted that the development of system and software requirements specifications to meet user needs requires time and resource allocation sufficient to do a good job. Frequently this portion of the software development lifecycle is underestimated and underfunded with the obvious results— namely, software products that do not serve the needs of the user.

The software requirements specifications document should be carefully crafted and be as complete as possible, and maintain consistency between and among the several parts of the design. As many aspects of the system should be specified as possible, as well as all the functions that the system must perform. Conflicts in the software requirements specifications documents should be resolved through trade-offs and priority setting by the user in conjunction with the software designers at this stage in the software requirements specification development. In actual practice, it is not likely that we will achieve software requirements documents that are free of errors. Failure to give adequate attention to error reduction and conflict trade-off at this stage of software development often leads to disastrous consequences downstream in the development process.

Heninger [1980] has provided a guide to software requirements documentation and has presented six necessary conditions that must be met if satisfactory software requirements specifications are to be developed for the software development process:

1. External system behavior must be specified.
2. Implementation constraints must be specified.
3. Changes in the requirements specifications should be easy to make.
4. System maintenance should use this as a reference document.
5. The lifecycle of the system should be part of the document.
6. Acceptable responses to undesirable events should be included.

In addition, there should be an understanding of the environment in which the functional system will operate and some understanding of the volatility of this environment.

The software requirements specification document restates the system requirements specifications as agreed to by the user and translates these into technical terminology for use in the design development. Thus, there must be a direct relationship between the system requirements specifications and software requirements specifications so that the latter document will serve the needs of the design and also serve as a reference tool throughout the development lifecycle.

There are any number of guidelines for the development of the software requirements specification document, and several of these may be used successfully in the management of the software design process. The most important aspects are:

1. Tailor this document to the specific system to be designed.
2. Make certain that it represents the user defined system.
3. Be sure that all functional and nonfunctional system behavior constraints are met.
4. Follow through with validation and verification procedures.

Construction of a software requirements specification document would include, but surely not be limited to, the following technical topics:

System Description

The system should be described in general terms consistent with, and generally the same as, the system requirements specifications prepared earlier.

Hardware Description

The intended hardware or any constraints related to hardware are to be presented in this section.

System Structural Model

The system should be graphically modeled using one of the techniques described in Chapter 4. For example, dataflow diagrams, entity–relationship diagrams, Jackson system diagrams, or other structured techniques.

Functional Requirements

These imply a needed output behavior of the system (as a function of, or in terms of, input behavior) in terms, such as $O = f(i)$, where O = output, i = input, and f = the function for those simple cases where quantitative modeling is possible. As noted in Section 3.4.1, the functional requirements can include data, system activities measurements and test conditions, and internal processing and performance requirements.

Nonfunctional Requirements

These describe requirements associated with constraints, alterables, or limitations such as 1) quality factor requirements 2) external interface requirements, 3) external performance requirements, 4) external operating requirements, 5) economic requirements, 6) structural requirements, and 7) political constraints.

Installation and Maintenance Environment

The installation and maintenance environment are described, as well as any anticipated hardware migrations or changes in user needs. Installation and maintenance requirements are nonfunctional requirements, even though they effect functionality.

In addition to technical requirements for software development, process management requirements are needed as well. A major need in a software specification is cost and schedule information. This may be obtained from one of the cost models discussed in Chapter 10. System management needs should also be described. Chapter 9 is concerned with issues associated with software process management.

3.6 ACTIVITIES AND PRODUCTS FROM SOFTWARE REQUIREMENTS SPECIFICATIONS

During the process of developing the system and software requirements specifications, the major task of software requirements specifications analysis must be conducted. The objectives of this segment of the software requirements specifications phase are to (1) recognize and address any problems that have been identified during the analysis and evaluation efforts, (2) evaluate the plan and synthesize the approaches and solutions for the software development, and (3) prepare as concise a set of conditions as is feasible for the detailed software design phase. These activities are best met by utilizing the software requirements specifications document prepared according to the system requirements specifications from the user group as a guide.

3.6 SUMMARY AND CONCLUSIONS

The identification of system-level requirements specifications and software requirements specifications represent the first phase in production of a software product. The process of identification of the system requirements specifications is, to a great extent, a knowledge acquisition procedure. As such, it is subject to all the problems and issues associated with human interaction and subjective interpretation of information. Careful attention must be given to the process of knowledge acquisition to do the job correctly.

Once the system requirements specification document is prepared, there are several support tools that may be used to aid in the conversion of these to software requirements specifications. These tools provide a means to answer questions from the software developer related to interface problems, complexity problems, consistency of specifications, and other issues that must be resolved. Clearly, a given set of user system requirements specifications can have many correct software requirements specifications. Available tools usually permit the developer to use the procedure embedded in the tool to provide only one, or a few, such specifications. There is a major need for robust tools to enhance the development of software requirements.

The system and software requirements definition and specification documents that form the final deliverable of this phase of software systems engineering activity serve as the input, control, and evaluation documents for the remainder of the software development process. Our discussion of system and software requirements specifications development has emphasized the interpersonal interactions between the user and the software systems development team. It is important that the system and software requirements specification documents developed by this process are correct, consistent, modifiable, traceable, unambiguous, and verifiable [Fairley, 1985]. The methods that we have covered are important for the proper development of these requirements specification documents.

3.8 PROBLEMS

3.1. Explain why the requirements engineering phase is subdivided into two parts: system-level requirements identification and software level requirement specifications.

3.2. Who is the "user" of applications packages for personal computers? Who serves as a surrogate for the end user and is responsible for identifying requirements for these applications packages?

3.3. Why is it important that requirements analysis, design, test, and maintenance of applications systems software be concerned about being in an economics-driven context? Is it important that computer systems software be so concerned?

3.4. Relate the activities shown in the matrix of Figure 3.4 to the systems engineering approach to problem identification, analysis, and solution covered in Chapter 1.

3.5. Interactive approaches to the acquisition of knowledge are generally considered the most appropriate techniques. Explain how one or more of these approaches are implemented.

3.6. What are the differences between nominal group techniques and the other methods of inquiry?

3.7. How would you go about the process of eliciting information from experts steeped in procedural and rule-based knowledge that is essential to the software development project system-level requirements identification? Is this a dichotomy? Are experts ever steeped in procedural or rule-based knowledge? Or does this merely describe proficiency? (See Chapter 9.)

3.8. Indicate the different approaches that may be taken by individual software systems engineers toward the development of requirements specifications.

3.9. Why is it desirable to develop two requirements documents-one for system requirements specifications and the other for software requirements specification?

3.10. What are some of the basic issues that impair our ability to prepare a good set of software requirements specifications? How will you overcome these issues to ensure adequate software requirements specifications?

3.11. Explain the difference between functional and nonfunctional requirements.

3.12. Within functional requirements, we have listed a category called *data requirements*. How are data requirements selected? What metrics can we use to ensure that we have complete and consistent data requirements?

3.13. A requirements engineering process model is presented in Figure 3.9. Trace the steps through this model and develop a systems engineering lifecycle model for this process.

3.14. What are the types of errors that account for the majority of problems in system-level specifications and software requirements specifications?

3.15. Explain the use of the system and software requirements specification documents for testing the system and validating the user needs.

Chapter 4

Conceptual and Logical Design and Detailed Design

4.1 INTRODUCTION

In the process of transformation of software requirements specifications into executable code, it is desirable to undertake conceptual and logical design efforts in order to produce architectures that provide specifications for the detailed design and coding phase. Each of these areas has been the subject of significant development activity over the past several years. This has resulted in several structured approaches to conceptual and logical design and detailed design, which we will cover in this chapter. Extensive use of software lifecycle models for software product development has provided the stimulus to develop toolkits that can automate various parts of the software development lifecycle. We will discuss some of these toolkits here.

In Chapter 2, on models for the software lifecycle, we have examined several software development lifecycle models in detail, particularly the waterfall model and the derivatives that have come from it. In Chapter 3, on software requirements analysis and specifications, we have seen that the development of user-driven requirements definitions and specifications form an essential and critical part of the software development lifecycle. Without good user-centered requirements definitions and specifications, the resulting software product is not likely to satisfy the user, no matter how well the internal design is conceived.

The purposes of this chapter are to provide the background and information necessary for (1) conceptual and logical design of software, (2) detailed design approaches, and (3) understanding various methods that have been developed to implement these approaches. The inputs to the conceptual and logical design phase of software development are the detailed software specifications that were formulated as a result of the software requirements definitions and specifications phase. The outcomes of this phase are detailed design specifications that are used as inputs for programming and testing operations that follow in the detailed design and coding phase.

The approach we will take is to first look at techniques that feature functional decomposition of the requirements specifications. Functional decomposition techniques are generally oriented towards the development framework associated with the waterfall lifecycle model, as organizing themes for the various logic approaches and automated toolkits. The standard waterfall software development lifecycle is shown in Figure 4.1, and was presented before as Figure 2.3. Phase 2 of this model is conceptual and logical design and phase 3 is detailed design.

During the past several years, much attention has been given to automation of the conceptual and logical design phase and the detailed design phase. One of the major outcomes of these efforts to achieve automation, which is of particular importance to software systems, is the notion of a development environment. This environment includes, but is not restricted to, the tools that assist the software developer in achieving a consistent and correct software design product. We will present several of the automated approaches to support these design functions in this chapter. In Chapter 7, on software environments, we will present several commercial CASE tools and provide discussions of the use of these automation products. As we noted in Chapter 3, automatic translation of requirements specifications to conceptual and logical design and detailed design products has been successful in very restricted

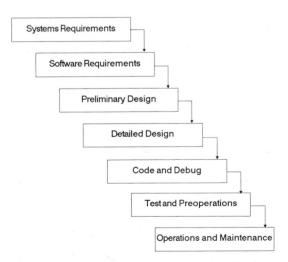

FIGURE 4.1   Waterfall software development lifecycle due to Boehm

application domains. Additionally, there have been major efforts directed at code generation and these will be considered in Chapter 5.

Top-down design takes advantage of the hierarchical characteristics of system functions. Design commences at the highest level of abstraction of the system and proceeds through system decomposition until the most primitive level is reached.

It is not, however, practical to decompose large-scale software system development projects through application of *only* a top-down approach. Hence, just as in the bottom-up design approach, the top-down approaches are not used exclusively, rather they are used in conjunction with the "bottom-up" approaches. These approaches complement one another and tend to assist in reaching the best possible design allowed by a fixed upper limit on resources that may be expended.

The top-down approach does lend itself to small projects that are truly hierarchical in nature. For these smaller projects the top-down approach may be used to the exclusion of the bottom-up approach. In this case, system decomposition commences at the start of the conceptual design effort in order to provide as detailed information as possible concerning the requirements definitions and specifications. Once top-level design requirements are determined and validated, the detailed design activity is activated. Following detailed design of the system at the initial stage of decomposition, the process is repeated until the abstractions are removed and the details of each design level are revealed. This process is continued until the lowest level of abstraction has been reached and detailed design specifications have been prepared. The representation at all levels of decomposition must be clear, concise, and unambiguous in order to be certain that the design process has been concluded in an orderly way and that it will produce a system design that will satisfy the user or system requirements specifications.

As we have noted, detailed design using this approach is concerned with the identification of modules and the relationships that exist between modules, the interfaces, and the data requirements. Any constraints related to hardware are introduced early and handled during system-level considerations. In the top-down approach, detailed design and the integration of modules continues in a progressively detailed fashion until the entire system is sufficiently well articulated that it may be implemented into code and made ready for test. As with the bottom-up approach, the top-down approach is particularly amenable to the several structured design methods covered in this chapter.

We begin with a discussion of conceptual and logical design approaches and associated functional decomposition design methods. This is followed by a review of the automated tools that have been developed to implement conceptual or functional design. Next, we turn our attention to detailed design considerations that enable implementation of the results of functional decomposition techniques. Finally we will present one of the more recent developments in software design, object-oriented design methods.

4.2   STRUCTURED LOGICAL DESIGN FOR FUNCTIONAL DECOMPOSITION

The purpose of the conceptual design phase of the software development lifecycle is to obtain logical design specifications for a software product. This enables (1) determination of the structure of the software, and (2) its hierarchical decomposition into functions that will later be converted into source code. Notions of structure are essential for control in detailed software design. An effective way to provide for structured flow control is to apply a top-down, modular approach to the software requirements specifications that will result in detailed design requirements for software product and process development. In this approach, major functions or procedures are identified that, when connected together in an appropriate way, will result in a *logic design* for the software system. This procedure is typically called *functional decomposition*. The resulting functions are then further broken down into subfunctions or subprocedures at ever lower levels in the solution hierarchy. This decomposition continues until all the functional program modules required to implement the software requirements specifications have been identified. The interfaces to each function must also be defined. Generally, it is desirable to do this in such a way that each functional module is independent of other modules in the system, as this will allow each of the functional modules to be coded independently of other functional modules.

4.2.1   Structured Design Tools

Several important structured procedures for functional decomposition are:

Flowcharts
Data flow diagrams (DFDs)
Data dictionaries
Process specifications
Data structure methods (DSMs)
Entity–relationship diagrams
Data structured systems development (DSSD)
Jackson system development (JSD)

We will discuss each of these techniques and approaches to functional decomposition for structuring conceptual and logical design specifications.

4.2.2   Flowcharts

Flowcharts are the most widely used technique for documentation of the design specifications that emanate from logical design. Flow chart symbols have been standardized and are defined in American National Standards

[1970]. A set of ANSI X3.5-1970 system flowcharting symbols is presented in Figure 4.2. There are four elements that comprise the ANSI flowcharting standards. Their names and purposes are:

1. *Process*—indicated the particular procedure that will be taken on the input to transform it to the output
2. *Collection point*—indicates two or more inputs into a single node with one output
3. *Decision point*—indicates that a choice between "yes" or "no" must be made
4. *Expansion point*—indicates that one input is amplified to two or more outputs

There are many flowcharting methods, only some of which have been applied specifically to software development.

One of the earlier uses of flowcharting-like methods is the Nassi–Schneiderman (N–S) [1973] chart. This method was initially employed, in part, as a means to eliminate GOTO statements that result from traditional practices of programmers trained in unstructured approaches, and make for poor design. More importantly, though, the N–S chart approach assists in determining and implementing appropriate structural relations, including branching for software modules. These procedures generally call for single exit/entry points and enhance the resulting modularity of the program structure. The standard structured programming control structures, mentioned before, are included. A typical blank N–S chart is depicted in Figure 4.3. The task of logical software design is to fill in the entries shown in Figure 4.3 for the specific software product being designed. Typical entries may be found in Nassi and Schneiderman [1973].

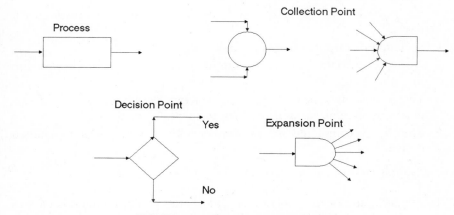

FIGURE 4.2   Flowcharting symbols

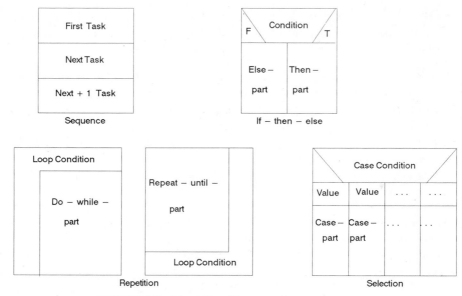

FIGURE 4.3 Nassi-Shneiderman chart components

The N–S chart is used to provide transitions of requirements specifications to flowcharts. Through use of the standard N–S charts, as depicted in Figure 4.3, tasks are defined along with conditions and logical operations in order to provide a means of delineating logical flow of the program code. The essential steps involved in using a N–S chart are:

1. Tasks are defined and delineated as to the sequence of operation.
2. Logical functions that apply are defined.
3. Loop conditions are identified using do__while and repeat__until loops.
4. Selection of case conditions is made.
5. Alternatives to the logical functions are reviewed for incorporation into the final design.
6. These steps are repeated until a satisfactory design is found, as determined by minimization of the logical functions for the design.
7. The chart is completed and software development moves on to detailed design.

The advantages of the N–S charts are:

1. The structure of the program is represented graphically and is easy to read and interpret.

2. The basis of alternative selection, and the impact of alternatives on other modules of the program, are explicitly defined.
3. The scope of iterative processes is well defined and viable.
4. The scope of the local and global variables is evident.
5. Arbitrary transfers of control are not possible.
6. Complete thought structures are confined to a relatively simple and easy-to-read chart on one page.
7. Recursion has a very simple representation.

There are five primary uses for the N–S charts: (1) creating logic designs; (2) programming from the charts, including both coding and testing; (3) functional design; (4) writing program documentation, including high-level design and procedural documentation; and (5) walkthrough inspections and program design reviews.

There are two potential disadvantages resulting from use of the N–S charts:

1. Maintenance of the resulting program code may not be a simple task since any changes resulting from a modification of a task or a logical function requires iteration of the entire set of steps that comprise the N–S procedure.
2. Programmers are not normally trained in this relatively sophisticated form of charting and, as a result, may not be able to easily understand or prepare these charts.

Nevertheless, this is a potentially very attractive method. The ease of interpretation of the DO—WHILE, IF—THEN—ELSE, and DO—UNTIL symbols is particularly evident in Figure 4.3.

There are other charting approaches. Pseudocode can be used for example, as can hierarchical-input-process-output (HIPO) charting. Let us look at some of these other approaches.

4.2.3 Data Flow Diagrams

The data flow diagram (DFD) [Yourdon, 1986], which is sometimes also called a *program graph* or *bubble chart*, is intended to show the flow of data through a program or system. These diagrams provide an easy, graphic means of modeling the flow of data through any system. They may be either implemented manually or automated, or as a mixture of each [Yourdon, 1986]. The basic elements of a data flow diagram are sources or sinks of data, data flows, data processes, and data stores. A typical system requires several levels in order to depict an accurate and complete picture of the entire data flow process. Standard symbols for data flow diagrams are derived from electric circuit diagram analysis and are shown in Figure 4.4.

The fundamental notion imbedded in a data flow diagram is that infor-

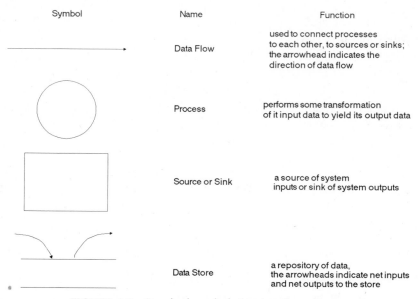

Symbol	Name	Function
	Data Flow	used to connect processes to each other, to sources or sinks; the arrowhead indicates the direction of data flow
	Process	performs some transformation of it input data to yield its output data
	Source or Sink	a source of system inputs or sink of system outputs
	Data Store	a repository of data, the arrowheads indicate net inputs and net outputs to the store

FIGURE 4.4   Standard symbols for data flow diagrams

mation, as it moves through a module or system, may be stored, transformed, processed, or connected to some other portion of the system. Data flow diagrams represent a graphical technique that shows these information flows and transformations that result from data moving through particular processes. Data flow diagrams may be used to show the system in its entirety, or in part, and at any level of abstraction. Each of the various levels retains a parent–child relationship with preceding or succeeding levels. This continues throughout each level, until either the top- or bottom-level information detail is reached.

Generally, a data flow diagram is identical to a conventional system flowchart. However, data flow diagrams do not indicate whether the processing activities will be implemented as modules, programs, or job steps. They do not indicate the equipment on which the process will be implemented, nor any temporal effect of data flows. Data flow diagrams do not indicate data flows between processing steps that will be implemented in terms of tape files, disk packs, modems, core memory, or similar equipment. In other words, the data flow diagram is a logical, abstract system flowchart only; the aforementioned details are normally left to the actual software design. Typical flows depicted in the data flow diagram approach are shown in Figures 4.5 and 4.6.

The essential steps involved in using a data flow diagram are as follows:

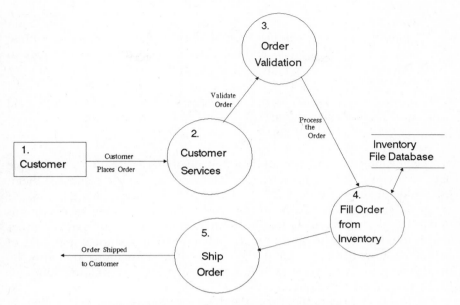

FIGURE 4.5   Data flow diagram 01 level

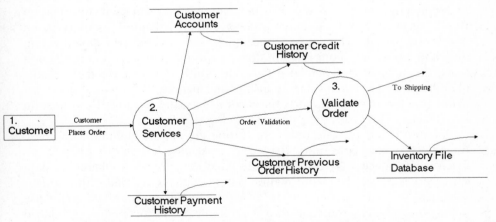

FIGURE 4.6   Data flow diagram 02 level for customer services

1. *Sources and sinks of data are identified*. These usually represent activities that either provide or use information furnished by the system.
2. *The path of information flow is identified*. We require information flow from the source and to the sink to be transformed or stored. Logical AND and OR functions may be used to direct the data flow, and there may be more than one input or output.

3. *Transformation of data is accomplished.* This means that the information from the source or sink has been directed along a path to be modified from its present form to another form as characterized by an action verb that operates on an object noun; for instance, ENROLL the STUDENT.

4. *Information is initially stored in a database* where it is temporarily held until required for another data flow and transformation. Any information that is "used" finally goes to a sink.

The advantages to the use, of data flow diagrams are that they are simple and easy to use, and require that few elements be used to represent them, especially for simple systems. Use of this approach requires that the designer views the design from a structured perspective. The number of operations that are to be performed are four in number, as just described, and are rather simple to understand and perform. The identification of sources and sinks of data, data flows from one element to another, transformations to modify the data, and the use of database repositories form the entire set of four operations for this graphical technique.

The disadvantages to the use of the data flow diagram approach to logical design reside in the way this structured approach handles information flows and the way in which one can use it to deal effectively with highly complex systems. First, data flow diagrams attempt to project all data flow as occurring in a sequential manner, as shown in the data flow diagram itself. Information flow is certainly not a sequential process; rather, it is more likely to be an asynchronous one. This makes conceptualization of the data flow diagram difficult from a logical information flow perspective. For highly complex systems, the systems designer must have an intuitive perspective that permits identification of hierarchical relationships and increasing levels of abstraction. While graphic analysis supports these constructs, the resulting flow diagram is difficult to visualize.

A data dictionary is desirable for setting up and maintaining a database for any software application. It is most especially desirable, perhaps even essential, for successful complex large scale systems development. A data dictionary is a specialized information system that is concerned with the identification, standardization, and use of all data elements and entities for use in the processing environment. As a general rule, a data dictionary is produced with *predefined schema* and with specialized programs for dictionary information. In the instance of data dictionaries, a *schema* is defined as a stored data description. Examples of schemas are types of objects and the possible relationships that exist between them that are stored in a database. Important features of the data dictionary are:

1. The scope of data entities that extend usage beyond individual data items.

2. The dictionary, in addition to describing all data elements and entities

for an organization, may include other organizational information that supports information resource management of the enormous variety of reports provided.

3. The provision for maintenance, modification and transformation of software for data processing applications.

The ideal data dictionary provides all the features just noted as well as an active software component that serves all design applications relative to data and entity needs. A data dictionary may also assist in information resource management processes through the tasks of data error reduction, program modification support, and maintenance of data items.

In order to be able to effectively utilize the data flow diagram method for other than very simple applications, it is essential that some representation of the content of the information in each portion of the data flow diagram be provided. For this use, a data dictionary is an organized collection of logical definitions of all data names that are shown on the data flow diagram, including a representation of the content of each arrow. The data dictionary is a quasi-formal grammar for describing the content of information to be used within the system under consideration.

Page-Jones [1980] defines a data dictionary as follows:

> The data dictionary contains definitions of all data mentioned in the data flow diagram, in a process specification and in the data dictionary itself. Composite data (data that can be further divided) is defined in terms of its components; elementary data (data that cannot be further divided) is defined in terms of the meaning of each of the values that it can assume. Thus, the data dictionary is composed of: definitions of data flows, files (data stores), and data used within processes (transforms).

One popularly used approach to data dictionary processes and procedures is that of DeMarco [1979]. In this approach, there are likely to be several thousand data definitions. These definitions enable the analyst to represent data in one of three ways:

1. As a sequence of data
2. As a selection from among a set of data
3. As a repeated grouping of data

Each data type is a part of one of these three representations and may be a composite of these representations, as in the parent–child sense of logical design. The data dictionary also contains logic notation that enables operations to be included as part of the information contained in it. The mathematical operators used within the typical data dictionary are defined in Table 4.1. Thus, a data element dictionary description tells us what records in the data dictionary consist of and the logical relationships that pertain to each particular element.

TABLE 4.1   Typical Data Dictionary Notation and Mathematical Operators

Notation	Meaning
$x = a + b$	x consists of data elements a and b
$x = [a/b]$	x consists of either a or b
$x = (a)$	x consists of an optional data element a
$x = y\{a\}$	x consists of y or more occurrences
$x = \{a\}z$	x consists of z or fewer occurrences of a
$x = y\{a\}z$	x consists of between y and z occurrences of a

In order to utilize a data dictionary as part of the software development process, it is necessary to have a reasonably clear notion of the intended uses of the data that are to be classified and stored. The development of the data dictionary begins with formation of lists of desired data items or fields that have been grouped in accordance with the entities that they are to represent. A name is assigned for each of these lists, and a brief statement of the meaning of each is provided. This statement is especially important as constraints relative to length of fields in the database management system (DBMS) may necessitate severe abbreviations, thereby making it difficult to interpret them in terms of an extended meaning. Of course, this is desirable regardless of whether a data dictionary is used.

As a first step in constructing a data dictionary, the data items needed and their intended usage should be identified. This list should contain each data item name and an explanation of its meaning. Next, the relationships between data elements should be described and any keys or pointers should be determined. Finally, the type of DBMS is selected and the dictionary is implemented within the DBMS.

These steps toward generating a data dictionary also provide for the arrangement of information for use in software development. This is accomplished by cross-reference and by program object through entity modeling. A properly functioning data dictionary will provide for consistency and compatibility of data items and entities. These requirements are checked through the data dictionary when program changes are made. The three functions of a data dictionary lead directly to the steps needed to construct the data dictionary. The essential steps in generating a data dictionary, and incorporating it in one of the other approaches, such as a data flow diagram, are as follows:

1. The system to be designed is approached from a top-down perspective. It is decomposed to form the most primitive operation of the system. The result of this decomposition is a logical model of how the system functions in accordance with the intended conceptual design approach,

such as the data flow diagram approach, if the data dictionary is intended for use with a data flow diagram.

2. This data dictionary framework shows all entities, data stores, outputs, and transformations appropriate for detailed design.

3. Data structures are established for all data required for the system functions.

4. Once the data structures have been established, a data dictionary is constructed to represent all data elements and entities. The use for which the dictionary is intended, and provision for maintenance and modification of data and entities, is made.

As the data flow diagram construction progresses, the data dictionary is expanded until it contains an unambiguous characterization of all data elements included within the process described. The logical relationships between basic elements and composite elements is also specified so that all terms are fully defined and referenced for all purposes.

For very large system designs, it is necessary that the data dictionary development process be automated. A typical data dictionary for a large system may include several thousand entries. It is physically impossible to manually maintain a dictionary of this size or to retain consistent and unambiguous terms for each data element or composite of data elements. Therefore, automated tools are needed for efficient and effective development and maintenance of a data dictionary.

Process specifications are short descriptions of the processes and procedures developed through the data flow diagram analysis. The purpose of the process specification is to permit the analyst to describe the procedures and policies represented by the bottom level elements of the data flow diagram.* Process specifications do not include the implementation tactics to be employed to accomplish the activity.† These bottom-level process functional elements represent descriptions and are often referred to as "mini-specifications," since each one is a miniature functional specification.

One basic approach to the construction of a data flow diagram is to use a natural language to describe each function (transform) that is to be represented in the data flow diagram. One of the most used languages is a *Program Design Language (PDL)*, such as that due to Van Leer [1976] or Linger, Mills, and Witt [1979]. These English-like languages incorporate structured English and includes basic procedures, such as sequence, selection, and repetition, together with English phrases. The goal is to make the description comprehensible to the average user.

The *process specifications* may be written in a variety of forms that include:

---

*Here the term bottom level is used to indicate that we have reached to primitive level of the data flow diagram.

†In the context used here, activity refers to the use of structured approaches to view the design.

- Formulas
- Graphs
- Decision tables

The usual form of expressing a process specification is in structured English. This consists of a limited set of nouns and verbs that are organized to represent a compromise between readability and rigor [Yourdon, 1986]. Process specifications results have also been referred to as *data structure diagrams* (DSD) [Shere, 1987]. The process specifications or data structure diagrams are graphic tools that are capable of portraying, in a concise manner, the logical design of the database structure, decision trees and structured English. Each mini-specification uses these methods to describe the piece of the action pertinent to that particular activity. The aggregation of all the mini-specifications accounts for the total process specification for the design being developed.

In its most sparse form, structured English consists of a very limited set of elements. These include (1) a limited set of action-oriented verbs, such as find or print; (2) structured programming control constructs, such as IF__THEN __ELSE, DO__WHILE, and other like control commands; and (3) data elements that have been defined in the data dictionary.

Without specifying how the process eventually will be built, properly written mini-specifications indicate what the process must accomplish. Structured English is often combined with natural-language descriptions in order to provide a complete description of the function being developed. This enables us to easily add procedural detail during the software design phase of the development lifecycle. The essential steps in using the process specification approach are as follows:

1. After development of the data flow diagram, examine the transformations, and identify and name the elements in the process as nouns or verbs.
2. Determine the physical data transformations; that is, identify those processes that physically change the data from input to output of the "bubble"* using mathematical formulas or procedural rules.
3. Determine the logical data transformations through use of logical functions AND and OR.
4. Label all process specifications as they are identified.

The advantages of the process specifications approach to data structure diagrams are that it supports the development of structured design and data flow diagrams in a constructive way. This provides for conversion of abstract ideas

---

*As used here "bubble" refers to the transformation or process of changing data either physically or logically.

from the data flow diagrams into program constructs that permit solution to identified data flow diagram problems. As process specifications and data structure diagrams are applied, new information, such as additional control information, will often be discovered. This will often require modification of the structure chart for the data structure diagram.

Disadvantages in the use of process specification approach to data structure diagrams are that it requires a fairly sophisticated level of experience on the part of the designer. We noted this earlier relative to the use of the N–S chart. This is true because the decision as to what should be considered as input transformations is a difficult task. Often it is not clear what nouns and action verbs are proper for the particular transformation under consideration. Finally, it is difficult to know when a "best" solution is at hand, or even what the term "best" denotes.

4.2.4 Data Structure-Oriented Methods

Data structure methods result from examination of software development processes and procedures from data structure aspects, rather than from the perspective of data flow processes. Just as with the data flow diagram methods, there are several tools that support these approaches. These data structure approaches assist the software developer in (1) identifying entities and processes, (2) structuring data in an hierarchical format, (3) formalizing the data structure representation, and (4) providing a systematic approach for developing program structure from the hierarchical data structure.

In this way, data structure methods provide for software design with due concern for architectural and procedural needs. The early work in this field of Warnier [1977, 1978] was extended by Orr [1977] and is termed the *Warnier–Orr method*. The Warnier diagram provides a notation for representation of the information hierarchy that permits software structure to be developed directly from data structure. Orr's approach in extending the Warnier diagram concept has evolved into the data structured systems development (DSDD) method.

Warnier [1977] diagrams allow the representation of data structure hierarchy in an easy to use format, especially because of the extension of Orr [1977]. A hierarchical data structure is utilized for analysis of the information content of software requirements and specifications. This diagram may be used to represent hierarchical data at any level of detail. Common notation is to use the brace ({ }) to differentiate between the several levels of data abstraction. Each data item may be a sequence or collection of data items or an elementary item at the base level of the hierarchical data structure. A typical Warnier–Orr diagram is shown in Figure 4.7.

The fundamental steps involved in construction of Warnier–Orr diagrams are as follows:

1. All database storage and retrieval activities are noted and classified.

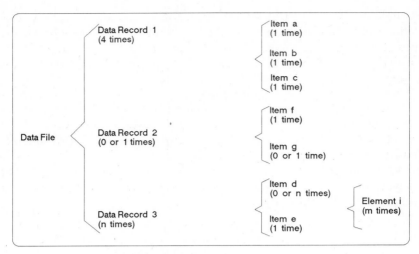

FIGURE 4.7   Warnier–Orr diagram

2. Any inconsistencies in data elements are resolved.
3. Data and activities are examined to determine use of the data in order to eliminate redundant operations.
4. The Warnier–Orr diagram, based on the derived data, structure is built.

Now that we know how to build the Warnier–Orr diagram, it is important that we be able to use it. The steps involved in using the diagram are as follows.

1. Data files are decomposed into data records.
2. Data records are decomposed into data items.
3. Data items are decomposed into data elements, which represent primitives of the data files.

The Warnier–Orr diagram views the system from a functional perspective, that is, a perspective in which the structure of the data itself is used to determine the functional structure required to process the data. It is a top-down approach that identifies data elements, and the operations on these data elements. It is an approach that brings order to these through organized data structures.

4.2.6   Entity-Relationship Diagrams

A major structured analysis tool is the *entity–relationship diagram*, often abbreviated as the "E-R diagram" [Chen, 1976]. An example of the notation for an E-R diagram is shown in Figure 4.8.

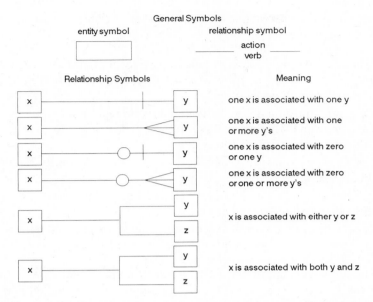

FIGURE 4.8 Entity-Relationship (E-R) diagram symbols

The purpose of the E-R diagram is to be able to identify and highlight the major objects or entities of stored data with which the system must deal. The E-R diagram also serves to highlight the various relationships that exist between objects. The process in initiated with the most abstract view of the system. We proceed to decompose the system into its primitive activities as more and more becomes known about the relationships and entities. We construct charts as a group of entities and their relationships, beginning with the central entity representation. The box or square brackets ([ ]) notation for E-R diagrams is common. Relationships are represented as straight lines with a verb indicating what is to be done with the entity.

Those systems that interface the system under consideration are constructed as other charts. Connections to any other system is indicated by an arrow, or directed flow from the central E-R diagram. The data to be transferred over the interface are directed, with the direction of the arrow indicating the direction in which the information flows. Sequences of interface interactions may be specified by using numbered sequences next to the interface data (e.g., 1, 2, . . . 1a, 2a, . . .).

The data flow diagram and the E-R diagram each highlight a different aspect of the same system. As a consequence, there are one-to-one correspondences that must be checked by the systems analyst to ensure that an E-R diagram and a data flow diagram are consistent over all applications. This suggests that it is desirable to use both methods such that we can view the logical issues from the two perspectives generated by these approaches.

Figure 4.9 depicts an example of the use of E-R diagram. The steps involved in using the approach are:

1. Examine the design project at the highest level of abstraction available. If this is the top level of the system, it is termed the "0-level." Prepare an initial data flow diagram.
2. Identify all the data flows, including the sources and sinks and processes, and determine whether this is a repeat of existing information or additional information for the system.
3. Construct E-R diagrams for all processes, using the entity-relationship notation described above.
4. Validate the E-R diagrams and determine that the lowest needed level of decomposition has been achieved.
5. Repeat the process until the primitive level diagram has been found and that all entity relationships have been found and are retained.

The major advantage of the E-R approach is that it provides a realistic view of the structure and form of a development project that should result in appropriate software. In addition, the approach leads to the development of a data dictionary that will ultimately serve the user in other ways. The primary difficulties that may impede easy use of the E-R diagram method are in the need for selection of appropriate verbs for relationships, elimination of redundancy of entities, and assurances that all the needed entity relationships have been determined and properly used. Although all these activities are regarded as useful, the search for them in a large scale software development project may be a disadvantage because of the length of time that must be invested to resolve these issues.

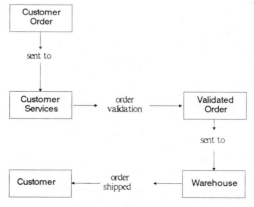

FIGURE 4.9 An E-R data diagram for the data flow diagram of Figure 4.5

4.2.7 Data Structured Systems Development

Data structured systems development (DSSD) is a combination of the War-nier–Orr method and the E-R diagram. The data structured system development process begins [Warnier 1974, 1981] first by looking at the application for which the system is intended. Specifically, we examine the manner in which data move between the place where they originate and the place where they are used. Following this, the functions are reviewed through use of the Warnier approach. This allows us to identify data entities and the processing requirements for this data. Next, the results of the application are embedded in a Warnier diagram, such as shown in Figure 4.9. Appropriate steps to follow in using the procedure have been covered in the preceding section on Warnier–Orr diagrams. These steps provide for the examination of data flow, data content, and data structure in a manner similar to the data flow diagram structured approach. There is a need to check for consistency between the data flow diagram and the data structure systems diagram to ensure model consistency over all applications.

As with the E-R diagram, the DSSD serves to organize a data structure systems development diagram in a manner quite similar to that which would result from use of data flow diagram techniques. The DSSD and E-R diagrams provide information as to:

1. The data entities that are to be processed
2. Where the data originates
3. The destination for the data
4. The context of the data entities
5. The various interfaces to other potential users

Entity diagrams use boxes or square brackets ([ ]) in order to denote the users and originators of data entities. Arrows are used to point to information flow between "sources" and "sinks." Interfaces are shown on the E-R notation diagram between each of the application functions,* as shown in Figure 4.8 and the example shown in Figure 4.9. The application functions that are to be implemented† to accomplish the purpose of a software part‡ are named on the arrows that connect the intended application. Data structured system development uses Warnier-Orr notation or an *assembly line diagram* (ALD) to couple information flow and processes or operations that must be applied to the information. Using Warnier–Orr notation, the ALD proceeds from

---

*An applications function is an identifiable discrete part of a system that interfaces with another system part.
†The applications function is implemented by identifying the function and its relationships, such as an execute command that transforms an input to an output.
‡The purpose of the software part is determined by the function that is to be performed, such as update database.

the most detailed hierarchical level to the top level of data structure to show the specific application chain. Each process in the chain is refined by developing a narrative that gives pertinent information on such concerns as: input, process to be performed, output, data flow, and frequency of activity.

The fundamental steps in using the data structure system development diagram are a combination of the steps noted for the Warnier–Orr diagram development and the entity-relationship approach discussed above. We have just described these steps and will not repeat them here.

Through use of these steps, the analyst constructs a manual model of the functional elements of the software system output. This model identifies the organization of the data structure and the entities that comprises the output. Once this prototype system model is completed, a Warnier–Orr diagram is used in order to model the hierarchical data structure.

This approach models the system from a logical view. Data structured system development diagrams also provide for hardware considerations as a part of the analysis process. This includes such parameters as performance, reliability, system security, actual hardware required, and the necessary interfaces between databases, hardware, and networks. The advantages and disadvantages associated with use of data structured system development are the same as those associated with Warnier-Orr diagrams and entity-relationship approaches.

4.2.8   Jackson System Development

Jackson system development (JSD) is based on the work done by M. A. Jackson [1975, 1983] related to information domain analysis and the various relationships that exist between program development and system design. This approach is similar in many ways to that associated with data flow diagrams and data structured system development diagrams. JSD provides a logical approach to the organization of information as well as a model to develop the information flow, data entities, and interface requirements.

Five fundamental steps are involved in conducting Jackson system development:

Entity Action

The entities and actions are identified. These include information production activities from organizations, people, and objects.

Entity Structure

The actions that operate on entities are ordered by the time of application and represented with Jackson diagrams as logical tree structures.

Initial Model

A model, based on the defined actions from the first two steps, is developed.

System Timing

Process schedules are developed, assessed, and specified.

Implementation

All parts of the system implementation are specified, including both hardware and software.

As may be seen from the five steps, many similarities exist between this approach and that of Warnier and Orr. In particular, entities and relationships are determined, including all the actions to be taken. This approach relies on functional decomposition in the same way as other data structured approaches. Of course, one would expect that the results using several approaches to be similar in that each was conceived to resolve essentially the same logical issues.

The JSD procedure begins with a brief statement of the logic design problem in natural language (e.g., English) form. From this statement, all entities are selected by reviewing all the nouns used in the problem description and simply calling them "entities." Through a selection process specific nouns are selected as representative of the model of information that is to be acted on. Actions are determined through a review of the verbs that are contained in the problem description. Action verbs serve as candidates for selection, and, as in entity selection, these verbs must operate on the model of the information flow. Entity structure identification commences once the entities and actions have been defined. This structure will normally be modified as more information concerning the logic design problem is developed.

The next step in use of the JSD method is to identify the entity structure. This structure describes all that is known concerning the actions of the entity over time. Jackson diagrams are used to show the action sequences that take place over time. Actions are applied to entities as sequences, logical actions (either/or), or as repetitive actions.

When completed, JSD diagrams show all the action steps carried on by the entity as a set of steps over time. Associated text may be used to add clarifying notes to each of the action–entity relationships.

The initial JSD step involves development of an abstraction of the actual situation under consideration. Entities and actions determined previously are selected and the relationship between them is ordered through structure diagrams. First, a specification of the actual system is constructed with a *system specification diagram* (SSD). This uses a special notation designed for this purpose. Following this, a *datastream connection* (DSC) is constructed in order to show the flow of information and the various processes to which the datastreams are subjected. As in other approaches, arrowheads are used to show the direction of information flow. JSD symbols are defined in Figure 4.10.

An entity defined as the *state Vector connection* (SVC) is applied when one process is examined by another process in order to determine the state

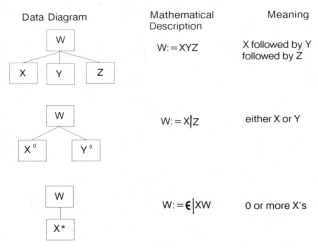

FIGURE 4.10 Jackson system development diagram symbols

of the first process. According to JSD conventions, *0* represents the actual process, and *1* represents the model of the real-world process. Datastreams are used to connect the model to the real world. Internal details of the model have been specified by Jackson as structure text. Structure text represents structure diagrams as text. A simplified version of a JDS notation and use in design is shown in Figure 4.11. The works of Jackson [1983] contain several examples of use of this approach.

The advantages and disadvantages of use of the approach are essentially the same as those for other data structured approaches. The major advantage of the Jackson system development approach is that it provides a view of the structure and form of the development project that approximate reality. Additionally, the approach uses the data structure itself to determine the functions for which the data are processed. The primary disadvantages to use of the JSD method, as with other data structured development approaches, lie in the difficulty inherent in the selection of appropriate verbs for relationships, the time required for elimination of redundancy of entities and the difficulty in relating the actual process to that of the real world model.

4.3 DETAILED DESIGN AND CODING

Most of the developmental activities of traditional software engineering, as viewed from the micro-enhancement perspective of influencing programmer productivity through such methods as structured programming, have been aimed at impacting detailed design operations. Detailed design is the culmination of significant preparatory activities that will result in all information

Structure	Representation
Sequence	left – to – right reading
Selection	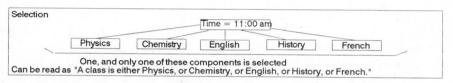
Iteration	
Hierarchy	

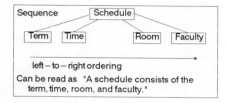

Sequence — Schedule

Term Time Room Faculty

left – to – right ordering

Can be read as "A schedule consists of the term, time, room, and faculty."

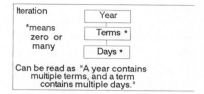

Iteration

*means zero or many

Year
Terms *
Days *

Can be read as "A year contains multiple terms, and a term contains multiple days."

Selection

Time = 11:00 am

Physics Chemistry English History French

One, and only one of these components is selected

Can be read as "A class is either Physics, or Chemistry, or English, or History, or French."

FIGURE 4.11 Jackson system programming notation

necessary for effective and efficient coding. Much has been accomplished in this particular phase of the software development lifecycle that has resulted in reducing and/or eliminating errors in (1) coding, (2) streamlining testing procedures, (3) introducing automated practices, and (4) ensuring that the code produced represents the detail designs that have been agreed on. We will cover the well-defined activities and then discuss integration and tool automation prospects for detailed design.

We will present an overview of detailed design practices and the various alternatives used for programming process, including programming tools and programming environments. We will examine detailed design approaches, software architecture, and various detailed design processes. We will look at some of the approaches that we have previously considered for logical design; namely, data flow, data structures, and other structured design methods as means of guiding the detailed design process to a successful conclusion. Success in detailed design means that we have produced a design that is programmable in an effective and efficient manner, and one that will meet the software requirements that have been identified. We will also examine object-oriented design and review that approach to detailed design. Object-oriented design practices are the most recently developed of the structured approaches to detailed design. This approach has found great favor because of its tendency to emulate natural thought processes of humans when dealing with organizations of entities and events under consideration. In addition we will examine top-down and bottom-up approaches to detailed design.

"Detailed design" refers to the processes and procedures involved in the conversion of the design specifications into detailed design that, in turn, leads to coding of the software product to be delivered. As noted earlier, the usual approach has been an ad hoc one of taking the requirements specifications and converting these into some form of flowchart and then commencing the coding operations.

Contemporary detailed design environments provide for precise activities, notations, and instruction that the programmer is to follow in writing the code that emulates the detailed design requirements. These include many of those methods presented earlier, such as data structured systems design, data flow diagrams, and an approach to be discussed later, that of object-oriented design. Use of these methods, and others, gives us a means of providing high quality designs, with a small number of errors, and efficient code.

Detailed design procedures are intended to define the modules and the needed interfaces for each module, so that these may be integrated to form the whole program. From detailed design features, program specifications for each module are prepared. These should be followed in order to produce a consistent logically programmed module that provides us efficient code, and with proper interfaces for the code modules.

Given the detailed design requirements specifications that have been prepared in earlier stages, the detailed design process follows along in several stages. These are:

1. Establish the subsystems that constitute the program modules.
2. Establish the subsystem interfaces between each of the proposed program modules.
3. Decompose each of these established modules and define the operations of each of these decomposed components.
4. Design each program for the component parts in terms of the interacting activities.
5. Specify any algorithms required.

The steps of the detailed design process are shown in detail in Figure 4.12. The intent of these steps is to indicate the relationships that exist between and among the several levels of decomposition in order to proceed from the design requirements definition to completion of the detailed design and coding activities in an effective and efficient manner.

As a general rule, the criteria that determine what constitutes a good detailed design are those that relate to the functions and constraints that have been established through the detailed design process. A good detailed design is one that meets the needs and constraints of the user specified requirements in the form of valid module specifications. From this we may define what is to be sought in a detailed design as:

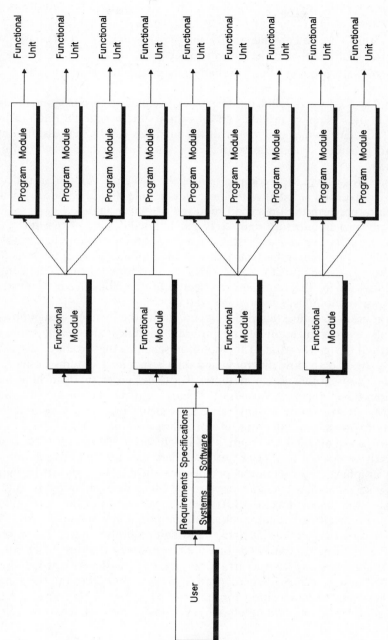

FIGURE 4.12 Decomposition levels leading to detailed design (coding)

1. A product that will lead to efficient code
2. A product that provides proper interfaces as defined in the requirements documents
3. A product that meets the quality and performance needs as established between the user and the systems designer
4. A software product* that is reliable, maintainable, and available.

The goals of a good detailed design process are met when a program module fits well in the system of modules and it exhibits the functional relationships assigned to that module and when all the modules can be successfully integrated to provide appropriate source code for the software product to be developed.

At the lowest level of decomposition of the design development process, this means that each element of the program module should be necessary and sufficient to perform the operation required of that module.

The software architecture realized in the detailed design process possesses two important latent characteristics of a computer program that is to be developed: (1) the hierarchical structure of the modules and (2) the structure of the data. These architectural structures are developed through the continuing subdivision of the requirements specifications from the most abstract levels down to modules, submodules, and elements.

The program structure that is developed during the detailed design process represents the organization of the program modules that result from the architectural design. Several of the notation schemes that we have discussed earlier, such as data flow diagrams and data structured systems design, are the products of various design methods. These design methods include Jackson system development, Warnier–Orr charts, entity-relationship diagrams, and DeMarco structured design. These approaches present a logical decomposition of software architecture into program structure.

Processes are depicted in Figure 4.13 in which the overall problem is successively decomposed to the level of elements that are to be programmed. From a graphical representation perspective such as that shown in Figure 4.13, we see that a particular software problem determination is initially depicted at the highest level of abstraction for this stage of the development process. The resulting structure is then decomposed into simple structures as represented by the bubbles labeled p1 through p5 in the figure. These structures are, in turn, decomposed into their primitive structure, such as the examples represented by structures 1, 2, and 3 in Figure 4.13. It is the role of detailed design to provide guidance for programmers through the suggestion of problem decomposition through the p1, p2, . . . , pn levels. Then, the detailed design and coding phase completes its needed activities.

---

*In Chapter 8 we will use the term "softproduct" to denote software product. We will also identify another useful byproduct of software development, software process, and call it "softprocess."

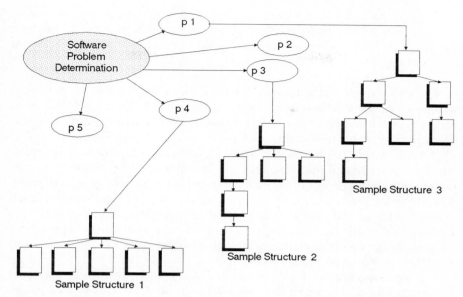

FIGURE 4.13   Problem decomposition for software solution structure

As we have noted earlier, the most effective approach to good software development is accomplished by consistent integrated application of a single lifecycle methodology. We have outlined a number of phases and steps within these phases that make up a framework for implementation of the methodology. There are a number of methods or approaches that may be useful as tools in implementing these steps.

The most popular generic approaches in use at this time for detailed design are:

1. *Data flow design*—uses data flow diagrams developed by the systems designer to produce a program structure that is typified by that depicted in Figure 4.14

2. *Data structure design*—uses hierarchical data structures associated with the particular problem being analyzed to produce a data structure chart such as the one shown in Figure 4.15

3. *Bottom-up approach*—moves to the lowest level of decomposition first then going up the levels until the entire system is addressed as is shown in Figure 4.16*a*

4. *Top-down approach*—implements a system design from the functional viewpoint starting with the highest-level perspective and progressing downward to the least element of the program as is shown in Figure 4.16*b*

Object-oriented design approach—views the system as a collection of objects rather than functions with messages passed between objects, and each object possess its own operational characteristics as is shown in Figure 4.17.

The data-driven methodologies form the basis for the use of structured design approaches as developed by DeMarco [1979], Yourdon [1982], and others. The bottom-up approach is little used anymore except on the simplest of projects. For this reason they will not be discussed here. These are not at all representative of the classic waterfall software development lifecycle, which is basically and fundamentally a systems engineering "top-down" approach. Of course, it would be possible to use a bottom-up approach within one phase, such as detailed design and coding, given that a top-down approach is being used for the overall development phases. Generally, however, this is unwise. For sufficiently small programs where a bottom-up approach to detailed design might work, the overall effort is probably too tiny to warrant a systems approach to the lifecycle.

The top-down approach to detailed design is implemented by a functional decomposition of the conceptual system design product. This is used as the basis of design approach in many of the CASE toolkits, a structured approach to design.

Object-oriented approaches represent a relatively new approach to detailed design. It shows considerable success potential, as it possesses the inherent parent–child relationships that exist among data elements, functions, and interfaces.

No one detailed design approach is the "best" for a given software development project, however. The factors that must be examined to determine

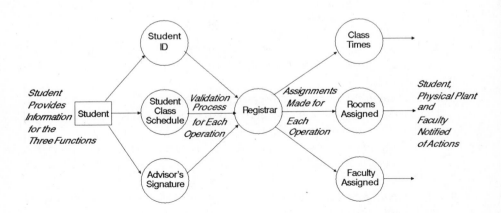

FIGURE 4.14 Data flow design diagram for class selection

Note:

Student record is comprised of a header record, a data record, and a trailer record. This data structure may be represented by the program structure shown in the lower part of this figure.

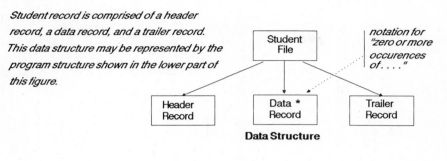

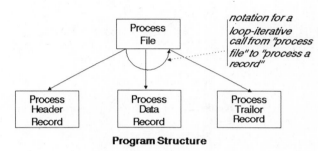

FIGURE 4.15 Data structure design

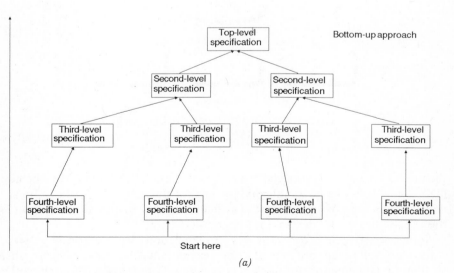

(a)

FIGURE 4.16a Bottom-up approach to system design

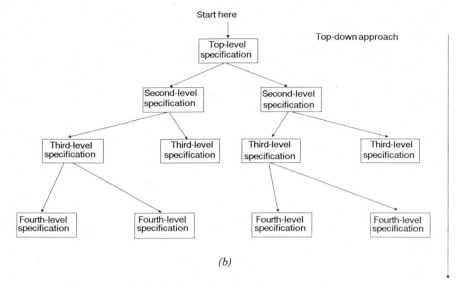

(b)

FIGURE 4.16b   Top-Down approach to system design

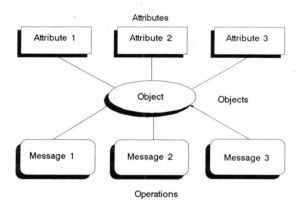

FIGURE 4.17   Object-oriented design notation

the most appropriate approach for a particular detailed design process include (1) examination of the complexity and size of the project, (2) the software development support environment available at the time of design, and (3) the capabilities of the design and programming staff.

Generally speaking, for most large organizations working on large-scale software development projects, the approaches that will yield the best results, all things taken equally, are the highly structured ones. They will provide the most consistent and integrated set of design and programming activities and will give management the best visibility into the total design and programming process. We will now present an overview of data flow design and data structure processes for detailed design. We will cover object-oriented design in somewhat more detail.

4.3.1 Data Flow Design Approach

The data flow design approach is based on traditional engineering analysis for electrical circuit design or fluid flow as derived from electrical and mechanical engineering. The basic idea was articulated by International Business Machines (IBM) and described as *hierarchical-input–process–output* (HIPO) systems analysis. In this approach a system having one or more inputs, that processes these inputs in a particular way and then has one or more outputs is analyzed. The basic elements of data flow design are similar to those used in electrical engineering circuit analysis. In data flow diagram notation, the basic process unit is a blackbox, a device that receives inputs, operates on these and delivers outputs, the data store is depicted as a capacitor, a device that stores energy, the connecting links are similar to electric current arrows that show the direction of data flow, and finally the sources and sinks of data are similar to voltage and current sources.

The use of HIPO data flow design begins with the identification of data entities and the relationships that exist between the data elements. This is followed by defining the nature of the inputs and outputs for the system under consideration. Next a data flow diagram showing the highest level of abstraction is constructed. This shows the basic data inputs and outputs and operations that will occur on the data. Next the system is decomposed by showing all the processes that must happen to construct the system being considered. Following this, each subsystem is expanded and all data flows to and from these process units are depicted. This procedure is followed until we have only data inputs and completed processes as outputs. This results in the construction of a HIPO data flow diagram that uses the following step-by-step procedure:

1. Develop the highest-level flow diagram that includes all data and information flow and provides all sources and sinks and interfaces.
2. Develop an event list for all events that occur within the system.
3. Refine the model to the second and third levels of detail.
4. Prepare graphic notation (as appropriate) to enable visualization of the system.
5. Review the flow diagrams and state diagrams to make certain that all the functions are represented and that the system is consistent and integrated.
6. Describe all data objects and procedural content of the system using

such devices as the data dictionary. Processing languages such as structured English or PDL, decision trees or decision tables are useful in determining the procedures that are to be invoked.

7. Prepare the system architecture based on the flow models used to develop the program.
8. Perform reviews and checks as necessary preparatory to testing.

Such a system is represented in Figure 4.17, which shows how a data flow diagram for a student seeking a class schedule is constructed.

The procedure begins with a listing of all inputs and outputs for the system under design. In Figure 4.18, the inputs would be student name, student ID, student class needs for the specific term, and times available to the student for taking classes. The outputs would be the final class schedule showing the time of day of the class, the faculty member who will teach the class, and the room number of the assigned class. The process is to produce a class schedule by the registrar.

We have covered the development and use of flow diagrams in some detail earlier in this chapter. Consistent and complete notations are essential for the development of these, including the abstract objects that are represented by them. With the utilization of data-flow-diagram-like structures, such as a

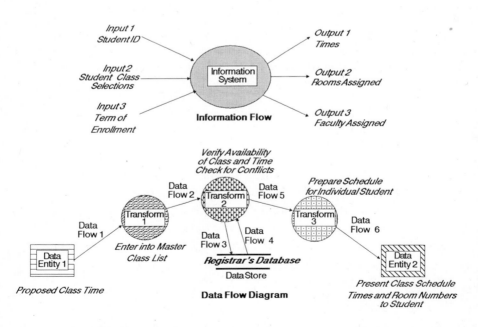

FIGURE 4.18 Data flow design notation for student enrollment

HIPO diagram, designs may be evaluated, compared, and tested. The need for structure is particularly acute for large complex detailed designs in which the system is to be decomposed into its several functional modules for ease of coding. While the use of data flow diagrams does not represent a unique way of considering software system detailed design, it is one of the preferred approaches by software designers.

Many CASE tools utilize this approach in the realization of software system design requirements and products. Difficulties that are experienced with data flow design occur with very large systems that have complex interactions. It is difficult to keep track of the many processes that take place and be certain that we have identified system primitives and are not a higher level of abstraction, and that the entire system design is considered. Automated CASE tools make these bookkeeping entries a much more orderly process, but still do not account for failure to obtain an acceptable design for a large complex system that is due to improperly identified user requirements.

4.3.2 Data Structure Design Approach

Data structure design approaches view data as means of describing the logical data structure that should occur in a data dictionary. The primary use of the data structure design approach is to permit orderly access to a data dictionary or system database and determine the manner in which the system responds to query inputs. The primary purposes of this approach are to (1) identify the minimum data set necessary to describe the system under consideration, (2) arrange data around centers of use so that data that normally are used together will be together, and (3) establish the correctness and consistency of the data descriptions in the data dictionary (or database) through use of data structure diagrams. The data structure approach makes the assumption that the designer is using hierarchical data structures and uses these data structures as the initial step in the development of the structure design approach.

Using the design strategies of the data structure approach, the entire procedure is combined with documentation techniques, evaluation criteria, and heuristics to form the overall data structure design approach. The methodology differs from the data flow approach in that data structure approaches seek the logical model of the data itself, rather than pursuing the flow of data from process to process as occurs in the data flow design approach.

The use of the data structure design approach commences with the identification and description of all data access functions. Each data item that goes into or out of a datastore operation is noted. Identification is made of data that goes into or out of or both into and out of a datastore, and these are all checked for consistency. This is followed by attempting to reduce the data set to the minimum data model that will describe the system under design. Finally, all data elements that may be derived from other data elements are eliminated from the system. The result is a model of the data element relationships and the ways in which database access is handled for these data. Thus the final outcome for detailed design using data structure design approach is a view of the way in which the data are organized as a logical flow process, not the way in which the data elements are stored in a database. A typical data structure design diagram is shown in Figure 4.19.

4.4 OBJECT-ORIENTED DESIGN APPROACHES

The design techniques that we have presented thus far represent functional views of the system. For these, system design is approached from a high level of abstraction that is successively reviewed and decomposed until primitives are reached. Data flow and data structure approaches are representative of these functional decomposition techniques, and the design methodologies that are utilized include data flow diagram, data structured system development, Jackson system development, and others discussed earlier in this chapter.

Object-oriented design approaches differ from the functional approaches described earlier that are intended to use programming languages, such as FORTRAN, COBOL, or ALGOL. These higher order languages model the problem domain using predefined data and control structures. In these higher-order languages, software design uses a functional decomposition approach and is accomplished using procedural processes involving the specific language to be used to develop the software part. The evolution of higher-order languages brought about the introduction of concepts that included abstraction and information hiding, together with data flow and data structure design approaches. The development of Pascal and other high-order languages brought on a greater variety of data structures and strong data typing.

During the 1970s, the development of discrete event digital simulation languages such as GPSS and SIMULA, and later Smalltalk 80, introduced the notion of data representation as objects and classes of objects that were acted on by procedures called "operations." GPSS and SIMULA are discrete event simulation languages. Smalltalk 80 is a true object-oriented language developed for this express purpose.

This powerful notation has led to the use of object-oriented design for software systems design applications. Object-oriented design methodology relies on the precise definition of objects and the relationships between objects and operations. Object-oriented languages allow us to achieve functional decomposition in a simpler more natural way then second-generation languages and third-generation languages, which necessarily involve many details not needed for object-oriented languages.

Object-oriented design presents us with the strength of using class hierarchy and the high level of cohesion that derives from the definitions of classes. Objects provide a clear, concise, and limited interface to the problem domain in that the only way to interact with an object is through the operations or messages to the object. These messages call for operations that may result in

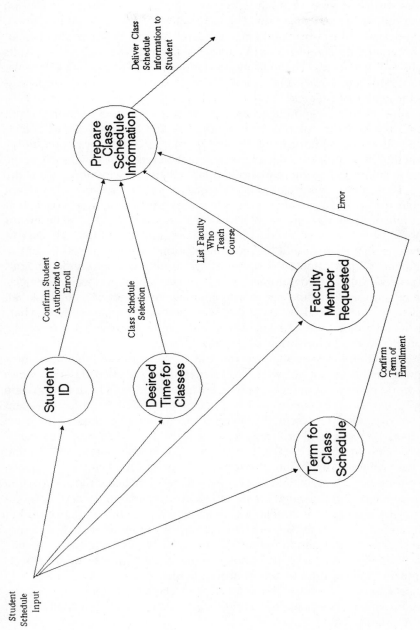

FIGURE 4.19 Data structure design

a change of state in the object in question. This message will affect the particular object called and only that one, as no other object is affected. This provides a high degree of modularity, and increased ability to verify and validate outcomes, and thus provides an increased sense of reliability in the derived design. Object-oriented languages are, for the most part, very-high-level programming languages used to accomplish precisely the same results as high-level languages. By focusing on the entities of objects and the relationships between objects, they often provide a simpler way to describe precisely those elements needed in detailed design procedures.

The object-oriented approach views a system as a collection of objects with messages passed from one object to another. A key characteristic of object-oriented design lies in information hiding [Parnas, 1972]. Information hiding is the ability of an object to have information isolated from view, such as the particular state of the object or operations that may be performed on the object. Thus, there exists within a particular object information that is not available for view except at runtime. It represents a design approach that utilizes late or dynamic binding of logic control and data structure. This means that objects may be considered as independent entities and thus are easy to modify as design changes and that communication between objects is kept to a minimum. Object-oriented design is programming language independent, while object-oriented programming is, of course, language-specific. Object-oriented languages include such programming languages as Smalltalk 80, SmallTalkV, and SIMULA. Ada and Modula-2 contain some of the characteristics of object-oriented languages and have features that permit the implementation of object-oriented design.

Object-oriented design signifies the use of software architectures, programming languages, or software design methodologies that describe views of the world in terms of objects that possess inheritance and have information hiding. *Object-oriented languages* (OOLs) are of special interest for programming activities and represent the division of entities into classes that have prescribed attributes and are capable of being addressed through messages. *Object-oriented design* (OOD) is a representation of the system domain and maps the problem domain into the solution domain. OOD connects objects, or data items or entities, and the operations on these, such that the information and processing is concentrated on the object classes, attributes, and messages that transfer between them. The attributes that set OOD apart from other structured techniques are the capability of object-oriented languages to support abstraction, information-hiding, and modularity. OOLs provide the only design tools that give these attributes without compromise to other aspects of the method and without compromising the processes.

Object-oriented design uses the concept of classes, attributes of objects, operations, and messages to implement the procedures of design applications. The notation for OOD is:

1. *Objects*—abstracts or physical entities that pertain to the domain of the system

2. *Attributes*—characteristics of objects
3. *Operations*—dynamic entities that may change with time
4. *Messages*—a request to the object to perform an operation

Objects may be abstract or physical entities that are a part of the domain of the system to be designed. Objects are equivalent to nouns in English language structure and are considered to possess information concerning their status in the problem domain. Objects then are real-world entities such as machines, files, products, signals, persons, things, and places and may be either physical entities or abstract representations. The attributes are characteristics that describe the properties ascribed to objects. Each attribute may be dynamically associated with a numerical value and the combination of these values together with the description of the object in the problem domain presents the state of the object. Thus, the attributes are related to the object as subobjects. Attributes include such things as the name of the object, the number of specific objects in a file, and the name for the place. The basic attribute, one that may not be further decomposed, is called a primitive object or subobject.

Operations consist of processes and data structures that apply to objects to which they are directed. These are dynamic entities whose value may change over time. Each object may be subjected to a number of operations that provide information relative to control and procedural constructs that are applied to the object. Information hiding is achieved by defining an object to have a private part and then assigning a message to address the appropriate processing operation.

Messages are passed between objects in order to change the state of the object, address the private data parts of an object, or otherwise modify an object. Modularity is provided by this design approach. This is accomplished inherently through the assignment of class structure and well-defined interfaces through messages. The application of OOD occurs through a message being sent to the object containing the operations to be performed that will result in a change of state of the object. An example of the relationships between objects, operations, and messages is shown in Figures 4.20 and 4.21.

Objects are given the distinction of belonging to classes, instances of those classes and are given inheritance characteristics by way of belonging to a specific class. As an example of the use of the concept of class, we will examine a knowledge-based decision support system for a model management system. The capabilities of the model management system include the capability of (1) adding and deleting particular models, (2) performing simulation and testing operations, (3) naming and renaming object classes, and (4) modifying and updating operations. The class, model, has two subclasses: quantitative models and qualitative models. These, in turn, contain a number of subclasses that are related to these. For the subclass, quantitative models, the subclasses include time-series models, operations research models, and other analytical models. In turn, the subclass, operations research models, contains such

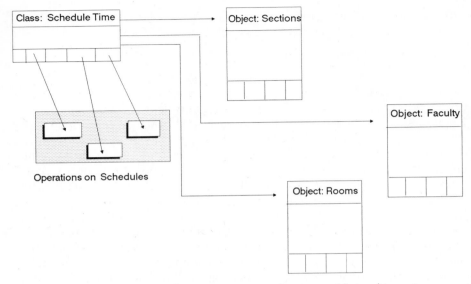

FIGURE 4.20 Object, operation, and message relationships

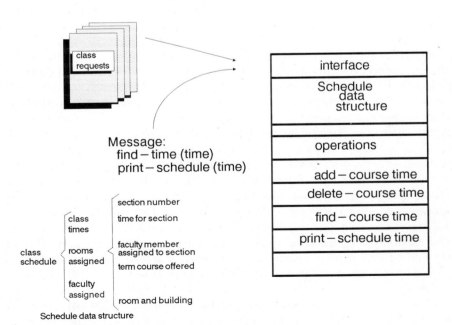

FIGURE 4.21 Object-oriented design perspective

models as linear programming models, nonlinear programming models, and dynamic programming models. For the subclass, qualitative models, we may have such subclass models as graphic models, artificial intelligence models, or descriptive models. The relationships between the class, model, and its several subclasses is shown in Figure 4.22.

In use of this system, the user is asked to identify the nature of the problem that is to be analyzed and select a model. Associated with each model class are instances of information that determine the types of problems for which the particular model may be used. The methods that are available for this system include select, view, add, delete, and external access.

A problem description may be entered into the system from the user that describes the content of the problem to be addressed. From this input, the model management system, through the "select" method, suggests a specific model for the problem. For example, if the user has a problem that is determined to require a linear programming model, the model management system will select the Simplex Model. This model may be "viewed" to determine if it is applicable to the problem under consideration. If this selection is not desired by the user, all linear models may be viewed for alternative selection. If one of these models is determined to be appropriate for the problem at hand, the method "external access" provides navigation to an external database that contains the entire model ready for use. If other models are found that are considered to be useful in the model management system, they may be added by implementation of the "add" method. Models that are never used may be removed by use of the "delete" method.

In addition to possessing characteristics of classes, objects also possess the properties of inheritance, which is essential for the implementation of OOD. This characteristic permits the use of hierarchies of objects and subobjects to form an extensive family for a given class. In the previous example, using the model management system as a class, extensions could be made both upward and downward in the classification schema by adding other instances of the class. Thus, model management systems belongs to a higher-order level of class that may be termed as general needs for decision support systems, while under the general classification of artificial intelligence models, there may be a further subdivision for natural language parsers. These classes could be extended to include all the models and methods necessary for full operation of a model management system for a decision support system. As more models are classified, the addition of these to the class is relatively simple, provided we know about the inheritance of characteristics from other subobjects. The same is true in the classification of other classes that form a problem domain for other software products to be constructed from the user requirements. The need is to understand the relationships that exist and make these explicit in the classes, attributes of the classes, and the messages that operate on the classes. It is also possible to have inheritance from more than a single class. This is defined to be a multiple inheritance characteristic. It is desirable to have the ability to represent multiple inheritance; that is, the class would be

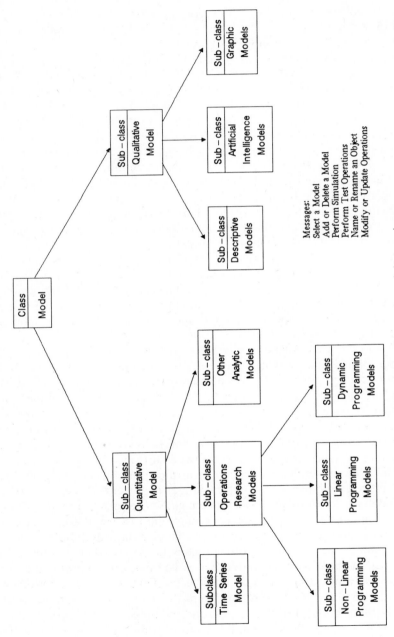

Messages:
Select a Model
Add or Delete a Model
Perform Simulation
Perform Test Operations
Name or Rename an Object
Modify or Update Operations

FIGURE 4.22 Object-oriented design classes

able to inherit the characteristics of more than one class. For software development this is a needed characteristic and forms the very foundation of OOD as an important design methodology.

In addition to objects having the distinction of belonging to classes, relationships exist between and among classes. In order to normalize and understand the problem domain and be able to comprehend the various relationships between and among objects, it is necessary that the objects be classified according to some schema and that the instances of this classification schema also be described. The ability to do this stems largely from the classification concept that is used and the ease with which the classification schema is able to be related to all members of the class. It is possible that many objects will have similar characteristics and will do similar operations in any problem domain. It is necessary to examine any of the familiar scenes to realize this situation. For example, consider a library of software parts. In the class of software parts, it is possible to have code, specifications, test routines, documentation, and many other classifications of software parts. Within any of these software parts, it is possible to have many subobjects and instances of the primary class. Thus, in the class specification, subobjects could be structured specifications, data structure information, or verbal specifications, to name but a few of the subobjects that have all the characteristics of the class specifications. Instances of the class specifications could include data entity specifications, interface specifications, and storage specifications. Thus, a class should be a larger group and subobjects in that class inherit all of the characteristics of the larger class, while instances of the class have all the characteristics of the larger class as well as attributes peculiar to the instance of the class itself. It is this ability to describe the problem domain in classification schema, and develop the inheritance characteristics within the class of objects, that makes OOD so attractive for software design.

From this, it is not difficult to realize that the classes may be reused as the need arises for design operations that invoke the class or similar classes from time to time. We will discuss the concepts and practice of reusability in a later chapter.

For OOD, complexities within the problem domain are handled through the use of classes, attributes of these classes, and the operations that may be assigned to them that cause a change of state in a given object. In OOD, the logical grouping of objects into classes is essential to understanding the problem and representing this problem in a real-world domain. The concept of class permits us to describe all the attributes of a particular class in one place and to describe all the operations of that class. The concept of type and class is quite similar in that type is associated with a number of operations that can be performed. If subtypes are present it may describe these as well. As we have noted earlier, however, only predefined operations may be performed in OOD languages. In OOD approaches, each problem domain class has associated with it a set of operations that affect only that class. This, in turn, ensures that system modularity will be preserved and further, establishes the concept of information hiding for each of the objects within a domain class. These properties allow a system design philosophy that encourages changes within classes without changing all other aspects of the problem, and that is easier to maintain because of modularity. These properties also limit changes to a particular piece of information, such as an algorithm within the object, to be isolated to a single class permitting experimentation without impacting other parts of the design process.

Object-oriented design concepts require the identification of objects, operations, and messages to describe the real-world problem domain. Objects often have similar characteristics or inherit characteristics from other objects or perform similar operations. Therefore, we define object classes and instances of the class to relate these characteristics in an orderly and understandable way. Inheritance permits us to relate the attributes and messages in a way that orders the classes and provides both modularity and information hiding. The implementation of OOD generally follows all of the several methods that we have presented earlier in our discussion of the logical design approaches: data structure design, architectural design, and procedural design. The identification of objects relates to the development of data structures; operations produce modules and structure for the design; and messages describe the interface requirements.

Steps in implementation [Booch, 1986] of OOD are:

1. Define the problem and identify the objects.
2. Identify the attributes of the objects.
3. Analyze the class of objects and identify higher-level classes.
4. Identify the operations.
5. Associate operations and attributes with the class.
6. Define the implementation of objects and operations.
7. Determine lower-level objects in the class.

These steps in the implementation of OOD have provided us with the entire system decomposition and ordering into its hierarchical relationships. OOD is based on information hiding, which provides objects with their own private state, which may not be accessed except by use of operations that address them. The objects that we have determined in our design process may be distributed and may be operated on in sequence or in parallel. Once the decomposition has been completed, the system is programmed in one of the OOLs for execution.

Identification of the objects represents the development of requirements and performing requirements analysis on these. The various approaches previously covered are more than adequate to present the identification of the real-world problem domain for object identification. The additional capability that OOD provides is a precise framework within which to describe the requirements for the software product. As noted earlier, OOD does not give a functional decomposition of the problem domain to resolve a given situation. Rather, it decomposes objects into subobjects, operations, and messages and then into the solution space from the problem domain. Once the objects are identified from the requirements analysis, we move to the detailed determination of the attributes of the identified objects.

It is necessary that the objects and their attributes be defined as precisely as possible prior to initiating the identification of operations. The objects and attributes are derived from the nouns and noun phrases that were developed as part of the requirements analysis. A common noun is by definition a class of things or persons and can be a proper name, a name of a thing, or an abstract noun that describes items such as quantity. Nouns may be thought of as generating inheritance among the objects in a class and as having more general or more specific attributes in relation to the inherited characteristics. In earlier examples on software parts and model management, it was essential to accomplish identification of the objects prior to ordering these in classes. Once all the objects are identified, an object table is constructed and objects are determined to be in either the problem domain or the solution domain. Attributes are determined by reviewing all the adjectives that are associated with the noun in question. Attributes are also determined by considering the problem constraints that apply to the particular object. It is important to note that not all nouns or objects described on the initial pass will survive for the final set. Some objects will be ancillary to the problem and the solution, others will become redundant as the iterations are performed, thereby leaving the actual objects of interest to the software design program.

After all the objects have been identified and determined to be necessary for the solution of the problem, the operations that act on these objects are determined. Operations are found by looking at all of the verbs that affect a given object. Verbs determine action or occurrences that operate on objects. Other actions that may impact objects are found in verb-phrases and predicates (e.g., "is the same as."). Examples of verb-phrases and predicates are found in operations such as "is equal to or less than," "is greater than," "read," "calculate," and other similar constructs. All of the verbs, verb-phrases, and predicates are captured in a table and termed "operations" for the object in question. If objects and/or operations are found in the final iterations that are performed to link these together, it is most likely that not all of the objects and/or operations have been discovered through the requirements analysis. Other reasons for left-over parts could be misidentification of the object or operation, or unrecognized relationships, or the decomposition has not progressed to the appropriate level to accommodate the precise activity. Should this be the case, it is necessary that the design steps be repeated until the entire system has been defined.

The various activities and outcomes that have been developed for OOD may be represented graphically through the notation suggested by Booch [1983]. These are shown in Figure 4.23. The graphical notation shows the dependencies between program components through a series of object de-

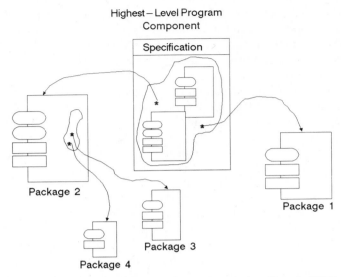

FIGURE 4.23   Object-Oriented Design notation (Booch 1983)

compositions until the lowest level of decomposition is mapped. While the use of graphic representation is not essential to OOD, it does provide a quick and accurate look at the state of development and relationships that occur. If the decomposition continues to include too much detail for easy use, a PDL, such as that found for Ada or FORTRAN, may be used for the design representation, as with other approaches.

Implementation follows along the path that we have described for other detailed design methods. Interfaces between modules and objects are defined in detail, data structures are specified in detail, and algorithms are prepared for various operations to be performed. As noted earlier, these activities may be isolated to any one object and applied iteratively until it is determined to be correct. This is one of the essential differences that sets OOD apart from other structured approaches and is the strategic foundation that makes this approach so successful. This process permits a level of design and data abstraction to be determined from which the implementation procedures may be developed. The design modules should be of a size that may be handled easily and not be so cumbersome as to offset the very attributes of OOD that make it attractive. A common rule of thumb is that 200 lines of code or less should be the maximum amount that is required for a particular design module.

Object-oriented design has the capability of handling not only passive objects such as those given in the various examples, but will accommodate active objects as well. An active object is one that has characteristics of independent concurrent behavior. Most common objects have combinations of data structures and subprograms, attributes and operations, that operate on the data structure. Active objects have all these characteristics and in addition possess independent control activities, such as tasks. This permits the design consideration of concurrency and synchronization through the definitions given by the source code–operating system used for implementation of the system under design.

The fundamental qualities of good software design developed from other approaches also apply to OOD. These include the ability to incorporate module fan-in, module fan-out, and cohesion. Classes are automatically highly cohesive and loosely coupled. Many benefits occur from the use of OOD include:

1. Reusability of previously designed parts; libraries of parts may be created and called *"reusable parts."*
2. Commonalties are made readily visible via class structure; therefore OOD structures are easier to understand.
3. The ability to isolate and modify any already defined class, changes to the design of a system have only limited impact because of the modularity, and maintenance is made easier.
4. There is a high level of cohesion and weak coupling, which is a property of class.
5. Modeling of real-time systems is supported through the high level of interaction between objects.
6. Testing and modification are easier because of the modularity, hence reliability is improved.

In summary, OOD provides a model of the real-world problem domain that may be realized in software. Objects, operations, and messages describe the problem domain in human-like thought association. OOD involves a three-step approach that requires the user to state the problem, define the solution strategy, and apply the strategy through the identification of objects, operations, specification of interfaces, and spelling out the implementation details for data and procedural abstractions. These steps are iterated until a satisfactory detailed design for the software product is achieved.

4.5 AUTOMATED SOFTWARE DEVELOPMENT TOOLS

A number of commercial products support the conceptual and logical phase of the software development lifecycle. These are generally designated as *computer-aided software engineering* (CASE) tools and intended to support many phases of the software development lifecycle. As we have seen in Chapter 3, several automated tools support requirements specifications activities and other phases of development as well. We will cover in detail the use of automated CASE tools in software systems engineering development environments in Chapter 7. For our purposes here, we will provide only the characteristics of those CASE tools that support conceptual and logical design and detailed design for software system development.

Most CASE tools that address requirements specifications functions also address the design development phases as well. As such, these tools carry forward many of the attributes that were found to be so useful in that phase. The major ones that are continued are (1) the data dictionary, (2) text editing capability, (3) graphical tools for representation of logical structure, (4) a central database for system development, and (5) report generation capability.

These tools are intended to support a specific method, such as data flow diagrams or Jackson system development, or they may support a number of approaches to design, such as data flow diagrams, data structured system development diagrams, and entity-relationship diagrams. Typically, CASE toolkits for logical and detailed design provide support for the following functions:

1. Continue the development of the data dictionary established in the requirements specifications phase and maintain this database for all entities and relationships that have been developed during design

2. Expand on the report generation capability from the requirements specifications activities to include the ability to review designs and generate documentation regarding these

3. Provide for the capability to bring information into and out of the system to encourage reuse of designs and exchange information concerning other development projects and other software development environments

4. Provide the ability to browse databases and various versions of stored design through a high level query language facility

5. Provide graphical capability for developing flow diagrams of various kinds, including the ability to store specific information about entities and the relationships that exist among them in a central database

6. Perform consistency and logical verification for data entities and their relationships, including error checking and omission of design attributes, such as datastorage required and none shown for a store function

Although there are no reported studies as to the capability to provide significant increases in software productivity through the use of automated toolkits, there are instances where such use can improve the software product and probably will improve software productivity. These instances occur when a software development shop employs a consistent approach to software design and development and uses a particular set of CASE tools over a long period of time. Accomplishing this will certainly lead to consistency in design, increased competency by the designers in the use of the tool, and amortization of the initial cost of the tool over a significant number of software development projects.

Use of these tools has an expense associated with them that extends beyond the initial cost. Users of these tools must be trained and kept current on the best use of the tool for the particular project to be developed. The tool itself must be maintained to ensure that it provides the user the ability to work as effectively and efficiently as possible. The design shop must have a set of standard operating procedures that incorporates the best features of the tool in order to exploit any potential productivity gains.

Software development environments generally include CASE toolkits of several varieties. The way in which these environments are integrated to include CASE tools for conceptual and logical design and detailed design operations will be covered in Chapter 7. OOLs represent a development environment for OOD, and, as such, may be considered to be a form of CASE tool.

For our purposes in this chapter it is sufficient to recognize the importance of these tools and the significant amount of development that has gone into CASE tool development. Certainly CASE tools, as they continue in their development, represent a potential for substantial improvement in the design process.

4.6 SUMMARY

In this chapter we have been concerned with conceptual and logical design of software, including various approaches to the detailed design process. We have considered both functional decomposition design approaches and object-oriented design techniques. By far the most used approach in contemporary design activities is the functional decomposition approach. This process is characterized by the use of structured design approaches that include data flow diagrams and data structure methods. Object-oriented design approaches are gaining in popularity, especially with the current emphasis on the use of Ada for software development by the U.S. Department of Defense and other Federal Agencies. Although not a purely object-oriented language such as Smalltalk 80, Ada has many of the essential language features that support object-oriented design. These are covered in Chapter 5.

While claims for increased software productivity as a consequence of using any of these approaches remain unsubstantiated, there can be little doubt of the efficacy of these design processes to affect the usability of the design output for the coding and testing phase. Use of any of these techniques ensures higher degrees of consistency of the design itself and a significant reduction of errors due to omission of design parts and in design logic.

4.7 PROBLEMS

4.1. Compare the attributes top-down and bottom-up design approaches. Why do you think it may be desirable to include both approaches in the design of a large-scale software system?

4.2.   What are the primary attributes of structured design tools that make them particularly attractive for conceptual and logical design and detailed design activities?

4.3.   Describe how to use a Nassi-Schneiderman chart and explain the use through the example of a temperature controller for use in home comfort systems.

4.4.   Construct a data flow diagram for a simple task such as how to change the oil in an automobile. Be sure you include all steps from procurement of the oil to its final disposal.

4.5.   In the text an example of a new student obtaining a class schedule was used to describe the data flow diagram. Compare the data flow diagram for these operations to those that you follow to obtain your class schedule.

4.6.   A data dictionary is an important feature of conceptual and logical design and detailed design. Define a schema for the data entities developed in Problem 4.5.

4.7.   Propose data dictionary data entities that are examples of the mathematical operators shown in Table 4.1.

4.8.   Prepare a mini-specification for the new student enrollment example used in the text.

4.9.   Indicate how data flow design methods are similar to data structured design methods. Indicate how these two methods differ.

4.10.   Compare the view of the software design developed from data flow design methods with those from data structured design methods. Why do you think it is desirable to have both views for a complex software system design?

4.11.   Entity-relationship diagrams may by used for a number of applications. We have presented its use for software systems design. Show how E-R diagrams could be used for computer hardware system designs.

4.12.   Compare the Jackson system development method with the data flow diagram method.

4.13.   Discuss the extension of data flow design method from conceptual and logical design to use in detailed design activities. What are the key characteristics of the conceptual and logical design that must be carried over to detailed design?

4.14.   Describe how to use the hierarchical-input–process–output design method is applied. Use this method to prepare diagrams for the oil change design problem given in Problem 4.4.

4.15. Compare the HIPO diagrams of Problem 4.14 to those that you derive for a data structure design approach.

4.16. Using the oil change example of Problem 4.4, develop an object-oriented design showing the objects, messages, and operations.

4.17. Compare the attributes of Ada and SmalltalkV as object-oriented languages. Which are true object-oriented languages?

4.18. Compare CASE tools for structured design methods with object-oriented design methods. What are the attributes of OOLs that provide a design environment? What are the shortcomings of OOLs as design environments?

Chapter 5

Programming Languages, and Testing

5.1 INTRODUCTION

Thus far in our presentation of the various phases of the software development lifecycle and the effect of micro-and macro-enhancement considerations on software productivity, we have emphasized the overall systems development process and the functions that lead to good design practices. The outcomes of the detail design phase of software development form the essential inputs for programming and subsequent testing of the programmed modules, sub-systems, and systems of the evolving software.

It is in this area that the most significant investments of time and effort have been made. The purpose of this is to enhance software productivity. The area of programming has a long history in computer science, beginning with the first machine language programs that were implemented more than 40 years ago. The process of coding is an informal one and has been resistant to automation attempts. While a great deal is known about the way in which programmers function, it has not been possible to capture this knowledge in any effective way that supports the provision of automated assistance. What we have been able to do is to develop higher level languages with increasing functionality and by this approach systematize much of the programming effort. These languages have been considered in depth by a number of authors and reported in a number of excellent texts and articles that are directly concerned with these micro-enhancement approaches to software engineering [Sommerville, 1989; Peters, 1987; Jones, 1985; and Pressman, 1987].

In our discussion of this important phase of the development of software, we will consider the characteristics of programming languages that are essential to good programming practice and the verification testing that is required to affirm the design. As in earlier chapters, we are not preparing a "how-to" manual on programming or coding. Rather we present an overview of this important activity.

At this point in our development of software systems engineering, we have examined an overall software systems engineering approach to the development of software, the requirements definition and specification phases, several approaches to conceptual and logical design, and some of the most useful detail design techniques. The overall system development phases that we have covered to this point involve:

1. Overall development of project objectives that need to be satisfied by the hardware and software to meet client needs
2. A means of transforming these high-level system objectives into system specifications for hardware and software specifications
3. Approaches to effective and efficient conceptual and logical design practices that lead to detail design activities that interpret the design for programming and testing

The activities associated with these phases have enabled us to formulate problems, develop requirements definitions and specifications, provide conceptual and logical structure, and complete detailed design operations. In Chapter 4, we examined ways in which the requirements specifications may be transformed through a series of phases into detailed design requirements and design parameters for coding and testing. These activities have provided mechanisms that lead us to

1. An understanding of the structure of information flows throughout the software system
2. A way to identify the various software modules associated with this structure
3. A means of defining the various control and data interfaces that exist between these modules
4. A mechanism for the determination of design constraints on the various software modules, including such important items as storage requirements and limits and execution times
5. A management structure that will enable us to develop the required modules

This amounts to a detail design of the complete software system. This now becomes the input to the next phase of development, which involves programming of and testing the design of the code. The output of this phase of software development will be properly coded modules, subsystems, and systems that have undergone verification testing to remove detailed design induced errors. From this point forward in the software development lifecycle, the software is a complete product that is ready for installation and overall system testing for requirements validation. Following installation at the client site, and associated test and evaluation, the software product enters into operation and maintenance for the remainder of its useful life.

In our approach, we view coding operations and testing functions as the culmination of significant preparatory activities that enable implementation of the design. Often this occurs through application of automated coding techniques. Much has been accomplished in this particular phase of the software development lifecycle to reduce and/or eliminate errors, streamline testing procedures, introduce automated coding and documentation generators, and assure that the code produced represents the agreed-on design specifications.

One of the major issues that remain at this phase is development of metrics to insure that the testing process measures what is required of the software product. Many of these metrics relate to concerns of software reliability, maintainability, and quality. These are covered in detail in Chapter 6. Here we will develop the testing plan and procedures that relate to the determination of the way in which the software product meets the detail design specifications. This is called *verification testing*.

We will examine structured programming methodologies, including questions of coupling and cohesion in program modules. Also, we review the pertinent characteristics of programming languages that may be used in the coding process. In our consideration of programming languages, we address the features of various languages that lead to good programming practices, such as the way in which languages handle various complexities. These complexities include the ability to handle specific attributes such as declarations, abstractions, control constructs, and exception handling. Properly utilized, these characteristics may have a direct positive effect on the readability and reliability of the program to be developed. Usually this occurs through presentation of the program in a clear, concise, and logical form. Finally, the subject of programming environments is presented to provide an integrated perspective of the overall programming activity. Total software engineering environments, of which programming environments are a significant part, are covered in detail in Chapter 7.

In the final parts of this chapter, we examine testing of software products to determine whether the modules, subsystems, and systems meet design objectives. As we noted in Chapter 3, the testing regime should have been determined previously from the requirements documents. This provides us with a guide for the conduct of testing and definition of the testing environment.

Testing is involved with exercising the program modules to determine that the module under test meets all design requirements, constraints, and special conditions related to the operating environment. The goals and objectives of the testing process are to be met by establishing measurement characteristics that will determine the extent to which our expectations about the software product are fulfilled. Once these objectives are determined, tests must be designed to:

1. Verify that the programming design meets the detail design requirements
2. Verify the design logic
3. Verify the interface design
4. Verify adherence to design and documentation standards
5. Establish test measurements
6. Identify the types of errors found in the program

5.2 CODING PRACTICES

5.2.1 Introduction

Traditionally, coding practice has been viewed as an art practiced by experienced persons skilled in programming. Often, the programming group or the individual programmer are viewed as creating a credible software product. This perspective has been changing with the introduction of a variety of automated coding processes, reusable software parts, and automated documentation capabilities. Automated tools for programming are examined later in this chapter. Reusable software is covered in Chapter 8, and automated documentation is part of an integrated software development environment that is covered in Chapter 7.

Certainly, the use of any of the several CASE toolkits that provide for detailed design of the program modules in Chapter 4 will furnish us with a good set of detailed design specifications for the programming process. These detailed designs give us cohesive, purposeful, and explicit instructions with regard to coding that serve to produce a capable, reliable, and high-quality software product with less reliance on a particular programming group or on a single skilled programmer.

These detail designs also lend themselves to the use of automated techniques for the production of code. Nonetheless, most of the software products developed today, and likely to be developed in the near term, are still produced by individual programmers or groups of professional programmers plying their art to produce a high-quality reliable software product.

In this section we will present an overview of program design practices and the various alternatives used in the programming process. We will examine the way data structure affects programming modules. We will also introduce structured programming approaches and discuss the effect cohesion and coupling between modules have on program design implementation.

5.2.2   Data Structure

In Chapter 4 we presented several approaches to structured design that included use of systems concepts for data structure. We have seen that a data structure is the representation of the logical relationship between the data entities that has been defined for the program. The nature and kind of relationships that exist between the data elements will dictate much of the organization of data in the program and access possibilities.

It is in this arena that the talent of the software designer and programmer come to the fore. The organization and degree of complexity are truly dependent on their knowledge and expertise. We will utilize data structure approaches in order to present an organized way to code modules. This approach relies on the use of data elements as fundamental items with which we deal in the programming process.

Data elements are items such as scalar items, vector items, *n*-dimensional matrices, or linked lists. They may be organized in a hierarchical data structure, a relational data structure, or other forms. These data forms may be represented in varying degrees of abstraction depending on the level of design detail, internal workings of the module, and interface requirements for access to the data. As we shall see in the sections that follow on structured programming approaches and attributes of high-level programming languages, the way in which the data elements are defined and structured dictates the way in which the program module develops.

5.2.3   Structured Programming Approaches

Structured programming is the first of the organized approaches to be developed and used for detail design and coding. It was defined by Dijkstra [1968] and others [Wirth, 1971; Bohm and Jacopini, 1966] in order to overcome limitations on the use of language constructs in programming. In this way, program modules will be easier to read, thus enabling novice programmers to review the function of the module and the logic used. So-called spaghetti-code programs would be eliminated when structured programming constructs are used, and this would result in code that is much more easily read and understood by those who did not write the code initially.

The term "structured programming" is a generic one that involves the use of specific constructs for coding. Structured programming practices were implemented to provide programmers with a consistent organization to good practice that utilized a top-down approach to module programming, used programming constructs such as DO__WHILE loops and IF__THEN__ELSE statements, and eliminated frequent use of GOTO statements.

The Jackson System Development (JSD) [Jackson, 1983] approach typifies the embodiment of structured programming practice. Typical structured programming constructs from the Jackson approach include the use of (1) left to right reading for sequences, (2) use of blocks with ovals on the right side to indicate selection, (3) blocks with solid ovals on the right side to indicate iteration, and (4) block diagrams to show hierarchical relationships.

These notation conventions for the Jackson structure programming approach are (1) sequence, (2) selection, (3) iteration, and (4) hierarchy, and are as shown in Figure 4.11. The interpretation of JSD notation leads to program structures such as those shown in Figure 4.11. In this figure, selection is shown as proceeding from right to left as in the development of a class schedule. The schedule is indexed by the term, time of day, room number, and faculty member in charge of the course. Iteration indicates that a year has multiple terms, and a term has multiple days during which courses may be offered. The selection is based on a particular time of day and the classes available during that particular hour. No more than one of these courses may be selected without conflict. Selection performs a logical OR function and provides a means for choice of one from among many.

The Jackson System Development approach is, like other structured design approaches, a top down approach. It is based on an analysis of data structure whereas many other structured design approaches are based on data flow analysis. JSD is a structured graphical technique that involves, as indicated in Figure 5.1, seven generally well specified design steps:

1. Entities and actions are identified
2. Actions are initially described, generally in natural language form
3. Entities are structured, such that actions that affect entities are ordered in time and represented by Jackson diagrams
4. Entities and actions are represented by an initial model and connections between this model and the real world are identified
5. Functions that correspond to defined actions are described

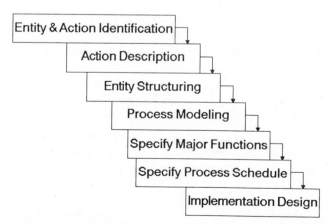

FIGURE 5.1 Essential steps in Jackson System Development (JSD)

6. Major functions, including process scheduling exemplars are specified
7. Implementation is accomplished by specifying the software (and hardware) design, initially in the form of structured psuedocode

The last three of these steps are detailed design and coding related. The first four are related to conceptual and logical design. For this reason, we introduced some JSD concepts in Chapter 4. Three graphical approaches are used in JSD and the steps of the JSD process follow the standard systems steps, as shown in Figure 5.2. The combination of these is well suited to the production of hierarchically well structured code, in any of several programming languages.

Hierarchical structure provides us with the top-down relationship between particular program modules. Other constructs that apply to the structured approach to programming in high level programming languages, include logic statements, read statements, and write statements. Most programs written in high level programming languages are composed of statements that combine (1) READ, WRITE, COMPUTE, FIND, and other simple statements, (2) IF_THEN_ELSE and CASE statements for decisions, and (3) DO_WHILE and DO_UNTIL statements for iteration. This logic is valid for PL/I, ALGOL, Pascal and other high level languages; however, COBOL lacks local variable and formal block structures and FORTRAN lacks IF_THEN_ELSE and DO_WHILE logic. It possesses only IF_THEN and counting forms of the loop. Thus, all programs would be capable of being written with these few structured constructs. Elimination of all (or most) GOTO or other branching statements is extremely valuable for preparation of simple logical programs that can be easily modified and understood by others.

Structured programming constructs and approaches have been adopted in virtually all high-level programming languages currently in use. The attributes may change from language to language; however, the approach remains the

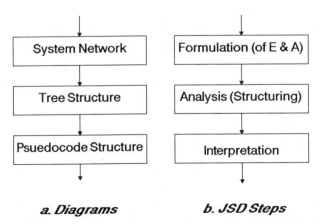

a. Diagrams   **b. JSD Steps**

FIGURE 5.2   Jackson diagrams and relation to systems engineering steps

same for good programming practice. Structured programming is particularly suited to the top-down approach and is frequently coupled with top-down detail design techniques for relatively small programs. For larger programming projects, a combination of top-down and bottom-up approaches is combined with other structured approaches.

5.2.4 Module Coupling and Cohesion

Module coupling and cohesion are two essential design concepts that must be handled. *Coupling* is the interaction that occurs between modules, while *cohesion* facilitates the determination of whether the programs in a module are essential for operation of that module. Taken together, coupling and cohesion provide a mechanism for judging the quality of the module design and function.

Program elements are foundation program units that may be grouped together to form an application module. Modules may include such activities as table look-up, file sort, evaluation of an algorithm, actions performed at the same time (synchronization), and subroutines. The assemblage of elements into modules that perform logic functions, such as data representation or detailed algorithm implementation, is followed by assembling modules into the next higher order of program functioning. To the extent that these modules require strong interactions one with the other, the modules are grouped into tightly coupled systems and form a tightly coupled group of modules. To the extent that they require loose interactions, they may be a loosely coupled system of modules that form a weak coupling relationship between modules. Whether tightly or weakly coupled modules are produced by the design process will depend on the nature of the approach to program design that is taken.

There are severe disadvantages to an approach that results in a tightly coupled set of functions. These disadvantages arise as a result of the interdependence of the functioning of one module with the functioning of another. The real challenge is to choose a particular approach that avoids tight coupling. To see that this is true, we have only to examine the impact of changing one module that is strongly dependent on another. Changes in the functioning of one module may have unforeseen effects on the other due to the strong interaction between them. Consider the situation in which one module begins to execute a subroutine that makes calls to another module for certain essential parts of the subroutine, and then returns control to the first module. Should the second module require modification for reasons other than its interaction with the first module, there is no reason to believe that the operations originally called will remain unaffected.

Coupling is a measure of the strength of the interconnectedness of the modules that constitute the program structure and, as we have noted, it is generally considered to be poor design practice to couple modules together in inappropriate ways. In a system of tightly coupled program modules, it is nearly impossible to modify any one module without impacting all other modules bound to it through tight coupling, unless the coupling is for shared data use or for real-time design. In the latter two instances of coupling, coupling is desirable and the effect of design modification is minimal, as we shall see when we discuss these coupling types.

Several types of coupling have been identified, some of them having a quite deleterious impact on the design, while other may indeed be beneficial. The various levels of coupling are [Peters, 1987]:

1. *Content*—information in one module uses or modifies information in another module.
2. *Control*—information is used by one module to signal another that a certain condition has occurred, that is, a *flag* is passed between two modules or when information enters from a device outside the module such as, an I/O device.
3. *Common*—data are passed from one module to another from a common database.
4. *Data*—passing of unstructured information between modules.
5. *Information*—passing of information between synchronizing modules.
6. *Synchronization*—coordination among modules occurs when two or more modules must be coordinated for other than a CALL/RETURN process.
7. *Stamp*—data that have some structured characteristics that are not fully utilized pass between two modules.

Content, control, and common coupling are generally considered to be poor designs that will potentially lead to severe problems during operation and maintenance of the program. Synchronization, information, and data coupling are generally considered to be good designs if they are appropriate to the particular design situation.

A design that calls for content or tight coupling is representative of the situation in which data in one module are used or modified by other modules. This means that invoking of one module calls for a circular movement of information around each of the modules contained in the system. The resultant outcome is that no information transfer may be isolated and examined without impacting some other module. Content coupling is to be avoided at all costs as it leads to nothing but trouble. It is extremely difficult to correct and makes a program nearly impossible to change or be maintained.

The most common form of coupling that is found in programs is control coupling. This is characterized by the passing of control from one module to another via a flag on which decisions are made by other modules. External control coupling occurs through I/O to specific devices, formats, and communications protocols.

Common coupling occurs when a number of modules refer to a common database. These forms of coupling are not necessarily bad, however, it is necessary that we take all such coupling activities into consideration in order to avoid problems.

Synchronization coupling occurs in the design of real-time systems. It is required whenever two or more modules are called by the operation of system hardware, such as sensors that provide input information in control center operation, or called by the language used in the design, for example, real-time interrupts from Ada, or calls made by the operating system, such as those related to sequence timing parameters. In these instances, synchronization coupling is critical to the operation of the system. Therefore, it is then considered appropriate to the design function. When synchronization coupling is considered for other than real-time systems, it is considered inappropriate and is, therefore, to be avoided.

Data coupling occurs when data elements are used between and among modules. This desirable form of coupling minimizes the number of data storage elements and makes these data available to any module that requires them without the requirement that the data be made part of the using module. For example, the execution of a computational algorithm requires data that may be in the form of tables. Other computational algorithms from different modules may use the same basic data elements. Since these data are in their own module that may be coupled to those modules that require them, storage is saved, computational efficiency is preserved, and the resulting program may have its data or algorithms modified without impacting other modules in the program.

Information coupling relates to synchronization coupling in that it describes the passing of information between synchronized modules. This type of coupling also supports such operations as the handshaking function in a procedure call. Generally, information coupling is required in real-time systems and is used in this context where there are competing needs for various modules.

Stamp coupling occurs when two modules utilize data structures that have some common attributes. In this instance, data may be used in a shared operation. This can be poor design practice and usually is to be avoided.

Cohesion in a system of modules is a measure of the strength of connectedness of the elements within a given system module and the way in which this module carries out the functions assigned to it. Elements within a module may express logical cohesion or functional cohesion. Logical cohesion implies that the logical design of a module is simple and is intended to carry out a single task. Functional cohesion implies that all the elements or instructions within the module are intended to support this single task. Other kinds of cohesion are possible; however, cohesion, such as temporal or communication, leads to poor program design and is to be avoided, except when they involve external devices. When a module is discovered to have a complex range of activities, it is probably best to break this module down into several modules for better and more efficient design. Modules should be designed with clear simple goals and provided with the means to accomplish these goals.

Cohesion is a natural property of information hiding, as was seen in Chapter 4 for object-oriented design. A cohesive module performs a single task within a software procedure, and requires little or no interaction with the procedures being performed by other modules.

Coupling and cohesion provide a measure of worth of program module. The presence of one demonstrates the absence of the other. Thus, it is highly desirable to have the absence of coupling between modules, and the presence of functional cohesion between elements in modules. For an in-depth discussion of coupling and cohesion in program design, the reader is referred of Peters [1987] or Yourdon [1982].

5.3   PROGRAMMING LANGUAGES

Programming languages are the basic tools of the programmer.It is necessary that software developers have at least some knowledge of the characteristics of the language currently being proposed for the system. Programming languages affect program readability, reliability, and usability. Selection of a programming language is one of the most important decisions facing the software engineer. Languages contain a variety of features that relate to this selection process, including the way the language handles such attributes as declarations, types, modules, control constructs, and exception handling.

Some of the more widely used languages are:

1. COBOL for business applications;
2. FORTRAN for scientific applications;
3. Pascal and C for systems applications;
4. Lisp and PROLOG for artificial intelligence applications
5. Ada for DoD embedded weapons system applications programs

There are, of course, many others. BASIC is an often used language for elementary applications but we know of no significant large programs written in BASIC. The major languages today are FORTRAN for scientific applications, COBOL for business applications, and C for almost everything new.

Initially, programming languages consisted of assembly code with the system designer, programmer, and operator being one person. Second-generation languages include FORTRAN and COBOL. These developments were followed in succession with more sophistication in language constructs and the capability of the language to perform such tasks as handling multiple users and background printing. Languages have continued to evolve until we are at the point of having fifth- and sixth-generation languages that support highly interactive operations and multiple users with distributed databases. The evolution of programming languages is depicted graphically in Figure 5.3.

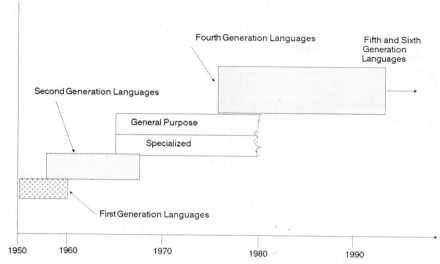

FIGURE 5.3   Generations of programming languages

In general, languages fall into five different categories: (1) assembly languages, (2) systems implementation languages, (3) static high-level languages, (4) block-structured languages, and (5) dynamic high-level languages. The higher the level of the language, the more likely it is to be portable from one machine architecture to another. Assembly languages are generally suitable only for embedded programs that are totally integrated into the operating system and machine architecture, as it is highly unlikely that this code will need to be ported from one machine to another. High-level languages may contain program parts that are intended to be as totally portable as possible. Other software parts may be designed to depend directly on the target machine architecture or make calls to the operating system or interact with other program modules.

Portability is characterized by a software module, subsystem, or subsystem that is completely self-contained and does not depend on other functions for operation. Portability or near-portability is highly desirable for some applications. This would be the case when we have an algorithm that is used to define the flight trajectory for a satellite launch, for example, that uses inputs from sensors for in-flight corrections. There is nothing embedded about this, and we may well wish to use this code on another machine.

One high-level language instruction usually takes the place of many equivalent instructions in machine or assembly language code. This normally permits the programmer to use more meaningful and more easily interpretable names for program variables and subroutines than is possible with machine languages. High-level language operations are usually independent of the format or style in which they are written. As a result of this naming capability and ability to format or stylize the form of the programs, high-level languages are easier to read, code, and debug than are machine or assembly languages. Language selection also has a great deal to do with the overall cost of the software project, control of the lifecycle development costs, and testing and maintenance. Languages with flexible naming conventions, structured constructs, and easy to read programs take less time to write and debug, and thus are less expensive to implement in terms of programmer time and cost. The choice of the right language for the software development project may serve to minimize the amount of coding required, control testing requirements, and make the program more readable and maintainable.

Language choice should be based on such factors as user requirements, availability of compilers, tool support, overall size of the project, functionality goals for the project in terms of quality factors, experience of the design group, testing requirements, application area (whether it is a real-time, transaction processing, or scientific application), and other factors important to the characteristics of languages. In the sections that ensue we will describe some of the needed characteristics of languages such as control structures, exception handling, information hiding, data types, data typing, declarations, initialization and constants, modules or subprograms, and pseudo-programming languages.

5.3.1 Control Structures

Control structures are available in most modern programming languages and are used to control the flow of the program to do what the designer and programmer intended to enable it. These structures establish the sequence in which programs are executed. Execution should be directed to perform the first program statement, followed by each subsequent statement in turn and exiting on the last statement. Control structures are essential for creating readable, maintainable, and testable programs. A variety of control structures are important to the writing of good programs, including loop controls, decision constructs, and exception handling.

The most common form of loop control is provided by the use of WHILE _DO and REPEAT_UNTIL statements. The FOR statement is used to execute a loop the number of times expressed in the control loop. Generally the use of the FOR statement is a safe construct and guarantees termination of the loop statement for most high-level languages. Problems arise in languages such as ALGOL60, in which the loop never terminates and this must be guarded against. In such languages as Pascal, this problem is circumvented by use of the loop counter.

In a high-level language, decision constructs allow a statement or group of statements to be selected for execution on the basis of some condition being true. The statements that implement this are IF_THEN and IF_THEN _ELSE. As a rule of thumb, there are no problems in using these statements.

GOTO statements present sever problems for programs and for operation and maintenance of programs and are to be avoided for most uses. Where the intended effect is beneficial, a prearranged GOTO may prove to save a great deal of time and programming effort. However, the unintended outcomes that occur from unbridled use the this statement make it one to be avoided. An unintended impact of a GOTO occurs when this statement is used to direct the operation of the program to a subroutine, but the programmer neglects to redirect the operation back to the step beyond the GOTO statement. The program will compile and not show any errors, yet it will not execute the intended operation.

In addition to the GOTO statement that causes troubles, the IF—THEN —ELSE statement may sometimes present problems, especially if it is deeply nested in a module. In complex situations, it is difficult to follow all of the ELSE possibilities associated with a specific IF. Recursion may also cause problems in that it may create a second activation of a module during the first activation; that is, the module invokes or activates itself as part of a defined procedure. The use of concurrency supports multiple tasks and general synchronization and communication between tasks, which is essential for real-time applications. Exception handling is a programming feature that traps user-defined conditions and passes these on to an exception handler program for processing.

Most modules should be designed to contain only a single entry and single exit point. This structure makes it easier to examine all aspects of a module, look at potential errors, and modify the module at a later time if this is required. A module with this type of simple interface is also much easier to test for design verification and operation than one with more than a single entry and exit point. If a module is too complex, it should be a candidate for further decomposition.

5.3.2 Exception Handling

Exception handling is important when an error or unexpected event occurs in executing a program. Exceptions may be due to either hardware or software errors that were not anticipated when the program was first written. Usually an unanticipated exception is given over to an automatic exception handler that resolves the problem. If the problem is serious and cannot be corrected in a short period of time, the program module containing this problem is usually eliminated, the problem searched out, and the module reprogrammed as corrected. If the exception is a known quantity, something that is known to occur with certain instances of input data, a programmer can code around the problem and the program can continue to execute. This is not good programming practice and "code-arounds" should not be part of the completed module.

5.3.3 Information Hiding

Information hiding is the ability to conceal the existence of certain pieces of information and deny access to it except under direction of specific rules that have been predefined. In general, it is desirable for each module to have access only to that information that is absolutely necessary for the operations that pertain to that module and to specific operations on that module. Information hiding occurs when the designer recognizes that certain data or information in the module is required only on selected call. The programmer then writes the program such that only those specific operations have access to the information that is not available except on call. Modules are specified and designed so that information that is contained within that module is not accessible to other modules unless there exists a need to know the information.

Hiding provides for effective modularity in the design process by defining independent sets of modules that communicate with any other module only the information necessary to accomplish the desired operation. It defines and enforces access constraints to both procedural detail within the module and any local data structure used by the module.

One of the greatest benefits that accrues from using information hiding occurs when modifications are to be made during the testing and maintenance phases. In these instances, the cohesion of the module permits modification without concern about the impact on other modules. This is so in modules of this design, since most of the data and procedures are hidden from other parts of the software and the introduction of inadvertent errors is not likely to propagate to other locations in the software. Thus, one of the real advantages to information hiding is that there is no way to corrupt the information from modules that are not to use the information. These programs tend to be more secure, have a high level of cohesion, and achieve a great degree of data independence.

5.3.4 Data Types

Another way in which we may judge the merit of a particular programming language concerns the syntax and breadth of its procedural constructs. The way in which data types are defined and supported is an important aspect of the quality of a given language. Data types and data typing are described by Fairley [1985] as "a class of objects together with a set of operations for creating and manipulating them."

In much the same manner as with object-oriented design procedures, data objects inherit attributes of the data type to which they belong. They may take on values that are within the range of values of the data type, and operated on by the procedures that apply to that type. Simple types serve to classify the object and the operations to which it is subjected.

Data types are used to group together data of a similar nature and simple data types can cover a wide range of values that include numeric types (e.g., integer, complex, real, discrete, or floating-point numbers), enumeration types (e.g., user-defined data types from Pascal), Boolean types (e.g., true or false, yes or no), and string types (e.g., alphanumeric data). Most programming languages permit the programmer to establish composite data types. These are termed arrays and form a sequential collection of the elements noted above. Arrays may be static or dynamic and multidimensional. The care with which we take in defining data types will go a long way in giving the program clarity and consistency.

5.3.5 Data Typing

Typing data enhances the ability to track, modify, and control data throughout the program design. Data definitions should be confined to one place in the program for ease of access and use, and all defined data types should be located in this position.

In addition to the definition of data types, data subtypes may also be defined as data objects. These defined subobjects inherit the characteristics of the data type itself. This serves to limit and constrain the use of the data and is most useful in checking routines. Data types may also be declared to be equal to a predefined data type. In this instance the data type derived from the existing one may be logically different from it, but will be able to undergo similar operations.

Type checking was introduced in ALGOL60, and much progress has occurred since then. Languages such as Pascal permit the programmer to define types and declare objects for that type. Once data types are carefully defined, rules for checking the various types may be defined and applied. As a result, abstraction is built into the program and both design and code are more readable and able to be error checked. Fairley [1985] has defined five levels of type checking that are commonly encountered in programming languages. The meaning and definition of these terms are as follows:

Level 0 Typeless programming languages that have no explicit means of data typing include BASIC, APL, Lisp, and COBOL. The user, however, is able to define data structures in these languages.

Level 1 *Automatic type conversion* is a type-checking that allows different mixed data types but converts operands of incompatible types, thus allowing requested operations to exist. PL/1 uses this approach to handle Boolean values.

Level 2 *Mixed-mode* type conversion is similar to the automatic type in that different data types within the same data type are converted to a single target type so that the called operation can occur. FORTRAN has this capability with regard to mixed-mode arithmetic.

Level 3 *Strong type checking* occurs in languages that permit operations to be performed only on the same data types. All operands, operators, and subprogram (modules) interfaces are checked for type compatibility at compile, load, and run time. Ada is a strong typing language, as is C.

Level 4 *Pseudo-strong type checking* has the same characteristics and strong type checking but is implemented through loopholes. Pascal checks interface compatibility for single compiled programs but does not do so for separately compiled procedures.

Most high-level languages provide the programmer with the capability to define their own data types. This permits freedom to classify objects and the operations that are permitted on the object. If the programmer violates any of the restrictions in the language regarding data typing, the program will not compile and error messages are printed out by the compiler.

5.3.6   Declarations

The *declaration* of names is used to provide information concerning the precise definition of the object, the way it is to be stored, and the way it is to be used in the program. Name declarations are closely associated with data type declarations. It permits the programmer to combine a data type with the declaration of an object. This allows a compiler to verify whether objects of the same type are properly used in operations. Error messages are provided when declarations are improperly used.

5.3.7   Initialization and Constants

Constants and variables are used in all programs and care must be exercised to ensure that these are given unambiguous descriptions to avoid program errors. To reduce programming errors, it is desirable to force initialization of all variables declared in the program. This removes any potential for the programmer to forget to build in the need for initialization. Some languages provide for initialization, (e.g., FORTRAN and Ada) but do not force the programmer to use it. If an initial value is not selected in these languages, it is assigned a value by the system. Pascal has no initialization features and the programmer must purposefully assign values.

Constants are entities that do not change and include such values as scientific and engineering physical constants, and might include standard rates of social security tax, state income tax rates, or other similar items. These values do not change during the execution of the program. Other constants include parameters that are used to derive a particular instance of a program. For example, a field may have a fixed length for a name in one instance of a program and require a different length in another instance of the program. This is accounted for by declaring the constant for the specific instance as a local constant. Constants may also be represented by variables that have been initialized and then not permitted to change during the remainder of the program.

5.3.8   Modules or Subprograms

A *subprogram* is a separately compilable program component that has both data and a control structure. Generally this is referred to as a *module* of the program. Modules contain objects whose values must be maintained and which do not change from one implementation to another. Values are declared globally and are generally accessible by any operation in the program. Modules represent entities in and of themselves and may be called or invoked in the same way as any program. Some modules are called in the same sequence every time the programs are run; others possess activation mechanisms that are distinct and enable the module to be invoked from anywhere in the program.

In most programming languages, a module is an entity in itself and operates on data in the way determined by the larger program of which it is a part. The most easily viewed case of modularity occurs in object-oriented design with the object being able to combine data and control structures in a specified way.

5.3.9   Pseudo-Programming Languages

It is sometimes useful to be able to represent a system design in natural-language-like statements. These natural language like statements are given the name "pseudocode." These are procedural languages in which the design consists of sets of procedures. The language may be that of an informal text description type, such as *programming design language* (PDL), or a precise language such as the predicate calculus. The goal in the use of these pseudo-programming languages is to precisely describe software implementation. The cost of writing pseudocode is intended to be low. Advantages in the use of PDLs are that the design closely matches the final code for implementation. This does not guarantee that the implementation is correct as the program is written. For precise languages, the advantage is that implementation may be assumed to be correct as the design is completed. However, implementation may be difficult to develop in these languages.

Jackson structured programming (JSP) presents us with a data structured view of the design problem and represents a PDL. It is based on data structure as a representation of the problem domain structure. JSP uses an informational viewpoint in addressing the application in the problem domain. It is used primarily in the business domain, where COBOL is the language of preference and is used for the design and implementation of code. It uses both graphics and text to show sequence, selection, or iteration within modules. It uses hierarchical structures to show program primitives at the lowest level of decomposition. Basically, JSP envisions a three-step method. Data relationships are defined first by examining and defining the input and output data structures and presenting these in graphic notation. Next, these graphs are converted to a basic implementation structure with the same graphics. Finally, the basic structure is filled in by listing the operations of implementation and assigning each to a component in the design. Figure 5.4 shows an example of the hierarchical structure for a personal computer. In this figure, the personal computer may be thought of as having many composite components, such as disk drives and random-access memory (RAM). The disk drives may be further reduced to include floppy disks and requiring a power

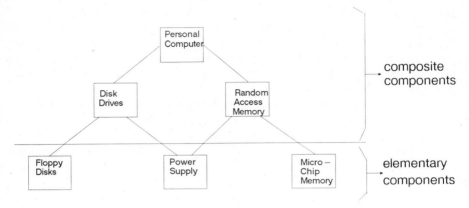

Hierarchies are structures having:
elementary components — lowest level of decomposition
composite components — higher level in correct order

FIGURE 5.4 High-level breakdown of a personal computer architecture using JSP hierarchy usage

supply. The RAM possesses microchips for its memory and shares the same power supply as the disk drives. A conceptual diagram showing a general approach to the JSP method is depicted in Figure 5.5.

A *program design language* (PDL) is a textual language that is sufficiently precise to describe a software implementation. PDLs were presented as a response to the need for a better way to design software than that afforded by flow diagrams. Use of a PDL presumes that the architectural design has been completed. PDLs are intended to enhance the quality of design through

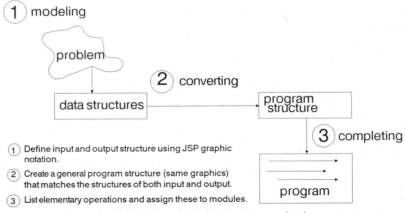

FIGURE 5.5 JSP programming method

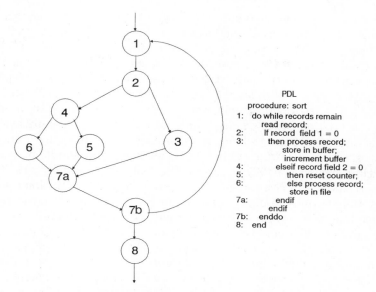

FIGURE 5.6   PDL translation into a flow graph

communication between designers using the same language. They are intended to increase the capability for completeness and consistency by conducting checks. Productivity improvements using PDL can be quite good compared to using flow diagrams in that the design is immediately visible. Translation of a PDL into a flow graph is shown in Figure 5.6. Additionally, if the PDL is close to the language of implementation, the coding is able to proceed quickly. PDL uses IF and DO language constructs and the processor uses control information of procedure calls. Use of PDL requires that the design be organized prior to implementation. Designs can be used to determine inconsistencies in the design and to evaluate and modify the design with relative ease.

5.3.10   Fourth-Generation Language Automated Program Generators

Automated program generators represent a move to automate programmer activities. As we have noted earlier in this chapter, the automation of the activities of the programmer has generally not occurred. However, one of the areas that has been subject to much of this effort is in automated program generators. Usually an automatic code generation is coupled to a *fourth-generation language* (4GL)* that enables simple natural language like input of the requirements, or the purposeful specifications for a program.

---

*A 4GL may or may not produce source code in a high-level programming language. Those that do not generally have a run-time interpreter to execute the statements written in the 4GL.

Although there is no standard definition as to exactly what constitutes a 4GL, there is a consensus of what a 4GL should provide and generally what 24GL should do. The major attributes of a 4GL are that it is a processing environment that provides a single, integrated systems development tool embedded within a comprehensive development facility [Goetz, 1987]. Users should expect to be able to learn how to use the 4GL in no more than 2 days, experience a "user-friendly" interaction process, and have a gain in productivity of at least an order of magnitude increase over the comparable time required using standard techniques as provided by one of the high-order languages, such as COBOL. Other major attributes that should be part of a 4GL include having a DBMS with automatic database navigation with a logical view or relational processing and an integrated active data dictionary–directory. It should possess a query facility with English-like language or a menu approach that supports Boolean selects; have a report generator, word processing, and graphics; and be able to support procedural and nonprocedural languages, while maintaining integrity, security and command structures. Thus, a language that exhibits these features is considerably more than just a programming language, it is a comprehensive software development facility.

A 4GL is often used in an automated programming environment that provides a software productivity improvement of at least one order of magnitude (10:1) over programming the same design in a standard 3GL or 2GL language. Many claims have been made as to the efficacy of 4GLs for increased productivity [Goetz, 1987]. While the 4GL code produced may well be written in a shorter period of time compared with the traditional approach, the translated code usually is much larger in size than the source code that would be written by a programmer. One of the major problems with 4GL and automatic program generators is that the code produced often requires longer run-time, as well as having more lines of code.

Several benchmark tests have been made of 4GLs, and the outcomes of these are not encouraging for the future, as compared to the use of higher-order (or 3GL) languages. Some of the results of these comparisons are:

1. The University of California, Los Angeles Graduate School of Management compared FOCUS to COBOL and reported a three-to-one (3:1) improvement time, but that FOCUS programs were 30 times slower in executing.

2. The FBI compared Natural (a product of Software AG) with COBOL and found a 5:1 increase in productivity; however, the transaction volume caused a performance degradation and the backlog was *not* reduced.

3. IDEAL (a product of Applied Data Research) advertisements states that IDEAL generates a 4.4:1 productivity gain compared to COBOL with 15% of the users reporting a gain of 10:1 or more in program writing efficiency.

All of this leads to the conclusion that present 4GLs are quite suitable for quick production of slowly executing code for a one, or at most a few, time operation. They do not appear to be a good choice for producing code that will be used over and over again.

Fourth-generation languages have a lot to offer, and the concepts and rationale on which they are based are excellent, and some good products are being brought to market for use. However, the results to date indicate that substantial improvements are required before these software development environments provide the gain in productivity that would make them truly cost-effective in the production of software that is to be used over and over again.

5.4 PROGRAMMING ENVIRONMENTS

Earlier we discussed the need for an integrated software systems engineering development environment. We will cover software engineering development environments in detail in Chapter 7. In this section we will examine that portion of the environment that contributes to programming and represents the integrated programming tools that aid in these operations. Most of the existing software systems engineering environments provide support for detailed design and programming activities. These functions are generally closely coupled in order to provide a uniform environment for the development of consistent, correct, and verifiable code. Much more emphasis has been placed on the development of automated assistance for detailed design than for the programming phase. This appears to be the case due to the acceptance of an individually customized approach to programming tasks.

Support environments for the programming phase may be considered as quite similar in concept and approach to support environments found in requirements definition and specification activities, in conceptual and logical design, and for detailed design phases, in that they support the activities to be accomplished. Major differences occur, however, through the significant increase in the scale of operations at the coding phase. Many more people are brought in to perform the programming implementation of the detailed design than are utilized on any other phase of software development.

The increase in personnel required to accomplish the programming phase presents a significant additional strain on the development organization, if it has not been planned to accommodate this increased level of activity. These strains are generally related to increased management requirements. Communication channels are stressed and strained and coordination of programming groups and individuals must be emphasized, much as management and organization support activities must be established to meet group needs.

When 4GLs or software part reusability is part of the programming effort, management and coordination take on a different role as the part of the programming staff is modified. In the case of 4GLs, automatic programming is accomplished, necessitating management oversight on the quality, effectiveness, and efficiency of the code produced. When software parts are reused, management needs are for oversight on retrieval of parts and the amount of effort required to adapt these to the current program. Reusability is covered in much more detail in Chapter 8.

Thus the software systems engineering support environment for the detailed phase, or programming, design and coding, is characterized by the increased need for management and coordination support. This aspect of the support environment is the most essential part and represents a substantial change from the needs for support environments in other phases. The support environment must also enhance design consistency and integration and provide constant verification checks back to the detailed design baseline. This means that a configuration that is robust is a necessity and not a luxury if the environment is to enhance the programming process and increase productivity.

The opportunity to improve programmer productivity through use of a programming support environment is due to the fact that individual programmer approaches are not uniform across programmers and the results are not predictable. Programming continues to be an individualized skill. A programming support environment must be able to support standardized methods that generally enhance productivity. In addition, the programming environment must not squelch programmer innovation and creativity. Thus, the environment must be flexible and tailorable to the needs of the individual programmer or group of programmers who are to implement the design.

As we have seen, there is no standardized way for performing these programming functions. Individual programmer creativity must be supported to maximize the opportunity for effectiveness and efficiency of program design. Therefore, it is important that the environment support the formulation and conceptualization of program design and program changes and provide structured programming capability, evaluation and checking, and automated processes for PDLs, storage, consistency checks, and program design changes.

Another important consideration for the programming component of a software systems engineering development environment is the ability to provide for program migration or portability. As we have indicated in earlier chapters, changes in both hardware and software are occurring at a very rapid rate. While the technology is changing at a rapid rate, the pace of acquisition, from conception to installation, for most software development processes has become increasingly slower. The time required to develop requirements definitions and specifications by the group determining the initial need often extends over a very long time. Added to this is the time to prepare and let contracts and begin the preparation of the conceptual design process. This means that the length of time that it generally takes for the development cycle of large-scale complex software programs is likely to be excessive.

Given the most likely length of time that it takes to develop a software project, this means that it is highly conceivable that we will see not only one but possibly several changes in target hardware during the course of a single procurement. From this we may infer that it is highly likely that the software will be operated on a different piece of hardware than that originally targeted. Changes in the way software is written, the use of reusable parts, new operating systems, and other modifications will also impact the nature of the software development process during the implementation phase. As a consequence of these factors, it is highly desirable to build in a high degree of portability and machine independence of a given software product.

Building in portability for software products may be feasible for some types of software projects but not for others. For example, an embedded system is highly unlikely to be a candidate for portability, while a product intended primarily for transaction processing is a good candidate for portability. Techniques for software portability to enable software use on different computer hardware systems include program emulation, compiling a program in abstract machine language then implementing the abstract machine on other machines, and using preprocessors to translate from one dialect of a language to another. Experience shows that none of these approaches is guaranteed to produce the desired outcome: complete portability of a specific software product. We find that even when standards are invoked and high-level languages are used for programming, it is most likely that machine dependencies will occur and require modification of the transitional program prior to successful operation. This is true because different machines have different architectures, different conventions for information representation, and a host of other variables such as different word lengths and different counting techniques. When these factors are known beforehand, it is a relatively straightforward task to establish detail design criteria to take many of the parameters into account. The problems occur when this information is not known in advance and then a requirement is given that programs are to be portable. Depending on the value of the program and its length and complexity, it is often more economical to discard the old program and simply bite the bullet and rewrite the software to fit the new conditions.

Other issues related to portability arise as a result of variations of operating systems found on machines from different vendors. Even with the use of high-level languages, most languages use calls to the operating system to conceal low-level machine details from the programmer. The major problem areas are libraries, files, input/output devices, and job control. Reuse of code also gives rise to problems; for example, if the code to be reused is a a large library database, the reusable software may make calls into the operating system. If this occurs on a regular basis and for a large number of queries, it may cause more problems than rewriting the program at the onset. Reuse of code fragments must be addressed as early as possible if reusability is to be a major consideration for the design of the particular software product.

The programming part of the software systems development environment is representative of a approach that is different from what we have seen in development phases that preceded it. A major consideration is for support of individual or group programmer creativity. Management considerations have a high priority in order to keep the implementation phase moving to complete the project within budget and on time. Issues of migration and portability become quite important as the length of time required for the total development project is extended. The implementation of reused code presents additional problems for the programming phase. The ability to accommodate to schedule changes and variations in target environments must be accommodated in order for the software product to be considered a successful installation.

5.5   SOFTWARE TESTING

There are two general types of software tests: validation tests and verification tests, usually termed "V&V." Validation testing is concerned with the confirmation that the software that is being designed satisfies system requirements. Verification testing is concerned with the confirmation that the outputs of a particular development phase authenticate the intent of the input to that same phase. Thus validation always refers back to the software requirements definition and specification documentation, while verification always refers back to the inputs of the phase undergoing authentication tests. In this section we are concerned only with verification testing for the programming phase of the software development lifecycle.

Software testing is a process that begins with the development of test requirements during the initial phase of the software development project and continues throughout the entire project. Ideally, requirements should be validated and verified at every phase of the process. In actuality, validation may be confirmed at the completion of the requirements specification process and not again until system tests, while verification normally occurs at each phase along the way.

It is a critical challenge to the software development process to provide a means for validation and verification (V&V) of requirements, design specification, detailed design, and coding. This needs to be accomplished in order to assure the user that the software product will meet the intended application for the software and be as error free as feasible.

The software testing techniques discussed in this chapter are intended to be a part of a verification process that exercises the program using data similar to that for which the system was designed. The various components of the system are observed, particularly the program inputs and outputs, to determine the existence of errors or failure of the program to meet the assigned task. Verification occurs as each module or algorithm is tested to determine that it is logically and functionally correct and achieves the desired goal of the software part under consideration. It must be kept in mind that even though various tests detect errors that are then corrected, there is no guarantee that the software is error-free. No testing program is able to show that the software is correct; the tests simply demonstrate the presence or absence of errors that may be detected by the specific test applied. A successful test is one that detects errors correctly, as intended by the test routine applied. An unsuccessful test is one that is applied and which finds no errors when there are errors, or which indicates that errors are present when they are not present.

Testing is a critical part of the total quality assurance effort that ensures that the software will be as free of error as possible when installed for operation. It is extremely important to the design of the testing regime that detailed knowledge of the program structure and intent of the software product be used to design the tests.

There are several necessary characteristics for software testing programs:

1. Testing is executing a program with the intent of finding errors.
2. A good test case has a high probability of finding as yet undiscovered errors.
3. A successful test is one that uncovers as yet undiscovered errors.
4. Testing cannot show the absence of defects; it only shows that software defects are present.

Those who are responsible for the design and implementation of the testing program should be involved in the overall design process in order to provide the necessary guidance to the detailed designers or Programmers. Testing is necessary before final review of the specification, design and programming efforts that has produced the software. It is used to perform the final (and often only) verification check on the soon-to-be-delivered software product.

The development of the software testing effort commences with the development of requirements definitions and specifications. As the software development continues through conceptual and logical design and detailed design, the test plans continue to be developed and refined. Test plan development follows software configuration, and a test configuration is prepared. The test configuration and the software configuration come together after the programming phase and the actual verification tests on software modules are conducted. The test plan contains not only the necessary tests to exercise the specific module but also the expected results of the test from the detailed design parameters for that module. Test results are then evaluated against the expected results. Errors are corrected through a debug routine. Reliability of the evaluated software product is next determined through use of a reliability model. The reliability model is exercised and the predicted reliability of the software is calculated. This process is shown in Figure 5.7.

It is not unusual to expend from 40 to 80% of the total coding cost on the testing process, depending on the intended use of the software. If the software product to be used where human life is at stake, or the software is to be human-rated, the cost of the testing program can cost from 3 to 5 times the

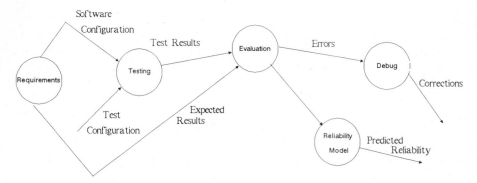

FIGURE 5.7 Test information flow

total cost of other portions of the software design and development project.For use in a business environment that is determined by the user to be noncritical, the test costs generally move the lower part of the range.

Once the test plan has been prepared and approved, testing of the software consists of several steps. Generally modules are subject to unit tests that are intended to determine whether the module functions in accordance with the detailed design requirements. This is followed by testing several modules together in integration tests. These tests are intended to determine whether the group of modules functions properly at the interfaces between them. Once this is completed, the assembled software may be subjected to validation testing. This last test seldom is accomplished for large complex systems. Validation testing usually requires the presence of the actual operating environment, and this is generally not feasible. Thus validation testing usually occurs at the time of installation and coincides with system testing. The several steps that we have discussed for a software testing approach are shown in Figure 5.8.

The types of tests that are performed during the approach outlined above are often divided into several groupings that tend to aid in performing the actual testing program. These test types are as follows:

1. Function testing
2. Module testing
3. Subsystem testing
4. System testing
5. Acceptance testing

Normally function and module testing are carried out only when full information of the intended operation of the module within the software product is provided. These tests seldom require a formal testing procedure, as these tests are performed to ensure that the function and module accomplish the

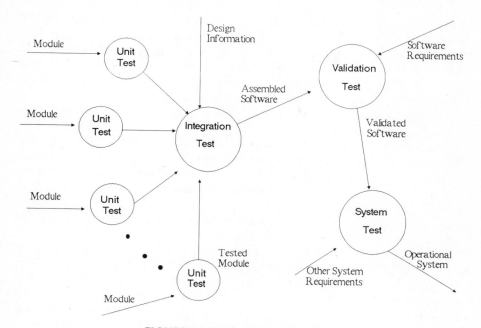

FIGURE 5.8   Software testing steps

tasks, as assigned. Functions are usually tested first, followed by assembly of appropriate functions to form a module, which is then tested as a stand-alone entity. Errors detected during these tests are corrected by the programmer responsible for the module implementation.

Subsystem testing is comprised of an assemblage of modules connected together, as in the final configuration, and exercised with appropriate parameters. Testing at this stage should concentrate on module or unit interfaces, as the functions and modules themselves have been tested previously and found (or corrected) to meet the test requirements. All interface functions, such as data transfer, calls from one module to another, and timing functions, are to be exercised during subsystem testing. Error correction for these testing procedures may be the responsibility of the initial programmer or of a group of specialists who are experienced in correcting interface problems.

Usually, system testing is conducted after completion of subsystem testing and is a test of the integrated system. The goal in this testing procedure is to locate any design or coding errors that have escaped earlier detection and correction. Validation testing may be performed during these operations to determine whether the integrated subsystems meet the stated requirements. Errors detected during this testing process are generally fixed by experienced programmers.

Acceptance testing involves the use of real data, rather than data prepared specifically for the testing regime. This test is the final verification check and the first attempt to get at validation of the software. Validation using real data generally results in errors that show whether the system will meet user requirements. These errors are most easily spotted at this time. Performance and functionality are also determined at this point, since this is the first real test for the assembled software in its final configuration. Any errors determined to be present at this late stage in the testing cycle are the province of a special troubleshooting group that prepares the software product for installation at the user facility.

In conducting tests on software, it is essential that a test plan or test strategy be prepared in advance of implementation of the test program. Generally a good strategy for software testing is to begin at the function and module level and work outward toward integration of the entire system. Other approaches may be used; however, any approach that is to be used must accommodate these low-level tests. They are essential in order to verify that a code segment or function has been correctly developed and implemented in the module. Strategies include the top-down approach, the bottom-up approach, and the incremental module approach. No one of these is satisfactory in and of itself. There are too many issues involved for a single testing model to be used. For top-down tests, the testing unit is required to construct stubs that simulate the lower level units that affect the input/output of these systems or subsystems. For bottom-up tests, the testing unit is required to construct drivers in order to provide appropriate inputs for these modules. The use of incremental testing combines some of the best of both top-down and bottom-up approaches. In this instance however, we may be required to construct both stubs and drivers, depending on the relative placement of the unit. There is simply no best way to conduct the testing program. Ultimately, all three strategies are used. The choice is clearly a function of the organization that is conducting the testing program and its experiential capabilities.

It is also desirable for the overall test strategy to include high-level tests that are intended to validate major system functions against user requirements prior to acceptance testing. As we have noted, this is often not feasible and validation tests are frequently relegated to the system test environment. When this is the case, the validation test plan is implemented at the user facility on target equipment prior to final acceptance by the user.

After all the testing is complete, all errors that have been detected are corrected. There are several observations that are pertinent relative to the occurrence or frequency of occurrence of errors. These are as follows:

1. Logic errors and incorrect assumptions that are detected during any of the test procedures appear to be inversely proportional to the probability that a program path will be executed.

2. For most software products, it is likely that all logic paths will be executed once the software is installed and in use. This means that if all logic paths are not exercised during the testing process, which is very likely unless major effort is expended, the probability of software malfunction due to undetected errors will be quite high.

3. Typographical errors are usually randomly distributed throughout the code and no test can be designed to detect all these errors. Thus, they will continue to be detected and corrected during the entire life of the software.

4. Finally, validation tests may not be completed until after installation at the user site. This may lead to the not uncommon finding that the delivered software product fails to meet the intended requirements of the user.

In the sections that follow, verification testing plans and implementation strategies are presented.

5.5.1 Function and Module Testing

As we noted earlier, testing at this level requires knowledge of the internal workings of the module so that the developed test design is such that it exercises all of the internal components of the module. This type of testing is the fundamental verification test which requires that the basic units that have been programmed actually meet the detail design for that part.

Function and module testing closely examines the procedural details of the internal workings of the module under test. This type of testing environment may be a static one that requires a detailed and disciplined review of module functioning followed by a detailed analysis of the results of the programming effort or a dynamic one that actually operates the program. For dynamic testing, all possible logical paths are tested, any conditions are considered and tested, and all loops are exercised as well. In addition, the status of the program is examined at various critical points along the execution path. For static testing the code may be mathematically verified, program inspections are implemented, and source code is examined and analyzed. Program execution is not required.

Methods employed for function and module testing include manual code reviews by the test group, structured walkthroughs for more complex functions, and path analysis. Path analysis tests include operations such as, loop analysis or basis path testing [McCabe, 1976]. This mode of testing may be extremely expensive to conduct. This is so even for small programs because of the potentially large number of single loop execution times possible for a given function. When considering this approach for a large complex system, great caution must be exercised to ensure that limitations are placed on the logical paths that are selected and exercised, as the potential for exceedingly long test times and costs are very high. A typical test case design will utilize the control structure embedded within the procedural design of the module under test to ensure the adequacy of the tests to be performed. As we have noted, there is no assurance that other paths are not present that will cause problems under full system operation. Minimally, for this testing process, the important paths must be exercised in order to give some degree of assurance that the module will perform the designed functions in a proper manner.

One approach to function and module testing is the application and use of whitebox or structural testing [Pressman, 1987; Sommerville, 1989]. In this approach, the test group must possess complete information concerning the code that is proposed for test. It is also necessary to have direct knowledge of the structure of the software part. One such method is termed *basis path testing* by its developer [McCabe, 1976]. This testing procedure involves the development of a flow diagram that shows the logical control structure of the program under test and the flow of data through the program. Generally we find that a procedural design language, such as PDL, is used to describe the control flow for relatively simple functions. However, the use of these languages becomes exceedingly complex as the logical complexity of the program grows, and this approach to testing becomes very costly and time consuming.

This process may be applied to procedural design or to source code. A typical logic structure for function testing in structured notation is shown in Figure 5.9. The various logic functions are:

1. Sequence prescribes left-to-right flow.
2. The **UNTIL** function denotes that the program continues until the next step is called.
3. The **WHILE** function indicates that the program continues operating while another function is operating.
4. The **IF** function is a conditional function.
5. The **IF__THEN__ELSE** function indicates a condition and a branch to another function.

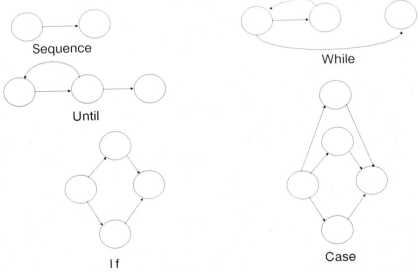

FIGURE 5.9 Structured constructs in flow graph notation

6. The **WHILE_DO** function indicates the program will do another function at the same time.

7. The **CASE_OF** function indicates the selection of a variable name on which to operate.

A flowchart and its accompanying flow graph for some of these simple functions are depicted in Figure 5.10. Nodes represent decision points, and edges or directed lines indicate the flow of control for the program. The steps that are followed in basis path testing are:

1. Using the design or code itself, draw a flow graph that corresponds to the flow of data in the unit.

2. Using McCabe's complexity measure, determine the cyclomatic complexity [McCabe, 1976] of the resultant flow graph, according to

Cyclomatic complexity = the number of edges − the number of nodes + 1

3. From this flow graph, determine a basis set of linearly independent paths.

4. Prepare test cases that force execution of each path in the basis set.

Loop testing is one of the more important of the white-box testing techniques. It focuses on the validity checking of all loops in the functional part

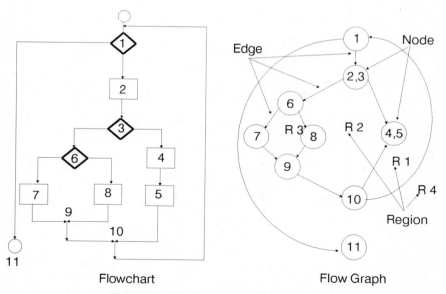

Flowchart   Flow Graph

FIGURE 5.10   Flowchart and flow graph

of the program fragment. Four basic loop types have been identified and are to be examined: (1) simple loops, (2) concatenated loops, (3) nested loops, and (4) unstructured loops. These loop types are graphically depicted in Figure 5.11.

Loop tests are intended to uncover errors such as initialization errors, indexing and incrementing errors, and bounding errors at the loop limits. With simple loops the testing procedure is relatively straightforward: skip it entirely or exercise it once. There is no need to do more than static testing with simple loops, since the path through them is easily viewed and confirmed. With nested loops, tests should commence with the innermost loop and continue outward as each loop is verified. When this is done, each nested loop may be considered as a simple loop when all paths for inner loops have been exercised. Concatenated loops may be treated as simple loops if the loops are independent or otherwise as nested loops. Once this determination is made, the appropriate test procedure is to be completed. Unstructured loops are not acceptable as good design practice and should be referred back to the designer for correction. In this instance, the complexity of the loop is such that unintended paths are likely to occur with possibly deadly impact on the program operation during testing at higher levels.

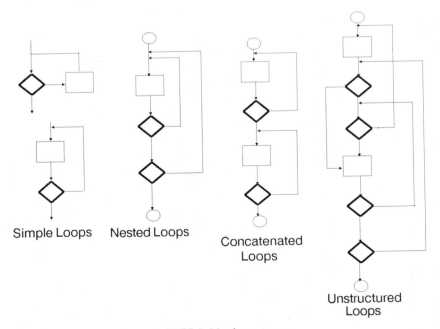

Simple Loops   Nested Loops

Concatenated
Loops

Unstructured
Loops

FIGURE 5.11   Loop types

5.5.2   System and Subsystem Testing

System and subsystem testing consists of knowing the specified functions and designing and implementing tests that are able to demonstrate that all these functions are fully operable in the module, subsystem, or system tested. Normally, this testing approach takes place at the interfaces of the software system. It is concerned with the execution of the program and the comparison of the results with the specifications. Functional operations and I/O are to be properly identified and correctly produced, and the integrity of external information, such as data files or databases, is to be correctly maintained by the test. These tests are intended to demonstrate that the program meets the operational requirements of the system at the subsystem or system level.

System and subsystem testing focuses on the functional requirements of each software part and, as such, presents a complementary approach to functional and module testing procedures. It is designed to detect errors such as missing or incorrect functions at the function level, interface errors at the module and subsystem level, performance errors, and initialization and termination errors. Generally this type of testing is applied late in the testing regime after module or unit testing has been completed and errors detected during these tests have been corrected. These tests are aimed at determination of functional validity, sensitivity to input variation, isolation of data boundaries, toleration of required data rates and volume, and the effect of specific combinations of data on system operation. Test cases are designed to indicate the presence or absence of classes of error and reduce the number of actual tests that must be run. Several ways of performing these tests have been developed and applied [Pressman, 1987; Sommerville, 1989]. These include equivalence partitioning, boundary-value analysis, cause–effect graphing, and data validation testing.

Equivalence partitioning divides input data into specific classes of data that are intended to show that classes of errors exist. In this way it is possible to uncover whole classes of errors without executing all possible tests in order to determine that a class of errors exists. As an example, if the range of a parameter is known, an equivalence test would be to examine inputs that are in the range; for example, four digits are always required. From this information test equivalence classes may be defined and then tested. An equivalence class may be determined to be input conditions that specify classes of errors that may be tested or exercising a table or simply the presence or absence of a parameter. Other possible cases might include a range for input parameters, with one valid and one invalid class defined; a specific value indicating that one valid and two invalid classes are defined; or a member of a set, which has one valid and one invalid class defined. Implementation of this test will provide information as to whether a class of errors exists for the input data of the test. Generally, a satisfactory test result for one data set does not indicate error free performance for other input data.

Boundary-value analysis testing calls for the selection of test cases that examine the extreme values for a particular function, module, or subsystem.

It is complementary testing procedure to equivalence partitioning testing. Experience from testing, completed on many software projects [Sommerville, 1989], shows that a large number of errors appear at the extremes of the error classes detected by equivalence testing. Thus, test cases should be designed to examine the areas just outside the expected range of parameters, rather than simply testing the input conditions only. Similar tests should be designed and implemented for the range of output parameters. The guide for selection of boundary value analysis is to choose parameters just outside the expected range, that is, above and below explicit values, or look at the values just above and below a minimum and maximum condition, or view an array at the boundary of the array rather than at the midrange. In this way the number of tests that must be conducted to ascertain the presence of such errors may be minimized.

Cause–effect graphing is intended to test concise logical conditions and the corresponding actions by representation of these functions in the testing regime. Causes and effects are listed and identified and a graph is constructed. Once the graph is completed, it is converted into a decision table and the decision rules are converted into test cases. The test cases thus derived are then exercised using the decision rules as developed.

Finally, data validation is used to cover areas not found by those just given. Data validation techniques include giving the system incorrect commands, incorrect syntax, correct syntax at the wrong time, omission of commands, system interrupts, and similar inputs. Data validation is particularly useful for command-driven systems.

No matter how complete and exhaustive the testing by these means has been, only the presence of errors detected by these tests will be corrected. Errors that have not been detected by these tests continue to exist in the system and await only the moment of execution to be potentially exercised.

5.5.3   Program Verification and Validation (again)

Verification and validation are well-defined terms and we now discuss them further. Verification is the process of determining whether the product of a given phase fulfills requirements established during the preceding phase. At each stage of the development process, verification means that the requirements of the previous stage have been met and faithfully carried out using good practice.* Further, with verification we are ensured that the design is both traceable to its sources and economical in the use of code.

Validation is the process of ensuring compliance with software requirements. Sound practices must be employed to confirm that the software meets the user requirements, as stated in the system level requirements. Additionally, quality and functionality goals are to be validated back to the user

---

*Good practice means that we have employed a consistent approach throughout the design and programming process and that we have used methods such as those we discussed in Chapter 4.

definitions of these. Validation assures us that the software product that has been designed and delivered will do what the user had in mind, but only as these are faithfully captured by the system level requirements definitions and specifications.

Verification is intended to demonstrate that the program is essentially correct by showing the correspondence between the program and the specification from the previous phase that defined the program. Verification answers the question "Are we building the product right?" Verification testing may take many forms, such as unit testing or integration testing, and may be applied either top-down or bottom-up, or by any combination of the test procedures that we have just examined.

A summary of these approaches is useful, as these apply to verification testing procedures. Unit testing is intended to verify interfaces, local data structure, boundary conditions, independent paths, and error-handling paths as shown in Figure 5.12. The approaches have been presented previously and they are the same for this application. It is considered as an adjunct to the coding step and occurs after source code has been developed, reviewed, and verified for correct syntax. Modules are not stand-alone units; therefore, driver and/or stub software must be developed for each test as shown in Figure 5.13. Test cases are prepared and given to the module under test as well as any driver that had to be designed and constructed for this purpose. Stubs must be designed and constructed so that the module may function in an environment as close to actual operation as possible. Test results are reviewed and any errors remaining are corrected.

Integration testing is a systematic technique for assemblage of the program structure, and at the same time conducting tests designed to uncover errors associated with module interfaces, as the system is assembled. There are three approaches to integration testing: top-down, bottom-up, and incremental test-

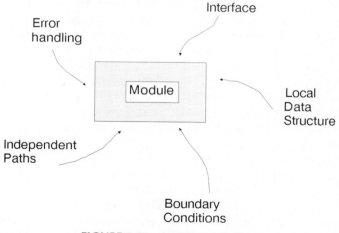

FIGURE 5.12   Unit test activities

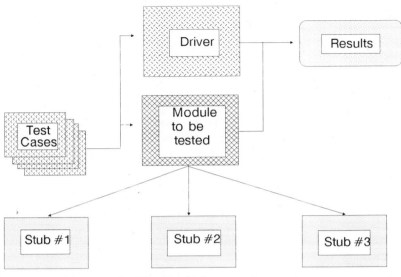

FIGURE 5.13 Unit test environment

ing. The objectives or these testing procedures are to place verified modules, subsystems, or systems into a configuration that represents the installed program and conduct integration tests.

Units that have been subjected to function and module tests are used to form the subsystem or system. The objective is to take verified unit modules and build the system structure, as called for by the design. As the initial assemblage of units is tested and the design verified, additional units are added to the system until the entire system is tested. This is a costly procedure and for this reason, is applicable primarily for smaller systems.

Top-down testing begins with the top-level system and proceeds to test the actual system using appropriate stubs and drivers to simulate lower-level components. This approach is sometimes referred to as the "big-bang" approach. It is the ultimate top-down approach and represents a full-system test with all the system modules connected as if installed. Top-down integration testing for verification is shown in Figure 5.14. In the big-bang approach, supreme confidence is exuded by the design team and the entire system is assembled and then tested for verification. This is a very costly and usually unsuccessful approach.

The third approach is called the *incremental procedure.* In this procedure, a module or system of modules that may have been tested for functional errors, is assembled and a test case is prepared. In this procedure we may start with one or several modules. We design appropriate stubs and drivers in order to perform the integration and verification tests. This approach is a combination of top-down and bottom-up integration testing. It begins some-

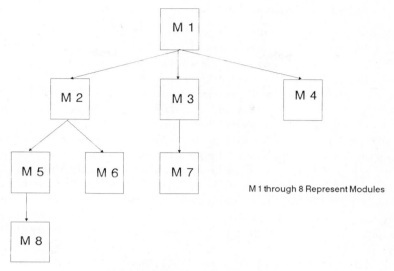

FIGURE 5.14   Top-down integration

where in the midrange of assemblage of modules and works both upward to assemble the system and downward to add lower-level modules. It combines the best features of either extreme and is the preferred approach for large-scale systems.

Validation is intended to demonstrate that the system meets the software requirements specifications defined at the onset of the development program. It is the most time-consuming and costly of all the testing applications. Validation responds to the question "Are we building the right product?" as the product is defined by the software specifications. Validation testing normally commences after all other tests are completed and any errors discovered by these tests have been corrected. This test succeeds when the software functions in accordance with the agreed-to software requirements specifications, as defined in the requirements specification documents. In most software development programs, validation test design commences at once on acceptance of the software requirements specifications. It is intended that this test ensures that all of the functional requirements have been satisfied, all performance goals have been met, all the documentation is correct and delivered to the user, and all the quality and functionality goals have been achieved (interoperability, transportability, maintainability, etc.), but only as measured from the (possibly incorrect) software requirements specifications. Validation test inputs are provided by the requirements definition and specification documents, the final integrated software product, and such user documents as are required to authenticate that the software product performs the functions, described by the software requirements specifications.

.4 Configuration Management

Configuration management is dedicated to the management of the software product after it has been verified, validated, and delivered. It is an essential part of the overall management of software development, and continues through the entire development process. When the software product is delivered for installation, a configuration review is conducted to determine that the product may be operated and maintained. A configuration review is conducted at the same time as the validation test is accomplished to ascertain that all elements of the software have been properly developed and designed, documented, and cataloged and support the maintenance activity. A configuration review commences with inputs from all the various phases. These inputs include requirements definition and specification documents; design documentation, test documentation, and other user documents as are necessary to confirm that the configuration meets the purposes of the design. A flowchart for validation testing and configuration review is shown in Figure 5.15.

The aspects of testing covered here comprise only that portion of a large-scale software development program that occurs during coding and testing portion of the software development lifecycle. There are many other tests and reviews throughout the lifecycle, which we will discuss in Chapter 6. The objectives are to uncover errors in coding and correct these. Errors at the coding phase may include unit, function, and module errors. Also, errors may be due to the integration of these fundamental building blocks that form the subsystem and system. Test cases are carefully designed to exercise a particular function or logic structure. These tests are undertaken until the entire system has undergone proper testing procedures. As is most often the case for large scale complex systems, the final validation test and configuration reviews are conducted on the target system.

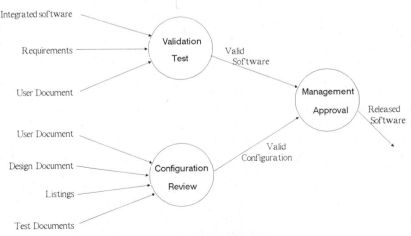

FIGURE 5.15 Configuration review process

5.6 SUMMARY

In this chapter, we have covered the essential constructs of coding practices and testing of coded modules. We have presented some needed characteristics of coding and of programming languages that are required to facilitate the programming effort. These characteristics include (1) data structures, (2) structured programming approaches to coding, (3) module coupling and cohesion, and (4) programming languages with the necessary attributes of these languages for good programming practice. These give us the means of transforming the detailed design specifications into code.

We have covered testing processes that apply to the programs developed during the coding phase. Testing provides us with the means of measuring what is delivered by the software product. It is concerned with exercising all the design requirements to ascertain that the module under test does what was intended by the design. Normally, testing does not exercise all possible paths through a particular module and as such is neither exhaustive nor complete. We have defined verification and validation testing at this phase of development and given methods to accomplish this.

Finally, we have addressed configuration management requirements necessary for production of trustworthy software products. Configuration management is intended to assure us that, once verification and validation tests have been performed on the programs generated during this phase, we may install, operate, and maintain the software product as prescribed by the software requirements specifications.

5.7 PROBLEMS

5.1. Enumerate the phases and steps within these phases that lead to the coding and testing activities.

5.2. Programming has been noted for being a profession steeped in individual creativity. Explain the meaning behind this perception.

5.3. The GOTO statement was used extensively in early programming efforts. Explain why this construction gave problems and how you would achieve the same end result without this construction.

5.4. Show, by example, that the logical constructs for high-level languages are sufficient for writing most programs.

5.5. Explain the difference between cohesion and coupling, and indicate how these two factors work together to give a measure of the quality of the module program.

5.6. Explain the differences between common coupling types, such as content coupling, control coupling, synchronization coupling, and common coupling.

5.7. What are the common attributes of most high-level programming languages?

5.8. Explain the need and use of control structures in high-level languages.

5.9. Information hiding has become a necessary part of "good" programming practice. What are the attributes that contribute to this practice. Are there problems that arise due to information hiding?

5.10. Explain the difference between data types and data typing.

5.11. Five levels of type checking are given in this chapter. Review these and explain the use of each for data type error checking.

5.12. How are pseudo-programming languages used to aid the programming activity?

5.13. 4GLs represent a major step forward in the development of automatic program generators. Explain the major advantages and disadvantages in the use of 4GLs.

5.14. What are the major attributes to be sought in a supportive programming environment?

5.15. Rank the types of programmer assistance aids determined in Problem 5.14 in order of importance for the programmer. Is this same order maintained from the perspective of the software designer?

5.16. Explain the difference between software verification and software validation.

5.17. In which phases of the software development lifecycle do you recommend application of verification and validation?

5.18. What are the cost impacts of application of verification and validation, and how do you justify expenditures for these activities?

5.19. Write a test plan for function and module testing detailed design and coden that is to follow.

5.20. What is the role of system and subsystem testing in the overall testing plan for software development.

5.21. Review the several types of tests that may be called for in system and subsystem testing, and explain the significance of each. Can certain of these tests be omitted without concern? Why?

5.22. Explain the role of configuration management in the design, development, programming, and testing of a software product.

CHAPTER 6

Software Reliability, Maintainability and Quality Assurance

In this chapter, we wish to introduce some very important notions relative to software productivity. There are many concepts that relate to this, among the most important of which are effectiveness factors, including reliability, maintainability, and quality assurance. As we have noted, these are non-functional requirements that ensure operational functionality and trustworthiness of the to-be-developed software. Cost and effort factors to produce software are of major importance as well. These will be considered in Chapter 10.

Our concern here will be with the *effectiveness* factors of reliability, maintainability, and quality assurance. There is little specific agreement concerning what these terms mean, although a general meaning seems relatively clear. We will begin our efforts, therefore, with some introductory definitions. Then, we will indicate some specific ways in which we can determine these quantities for a software development effort. Of particular interest are normative methods whereby we can identify appropriate software design and management efforts. Ideally, this would be done as part of the software requirements identification phase to ensure that the attributes of software functionality are at a very high level when the software is actually delivered to the client. Sadly, there is no completely satisfactory method to *ensure* this at present, although we can undertake efforts that will aid in enhancing functionality. We will discuss some of these functionality concepts here.

6.1 INTRODUCTION

Quality is like motherhood, god, and country. Everyone is for it, and wants everything that they do, or have, to possess this at a very high level. So, there is bound to be general agreement that *quality* should necessarily be the primary driver of the entire software design and development process. But quality is a very evasive expression. Many of us might say that we know it when we see it, even though we cannot define it. There are many problems with this sort of attitude, especially when we cannot act entirely as individuals but must function as part of a group or team. If we cannot define quality, then we will doubtlessly have difficulties in communicating it, or in assisting others to recognize it.

Quality is a subjective term and a multiattributed one as well. DoD Standard 2168 [1987] provides a very simple definition of quality:

- Software quality is the degree to which the attributes of the software enable it to perform its specified end-item use.

The IEEE Standard for Software Quality Assurance Plans [1984] uses a similar definition for quality assurance:

- Quality Assurance is a planned and systematic pattern of all actions necessary to provide adequate confidence that the item or product conforms to established technical requirements.

For the most part, these are very reasonable definitions. Each contains the notion of a metric to indicate the *degree of quality* or degree of conformance to the requirements of the user or client. Each is, however, not as specific as might be desired relative to the need for quality assurance of the software requirements specifications themselves. As software systems engineers, we must be concerned with an *engineering design* interpretation of software quality assurance.

We need appropriate metrics or indicators of software quality so as to be able to obtain an early warning indicator of potential difficulties and make appropriate design changes early in the software development lifecycle. Although not explicitly mentioned, it is our belief that the notions of conformity with standards of good practice, legality, and so on are intrinsic to these definitions. Also inherent in these definitions of quality assurance is the notion of *testing* as the primary tool of software quality assurance. This includes, as has been well noted by Beizer [1984], the notion of *software design for testability*. To do this requires appropriate software metrics. It is not good enough to identify attributes of software functionality; we must have attribute measures of functionality as well. While an attribute need not necessarily be quantifiable, an attribute measure should be. Thus the term *attribute measure* is synonymous with *metric*.

Software quality assurance and associated testing are related to, but quite different from, code debugging. A high-quality software design methodology should lead to a high level of software quality assurance and a high degree of coding error prevention. We recall from our earlier discussions that a methodology is an open set of procedures for problem solving. Clearly, there is something deficient in the methodology if the resulting design methods do not lead to a functional problem solution, and functionality includes quality assurance.

Software quality assurance indicators should lead to the detection of errors, if any, and the diagnosis of these, such as to identify them as coding errors or logic errors. Correction of coding, or logic, or specification errors is, however, an activity that should be performed by a very different group of people than those testing for quality assurance. This is the major reason for not including code debugging as a part of quality assurance. It is simply a part of the coding and unit test phase in the system lifecycle.

This leads to the notion of a three-stage process in software quality assurance and subsequent maintenance efforts. Software quality assurance will be primarily determined with *detection* of the existence of faults, and some efforts at determination of the location and type of flaw, that is to say, *diagnosis* of the fault. Software maintenance will be concerned primarily with fault *correction*, where correction is given a very general interpretation, as will be discussed. Figure 6.1 illustrates how these relate together to enhance software productivity.

Software quality assurance and associated testing can be conducted from either a structural, a functional, or a purposeful perspective. From a structural perspective, software would be tested in terms of micro-level details that involve programming language style, control, and coding particulars. From a functional perspective, software quality assurance and testing involves treating the software as a blackbox and determining whether the software performance conforms to the software technical requirements specifications. From a purposeful perspective, software must be tested to determine whether it does what the client really wishes it to do. This is generally known as *validation* testing.

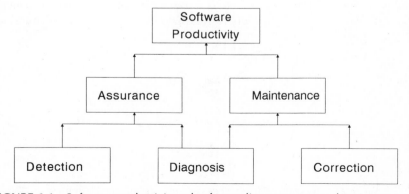

FIGURE 6.1 Software productivity roles for quality assurance and maintenance

These perspectives are surely not mutually exclusive, and each needs to be employed in a typical software quality assurance effort, as shown in Figure 6.2. There are problems in implementing each of these. Complete functional testing will often, perhaps almost always, be impossible in practice because this would require subjecting the software to all possible inputs and verifying that the appropriate output is obtained from each of them. There will generally be insufficient time to allow this, and there will often be other difficulties, also. For instance, we will generally not have sufficient ability and experiential familiarity with a particular application to identify all possible inputs.

Complete structural testing would involve identifying a number of tests such that each possible path through the code is exercised or is processed at least once. There will usually be a very large number of possible paths through any large program, and so complete structural testing is impractical. Generally, clients are not able to express perfect knowledge about their needs, and so complete purposeful testing is not feasible, either.

All this says is that we must recognize that we live in a real world. For precisely this reason, we must generally also reject formal proofs of software correctness. These generally rely on both structural and functional constructs, as they will usually necessitate very unrealistic assumptions in order to render the mathematics associated with a formal proof tractable. While these proofs of correctness may be useful for some small scale numerical analysis software development efforts, large-scale software developments will normally be much too complicated for successful application of proof of correctness approaches.

Notions of software quality indicators are quite closely related to notions of software process management. Generally, software quality indicators belong in the category of software productivity methods and tools. This was shown in Figure 1.1, which describes the three levels of software systems engineering. There are several dimensions on which to develop a taxonomy of software quality indicators. We have already mentioned the notions of structural, functional, and purposeful assurance. External versus internal quality indicators is another related dimension. The two are not independent concepts as the external quality of a software system is generally quite dependent on internal quality as well as knowledge of the purpose to which the software system will be put. Generally, this relationship is as shown in Figure 6.3.

FIGURE 6.2   Perspectives on software quality assurance

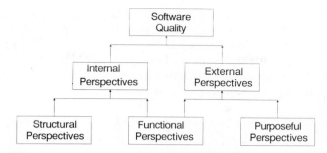

FIGURE 6.3   Internal and external quality assurance perspectives

Consistency and completeness of the code are certainly internal quality indicators, and they influence functionality, which is an external indicator. Even these internal notions are subtle in that it is not at all always clear what many of them, such as *completeness,* mean. When we consider the great variety of ways in which software can be *incomplete,* then we fully realize that the development of a *testable metric* for completeness will generally not be an easy task. This is not intended to imply that it is a simple task to develop an abstract theory of internal completeness,* but, as a pragmatic concept, completeness involves client purpose and this is an external concept. What we do infer is that, for a complex system, it does not appear possible to separate internal from external factors at all. The external factors are difficult to establish since they involve client or user needs, and the environment in which the system is to function. Once the external factors have been determined, these must somehow be translated into internal factors which, in turn, influence the external factors.

Generally, a client or user group will be initially concerned only with the *quality* of the software delivered to it in terms of usability of the *software product* for an assumed set of purposes, which are often difficult to specify in advance. But, the quality of the end product is a direct function of the quality of the *process* that produced the end product. Given that the fundamental quality of most of the computer and peripheral hardware components is quite high, the quality of an overall system will often be much more dependent on the quality of the software product than anything else. Since software development is primarily an information technology development, and since this is an intellectual technology with no real physical or material component, we see that *software processes may be the most important software product from design or management perspectives.*

As time progresses, the interest of the user group may expand to also include not only software product operation but also software revision to meet

---

*Doubtlessly, this will be very difficult.

evolving needs, and transitioning of the software product to meet new needs in an efficient and effective way. This introduction of time as an important dimension in software utilization leads to the hierarchically structured notion of quality assurance attributes, as we have indicated in Figure 1.8.

Useful rudimentary efforts towards quality infusion into software development efforts involve three steps:

1. Identification of quality attributes important for a specific situation
2. Determining importance weights for these attributes
3. Defining and instrumenting operational methods of determining the attribute scores for specific software development approaches.

When only a single software development approach is being considered, we need an evaluation of this approach. Often, we wish to select from among potentially competing software development approaches and the multiattribute utility theory approach [Keeney and Raiffa, 1976; Sage, 1977] may be quite useful for this. We will describe this approach in some detail in Section 6.3. We will also present two rather different approaches to the evaluation of software quality. One of these will be based on compensatory trade-off among performance across attributes. The other will assume that a fixed level of performance on each attribute has been established and a software product will be said to meet standards, or be assured, if performance is above the minimum established across all attributes included in the standard.

Software quality assurance is the name often associated with efforts that lead to the equivalent of a *guarantee* for a software product. Generally, this guarantee is with respect to the software quality attribute measures exceeding minimum performance standards on all quality attributes. But there are other approaches that allow compensatory trade-offs. *Quality control* is the act of inspecting an established product, that is to say the result of a specific software development process, to make sure that it meets some minimum defined set of standards. Here we are much more concerned, as engineers, with the more general term "quality assurance," which also implies design for quality, and not just inspections to eliminate the unworthy.

Quality assurance involves those systems management processes, systems design methodologies, and software development techniques and tools that act to ensure that the resulting software product meets or exceeds a set of multiattributed standards of excellence.

Software quality assurance activities are generally related to those software verification and validation activities that are conducted throughout all stages of the software development lifecycle. Since quality assurance also involves software management processes, this is a topic that must necessarily also be considered in Chapter 9, where we study software process management.

Software *verification* is the activity of comparing the software product produced at the output of each phase of the lifecycle with the product produced at the output of the preceding phase. It is this latter output that serves both as the input to the next phase and as a specification for it. *validation* compares the output product at each stage of the software In. occasionally only the final product phase, to the initial system requiremen. Often these activities are performed by people outside of the software de-velopment organization and the prefix "independent" is sometimes used in these cases. Figure 6.4 illustrates the difference in these important concepts.

Verification and validation generally do not address the appropriateness of the system requirements and may not, as a consequence, determine whether a system really satisfies user needs. While verification seeks to determine whether the software product is being built correctly, validation seeks to determine whether the right product has been produced from an assumed set of correct specifications. So, verification and validation are quality control techniques and a part of quality assurance.

The formal process of determining that a software product is suitable for an intended application is often termed *software certification*. The certification of software is a warranty or certification that the software will perform in accordance with agreed-on requirements.

Obtaining a high degree of software productivity requires a number of related software product assurance approaches. Our efforts in this chapter will proceed as follows. In our next section, we introduce a partial taxonomy for quality control and testing. Following this, we present some approaches

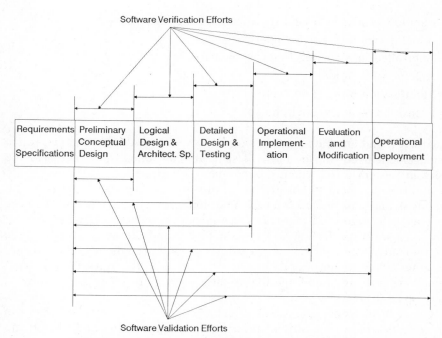

FIGURE 6.4 Range of verification and validation efforts

to testing software quality. This will naturally lead to a discussion of software maintenance concepts, the topic that follows next and which concludes this chapter.

6.2 A TAXONOMY OF ATTRIBUTES AND ASSOCIATED METRICS FOR SOFTWARE QUALITY ASSURANCE

In our introductory Chapter 1, we introduced a number of indicators of software quality. We identified 43 attributes there, and there are doubtlessly many more that could have been identified. In this section, we will provide a definition of these and some indication of how each can be measured or tested. In our next section, we will develop a multiattribute model for software quality assurance that will make use of these indicators.

There are many perspectives that can be taken relative to software quality indicators. It is possible to speak of the metrics that should be used at the different phases in the software development lifecycle. We realize that this would represent an internal assessment of quality. An external assessment of the developed and implemented software would generally need to be made also to ensure that concerns of software product revision and software product transition are addressed, as well as that of software operational functionality. This reflects the fact that throughout its lifecycle, software typically undergoes

Identification of need and specification of requirements

Initial design and development

Controlled introduction to a customer market

Release to customers

Modification to meet evolving needs

Transition to a new environment

Attributes, and attribute measures or metrics, are needed that serve project management needs during initial design and controlled introduction of the software system to the client group. There are also needs at the corporate level of management to ensure that a software product should be released, modified, and transitioned to a new environment and perhaps a new customer base as well. Figure 6.5 illustrates this management-oriented view of these phases in software evolution. From this figure and the discussion here, we see that software quality assurance efforts should serve the need of software program management in obtaining an efficient and effective software development venture and rapid solutions to difficulties at any phase in the software development lifecycle.

Upper-level management will often need software quality indicators in order to be able to quantify software development quality and to compare different and potentially competing development programs on the basis of

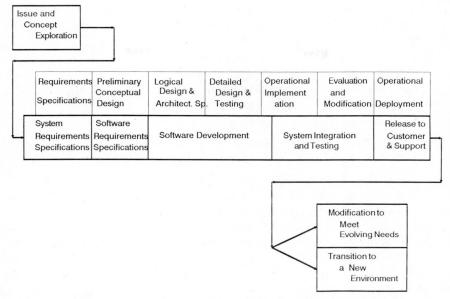

FIGURE 6.5   Expansion of a typical software lifecycle model

costs and effectiveness. These metrics allow management to select appropriately from among the potentially competing organizations that propose to assist in the support effort. The use of appropriate metrics allows for and supports the goals of better responsiveness to client and customer needs.

6.2.1   Definitions and Acronyms for Quality Assurance

There are a rather large number of acronyms in use today to describe various software quality assurance indicators. Among these, which we list alphabetically, are:

CDR = Critical Design Review   The software design description (SDD) is examined to determine the extent to which it satisfies the requirements of the software requirements specifications (SRS) in a critical design review (CDR). Special concern is associated with determining that all design specification change requests have been accommodated.

FQR = Formal Qualification Review   The formal qualification review (FQR) is an acceptance testing procedure designed to determine whether the final coded software system or subsystem conforms with the final system technical specifications and requirements.

FCA = Functional Configuration Audit   A functional configuration audit, (FCA), sometimes called a *functional audit* (FA), is an audit held prior to final software delivery to verify that all the requirements of the software requirements specifications (SRSs) have been met by each of the software subsystems and associated documentation.

IPA = In-Process Audit   At various times in the software development process, in-process audits (IPAs) may be conducted to evaluate consistency of the software design at that phase of the lifecycle, including:

1. Code performance versus design documentation
2. Hardware and software interface specifications
3. Functional requirements and design implementations
4. Functional requirements and review–audit prescriptions

It should be noted that an IPA involves both a functional configuration audit (FCA) and a physical configuration audit (PCA).

MR = Managerial Review   Managerial reviews are held periodically to determine the extent of execution of the software quality assurance plan (SQAP).

OTE = Operational Test and Evaluation   Operational test and evaluation (OTE) generally involves determination by an outside independent organization of the extent to which an operational software product meets the requirements and needs of the client or user. This is generally a purposeful evaluation.

PCA = Physical Configuration Audit   The purpose of a physical configuration audit (PCA), sometimes called *physical audit* (PA), is to evaluate whether the software and associated documentation are both internally consistent and suitable for delivery to the client. This audit examines actual detail code.

PDR = Preliminary Design Review   The purpose of a preliminary design review (PDR) is to enable an evaluation of the extent of acceptability of the preliminary software design, as specified by a preliminary version of the software design description (SDD). It represents a technical review of the basic design approach for each major software subsystem. Software development and verification tools are identified. If changes are recommended, particular care is used to determine their propagation throughout the system development lifecycle in a consistent manner.

SCM = Software Configuration Management   Software configuration management (SCM) is the process of identification of software system configuration at specific points in time along the lifecycle such as to enable maintenance of the traceability and integrity of the software configuration throughout the development lifecycle. While this is not formally a part of quality assurance, the specific steps to determine quality assurance activities are directly related to SCM results.

SDD = Software Design Document   The software design document (SDD) is prepared to indicate the design specifications for the software that is to be developed. A SDD defines the software architecture, modules, and interfaces for a software system that (presumably) satisfies the specified software requirements. It also contains the computer code that describes or specifies the software capabilities.

SDR = Software Design Review The software design review (SDR) occurs after configuration management has been accomplished and the SDD has been written. The SDR should describe each of the major subsystems that comprise the overall design specifications, such as databases and internal interfaces. Tools required for verification are also identified as a by-product of this effort.

SDP = Software Development Plans The processes, procedures, activities, and standards that are used for software management, including software quality assurance and management, are often denoted by the collective term "software development plans" (SDPs).

SQA = Software Quality Assurance Formally, software quality assurance (SQA) is the extent or degree to which a software product is in conformity with established (technical) requirements.

SQAP = Software Quality Assurance Plan The plan or systematic effort contemplated to determine, or measure, the extent of software quality assurance is known as the software quality assurance plan (SQAP).

SQPP = Software Quality Program Plan There is generally a meta-level planning activity that leads to the specific SQAP. The software quality program plan is the guiding force behind this effort. It is this program plan that leads to the projects that comprise the SQAP.

SRR = Software Requirements Review A review to evaluate, and determine the adequacy of, the requirements that are stated in the software requirements specifications (SRS) is called a software requirements review (SRR). Planning for software testing is accomplished here.

SRS = Software Requirements Specifications The software requirements specification (SRS) should clearly and precisely describe each of the essential requirements for the software as well as the external interface. Each of these specifications should be defined so that it is possible to develop an objective metric to verify and validate achievement level by a prescribed method.

SVVP = Software Verification and Validation Plan The software verification and validation plan (SVVP) describes the inspection, analysis, demonstration, or test methods that are used to:

1. Verify that the requirements in the SRS are implemented in the design expressed in the SDD, and that the design expressed by the SDD is indeed implemented by the resulting operational code.
2. Validate that the executable code complies with the requirements that are contained in the SRS.

SVVR = Software Verification and Validation Report The results of the execution of the SVVP and the results of all reviews, audits, and tests of the SQA plan are contained in the software verification and validation report (SVVR).

Figure 6.6 illustrates how these reviews and audits flow from one to another, and how they are matched to the various phases in the software lifecycle. The matrix in Figure 6.7, when completed, will contain the many activities

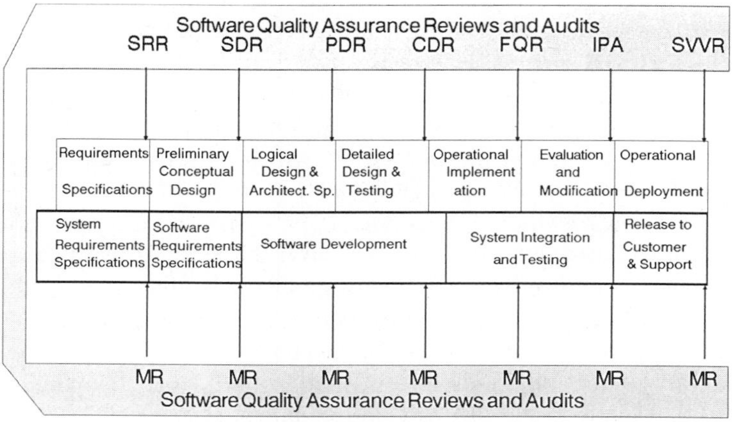

FIGURE 6.6 Typical sequence of software review and audits

	QUALITY ASSURANCE	PROJECT MANAGEMENT
PHASE 1		
PHASE 2		
PHASE 3		
PHASE 4		
PHASE 5		
PHASE 6		
PHASE 7		

FIGURE 6.7 Activity matrix to be completed as part of SQAP

involved in software quality assurance. A major objective in development of a SQAP is to complete the entries in this matrix, and accomplish them.

This concludes a brief discussion of the various plans, reviews, and audits associated with software quality and software quality assurance. Some of these may be implemented as metrics on a continuous scale, and some as metrics on a binary (acceptable or not acceptable) scale. Each has uses and a continuous scale may be more or less appropriate than a binary scale, depending on the intended use. Some of these are performed in a static fashion, through the examination of code, documentation, and requirements. Others may be performed through execution of the code itself. We will return to a discussion of this in the next section.

6.2.2 Software Quality Assurance Attributes, Errors, and Plans

Our efforts in Chapter 1 have led to the identification of a number of attributes of software quality and related functionality concerns. It would be possible to provide a brief definition of these to enable us to measure these for a given software product. A more appropriate method of approach is to structure these such that we obtain an attribute tree that will enable the meaning of each of these to become apparent through the hierarchical structure. Generally, a structure that relates important performance attributes should be developed for each specific software product to be evaluated as attributes of importance will vary from software system to software system. One of the first tasks that confronts us in developing this hierarchy is the decomposition approach. In Chapter 1 we developed Figure 1.8, which is repeated as Figure 6.8, from the perspective of *maintenance use types.* Here, software evaluation would be scored along the dimensions of *maintenance use type* dimensions of

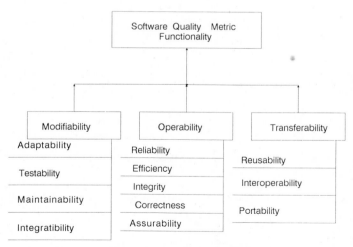

FIGURE 6.8 One possible software quality attribute tree

present operability, future modifiability, and *future transferability* (or transitioning) to a new environment.

This may be the most appropriate approach to structuring for quality assurance measurement. If, for example, one particular software system scored high on operability and modifiability but low on transferability, it should not be considered seriously as a candidate for transitioning. This is, of course, a quality control perspective on the software. From a design perspective, it would be acceptable to design software with a low performance on transferability if, for some reason, it is known that the software will never be a candidate for this use.

It would also be possible to structure the quality assurance attribute tree such that the first-level attributes are those of structure, function, and purpose. In doing this, we would tend to be evaluating the software along dimensions that resemble specific testing instruments that might be utilized to measure software acceptability. Figure 6.2 represents this sort of structure. Our next subsection will present a discussion of methods for software measurement and testing patterned after this structure.

Sometimes an initially identified set of attributes turns out to be difficult to understand for purposes of identifying quantifiable attribute measures and scoring. In this case, it is usually beneficial to disaggregate those at the lowest level that was initially defined into lower level attributes. Figure 6.9a–c shows this for each of the attributes defined in Figure 6.8.

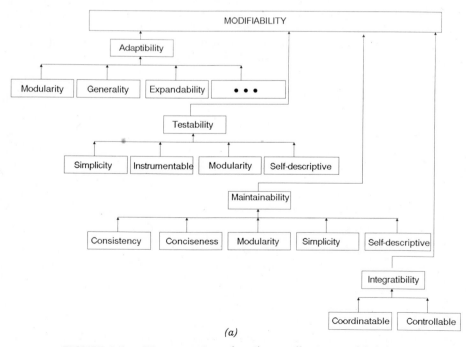

(a)

FIGURE 6.9a   Disaggregation of attributes affecting modifiability

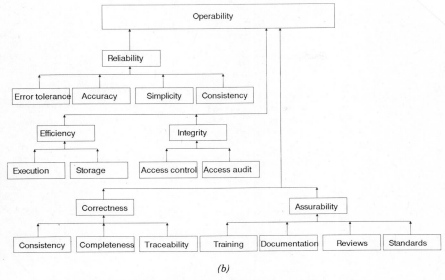

(b)

FIGURE 6.9b Disaggregation of the operability attribute

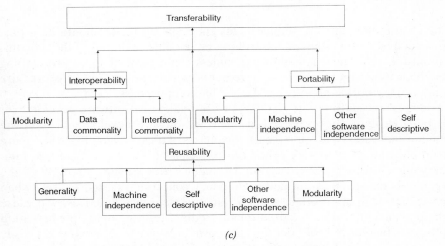

(c)

FIGURE 6.9c Disaggregation of the transferability attribute

Sometimes attribute measures are difficult to work with because the associated attributes are not *preferentially independent* [Keeney and Raiffa, 1976; Sage, 1977]. Decomposition on a different basis is then called for in many cases. It is also possible to disaggregate the quality attributes according to the phases of the system lifecycle. This would yield a structure like that of Figure 6.9*d*. A possible problem with this approach is that evaluation at

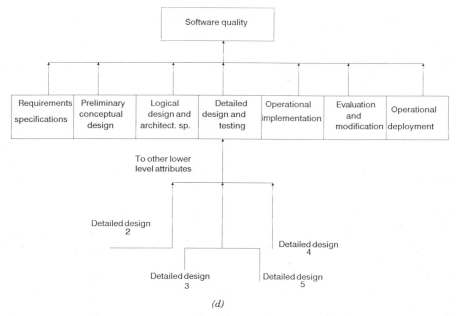

FIGURE 6.9d   Decomposition of quality attributes at each phase in the SLC

the system and software requirements specification phase should be a purposeful evaluation. Generally it will not be possible to do this at the time this initial lifecycle phase is completed, unless some form of rapid prototyping has been used to generate the requirements specifications. Thus, this structure may or may not be appropriate for evaluation purposes.

One of the unfortunate realities of life relative to software development is that the majority of effort consumed in software development is in the coding and testing and implementation phases of the software lifecycle. Figure 6.10 illustrates this in very general terms. One of the major hypotheses underlying software productivity improvement is that greater attention to the requirements specification and preliminary conceptual design phases, when associated with appropriate software quality assurance practices, will cause the percentage of time required for the coding, testing, and implementation phases to be reduced considerably, as shown in Figure 6.11. What is not easily apparent in these figures is that the total effort required is spread out more in time, as shown in Figures 6.12 and 6.13. Also, the cumulative effort for the coding and testing, and implementation, phases is reduced significantly. Figures 6.14 and 6.15 illustrate this, again in conceptual terms. This is also hypothesized to lead to overall effort reductions for the software development process, as well as the production of higher-quality software.

We believe that this will result primarily from the use of the macro-enhancement tools and effective software process management efforts, as we

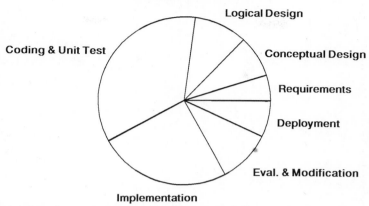

FIGURE 6.10   Typical percentage effort distribution by phase of the SLC

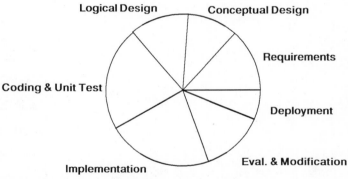

FIGURE 6.11   Potential effort distribution per SLC phase with enhanced issue finding (such as purposeful rapid prototyping)

noted before. Our discussions here suggest augmentation of this development such that we also specifically embed the notions of automatic production of code, systems design, and quality assurance approaches to contribute to a *software development process*, as shown in Figure 6.16.

Software quality assurance involves examination of software products, at various phases of the lifecycle of software development, to determine concordance with requirements and specifications. The *specifications* include system and software requirements specifications, documentation specifications,

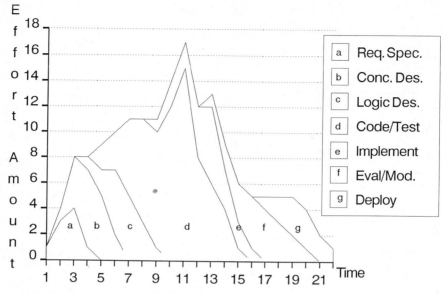

FIGURE 6.12   Conventional development cycle phased effort over time

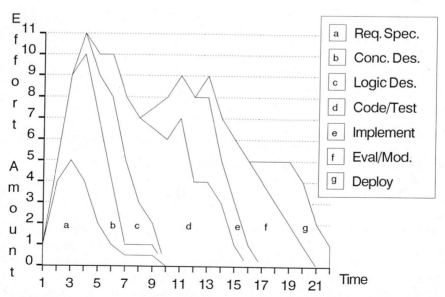

FIGURE 6.13   Enhanced requirement specifications -phased effort over time

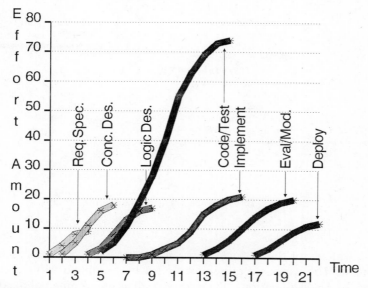

FIGURE 6.14   Cumulative effort amount by phase in conventional development cycle

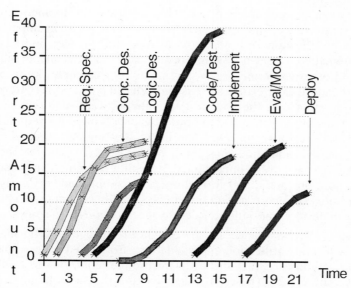

FIGURE 6.15   Cumulative effort amount by phase for enhanced requirement specifications

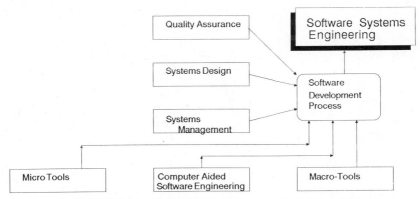

FIGURE 6.16   The software systems engineering process

and specifications for the various stages of software and systems design and management. The various requirements must be examined with respect to their concordance with various standards as well as environmental needs and user needs. When any aspect of a software product is incomplete, inconsistent, incorrect, or otherwise *imperfect*, errors will almost surely occur.

These errors may be associated with either of the three fundamental systems engineering steps of formulation, analysis, or interpretation. And, of course, errors may occur at any phase of the software development lifecycle. The most significant errors are generally those that result in imperfect requirements specifications. These errors include, but are not limited to, incorrect statements of user needs and result in incomplete, inconsistent, infeasible, and otherwise *imperfect* requirements. For example, let us assume that analysis and design errors are first introduced by imperfect translation of user requirements, at the system level, into software requirements. This results in an incomplete, inconsistent, or infeasible set of design requirements. When these are not detected until late in the development lifecycle, it can be very expensive and time-consuming to correct errors; as we noted in Chapter 3. Thus, it is very important that quality assurance and associated error detection, diagnosis, and correction, be accomplished very early in the lifecycle. Major cost overruns and time delays are almost impossible to avoid because of imperfect translation of design specifications into source code.

Software quality assurance can be enhanced through walkthroughs and inspections, formal verification and validation efforts, and other approaches that provide confidence that the software product conforms to established technical requirements. These are expensive and time-consuming activities. They must provide benefits that justify their cost, or their use may be counterproductive. This is especially the case when they result in software development delays without a corresponding increase in software functionality. *It is very important that we keep the normative component of quality assurance in mind. While it is important that we detect and ultimately correct errors, it is much better to establish lifecycle design and development procedures so that error occurrence is minimized.*

As we have already noted, preparation of a SQAP is a fundamental task in software quality assurance.

The duties of a software quality assurance team, which may often both write and implement the plan, include:

1. Development and implementation of quality assurance standards for a specific software development effort, including the practices, procedures, and policies that comprise the software quality assurance plans
2. Development and implementation of metrics, testing tools, and other quality assurance techniques
3. Implementation of the resulting quality assurance plan, including documentation of a final quality assurance report

The essential components of the SQAP include:

1. Identification of the scope and purpose of the plan
2. Identification of the organizational structure for implementing the plan, including specific tasks to be performed by members of the group
3. Identification of documents that need to be prepared, and methods to determine quality and adequacy of this documentation
4. Identification of metrics, standards, procedures, and practices, including reviews and audits, that will be used in implementing the plan
5. Identification of methods that will be used in collecting, maintaining, and recording quality assurance information
6. Implementation of each of these

In order to implement the approaches suggested here for software quality assurance, we need to be concerned with development, evaluation, and measurement approaches to enable instrumentation of software quality assurance as a viable approach. This requires identification of associated methods for software measurement and test. In these efforts, it is critical to develop approaches that will increase the possibility of early detection of the potential for errors. We must also be able to apply appropriate diagnosis and correction at these early phases, where such changes are much less consumptive of time, effort, and money than they are at the later phases of the lifecycle. We will turn our attention to these topics in the next two sections of this chapter and in our subsequent efforts in later chapters.

6.3   A MULTIATTRIBUTE APPROACH TO QUALITY ASSURANCE EVALUATION MEASUREMENTS

The purpose of quality assurance approaches is to provide tools for improving software performance in the sense of enhanced and assured quality. One class of evaluation techniques is decision analysis based on multiattribute utility theory (MAUT). One of the most useful features of the MAUT-based approach is that it provides guidelines and a framework for selecting relevant alternatives, that seek to assure software quality, by means of analyzing the outcomes that result from using these alternative approaches. As a by-product of this, we obtain an evaluation measure for each alternative considered. Decomposition is essential for the analysis of complex alternative evaluation problems. This multiattribute-based approach presumes that candidate alternatives can be studied in terms of different dimensions or attributes of software quality. By decomposing the decision space, and subsequently analyzing the relative preferences of persons responsible for picking a quality assurance strategy on each dimension and across the different dimensions, MAUT-based decision analysis offers a prescriptive procedure for alternative selection on the basis of normative behavior for rational choice.

Information requirements are determined primarily by the functional form of the quality assurance situation structural model that is used for evaluation. Consequently, the coordination of the assessment step would be a straightforward process if all relevant information concerning all important aspects of quality assurance were precise and readily available. There are several real difficulties in obtaining consistent numerically scaled utility functions, even for a single-dimensional attribute or utility space. Also, related difficulties in the assessment of probabilities and risk attitude coefficients often impose barriers to obtaining the precise, consistent, and complete information that is needed for direct veridical use of the MAUT process. In part for this reason, many of the applications of MAUT to software evaluation efforts do not attempt the scaling truly needed to ensure that the results of the evaluation process are as sound mathematically and behaviorally as they might be. Nevertheless, many studies show that even use of improper scaling approaches yield quite robust solutions to evaluation problems that are better than those that result from wholistic judgment [Dawes, 1979; Sage, 1981].

In this section, we examine several operational and behavioral issues in the use of MAUT-based evaluation models.

6.3.1   The MAUT Framework for Decision Analysis

In the decision analysis and alternative evaluation paradigm [Keeney and Raiffa, 1976; Sage 1977], it is assumed that a set of feasible alternatives $A = (a_1, \ldots, a_m)$ and a set $(X_1, \ldots, X_n)$ of attributes or evaluators of the quality assurance alternatives can be identified. Associated with each alternative a in A, there is a corresponding consequence $[X_1(a), X_2(a), \ldots, X_n(a)]$ in the n-dimensional consequence space $X = X_1, X_2, \ldots, X_n$ of software quality attributes.

From this perspective, the software quality assurance problem is to choose an alternative a in A so that the payoff $[X_1(a), \ldots, X_n(a)]$ will be "satisfying" or perhaps even the largest possible value. It is always possible in principle to compare the values of each $X_i(a)$ for different alternatives but, in most situations, the magnitudes of $X_i(a)$ and $X_j(a)$ for $i \neq j$ can not be meaningfully compared since they may be measured in totally different units. Thus, a scaler valued utility function defined on the attributes $(X_1, \ldots, X_n)$ is sought that will allow comparison of the alternatives across the attributes. The existence of this scaler valued function, as a mechanism for representation and selection of alternatives in a utility space, follows from the fundamental representation theorem of simple preferences.

A primary interest in the literature on MAUT is to structure and assess a utility function u of the form

$$u[X_1(a), \ldots, X_n(a)] = f\{u_1[X_1(a)], \ldots, u_n[X_n(a)], k_1, \ldots, k_m\}$$

where u_i is a utility function over the single attribute X_i, k_j are scaling constants, and f aggregates the values of the single attribute utility functions so as to enable one to compute the scaler utility of the alternatives. The utility functions u and u_i are assumed to be monotonic and bounded. Usually, they are scaled by

$$u(x^*) = 1$$
$$u(x^0) = 0$$
$$u_i(x_i^*) = 1$$
$$u_i(x_i^0) = 0$$

for all i. Here $\mathbf{x}^* = (x_1^*, x_2^*, \ldots, x_n^*)$ designates the most desirable consequence and $\mathbf{x}^0 = (x_1^0, x_2^0, \ldots, x_n^0)$ the least desirable. In a similar way, the symbols x_i^* and x_i^0 refer to the best and worst consequence, respectively, for each attribute X_i, that is, $x_i^* = x_i(a^*)$, where a^* is the best alternative for attribute i, and $x_i^0 = x_i(a_0)$, where a_0 is the worst alternative for attribute i.

We have very briefly described the case where associated with each alternative there is a known consequence that follows with certainty from implementation of the alternative. This is often called the "certain-decision" case, and is the case of most interest for software quality assurance efforts.

The foundations of principles for decisionmaking under risk are provided by the classical work of von Neumann and Morgenstern [1953]. The implications of this work are that probabilities and utilities can be used to calculate the expected utility of each alternative and that alternatives with higher expected utilities should be preferred.

6.3.2 Independence Concepts

Multiattribute utility theory provides representation theorems, based on various forms of independence across the attributes, that describe the functional form of the multiattribute utility u as an additive, multiplicative, or multilinear function of the conditional single attribute utility functions u_i [Keeney and Raiffa, 1976; Sage, 1977].

We provide an overview here of independence concepts and related implications for the case of certainty and for the case involving risk in a decisionmaking context. Following this, we provide some specific illustration of computations of software quality using these approaches. Our first two independence concepts concern simple preference judgments among alternatives. They imply invariance of simple preference orders with common changes in attribute levels.

> *Preferential Independence*   Given a set of attributes $X = \{X_1, X_2, \ldots, X_n\}$, a subset of attributes Y is preferentially independent of the complementary set Y^c if and only if the preference order of consequences involving only changes in the levels in Y does not depend on the levels at which attributes in Y^c are held fixed.

We are mostly interested in the case where the subsets Y are the attributes $X_i, i = 1, \ldots, n$. This is the case where each attribute X_i is preferentially independent of its complement. This interest occurs because of the following reasons:

1. It is the weakest form of independence that we can have
2. It holds naturally in most decision situations
3. It is relatively easy to check for independence in analytically and behaviorally relevant ways.

> *Mutual Preferential Independence*   The attributes $X_1, X_2, \ldots, X_n$ are mutually preferentially independent if every subset Y of these attributes is preferentially independent of its complementary set Y^c. Obviously, this is a stronger condition than preferential independence, and more difficult to justify.

We now discuss independence concepts relevant to the case involving risk. These concepts describe preference behavior of the software quality assurance evaluator involving lotteries instead of consequences that occur with certainty. By a lottery x^j we mean a set of possible consequences, each associated with a known probability value. Preferences over lotteries reflect both strength of preference and risk attitude behavior of the software quality assurance evaluator.

> *Utility Independence*   A subset of attributes Y is utility independent of its complement Y^c if the conditional preference order for lotteries involving only changes in the levels of attributes in Y does not depend on the levels at which the attributes in Y^c are held fixed.

Similar to the certainty case, the case where the subsets Y are the attributes X_i, $i = 1,2, \ldots , n$, that is, the case where each attribute is utility independent, is of significant importance in that it is the weakest form of independence for the case involving risk. Utility independence is a generalization of preferential independence for the certainty case. Some important definitions are:

> *Mutual Utility Independence*   Attributes $X_1, X_2, \ldots , X_n$ are said to be mutually utility independent if every subset of $(X_1, X_2, \ldots , X_n)$ is utility-independent of its complement.
>
> *Additive Independence*   Attributes $X_1, X_2, \ldots , X_n$ are additive-independent if preferences over lotteries involving levels of $X_1, X_2, \ldots , X_n$ depend only on the marginal probability distribution of each attribute and not on their joint probability distribution.

Additive independence is a very strong assumption, and it most likely will not hold, in any strict sense, in most real alternative evaluation problems, including those associated with quality assurance. We might expect that preferences over lotteries involving consequences in $X_1, X_2, \ldots , X_n$ depend not only on the marginal probability of the respective attributes but also on their joint probability distribution since in fact they occur conjointly. In addition, additive independence is often very difficult to test in practice. Nevertheless, it is a very desirable goal in practice to identify, define, and structure a set of attributes that are additively independent, or nearly so.

6.3.3   Additive Representations

The simplicity of additive decision models has motivated the development of a wide variety of methods for solving complex multiattribute decision problems based on this very simple representation. It would be a simple task if we could calculate the utility of the alternatives in A by merely calculating the utility on each attribute separately using preference information on these, and then adding them. This special case of the more general representation problem is usually referred to as the *additive conjoint* representation.

We review here some of the works concerned with finding conditions that are necessary and/or sufficient for the existence of an additive representation in decision models and relate them to the structural conditions that these impose in the problem.

The following theorem, relating mutual preferential independence and the existence of an additive representation, is presented in Keeney and Raiffa [1976]:

> *Additive Representation Theorem*   Given attributes $X_1, X_2, \ldots , X_n$, it can be shown that an additive utility function

$$u(x_1, \ldots , x_n) = \sum_{i=1}^{n} k_i u_i(x_i)$$

exists if and only if the attributes are mutually preferentially independent, where:

1. u is normalized by

$$u(x_1^0, x_2^0, \ldots, x_n^0) = 0 \quad \text{and} \quad u(x_1^*, x_2^*, \ldots, x_n^*) = 1$$

2. The expression

$$u_i = u_i[X_i(a)]$$

is that of a single-attribute utility function normalized by

$$u_i(x_i^0) = 0 \quad \text{and} \quad u_i(x_i^*) = 1$$

3. Finally, the multiplicative scaling constants are determined by

$$k_i = u(x_i^*, x_i^0), \, i = 1,2, \ldots, n$$

In theory, there exists a feasible way to test conditions for the existence of an additive representation such as this. However, the number of empirical tests required to determine whether the attributes are mutually preferentially independent may grow very rapidly with increases in the number of alternatives m and the number of attributes n. For example, if $m = n = 5$, we will have to make 375 tests of preference orders while for $m = n = 6$, the number is 1116. In practice, care is given to identify attributes that appear to satisfy this property. Usually, there is no detailed validation of the additivity requirements. Fortunately, there is evidence that the results obtained by using the various preferential independence assumptions are quite good, even though the assumptions may not be precisely satisfied.

This section has presented a brief overview of representation theorems of multiattribute decision models. Clearly, this is a deep and specialized subject. Often, claims are made that suggest such desirable occurrences as *additivity* and *independence* without clearly stating, or perhaps even recognizing the several types of independence and representations. *It is very helpful to be aware of this.* As might be expected, the simpler the functional form of the model, the more restrictive the assumptions on the structure of the decision situation and about the software quality assurance evaluator's behavior in judgment and choice. No representation theorem exists that describes the form of u for the weakest independence condition in the certainty case, namely, preferential independence. In the case involving risk, utility independence resulted in the multilinear representation and mutual utility independence in the multiplicative representation. While these independence conditions are relatively weak and may hold in a large number of cases, they result in rather complex functional representations.

The simplest representation, the additive model, required the conditions of an additive conjoint structure in the certainty case and additive independence in the case involving risk. Additive independence, besides being very difficult to show, is often intuitively unjustifiable. The conditions of the additive conjoint structure are very restrictive, at least in the context of multiattribute decision problems. This suggests that the discretization of a multiattribute decision problem can not be arbitrary if it is represented by an additive model. Or, if the problem is naturally discrete, it must have the special characteristics implied by the additive conjoint structure.

6.3.4   Dominance and the Efficient Frontier

We will now discuss various methods intended to screen candidate alternatives in evaluation activities. Some of these are based on the concept of dominance defined as follows. We suppose that there are many alternatives, and let alternatives a_1, a_2 be represented in the consequence space as

$$a_1 = [X_1(a_1), \ldots, X_n(a_1)]$$
$$a_2 = [X_1(a_2), \ldots, X_n(a_2)]$$

We say that a_1 dominates a_2 whenever a_1 is at least as good as a_2 for every consequence $X_i, i = 1, \ldots, n$, and strictly better for at least one consequence.

We note that the notion of dominance requires knowledge of only the ordinal preference of the alternatives for each consequence and not any comparison or trade-off among consequences. The notion of dominance is very often used to generate the set of nondominated alternatives and discard those that are dominated since they, presumably, cannot be candidates for the best alternative. It is possible to show that the concept of dominance as a criterion for the generation of the nondominated set of alternatives implies at least preferential independence across the attributes, a condition that does not always exist.

For any feasible alternative a_i in the alternative space A, there is a corresponding consequence $[X_1(a_i), \ldots, X_n(a_i)]$ representing that alternative in the consequence space X. Let R be the set of consequences in X whose members are associated with alternatives in A. The set R is the so-called range set of the vector mapping defined on the domain A. The set of consequences of R that are not dominated is called the efficient frontier of R or the Pareto optimal set.

6.3.5   Decision Analysis Methods

The method of decision analysis, based on multiattribute utility theory, consists of four major steps:

1. **Identification of the Decision Problem** This includes the generation of

alternatives and the specification of objectives and hence attributes to be used in the evaluation of alternatives.

2. **Assessment of the Possible Consequences for Each Alternative** In the case of certainty, this consists in specifying the unique known consequence that follows for sure from implementation of each alternative. When various possible consequences may occur, a probability distribution function over the set of attributes for each alternative must be determined.

3. **Determination of Preferential Information** The structure of the model is determined and the quantification of its parameters is made. This step requires relevant, precise, and consistent information about value assessment, value trade-offs, and risk attitude.

4. **Evaluation of Alternative and Sensitivity Analysis** The information gathered is synthesized by use of the expected utility criterion. The alternative with the highest expected utility is the most desired. Finally, the sensitivity of the decision, to a variety of changes, is explored in order to gain some confidence concerning the recommended evaluation or decision.

Figure 6.17 presents a graphic description of the steps of decision analysis, sequenced in the order in which the steps are usually accomplished. As is apparent, these steps simply correspond to the basic systems engineering steps of formulation, analysis, and interpretation. Figure 6.17 does explicitly show the iteration and feedback made possible by the sensitivity analysis, and the subsequent revision of the outputs of these steps as a result of this.

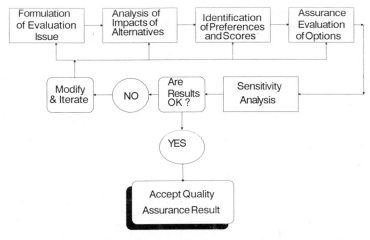

FIGURE 6.17   Steps in the evaluation of software quality assurance alternatives

6.3.6   Assessment Methods

In applying the decision analysis paradigm for the resolution of complex decision problems, assessment methods to obtain precise utility values are needed. The fundamental results for the representation of simple preference and degree of preference, and the classical results of von Neuman and Morgenstern [1953] when risk is involved, guarantee the existence of a real-valued utility function that quantifies value judgment and risk attitude of the software quality assurance evaluator. These results give rise to the development of various assessment methods to quantify precisely the underlying utility functions. The precise assessment of utility values is deemed necessary in order to operationalize these results in effective decision aids. In this section, some of the most widely used methods for utility assessment are briefly overviewed.

Direct Elicitation   The software quality assurance evaluator is asked to assign objects from a measurable set to the levels of a set of attributes, thereby indicating its relative utility. The assignment might be into preassigned categories (e.g., fair, good, excellent), each associated with a particular worth score. This technique is used extensively in psychometric studies, and its application in decision analysis is a direct extension of existing procedures in that field. The assignments could be also into numerical values on a predefined scale. The range of the scale could be anchored, with 0 to 100 being the most common anchor points used. Alternately this assignment could be left open such that it could then be normalized after the elicitation is completed. Direct methods can provide precise numerical scores and therefore are very attractive for their speed in application. Providing precise, consistent, and meaningful numerical values is a very difficult cognitive task, however.

Ranking Methods   In this method the evaluator orders the levels of a specific set of attributes from most preferred to least preferred. The ordering may consist of levels of a single attribute, as in the case of assessing single attribute utility functions. Or, it may involve combinations of the levels of two or more attributes, as occurs when investigating value trade-offs, or when assessing the utility of nonindependent attributes. As the number of attributes in the combinations to be ordered becomes larger, the task for the evaluator becomes more difficult, as does the likelihood that the heuristic process utilized to simplify the complexity of the task will be inadequate. Ranking methods are also employed to order the intervals between the attributes. This type of assessment measures the relative strength of preference of one preference relation with respect to another preference relation. While the ordering of levels of attribute combinations is a very acceptable and easy to implement task, the strength of preference concept presents serious operational problems. The major challenge in implementing this type of assessment is to have the software quality assurance evaluator focus on the exchange and not on the final out-comes. Given two pairs of alternatives (a_i, a_j), (a_k, a_l) such that $a_i > a_j$ (where the symbol $>$ means "preferred to") and $a_k > a_l$, we could ask the software quality assurance evaluator which exchange is perceived to be more favorable: a_i for a_j or a_k for a_l. If the first exchange is believed to be the favorable one, then the interval between a_i and a_j is larger than the interval between a_k and a_l. A common misinterpretation of this type of assessment is that instead of focusing on the exchange, the software quality assurance evaluator ranks the exchanges on the basis of the final outcomes a_i and a_k. For example, if the software quality assurance evaluator prefers an exchange of maintenance costs of \$1,000,000 for \$1,000,001 to an exchange of \$5 for \$500, then emphasis is often wrongly placed on the preference of \$1,000,001 over \$500 and not on the substitution of one outcome for another.

Indifference Methods   These methods consist of identifying indifference points in a decision space. Indifference methods may involve the joint assessment of several possible combinations of levels of attributes and determining indifference among these combinations. In this case, it requires judgment of "trade-off" between the utilities of various attribute level combinations. Strength of preference information is obtained exclusively when no risk or uncertainty is present. When risk is involved, indifference methods rely on the evaluator's ability to choose between a lottery involving uncertain outcomes with known probabilities and an alternative resulting on a sure outcome. In this case, we obtain what is called the certainty equivalent of a lottery, that is, the level of attributes for which the evaluator is indifferent to that lottery. Indifference judgments involving lotteries provide a combined assessment of strength of preference and risk attitude. We note, however, that indifference methods require the assumption of either continuity or restricted solvability on X. And they also require prior knowledge of the functional form of the decision model.

In standard multiattribute decision analysis, ranking methods are often used prior to the use of indifference methods. They provide a rough, imprecise assessment of the possible values of the parameters of the model facilitating the coordination of the subsequent precise assessments by means of indifference methods. Let us now apply some of the theoretical notions that we have just described to a quality assurance evaluation effort.

6.3.7   An Illustrative Software Quality Assurance Evaluation Using MAUT

Boehm, et al. [1976] are among those who provided early identification of key issues for software quality assurance. In order to ensure that utility theory approaches can be effectively utilized, it is desirable that the attributes of software quality be *measurable, (sufficiently) nonoverlapping or independent,* and *capable of automated measurement.*

As we have already noted, we may consider a software product in terms of present operability. To determine this, we might ask

How efficiently, effectively, and reliably can an existing software product be utilized?

We are also concerned with how the product can be modified to meet evolving needs. This involves understandability, and reevaluation as well as modification. These are some of the general functions of maintenance, as we will discuss in Section 6.5. Thus, we ask

How efficiently, effectively, and reliably can an existing software product be maintained?

Finally, we are concerned with transitioning to a new environment and so we are concerned with portability. Thus, we ask

How efficiently, effectively, and reliably can an existing software product be transitioned to a new environment?

Figure 6.5 has illustrated this enhanced view of the software lifecycle.

We may, as we have noted, develop an attribute tree for this expanded view of the software lifecycle. This is essentially what Boehm et al. [1976] have accomplished in their development of a software quality characteristics tree, such as shown in Figure 6.18. As we see in this figure, several of the lowest-level attributes repeat themselves in that they connect to more than one attribute at the next higher level. We must partition these attributes into components, each of which supports only one higher-level attribute. This is needed to ensure that we truly obtain a tree structure. It suggests measurement difficulty with respect to these attributes, however, as only that component contributing to the attribute at the next higher level should be measured. To minimize this difficulty, each of these lowest-level attributes should be defined for each higher level supported attribute. To not do this, and to provide a definition valid across several higher-level attributes is to invite difficulties with respect to attribute independence.

It is easily seen that evaluation measures of the sort described here can be interpreted as either absolute measures or as relative comparative measures. The choice depends on whether some ideal standard or the best and worst of the alternatives being evaluated is used to anchor alternative scores on the lowest level attributes at 0 and 1.0.

If absolute measures are to be used, it is desirable to define a threshold of unacceptability as some fixed number, perhaps 0.5. Then the best possible performance measure is defined as having a value of 1.0 and the worst an-

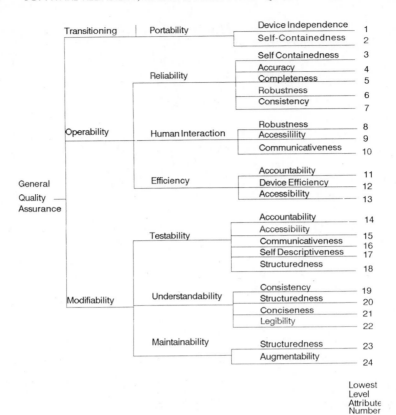

FIGURE 6.18   A possible attribute tree for software quality assurance

ticipated performance as having a value of 0.0. Figure 6.19 illustrates the fact that a nonlinear, not necessarily monotonic, function may relate these actual physical performance measures on each lowest-level attribute and the corresponding alternative score on this measure. A figure such as this should be constructed for each of the software quality assurance attributes. The values of the software quality assurance evaluator(s) are used to construct these figures. After this is done, it is possible to compare the performance difference between best and worst across all attributes at a given level that support a higher-level attribute. Attribute weights are assigned such that these attributes sum to one. Alternatively, the most important attribute can be assigned a value of 1.0 and other attribute weights assessed as necessarily less than one. Then, they can be easily scaled such the resulting attribute weights sum to one.

This is accomplished for all lowest-level attributes. Then, the attributes at the next highest level are compared and weights assigned. This is accomplished by either retaining the sum to one property initially or enforcing it later

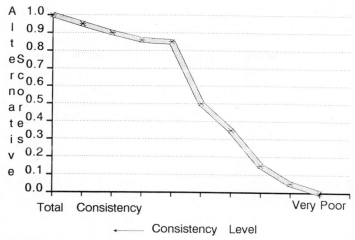

FIGURE 6.19   Subjective scales for worth of degrees of consistency

through scaling. There are a variety of ways to accomplish this, and we provide only a brief somewhat simplified description here. Sage [1977] and especially von Winterfeldt and Edwards [1986] provide much elaboration on the points mentioned here.

After performance metrics on the attributes and attribute weights have been identified, here on an absolute basis, we are ready to accomplish a specific evaluation for each alternative software product or software design and development alternative. This needs to be done for each lowest level attribute for each alternative. The overall performance of an alternative is then determined by computing the effective attribute weight for each lowest level attribute and then determining the score of the alternatives by multiplying each alternative score on each lowest level attribute by the appropriate weight, and then adding the results. Figures 6.20 and 6.21 illustrate this computation for the hypothetical attributes identified here. Figure 6.20 illustrates a set of hypothetical attribute weights that might be elicited from a software quality evaluator who has already identified performance scoring charts for the 24 attributes. One such chart has been presented in Figure 6.18. Figure 6.21 illustrates the final attribute weights that are obtained from Figure 6.20.

Figure 6.22 illustrates a hypothetical set of evaluation scores on the lowest-level attributes for two software products, or two proposed software development strategies. The overall software product evaluation score is obtained by multiplying the score for each attribute and the attribute weight and then summing the result. If it could be assumed that the process of eliciting the various weights was realistic, we should have confidence in selecting the alternative with the highest evaluation score as the best alternative.

In most cases, there would be reason to doubt some of the initially elicited

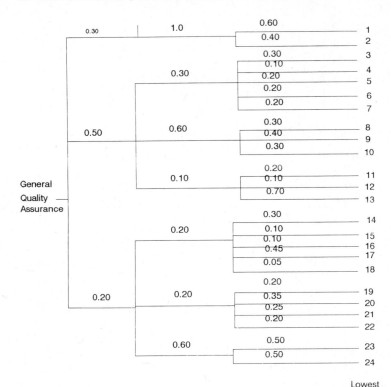

FIGURE 6.20 Illustration of the results of attribute weight assessment

values. In this case a sensitivity analysis would be performed by varying these values and seeing how much change is necessary before the evaluation decision switches. Through a sensitivity analysis of this sort, we can identify the most critical elements in an evaluation. Then, we can take extra care to ensure that these critical elements are measured very accurately.

This discussion has only touched the surface of a rather significant amount of research. There is a very extensive literature in this important area. It has seen a number of major applications and significant successes. Nevertheless, very little of the research that has been accomplished to date has been specifically applied to the software quality assurance area. The references by Sage [1977, 1987], von Winterfeldt and Edwards [1986], and Adelman [1989] should be consulted for contemporary discussions of decision analysis and evaluation research and for reference to some of the many contemporary efforts in this area.

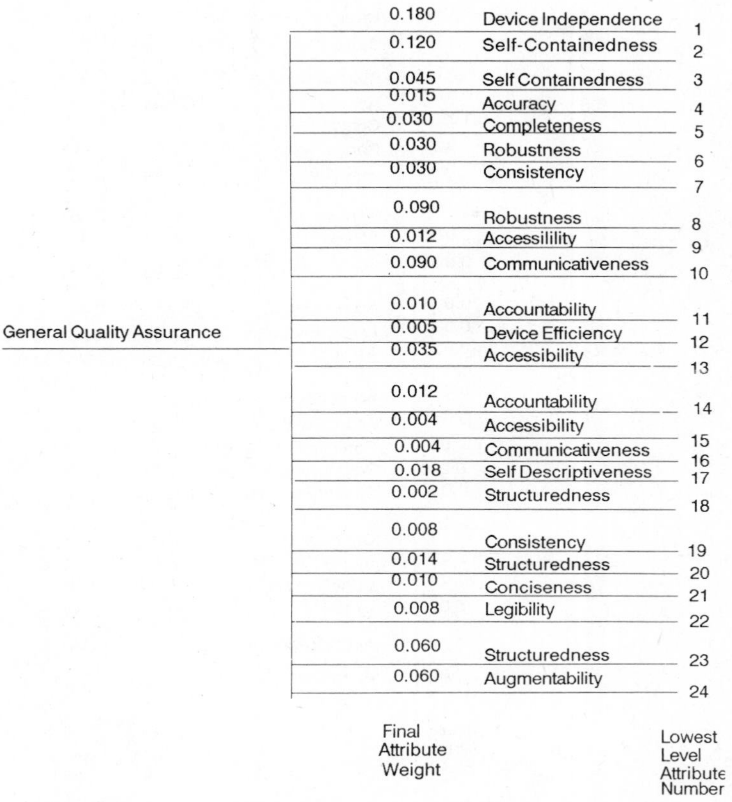

Final Attribute Weight	Lowest Level Attribute Number
0.180 Device Independence	1
0.120 Self-Containedness	2
0.045 Self Containedness	3
0.015 Accuracy	4
0.030 Completeness	5
0.030 Robustness	6
0.030 Consistency	7
0.090 Robustness	8
0.012 Accessilility	9
0.090 Communicativeness	10
0.010 Accountability	11
0.005 Device Efficiency	12
0.035 Accessibility	13
0.012 Accountability	14
0.004 Accessibility	15
0.004 Communicativeness	16
0.018 Self Descriptiveness	17
0.002 Structuredness	18
0.008 Consistency	19
0.014 Structuredness	20
0.010 Conciseness	21
0.008 Legibility	22
0.060 Structuredness	23
0.060 Augmentability	24

General Quality Assurance

FIGURE 6.21 Computation of aggregate attribute weights

6.4 METHODS FOR SOFTWARE QUALITY ASSURANCE MEASUREMENT AND TEST

The number of methods that may be used for measurement and test to determine software quality is vast. Perhaps more importantly, there are a considerable number of dimensions on which to develop a taxonomy of these measurements. The various perspectives from which a software product may be viewed suggest that this will be the case. An elementary and very useful classification scheme is according to structure, function and purpose. Our discussions will generally take this approach. For much expansion on the material discussed here, the reader is referred to Adrion et al. [1982], Beizer [1982, 1984], Chow [1985], Conte et al.[1986], and Fairley [1985].

There are a number of reasons that support software testing as a very worthy activity. Some of the applications of software testing are:

1. Validation of software requirements specifications

Final Attribute Weight	Attribute	Attribute Score for Alternative One	Attribute Score for Alternative Two
0.180	Device Independence	0.70	0.85
0.120	Self-Containedness	0.80	0.70
0.045	Self Containedness	0.50	0.60
0.015	Accuracy	0.80	0.80
0.030	Completeness	0.85	0.73
0.030	Robustness	0.65	0.55
0.030	Consistency	0.86	0.92
0.090	Robustness	0.65	0.75
0.012	Accessilility	0.74	0.44
0.090	Communicativeness	0.80	0.75
0.010	Accountability	0.65	0.80
0.005	Device Efficiency	0.75	0.85
0.035	Accessibility	0.85	0.70
0.012	Accountability	0.75	0.95
0.004	Accessibility	0.85	0.65
0.004	Communicativeness	0.65	0.95
0.018	Self Descriptiveness	0.85	0.75
0.002	Structuredness	0.85	0.95
0.008	Consistency	0.65	0.85
0.014	Structuredness	0.95	0.60
0.010	Conciseness	0.50	0.75
0.008	Legibility	1.00	0.65
0.060	Structuredness	0.75	0.80
0.060	Augmentability	0.50	1.00

Assurance

FIGURE 6.22 Attribute weights and alternative scores for SQA

2. Verification of the software product at each lifecycle phase
3. Determining whether the software does what the user thought it was going to do
4. Provision of useful information concerning operational implementation of the software
5. Identification of potentially critical issues for maintenance of the software and for transitioning it to a new environment.

Clearly, software testing offers much support for quality assurance. We will now examine some of the established testing procedures. As we noted earlier, we can view testing from a structural, functional, or purposeful perspective. We have already discussed structural testing in considerable detail in our earlier efforts concerning coding and unit testing. Our concern here is much more with functional and purposeful testing. Nevertheless, some summary comments concerning structural testing are in order here.

6.4.1 Structural Testing

Generally, it is necessary to identify a sufficient number of tests to ensure that it is possible to exercise every path in the software at least once. Immediately, we see that this is going to pose an academic problem since one write code such that some loops in the software might not ever terminate. This is certainly not done intentionally, of course. Although complete path testing can be done for some code, in general this is not possible. *Path testing* and *loop testing* represent the two principal approaches to structural testing.

A path through a segment of code, or *routine*, is any executable sequence of instructions through the routine. It is important to note the restriction that a path be executable in the sense of starting at some particular point and ending at another. Because of inadvertencies in code implementation, there may be paths that are never exercised in practice no matter which data are used. These are called *infeasible paths*. A special problem occurs with *virtually infeasible paths,* that is to say paths that are unlikely to be traveled. This is a special problem when there exists the possibility of bugs in these paths! One of the primary purposes of structured top-down design of code is to obtain modules that are of low complexity and sufficient simplicity such that all paths, exclusive of loop iteration, may be tested and such that infeasible paths are avoided.

The primary purpose of path testing is to ensure that the actual structure of a segment of code matches its intended structure. Realistic path testing demonstrates the correspondence between reality and desire or intent. The major design issue in path testing is that of selecting and exercising a sufficiently small set of path tests, while ensuring that the code structure is "*correct.*"

The control structures that determine flows are most conveniently represented by flowcharts. A flowchart, in the context used here, is a graphical representation of program structure and represents one of the earliest approaches that show how parts of a program are related to other parts, and how some parts are to continue to be executed until some condition is met. A flowchart can be constructed at a very high level illustrating only relationships among large segments of code or can be so detailed that it represents essentially a statement by statement account of a program.

As we have noted in Section 4.2.2, there are four fundamental elements in flowcharts: *decisions*, *events and activities*, *logic*, and *time sequences*. Most computer terminology uses the term process to represent either events or activities. Figure 6.23 illustrates typically used symbols for these elements that are defined as:

1. A *decision* element represents a point in code at which data flow diverges. IF-THEN-ELSE, WHILE, and UNTIL constructs are typical of decision elements.

2. A *process* is an element that has a single input and output. Inside an

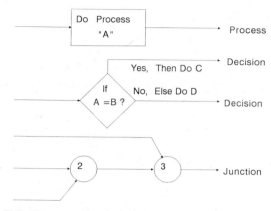

FIGURE 6.23   Symbols for process flow graphs

    element can be a single line of code or multiple instructions that are unbroken by decisions or logic branches.

3. A *logic* element is a point in code or a program where the flow converges. Logic AND, OR, or EXCLUSIVE OR logic statements can be used and the GOTO statement is a particular form of logic.

4. *Time arrows* are used to indicate direction of data flow or connecting linkages in flow graphs.

Two other elements are sometimes used. A connection matrix is sometimes used to indicate fan-in or fan-out of a large number of logic inputs or decision outputs. A simple connection matrix is a junction. A ground symbol is sometimes used to indicate the cessation of processing. We will use junctions but have little use for grounds or connection matrices here.

    Usually, these elements are abstracted further such that logic and decision elements become nodes and process elements, together with time flow arrows, become links. The resulting graph theoretic representation of a program is convenient in that it can be automatically generated as long as the program does not contain absolute address computations and associated control flow changes. Figures 6.24 through 6.26 illustrate a simple bubble-sort flowchart, BASIC language subroutine, and the associated directed graph. The BASIC program here is virtually identical in form to the code that would be written in FORTRAN or Pascal for this simple problem. There is really little more than is shown in the flowchart that is not contained in the source code listing. For a much larger program where the flowchart would be a highly abstracted version of the source code, there might well be advantages associated with easy interpretation of the flowchart, and potential use of the flowchart in writing the source code.

    The minimum requirements for path testing are that each instruction in the program be tested at least once, and every decision be taken with each

```
1.  'Subroutine Bubble Sort
2.  'Inputs : X, N
3.  'Outputs: X
4.  'Locals: J, P, S
5.  'Initialization
6.  S = TRUE
7.  FOR P = 1 To N
8.     IF S = FALSE THEN RETURN
9.     S = FALSE
10.    FOR J = 1 TO N-P
11.       IF X(J) > X(J+1)
12.       THEN S = TRUE
13.          TEMP=X(J): X(J)=X(J+1): X(J+1)=TEMP
14         NEXT J
15.    NEXT P
16.    RETURN
17.  'Endsub
```

FIGURE 6.24   Basic language program for simple bubble sort

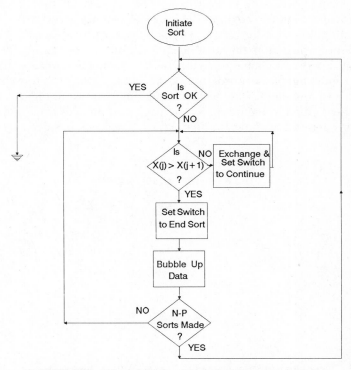

FIGURE 6.25   Flowchart for simple bubble sort algorithm

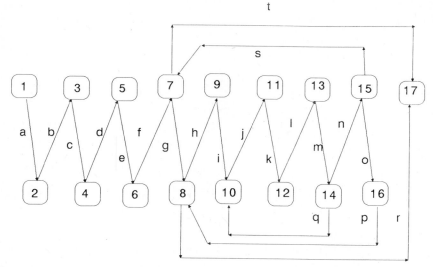

FIGURE 6.26   Control flow graph for bubble sort program

possible outcome occurring at least once. The set of paths that meets these criteria provides complete cover of the program, but *not necessarily* complete testing of all paths. In other words, complete cover assures testing the components out of which all paths must be created, but not necessarily all paths. A reasonable path test plan must simply require complete coverage. Consider again the simple bubble sort program shown in Figure 6.24. A flowchart that corresponds to this simple bubble chart program is shown in Figure 6.25 and a control flow graph in Figure 6.26. The node and link coverage for various paths in this network is shown in Figure 6.27. Each link has been associated

Paths	Dec 8	Dec 11	Dec 16	Linkages
abcdefghi	Yes	No	No	abcdefghi

FIGURE 6.27   Analysis of coverage of links and nodes

with a letter and each node with a number in Figure 6.26. The research of Beizer [1982] shows that path selection must be made such that we:

1. Select a sufficient number of paths in order to obtain complete coverage
2. Select short and functionally meaningful paths
3. Minimize the number of changes from path to path with ideally only one decision changing from path to path
4. Avoid complicated paths at the expense of a larger number of simpler paths.

Some particular illustrations for the simple example considered here will convey these points. Additional details can be found in Chapter 4. Suppose we use the test data set $S_1 = \{A(1) = 5, A(2) = 2, N = 2\}$. It is clear that complete coverage is reached. However, the test is not infallible. For example, if we replace the greater than decision statement, with just an equals statement, the program still functions correctly on this specific data, but is an incorrect program. The data set

$$S_2 = \{[A(1) = 5, \quad A(2) = 2, \quad A(2) = 2, \quad N = 3],$$
$$[A(1) = 3, \quad A(2) = 6, \quad N = 2]\}$$

will yield complete coverage. However, it still does not uncover the error incurred by replacing the greater than decision(s) by equal decisions.

This observation leads to the conclusion that it will be generally necessary to determine the *goodness* of a test data set and that statistical generation of data and testing will often be needed. The text by Shooman [1983] provides many discussions relative to statistical testing of software. Error seeding, in which known errors are introduced into the code such that their placement is statistically similar to that for actual errors [Mills, 1972], is another related approach to achieve the ends just described.

Loop testing is a particular form of path testing that is specifically designed to find the bugs that occur in loops. It is desirable since path testing is likely to lead to inconclusive results. Testing a single loop should cover one pass through the loop, two passes through the loop, and some typical number of passes. This is needed since a single pass may not necessarily uncover loop initialization errors. Loop testing should also involve an input that causes the loop to be bypassed. If there is a maximum number of passes through a loop, then loop testing should occur for data that would require one less than the maximum number of passes, the maximum number of passes, and one more pass than the maximum number that the loop will process. This type of testing will uncover endpoint bugs.

There are also nested loops, that is to say loops within loops, and these require special attention. Unstructured loops result from programming practices that allow branching from the middle of one loop to another loop. It is very difficult to test such loops and, for this reason, good structured programming practice will seek to avoid such loops.

Automated testing procedures that will accomplish path and loop testing are clearly desirable. Generally, it will be necessary to learn typical input sequences and to be able to potentially modify them in order to determine reasonable test input sequences.

Our discussion of *structural testing* is brief, both because we have covered closely related material in Chapter 4 and because our emphasis here is on functional and purposeful evaluation of software quality assurance.

6.4.2   Functional Testing

The ubiquitous program flowchart elements of decision, process, and logic are most often used to represent a structural description of a program. However, they can also be used to yield a functional or *transaction flow* description of program description. The major difference between the two approaches is that it is necessary to show all details of program flow in a structural description. In a process description, only the user perspective on transaction flow is illustrated. A brief look at the bubble sort flowchart of Figure 6.25 indicates that it is really drawn more from a functional perspective than a structural perspective. If we are to use a flowchart as a tool to enable program construction, it would seem more appropriate for it to be initially constructed from a transaction flow perspective, such as to guide the later writing of detailed source code.

Transaction flows can be represented in the same fashion as path flows. Thus, the discussions of our previous subsection are applicable here also. A variety of transaction flow representation tools may, potentially, be used. Among these are HIPO charts, which we briefly discussed in Chapter 3. Functional test requirements are requirements specifications driven. Thus, typical operating environments and conditions, and typical system inputs and outputs, will be needed in order to conduct a functional test. While structural testing can be done at a *micro-level,* any robust approach to functional testing will have to include both micro and *macro-level* details.

Generally, it will be possible to conduct unit tests on individual software subsystem modules in order to accomplish *structural evaluation* for software quality assurance. This will often, but not always, be the case relative to *functional evaluation.* When the software requirements specifications have been appropriately disaggregated into functions, as they should be, then unit functional testing is possible. *Purposeful testing* and complete functional testing require evaluation of the overall software product. Generally, it will be necessary to integrate several software modules in order to obtain a complete software product. Thus, *integration testing* becomes an important part of purposeful testing. To complete the picture, we validate software through *validation testing* and then accomplish *system-level testing* on the validated software in order to complete software quality assurance testing. Figure 6.28

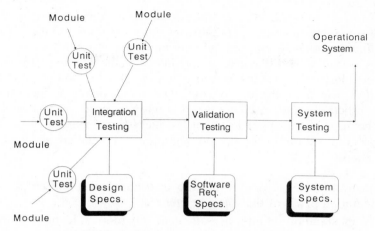

FIGURE 6.28   Typical flow of tests in SQA

illustrates these various stages of software testing and software quality assurance.

6.4.3   Integration Testing

One of the fundamental assumptions underlying good software engineering, and the scientific method in general, is that it is possible to break an issue into subcomponents, resolve the subcomponent issues, and thereby obtain a solution to the larger problem. Generally, things will not work out this smoothly due to errors in diagnosis of the initial issue and errors in making an appropriate decomposition. Thus, it is absolutely mandatory to accomplish integration testing to determine how well (or poorly) the complete software system performs. Integration testing is concerned with assembling unit tested software modules according to the design dictates of the requirements specifications, and then testing this assemblage.

More often than not, *bottom-up integration* is the game plan used to integrate the many component software modules of a system into a functioning software system. Bottom up integration testing would consist of unit structural (and functional) testing, followed by testing and evaluation of the associated system. This leads to what is often called the "big-bang" approach to testing, in which a large number of unit tested software modules are assembled into a single large system and the whole product tested at once. As we might suspect, software will often not work when assembled this way for the first time, and a major problem will then be to detect and isolate the source of the errors in the integrated product. But when the approach works, it is certainly efficient.

Top-down integration involves the incremental process of stagewise assembly and test of software. The primary routine and one or two immediate predecessor subroutines are thoroughly tested as *skeletons* and these become the *harness* for other subroutines that are immediately subordinate to these. Modules are integrated together by moving from the top down throughout the hierarchically structured software modules. This top-down approach allows us to verify major decision or control points very early in the evaluation process, especially since good software design will result in most major decisions being made at upper levels of the hierarchy. Figure 6.29 illustrates some essential features of top-down integration. Potential advantages to this approach are:

1. Integration and testing efforts are distributed over the entire implementation phase of the software lifecycle.
2. The most important interfaces are generally those at higher hierarchical levels, and these are the ones that will be evaluated first and most often.
3. The successfully evaluated and tested routines at the top level of the hierarchy become very natural test beds for lower-level subroutines.
4. New errors are localized to the new software modules that are being added to the system.
5. It becomes possible to field an operational system that can be field tested while it is still in a developmental stage, such as to aid in better identification of requirements specifications for updates to the system.

There will be many situations in which it will not be possible to always accomplish, completely, top-down integration. This is, perhaps, the only disadvantage to the approach that can be cited. Sometimes, this occurs because we simply lack sufficient time. This is a planning flaw. In other cases, not all lower-level modules have been delivered. This will often require some sort

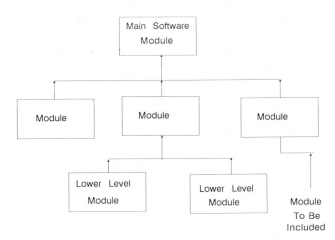

FIGURE 6.29 Iterative model inclusion in top down integration

of simulation efforts to model the results that would be produced by still missing modules. This reality has led to the development of what is often called "sandwich integration" as a hybrid of top-down and bottom-up approaches. Essentially, this is a top-down approach in which the most critical lowest level modules are built and tested first.

There are a variety of automated tools that can potentially be used in integration testing. These include module drivers, environment simulators, library management tools, and generators of operationally realistic test data. These are very needed in order to assist in the maintenance of various items such as code, test plans and cases, and test schedules.

6.4.4   System-Level Testing

Even after all of these efforts have been accomplished, there still remains the task of determining that the complete software system performance conforms to that of the requirements specifications, and that the statements in the requirements correspond to the real needs of the user. Our discussions in Section 6.3 provide approaches that may be useful for evaluation of complete system performance. Needed inputs for this evaluation may come from the detailed evaluation approaches discussed in this section.

In our initial discussion of this section, we mentioned structural, functional, and purposeful testing. Our actual discussions of testing procedures indicate that it would be possible also to describe five general stages in testing that are related to these three, as shown in Figure 6.30.

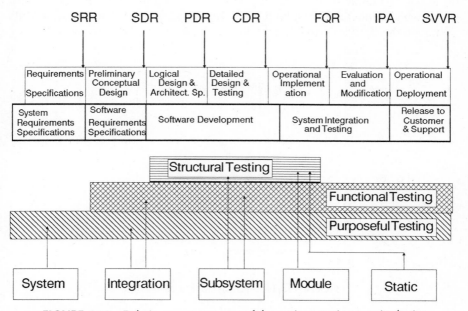

FIGURE 6.30 Relations among some of the various testing terminologies

It is also possible to develop a taxonomy of testing procedures according to the type of evaluation effort involved. A partial listing of these includes: code inspections and walkthroughs, static analysis of source code, and formal proofs of correctness. Efforts such as inspections and walkthroughs are highly pragmatic. Given a talented inspection team that is sensitive to human motivations and concerns, this can be a very satisfactory approach. Various complexity measures can be associated with static analysis of source code. This graph theoretic approach yields information that may be of some value but which does not seem to yield insight into how design should proceed. In a similar way, formal proofs of program correctness would have great value, if ever they could be obtained for realistic design situations. Even so, there would exist the difficulty of converting the proof of correctness information into useful design information that would have normative value. These, and a large number of other relevant topics are discussed in Beizer [1984] and Chow [1985]. At least four dimensions may be identified that may be used in classification of software quality assurance methods:

Static or dynamic testing

Informal or formal approaches

Functional, structural, or purposeful levels

Automated or manual measurements

Our efforts thus far in this chapter have concerned software quality assessment, especially through multiple attribute evaluation; and such related functionality topics as testing, reliability, and verification and validation. It is necessary that activities that support review, analysis, and testing to ensure quality be conducted throughout the software lifecycle. Figure 6.31 presents some of the activities that might be accomplished to determine a quality

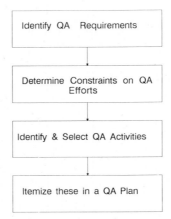

FIGURE 6.31   Steps in quality assurance

assurance, or validation, verification, and testing plan. In each of these steps, it should be remembered that it is the overall system needs and constraints that determine the quality assurance requirements. Also, the techniques and metrics that are to be used must be consistent with these needs and constraints, and the software project development and management approach. This technical direction and management approach will lead to various time and resource allocations that affect quality assurance approaches. Figure 6.32 indicates a typical table of contents for a quality assurance plan that might result from following through the steps detailed in Figure 6.31.

The last phase in the system lifecycle is operational deployment, and the modification to meet evolving needs and transitioning to meet new needs that often follows operational deployment. The *retrofit* of software that is needed in each of these three phases is often called "maintenance" and it this subject to which we now turn.

6.5 SOFTWARE MAINTENANCE

Software maintenance may be viewed from any of the following three perspectives:

1. Activities to be encountered to accomplish various types of maintenance and methods whereby the process can be made cost-effective
2. The costs that are associated with various maintenance profiles
3. The benefits or effectiveness indices associated with various maintenance profiles

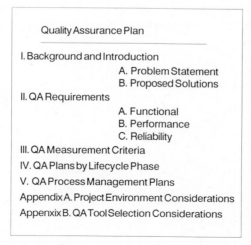

Quality Assurance Plan

I. Background and Introduction
    A. Problem Statement
    B. Proposed Solutions
II. QA Requirements
    A. Functional
    B. Performance
    C. Reliability
III. QA Measurement Criteria
IV. QA Plans by Lifecycle Phase
V. QA Process Management Plans
Appendix A. Project Environment Considerations
Appenxix B. QA Tool Selection Considerations

FIGURE 6.32 Typical table of contents for a hypothetical QA plan

We can simply define maintenance as *modification activities that follow the operational deployment of software.* From this perspective then, software maintenance involves those activities that occur after design, development, and release of a software product. The purpose of these activities is fourfold. First, it is necessary to bring a software system to an operational state, if it is not in this state when the software product is delivered. This involves *corrective maintenance.*

It is also necessary that a software product be *responsive.* The software system should be responsive to changing internal needs within the original environment, such as those brought about by a modified operating system. This is often called *adaptive maintenance.*

Perfective maintenance is the term often used to describe modification of the software such that it is able to meet external evolving user needs.

Although not as commonly used, we suggest the term "proactive maintenance" as the effort associated with system redesign to transition it to a new external environment. It also involves sensing the need for this and having the software capable of being transitioned on or before there is a need for transitioning.

In a very loose sense, proactive maintenance could also be termed "preventative maintenance." This term, however, is often used with hardware systems and implies such things as lubrication of parts before need occurs; or automatic replacement of banks of lightbulbs before they start to individually burn out. Since software does not degrade in quite the same way as hardware and does not need maintenance to maintain a presently established level of functionality, we choose not to use this term here. Many studies indicate that cost distributions among these four types of maintenance discussed and used here are something like that shown in Figure 6.33.

Software systems engineering efforts begin at need identification and extend throughout a lifecycle of a software product until the software is no longer suitable for use. Maintenance is one of the fundamental phases in the

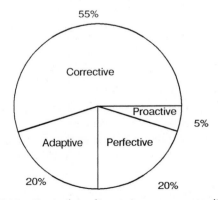

FIGURE 6.33 Typical quality maintenance cost distribution

software lifecycle. This phase of effort is characterized by four unique distinctive properties:

1. Maintenance must be performed within the environment of an existing software system and changes must be made within constraints imposed by this. One of the consequences of this is that aging hardware and software will result in special problems. Some of these are the lack of interoperability and horizontal integration across hardware and software of different vendors, especially as the system expands over time.
2. The time interval allowed for performance of software maintenance, particularly corrective maintenance, is often much less than the time allowed for performance of the preceding phases of the lifecycle. Occasionally, the time allocated for proactive maintenance will be lengthy.
3. There is often system operational data available for maintenance that is unavailable for other phases of the lifecycle.
4. Maintenance efforts have a set of miniphases all of their own that initiate with requirements identification, and proceed through redeployment of the maintained system. A complex maintenance effort, particularly of a perfective or proactive nature, may require as much or more time and effort as was required to deliver the initial software product although, as we have just noted, allocation of resources to maintenance is inadequate.

In many cases, maintenance of software will come close to involving redesign of software, perhaps even in a new language. As we know, it is possible to describe a software product as being systemic, structured or unstructured. *Unstructured software* is software that has been developed and deployed without benefit of a structured systems management process. If we have available source code only and the code has been written in unstructured COBOL, BASIC or FORTRAN, we have software in this category. If we are very unfortunate, even the remarks statements will be removed from the source code. Such code will be essentially unmaintainable. The situation could be worse. We might have only compiled code. In this case, we might attempt to use a disassembler to recover a version of the assembly code. Interpretation of this would be most difficult, indeed.

Semistructured software would represent software that has been written in a structured, or block structured language, such as Pascal, Ada, or C, or even newer versions of FORTRAN or BASIC. While the presence of program structure may make it much easier to determine what various segments of the code accomplish than would be the case for "spaghetti" code, still we will usually have major problems in determining the intent of the software designers. The best situation occurs when we have *systemic structured software* that has resulted from a software systems engineering process. The availability of documentation concerning the software and a maintenance manual should do much to enhance the efficiency and effectiveness of software maintenance.

This suggests a potential need for automated assistance in the conversion of unstructured source code to semistructured source code, and the retrofit of this semistructured source into systemic structured code. Computer-aided software engineering (CASE) tools that can accomplish this should support the conversion of old software, and software designed without the benefit of systems engineering approaches, into software that will have a much longer and more productive life expectancy.

For example, the Warnier–Orr diagram that we discussed in Chapter 3 can be used to document a program, structured or not. The documentation produced can be potentially extensive if a great level of code detail is used to produce the diagram. It can be used [Parikh, 1986] to answer important questions concerning design and documentation. If used before and after modification, it can be used to answer similar change questions.

Other automated aids to maintenance include text aids, debugging aids, cross-reference generators, comparators, linkage editors, and configuration management databases.

Often, a software maintenance team will be needed for a large software system. Whether the team should be employed by the software user organization, the software design organization, or some third party will depend on a number of technical and management factors. Regardless of the chain of command, software maintenance should be regarded as a very important function, and one as difficult and challenging as software design. Among the many responsibilities and needed capabilities of a software maintenance team are the following:

1. Understanding the operational system
2. Locating information in documentation
3. Updating documentation
4. Determination of change need
5. Submission of change requests
6. Identification and translation of change need to change requirements
7. Maintenance scheduling
8. Adding new system features
9. Detecting existence of errors
10. Diagnosis of source of errors
11. Correcting identified errors
12. Quality assurance of maintenance products
13. Deletion of software modules that are no longer used
14. Enforcing documentation and coding standards
15. Planning for, scheduling, and managing maintenance

There are a variety of factors that influence maintenance costs. Figure 6.34 indicates some of these. Each of the attributes that influence maintenance

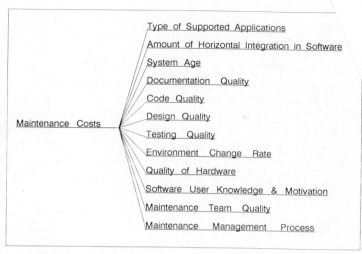

FIGURE 6.34 Factors that influence maintenance cost

cost can be disaggregated into lower level attributes. For example, attributes that indicate a lack of code quality include

Excessive use of DO loops
Excessive use of IF (THEN ELSE) statements
Excessive use of GOTO statements
Lack of structure
Code emulating code developed for older hardware
Hard coded parameters
Poorly commented code
Use of nonstandard language features
Meaningless variable names

Attributes of design quality are related to the attributes of code quality, for it is the design specifications that lead to the specification of modules and code. These attributes include:

Very large modules
Modules performing multiple functions
Multiple interactions between modules
Modules with multiple entry and exit points
Complex logic flow and program structure
Incomplete design specifications
Missing design specifications

Scoring functions for maintenance costs can be potentially determined on the basis of the multiattribute utility evaluation measures of Section 6.3. A primary use for such a measure would be to determine the nature and type of maintenance that should be performed.

There have been a number of efforts to determine empirical equations that might be used to determine maintenance costs. Belady and Lehman [1976] have related maintenance costs to the deterioration that occurs in a large system over time. They postulate an increase in system size and fragmentation of effort as maintenance personnel become experts in only one portion of a large system. The confounding of these is said to lead to an exponential increase in resources that need to be devoted to maintenance of the form

$$M = p + K e^{(c - d)}$$

where

M = total effort expended on maintenance

p = productive efforts that involve analysis, design, coding, testing, and evaluation

K = an empirically determined constant

c = complexity measure due to lack of a structured systemic approach

d = degree to which the maintenance team is familiar with the software

In the foregoing relation, the value of c is increased if the software system is developed without use of a systems engineering process. Of course, c will be higher for a large software product with a high degree of systemic structure than a small one with the same degree. If the software is maintained without an understanding of the structure, function, and purpose of and for the software, then the value of d will be low.

Many factors influence the nature and extent of problems involved in maintaining software. In one study due to Lientz and Swanson [1981], the 24 maintenance problem items shown in Figure 6.35 were identified and the most significant 13 of these aggregated into six maintenance problem factors as shown in the tree structure of Figure 6.36. Lack of user understanding and inadequate user training are the major contributors to maintenance problems in the form of *user knowledge.* Although demand for program enhancements and extensions is the single largest contributor in the 24 items, lack of user understanding and training, which leads to inadequate *user knowledge,* is the single major factor that accounts for approximately 60% of the common variance need for maintenance, as shown in Figure 6.37. This suggests, in the strongest of ways, that efforts to enhance user understanding of the software they are using will be well rewarded in terms of lower maintenance costs.

Planning software development projects for maintenance is very important. Designing software products to minimize the need for maintenance, provision

FIGURE 6.35 Important influencers of maintenance

Maintenance		
	User Knowledge	User Understanding Lacking
		Inadequate User Training
	Programmer Effectiveness	Maintenance Pgmr. Productivity
		Maintenance Pgmr. Motivation
	Product Quality	Maintenance Pgmr. Skill
		System Design Spec. Adeq.
		Original Program Quality
	Programmer Time Available	Documentation Quality
		Competing Demands for Pgmr
	Machine Requirements	Pgm Storage Requirements
		Pgm Processing Time Req.
	System Reliability	System HW & SW Reliability
		Data Integrity

FIGURE 6.36 Tree of thirteen important maintenance influencers

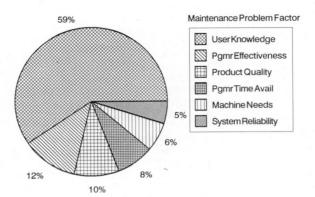

FIGURE 6.37   Importance of six critical maintenance influencers

of automated maintenance tools, and managing for effective maintenance are each very important activities in software systems engineering.

6.6   Summary

This chapter makes a transition to software system *process* issues. It discusses software quality, reliability, maintainability, and other software functionality perspectives. Clearly, a major thrust in the chapter is the use of multiple attribute evaluation and assessment procedures for evaluation of software functionality. In the remaining chapters in this text, we will continue this process orientation through an examination of various *macro level* concerns effecting software development.

6.7   Problems

6.1.   In his book on *Software Metrics*, Tom Gilb [1977] proposes an interesting specification matrix that will enable trade-offs between *quality factors* and their *criteria*. Investigate the use of this approach as a tool to enable determination of the requisite inputs to a MAUT analysis.

6.2.   In Chapter 1, we identified a rather long laundry list of functionality attributes of software:

• Acceptable	• Efficient	• Repairable
• Accessible	• Error-tolerant	• Reusable
• Accountable	• Expandable	• Robust
• Accurate	• Flexible	• Secure
• Adaptable	• Generalizable	• Self-contained

- Appropriate
- Assurable
- Available
- Clear
- Complete
- Consistent
- Correct
- Documentable
- Documented
- Effective
- Interoperable
- Maintainable
- Manageable
- Modifiable
- Modular
- Operable
- Portable
- Precise
- Reliable
- Survivable
- Testable
- Timely
- Transferable
- Understandable
- Usable
- User-friendly
- Valid
- Verifiable

One of the potential development problems is that we may not specify these attributes, either at all or perhaps not with sufficient specificity. Consider an appropriate software development lifecycle. At which phase should each of these attributes be specified, and measured? At what phase in the lifecycle will the impact of poor quality be realized, and noticed?

6.3. Consider again the attributes described in Problem 6.2. How could you use MAUT to determine the 10 most important of these attributes for a specific software development issue? Be sure to identify precisely the basis on which your choice of 10 attributes is made. Identify a hypothetical development issue and accomplish this evaluation.

6.4. A decade old Rome Air Development Center (RADC) study resulted in identification of a number of *quality criteria* for *software*:

Access audit
Access control
Accuracy
Communication commonality
Communicativeness
Completeness
Conciseness
Consistency
Data commonality
Error tolerance
Execution efficiency
Expandability
Generality
Instrumentation
Machine independence
Modularity

Operability
Self-descriptiveness
Simplicity
Software system independence
Storage efficiency
Traceability
Training

Propose an assessment of software quality based on these attributes. Please write a brief paper outlining how MAUT could be used with these attributes. Propose attribute measures for these and any templates or structuring tools desired. This particular RADC study suggested two scoring systems: one based on linear weighted sums and the other on a binary scoring procedure. Contrast and compare these two approaches.

6.5. Thomas J. McCabe [1976] has proposed a *cyclometric complexity measure* of software complexity that is based on graph theory. Please prepare a brief discussion of this and indicate how measures of cyclometric and essential complexity relate to and supplement measures of conciseness, simplicity, flexibility, and maintainability of code.

6.6. The attributes noted in Problems 6.2 and 6.4 could easily be used in a *checklist* like fashion to accomplish reviews and audits. Please write a formal plan to do this at each of the phases in a typical software development lifecycle.

6.7. What is *software configuration management* (SCM)? Four processes involved in SCM are *software configuration identification* (SCI), *software configuration control* (SCC), *software configuration status accounting* (SCSA), and *software configuration auditing* (SCA). How do these relate to the software development lifecycle? How do they relate to *verification and validation? Software quality assurance?*

6.8. There are a number of manuals that deal, at least in part, with software quality and its assurance. These standards documents include:

DoD-STD-7935
IEEE-STD-1008-1987
IEEE-STD-1987
IEEE-STD-730-1984
IEEE-STD-824-1983
IEEE-STD-829-1983
IEEE-STD-983-1986
MIL-STD-1521

MIL-STD-2187A

MIL-STD-2188

MIL-STD-38784R

MIL-STD-483

MIL-STD-52779A

RADC-TR-77-369

Please prepare a brief review of four of these. Develop the suggested taxonomy of quality developed in each of these and contrast and compare your results.

6.9. A term often used to describe Japanese work culture is *quality circle*. After searching for a few relevant items on this topic, prepare a discussion of *software quality circles*. What might they be and would they work?

6.10. Someone walks into your office and dumps 5000-line source of code program in C on your desk and says "This is the most miserable quality software that I have ever seen." Assist your friend in placing some qualitative and quantitative meaning to the expression. How could you go about determining the *quality* of this code?

6.11. Is it possible for software to be correct and not reliable or of high quality? Please explain.

6.12. *Requirements volatility* is a term first used by Barry Boehm to mean the tendency of the system level and software level requirements to change during the software development process. How does requirements volatility effect software quality, reliability, and maintainability?

6.13. Yourdon [1975] describes *antibugging* as the process of anticipating error conditions and developing error-handling paths that will either reroute or terminate processing when errors occur. What are some appropriate guidelines for *antibugging* and how do they relate to the detection, diagnosis, and correction activities that we have described. What are some advantages and disadvantages of including *antibugging* in software? How could we detect and correct errors in the *antibugging* part of a software system?

6.14. Obtain some code that you or a colleague wrote 2 or 3 years ago. Examine its functioning and suggest needed maintenance of the source code. Perform the suggested inspections during the retrofit phase for your old code. Describe the actual process used, including observed errors in coding and elsewhere.

6.15. Maintenance of automobiles is enhanced by having a *spare-parts depot*. Discuss the concept, if any, of a *software spare-parts depot*.

6.16. Prepare a plan for and construct a structured walkthrough of a software development that one of your colleagues is developing. Document this, perform it, and ask your colleague to critique your efforts.

6.17. From Halstead [1977] prepare a discussion of software science metrics. Contrast and compare these with the McCabe metrics you investigated in Problem 6.5.

Chapter 7

Operational Implementation, System Integration, and Environments for Software Systems Engineering

This chapter is primarily concerned with system environments and the integration and implementation of software systems. While operational implementation and system integration are activities that formally occur near the end of the system lifecycle, success requires appropriate attention to *concept development, identification of system specifications,* and *overall systems analysis and design* or operational deployment issues will generally be associated with the greatest of misfortunes.

So, we see that it will be important to understand the environment for software design and installation. Our efforts in this chapter will first be devoted to an examination of system implementation and integration issues. Then we will turn our attention to a discussion of software systems engineering environments. The chapter concludes with a discussion of *computer-aided software engineering* (CASE) tools for better environmental management and software development.

7.1 IMPLEMENTATION AND INTEGRATION

In the majority of cases, a system that is being deployed is *not* a totally new system concept which is being installed and where no other system has previously existed but, rather, a presumably improved version of an existing system. This *new system* will, therefore, evolve from an existing system in a fashion such as shown in Figure 7.1. Generally the new system is being delivered as a result of some contracted effort.

The result of the contracted effort will often be intended to be utilized in future efforts for implementation of some overall system integration concepts. Both technical and functional integration are generally achieved, each in an

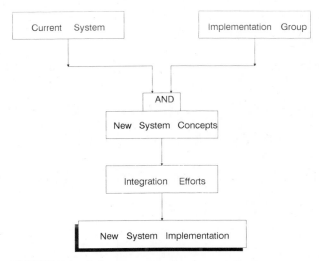

FIGURE 7.1   Software system implementation concerns

evolutionary manner, through systems implementation and integration efforts. The first deliverable relative to achieving this is generally a *system implementation and integration plan* that will identify, analyze, and prioritize technical and functional integration issues, and propose solutions to problems extant with the functional deployment of the developed software. To do this efficiently and effectively will require:

1. Outstanding capabilities in systems management
2. Thorough understanding of contemporary technology for the development of trustworthy systems architecture, systems integration, and software engineering
3. Technical direction and cost control abilities

These systems engineering capabilities must be present throughout the complete lifecycle of development of the system that is to be operationally deployed, as we have indicated in Figure 1.6, and the many models depicting the software system lifecycle that we discussed in Chapter 2. Not generally indicated in these discussions is the distributed nature of the effort, the system management–technical direction nature of the effort, the multiphase nature of the overall concept, or the iteration and feedback that must be provided back to earlier stages in the process. We have emphasized these in our discussions here.

Generally, it will be necessary for an implementation and integration contractor to provide integration concepts and designs. Often, the user group will have the contractual ability to approve or disapprove of these concepts

as they are developed. In many instances, the contractor will be
assist the user group in the future management and coordinatio
contractors, primarily through review of proposed subsystem desi{
cations. Figure 7.2 describes this systems management notion and indicates
the primary role of the integration contractor in the information technology
aspects that lead to development of an overall system concept, and the system
management and technical direction role that will often be required as a part
of a software implementation effort.

Both top-down and bottom-up approaches will generally be needed and
used for software system integration. The top-down approach will be primarily
concerned with long-term issues that concern structure and architecture of
the overall software system. The bottom-up approach will be concerned with
parallel efforts at making existing software systems more efficient and effective
such that they can be potentially incorporated into an overall integration
concept for the newly implemented software. The overall integration design
must be such as to take into consideration various existing hardware and
software that are not subject to change, and potentially other initiatives that
constrain the overall integration concept. This concept must, of course, be
consistent with both existing and evolving systems.

To be successful, the team accomplishing system implementation and integration should have a keen understanding of principles for the design of
integrated software systems that are often spatially distributed and multipurpose. They need also have systems management capability in order to assist
in the technical direction of the work of others, possibly subcontractors, should
this be required. This describes what is hoped for from a "primary" system
implementation and integration team. The central objectives in software system implementation are shown in Figure 7.3. Of particular importance here

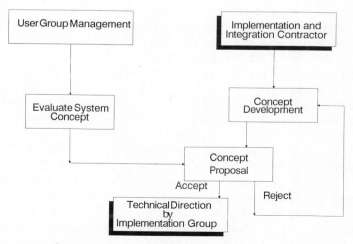

FIGURE 7.2 Interaction of implementation and user groups

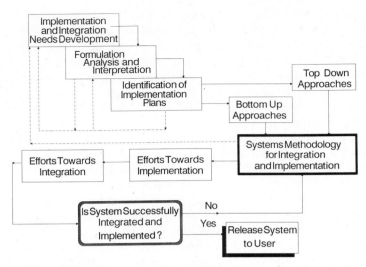

FIGURE 7.3 Typical effort flow for software system implementation

is the many feedback loops that will enable learning through experience, and the resulting improvement in the overall methodology for design implementation and evaluation as the experiential knowledge base grows.

Of central concern in an integration and implementation effort is the system level *information architecture* of the overall system concept. Conceptually, this might appear as shown in Figure 7.4. It should be explicitly noted that the operational system architecture will, more often than not, be very distributed spatially; what is shown in Figure 7.4 is merely a centralized representation of the system-level architecture.

The intended mission areas for support will, of course, vary from application to application. The primary systems engineering and technical direction activities of the software system implementation and integration team involve architectural design of the overall system and integration of specific individual new software systems into the overall system. The first of these activities calls for systems engineering activities on the part of the implementation and integration team. These technical tools and methodologies from information systems engineering involve primarily the "top-down" approaches identified in the initial phase of activity. The second of these activities encompasses systems engineering management and technical direction of other contractors and/or principally "bottom-up" approaches to the interfacing and interoperability of existing systems. The phases of effort associated with conceptual design and specification of the new components to be added to an existing system are related, as shown in Figure 7.5.

A number of systems technology and systems management issues and challenges are associated with this concept of *software systems implementation*

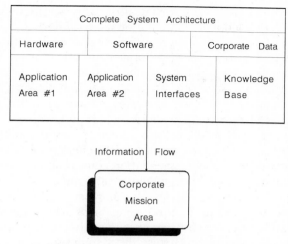

FIGURE 7.4   Representation of architectures

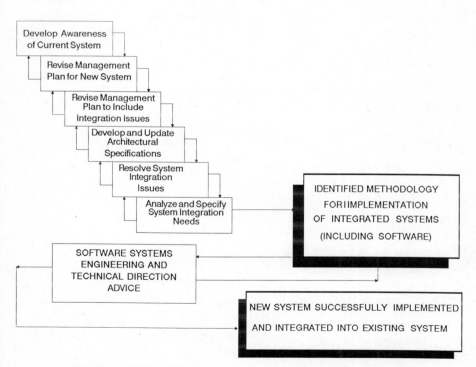

FIGURE 7.5   Activities in systems implementation and integration

and integration engineering. The technical issues generally involve the conduct, by the implementation and integration team, of impact assessments and the preparation of systems engineering reports on architectural changes and associated integration concerns. The implementation and integration team should also be capable of providing systems management support relative to technical and scheduling decisions. These will generally involve lifecycle costing studies of possible acquisition strategies and configuration management studies as they specifically relate to implementation needs.

When a positive "go-ahead" to an implementation decision is made, an implementation and integration contractor will generally be tasked to prepare design specifications and a recommendation concerning the method used to accomplish implementation. On making a subsequent decision concerning which implementation method to use, the implementation–integration contractor will generally assist in systems management and technical direction of the implementation effort. Involvement may include performance of an implementation task order, in which case the system user group will independently prepare the task order and determine the acceptance criteria. The implementation–integration contractor would then be responsible for management review and establishment of a management control system to ensure quality assurance provisions. This will include operational test and evaluation according to contractor prepared and user group approved operational test and evaluation plans. Figures 7.5 and 7.6 illustrate these implementation and integration contractor activities from somewhat different perspectives.

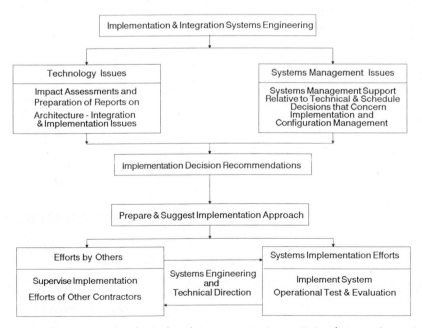

FIGURE 7.6 Technological and management issues in implementation

The very first effort should generally be to obtain, from a variety of relevant sources, identification of where the user group is, where the user group needs to be, and how it should get there relative to system implementation and integration. This *situation assessment* effort will result in definition of the problem in terms of the needs, constraints, and alterables specifically relative to the system implementation. Of course, at least a preliminary version of this effort must have been accomplished as an initial part of the requirements specifications effort that led to development of the software system that is now being implemented. Again, this emphasizes the fact that a system lifecycle is really a cornucopia-like diagram in which each of the phases within the lifecycle have a set of steps associated with them that are not dissimilar to the general activities accomplished within the overall system design phases.

With respect to implementation, there will generally exist a baseline configuration, which poses both a reference point and a set of constraints for the existing system that is to be modified through augmentation and installation of the new system. Thus, a necessary first task must be to identify potential alternative augmentations, additions, and modifications, of this existing system.

These will be subject to analysis and impact assessment activities in which the impacts of these identified alternatives on the effectiveness of the resulting operational implementation will be determined. This step should allow for some refinement of parameters within the assumed architectural structures for the alternative implementations, such that each of the alternatives is optimized for approximately best performance. These alternative systems and processes should be capable of being interfaced and interoperable with some existing systems, integrated with other systems, and compatible with still other systems. There is a major need for an evaluation and review methodology to verify and validate the software, the hardware, the human interfaces, and the trustworthiness of the resulting system.

Cost and effectiveness indices will be determined for each of the resulting refined alternatives. This will be in the form of a set of planning documents for augmentations of system resources that are currently operational. These documents will identify potential integration opportunities within the current technical environment of computer hardware and software, and communications. These impacts will be identified against a background of several alternative future scenarios for conditions that affect the system user group.

Also included with each evaluation should be an analysis of risk factors affecting implementation of each alternative. Risk is a very multiattributed concept, and relevant dimensions that affect operational functionality of the system being implemented should be fully explored.

Implementation and integration documents should be prepared. An appropriate system development lifecycle will be such that at least a preliminary version of these will have been prepared as part of requirements specifications. Now is the time to revise them! These documents will also include systems management plans for all phases of the system implementation lifecycle.

7.2 MANAGEMENT OF SOFTWARE SYSTEM IMPLEMENTATION AND INTEGRATION

Invariably, the goals of those working on a software systems engineering project will include the following:

1. Identify new technology approaches that will enhance operational functionality of a new system.
2. Identify significant "cost-drivers" that represent a high percentage of total costs.
3. Identify methods that will reduce costs while simultaneously retaining benefits.

The task of conceptual design of the system and, most importantly, the methodology for design of this system is basically a "top-down" effort that requires vigilant attention to software systems engineering management principals. The tasks of implementation of this concept will generally require detailed technical expertise for the many "bottom-up" tasks that are required. To neglect either is to invite failure in the sense of producing a system that will not satisfy the needs of the various users of the system. The best way to keep contract costs at a minimum *and achieve a satisfactory implementation of sound concepts* is to select a software contractor with the wisdom and experience to manage an effective systems management approach to the various problems that occur throughout the lifecycle. There will necessarily be tradeoffs among time schedules, standardization of the eventual product, and ultimate functionality and trustworthiness of this product in the operational environment. Thus, implementation and integration concerns need to be addressed as vital parts of the total effort. To do this effectively will require major efforts and environmental management throughout the entire software systems engineering lifecycle.

There will be hardware and software issues that will act as cost drivers. Without question, the software cost-drivers will generally be an order of magnitude more critical. In fact, quality software design procedures should enable relatively easy transfer of software from one machine to another as improved hardware evolves. One purpose of quality software design is to make the change of hardware virtually transparent to the system user. There are a variety of software design management needs and constraints. A major constraint is that the software design methodology and management must be such that effective and efficient design practices at the microlevel must be enhanced, and surely not inhibited. There is a very strong need for flexible standards for software of different scope and for different applications. A realistic software design and management methodology must recognize that standards that can prevent problems in operational software are necessarily different from standards that need be used in the requirements determination phase of the software acquisition lifecycle. We believe that it is possible to develop a *standardized software design and management methodology* that is realistic, unambiguous, consistent, necessary, and complete. It should be possible to develop a methodology that provides *interaction* and *feedback* among the several steps in the software design lifecycle, that involve *issue formulation, issue analysis,* and *issue interpretation,* and to use these through-out the system lifecycle.

To accomplish these objectives will require a software systems management team that is well versed in all relevant aspects of systems design and devel-opment, including implementation. Systems management activities must be such that a continuous, in-depth knowledge of relevant methodologies for the design, implementation and management of large software, and hardware, projects is applied. Required also may be the ability to integrate the results of various other software developers such as to ensure operational function-ality of the software subsystems that comprise the overall system.

The primary technical systems management issue here is the critical need to cope with the large existing and embedded repository of existing system resources that will generally have accumulated over the years. In many cases, several application software packages will have been acquired at a time when an integrated system was not a consideration driving system design. Therefore, there exists the need to become thoroughly aware of the existing system such as to be able to make knowledgeable recommendations concerning mainte-nance of the existing system and transitioning over time to a new and evolving integrated system.

To accomplish integration efficiently and effectively will require a very thorough identification of multiattribute metrics with which to evaluate the existing and current software system. Among these attributes will be those displayed in the attribute tree shown in Figure 7.7. Developing suitable us-ability metrics, that build on those initially identified as a part of requirements specifications, will be an important initial part of software system implemen-tation efforts. The result of this might well be a template that can be used to indicate the type of *maintenance* required for the existing system and the

FIGURE 7.7   Attribute template for usability of existing software

as it will be after implementation of the new system. As in Chapter
ıse maintenance in a very general context to mean correction, adaptation, enhancement, restructuring, or replacing, or an appropriate combination of these. Generally, application of an identified template for usability and reusability will be such as to enable one to answer questions concerning maintenance in the order given in Figure 7.8, as costs will generally increase as one moves down the maintenance hierarchy shown in this figure.

All of this is a part of the methodology for an integrated approach to software system implementation. It results in systems engineering and technical direction efforts in order that a formerly incompatible system can be successfully integrated into an existing environment. This is shown in Figure 7.9.

The concept of operational deployment, or system implementation, is an iterative and evolving one. It is not static over time. Thus it is that systems that once fit well into a complete software system at one point in time may not fit it at some future point. The evolving concept of implemented system software is shown in Figure 7.10. The iteration and feedback involved in this is essential and especially relevant in ensuring continuing functionality of the deployed system.

As we have noted, the primary cost-driver for many software intensive projects is the requirement to produce functionally useful and trustworthy software, to maintain existing systems, to integrate the existing software with other software, new and existing, and to enable hardware changes to be transparent to the system user. Thus, the efforts at the "tail end" of the software lifecycle are of major importance. Not only are they important in their own right, but the initial portions of the software lifecycle must reflect

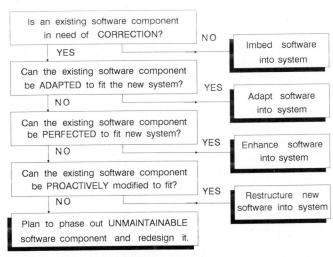

FIGURE 7.8 Maintenance as an evolving effort following operational implementation

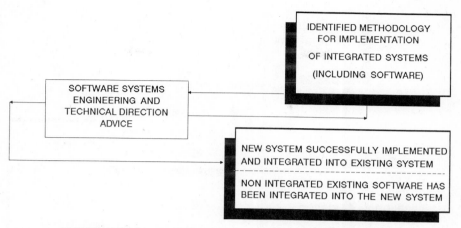

FIGURE 7.9   Integrating new software in with existing software

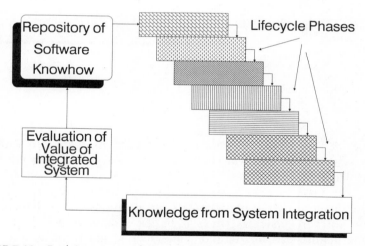

FIGURE 7.10   Evolving nature of systems implementation and associated learning

a keen awareness of these latter phases as well. Figure 7.11 illustrates some of the support made possible through an integrated development environment for software productivity.

7.3   INTEGRATION NEEDS IN SOFTWARE SYSTEM IMPLEMENTATION

Perhaps more so than any other modern high-technology system, a software system implementation effort is a very complex human-machine systems de-

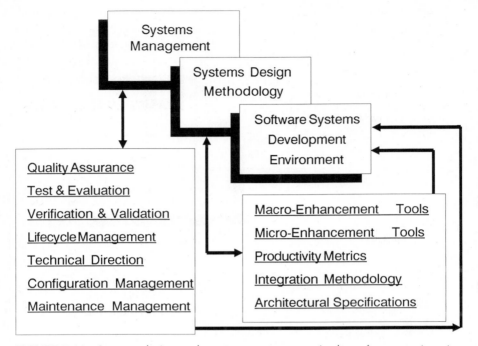

FIGURE 7.11   Systems design and systems management in the software engineering environment

sign issue. A very large percentage of the problems associated with large complex systems are, and will continue to be, associated with the human elements that are associated with operating, maintaining, and managing these systems. The tasks of operation, maintenance, and management are each strongly influenced by the requirements specifications and architectures selected for software systems. Thus, as has been already noted, there is a continuing major need for iteration, interaction, and feedback across and within the various phases of system activity associated with the entire lifecycle of a complex software system.

Several realities emerge from this:

1. It is very necessary to consider both the design of complex new software systems and the integration of existing and new systems, as well as the operation, maintenance, and management of these systems.
2. A *design support system* that enables system designers to anticipate and resolve operational, maintenance, and management problems prior to fielding large scale complex systems could do much to support high-quality software systems implementation and integration engineering.
3. Three types of knowledge are very important.

a. It is very important to understand the *practice* of software systems engineering design, that is to say, how existing software systems that form a part of an overall system have been designed, how this design affects operational functionality concerns, and how well existing designs meet existing and projected future requirements, including budget requirements.

b. To improve on existing systems and to design new information systems, it is also very necessary that we understand the *principles* of software system design. We need to understand both top-down and bottom-up perspectives on systems design, and why a hybrid of these two approaches will generally be needed. We need to be aware of a variety of approaches to system design, and how these may be integrated into a standardized "design for interoperability" approach that will enhance the integration of existing and new systems into an enhanced system concept and reality. In particular, we need to be very aware of the major potential improvements in systems design made possible by new high-level languages, such as Ada, and to be able to accomplish software systems design *for* the new high-level language, and not just to be able to write programs *in* the new high-level language.

c. To accomplish these effectively, we must also be aware of future *perspectives* that will enhance prospects for improvements in software systems to meet projected client needs in a timely and trustworthy manner. This will involve future projections of software and hardware technology base, as well as projections of client or user needs for the resulting system.

Although the word does not explicitly appear in this list of three desiderata for technical and systems management in implementation, *standards* is implied in each of the three.

The three approaches to system knowledge we have discussed interact together as indicated in Figure 7.12. One major objective of almost every software system production effort is to provide the software systems engineering technology and management capability to reduce implementation risks and enhance trustworthiness of the resulting system or process in resolving some particular issue or satisfying some need. Much of the development needed, for existing system retrofit and modification as well as for new system design, will involve software systems engineering. An appropriate high-level language should be used for this development, whenever this is at all possible. Essentially all precepts of software systems engineering support this notion, in a very general sense. As we have just noted, there will be two rather different perspectives associated with the implementation of program code in a new high-level language. One can write code and potentially also produce software *in* the new high-level language. Alternately, one can write code and potentially also produce software *for* the new high-level language. These are rather different approaches. The latter approach involves using the design philosophy and concepts as well as the new high-level language. The former approach involves just the use of the language.

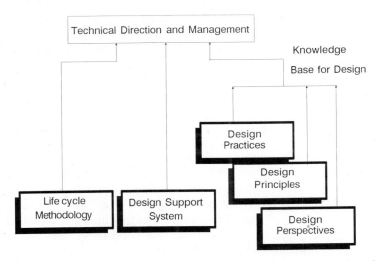

FIGURE 7.12   Principal design knowledge ingredients in systems engineering

For existing systems, decisions will often need to be made relative to whether overall client goals are best achieved by (1) modification of existing code, (2) recoding the original source code *in* the new high-level language, or (3) redesign and recoding the software system *for* the new high-level language. Many variables will influence this choice. To develop appropriate decision templates that assist user group personnel in making them will be a major goal for the software systems implementation and integration engineering contractor. There will necessarily be a multitude of attributes that comprise this template.

Let us continue this discussion by assuming that the new language in question is Ada. For new embedded defense systems, it is hard to imagine development in other than Ada as it is a *mandate* of the U.S. Department of Defense and not merely an alternative or optional language. The major advantage to this is the inherent power in the new language and the inherent standardization across many programmers, companies, operating systems, and hardware.

The major needs that will have to be satisfied in doing this include widespread education and training to use the new language and reeducation such that software system developers take more of a software systems engineering management perspective, rather than just learn to produce programs or code in Ada. The key words in this are *software systems engineering FOR Ada* and not just the production of code or programs in Ada. In this regard, it should be possible to produce an Ada program analyzer that will examine Ada code and, perhaps through use of a template, determine the extent to which the code is *in Ada*, rather than *for Ada*. This sort of ability would be part of a design support system. Generally, there would be a variety of technological components to this design support system, as shown in Figure 7.13.

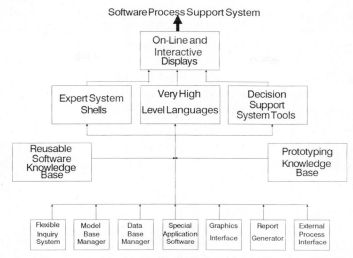

FIGURE 7.13   Some components in the support environment for software systems engineering

These could be used to enhance the ability to develop productive software, even when using very high powered software development tools. There is also a present lack of micro-enhancement software support tools in Ada, for example. These range from the need for fourth generation language type tools, including automatic program generators, to design completeness and consistency checkers.

Very needed as well will be the reusable software packages and prototyping capability that are associated with the macro-enhancement approach to software productivity.

There are some major technical challenges in this. Let us consider the situation that typically exists today. Choice of computer hardware will limit the selection of available database management systems. Alternately, the choice of a particular DBMS will constrain the hardware that may be selected as well as the operating system. A well-designed *integrated* software system surely needs DBMS independence. This would enable the system to use a variety of validated and verified (and interoperable) DBMSs. It would enable application software system expansion to be machine and operating system independent. This would foster greater competition among system vendors as well as do much to insure integrity of the resulting software systems. We will have a great deal more to say about this support environment, and needed support in it, in the remainder of this chapter.

It appears that this is an approach that is able to satisfy present and projected needs in contemporary software systems engineering software application environments, which is capable of efficiently and effectively coping with future user needs for hardware and software acquisition, and which will enable the identification, development, and operationalization of an integrated system and related needs. These include need satisfaction regarding implementation in contemporary environments:

1. Accommodating changes in external environment
2. Accommodating changes in user requirements
3. Use of product technologies that automate program construction
4. Use of technologies that reduce programming errors
5. Information management rather than data processing procedures
6. Evolving needs in the computer and software applications environment of the future

These evolving needs include:

7. Providing rapid turnaround for (re)development of applications
8. Describing the structure of multipurpose systems
9. Accommodating multiple users in distributed locations
10. Accommodating effective and efficient software maintenance
11. Enabling efficient and effective system implementation

We now turn our attention to a discussion of software environments.

7.4   SOFTWARE ENGINEERING ENVIRONMENTS

In this section, we will discuss *environments* for the design of trustworthy and responsive systems. We will summarize existing work in this area, much of which is to be found in the software engineering and systems engineering research literatures. To bring about some specificity to our discussions, we will consider a relatively specific application domain. In this connection, we will discuss needs for and requirements to be satisfied by appropriate environments for the design of complex automatic control systems of large scale and scope. At this point, it is advantageous to introduce a particular intended application such that we can describe some of the specific needs for this application environment as indicative of the sort of needs that would exist in other application environments.

The expression *environment for systems design* extends over a wide collection of interpretations. At one end of the spectrum is an interpretation that suggests a set of *computer-aided system design tools,* or perhaps just a very classic collection of design approaches that have not been subject to computerization at all. At another end of the spectrum are uses of the term that imply an adjuvant that provides *machine intelligence* or *expert system* type of support to aid systems design and development, potentially through the entire lifecycle phases of system evolution. These two notions are related.

The first refers to the environment of the designer, and the second refers to the environment of the client or system user. Still another common use of the term environment relates to the *surroundings* in which the designed system will be used.

Of course, an expert system would presumably need to have embedded within it knowledge of the operational environment of the user of the system, and knowledge concerning the system design and development process, both technical and management, of the software development organization. Otherwise, it becomes an "idiot savant," which is very knowledgeable about one particular perspective concerning a system but oblivious to either user or designer realities needed to design an efficacious system.

Needless to say, it will generally be a difficult task to understand either the environment of the designer or the user sufficiently well such that it becomes possible to model either of them in the knowledge base of an expert system. This is especially the case when we realize that systems must not only be designed, but they must be *integrated* in with other existing systems, and they must be *maintained* as a user's needs change over time.

For our purposes, we define environment as follows. *A system design and development environment is the set of methods, design methodologies, and systems management processes that, associated with the operational situation extant of the user, is used to produce a trustworthy system.* The methods portion of this definition represents those analytical tools that support the design process. For control systems design for example, this would include such design tools as root locus approaches, and the wealth of multiobjective optimization approaches, linear quadratic feedback algorithms, and stochastic control algorithms. Design methodologies represent the sets of open procedures that enable problem-solving, that is, the ways in which the methods and tools are used. The term "systems management" refers not only to the way in which problems are formulated but also to the way in which a problem-solving effort is formulated.

It is potentially important to note that this definition indicates that an appropriate systems design engineering environment is *much more* than an integrated set of methods and tools, regardless of their sophistication, that are useful throughout the technical lifecycle of a system. It is important, of course, to surround the system designer with an appropriate set of tools. But this alone will generally not be sufficient for the design of trustworthy systems that satisfy user needs and which are usable by the user.

A successful systems design team must necessarily be aware of appropriate methods, tools, and techniques. They need also to be aware of systems methodologies and design approaches that enable selection of appropriate methods, and appropriate human judgment at the cognitive process level of systems management. Thus, three functional components of systems design engineering are each necessary:

1. Systems science and operations research methods,

2. Systems methodology and design, and

3. Systems management.

Figure 7.14 shows an expanded conceptual model of the complete systems design engineering process that conceptually incorporates an awareness of the operational situation of the user. Thus, Figure 7.14 represents a conceptualization of an *environment for systems design engineering.*

The term "methodology" has appeared in our discussions, and it is important to discuss it. Methodology is sometimes a misused word, even in systems engineering. It is not simply an overly sophisticated synonym for method. As we use it, a methodology is an open set of procedures for problem-solving. Consequently, a methodology involves a set of methods, a set of activities, and a set of relations between the methods and the activities. To use a methodology we must have an appropriate set of methods. Generally, as we have indicated, these are the methods provided by systems and computer science and operations research. They include a variety of qualitative and quantitative approaches from a number of disciplines. Associated with a methodology is a structured framework into which particular methods are associated for resolution of a specific issue.

Systems engineering efforts will also be concerned with technical direction

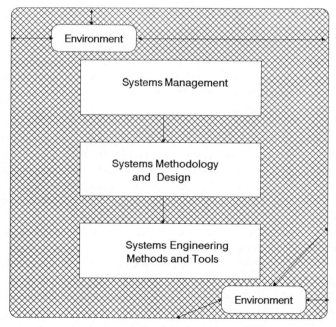

FIGURE 7.14 Three fundamental levels of systems design engineering and the environment for systems design

and management of systems design, production, and maintenance. By adopting the management technology of systems design engineering and applying it, we become very concerned with making sure that correct systems are designed, and not just that system designs are correct according to some potentially ill-conceived notions of what the system should do. Appropriate tools to enable efficient and effective error prevention and detection in a systems design process will enhance the production of system designs that are correct. To ensure that correct systems are designed requires that considerable emphasis be placed on the front end of the systems lifecycle, which involves issue or requirements identification, and on the environment for design.

In particular, there needs to be considerable emphasis on the accurate definition of a system, what it should do and how people should interact with it after it is produced. This should occur *before* the system is produced and implemented. In turn, this requires emphasis on conformance to system requirements specifications and the development of standards to insure compatibility and integratibility of system products. Such areas as documentation and communication are important in all of this. Thus, we see the need for the technical direction and management technology efforts that comprise systems engineering. In a previous effort [Sage, 1987b], we have referred to the need for technological systems design and management systems design and the appropriate use of design practices, principles, and perspectives.

To cope with these just mentioned needs, a number of methodologies associated with systems design engineering have evolved. Through these, it has been possible to decompose large design issues into smaller component subsystem design issues, design the subsystems, and then *build* the complete system as a collection of these subsystems. Even so, problems remain. Just simply connecting together the individual subsystems often does not result in a system that performs acceptably, from either a technological efficiency perspective or an effectiveness perspective. This has led to the realization that *systems integration engineering* and *systems management* throughout an entire system lifecycle will be necessary. Thus it is that contemporary efforts in *systems engineering* contain a focus on tools and methods, on the system design methodology that enable appropriate use of these tools, and on the systems management approaches that enable the embedding of design approaches within organizations and environments, such as to support the application of the principals of the physical and material sciences for the betterment of humankind. The use of appropriate tools, as well as systems methodology and management constructs enables *system design for more efficient and effective human interaction* [Sage, 1987a]. Clearly, this is a product of an effective systems design engineering environment. It is what we have attempted to describe in Figure 7.14.

A key issue in this is the design of critical technological systems and critical management systems to implement the technology such that human interaction concerns are dealt with in an effective way in a large variety of plausible contemporary environments in which a system is perceived to be a functionally

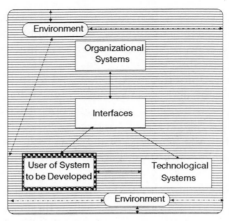

FIGURE 7.15 Needed integration of personnel, technology and organizations with the environment

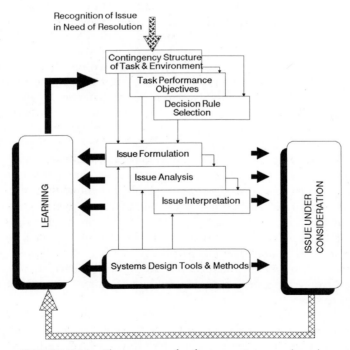

FIGURE 7.16 The process of software systems engineering

useful component. Figure 7.15 illustrates this conceptually. The major task of systems control engineering is to ensure appropriate integration across the levels of people, technological systems, organizational systems, and environment such as to ensure success in the software systems engineering process depicted conceptually in Figure 7.16. Thus, "appropriate" is, here, a very multiattributed term that encompasses such features as risk management, reliability, and modifiability.

7.5   ENVIRONMENTS FOR SYSTEM DESIGN

It is meaningful to discuss several types of design environments. One way to do this is to associate an environment with each of the seven phases of the systems lifecycle that we have discussed in Chapters 1 and 2:

1. Requirements specifications identification environment
2. Preliminary conceptual design environment
3. Logical design and system architecture specification environment
4. Detailed design and testing environment
5. Operational implementation environment
6. Evaluation and modification environment
7. Operational deployment environment

It will clearly be very difficult to provide tools, methodologies, and system management processes that are invariant across each of these different environments. We would expect to find, therefore, that one specific environment would support the different phases of the system lifecycle in differing amounts. At the level of tools, it is quite apparent that very general tools, such as text editors, will support all phases of the system lifecycle. However, the support from such a tool may be so very general that there is really little automation of the system development process, or achievement of standards of data interoperability.

To achieve truly useful system design environments, it seems a certainty that there will have to be specific tools that are primarily useful in only some system lifecycle phases. This suggests, strongly, the need for a systems engineering environment to support *transitioning* from one phase to the other, and to support integration and interoperability across phases and the products of different vendors.

The early phases of the system lifecycle are conceptual formulation or *framing* type efforts in which the primary tasks are associated with problem or issue characterization and representation. Then follows a detailed design and analysis, or *production* sequence of phases in which a system is actually produced. The final phases in the system lifecycle are devoted to interpretation and *evaluation* of the produced system and associated maintenance and modification of the system to make it more effective as time evolves. We can associate an environment with each of these, and we can also speak of a *generic* environment, and of tools associated with this environment. These tools would consist of very-general-purpose instruments that would be useful across the other more specialized environments. Figure 7.17 illustrates the general relationships among these environments.

There are other environmental taxonomies that have been identified. Dart et.al.[1987], for example, specify a taxonomy comprised of four elements:

1. *Language centered environments,* which provide integrated tools that support a specific high-level programming language, such as Interlisp for Lisp or Rational for Ada
2. *Structure-oriented environments,* which support
   a. The direct manipulation of program structure in a language independent fashion
   b. The generation of structure oriented environments
   c. Differing images of program structure at several levels of abstraction
3. *Toolkit environments,* which aggregate and make available a set of smaller tools that are primarily directed at code production and enhanced programmer productivity
4. *Methods-based environments,* which include either (or both) technology development methods for particular phases in the lifecycle, or methods for managing the development process, such as Excellerator and SREM

Our notion of four environmental phases is not unrelated to several of the other environmental constructs that have been identified. We choose this particular set of four since they so closely correspond to the general efforts

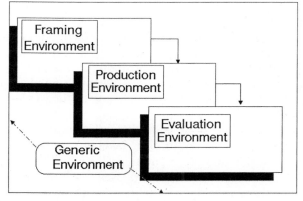

FIGURE 7.17   Support provided in various environments

of formulation, analysis, and interpretation that are the fundamental systems engineering steps. The fourth environment, a generic environment, corresponds to tools and support that are ubiquitous across the other three.

Let us examine these further. The *framing environment* consists of the tools, the methodologies, and the systems management procedures to accomplish the more conceptual parts of the system lifecycle. Among the activities involved in these phases are:

1. Identify the need for a system.
2. Identify the general requirements for a system in terms of user needs.
3. Identify design requirements for the system (conceptual design).
4. Identify functional and data requirements for the systems.
5. Identify resource constraints on system design and development in terms of cost, delivery time, software, and hardware.
6. Perform a cost–effectiveness, or cost–benefit, analysis of the system.
7. Identify a program and project development and management plan.

Identification or formulation, or *framing,* of an issue or problem is a very necessary first step in any problem-solving process. A problem statement should always be identified prior to the application of solution methods. Often, there is considerable merit in identifying the problem in terms of a number of interdependent elements that can be characterized as one or more of the *issue framing elements.* These include each of the following:

1. *Problem definition* elements (needs, constraints, alterables)
2. *Value system design* elements (objectives or objectives measures)
3. *System synthesis elements* (activities or controls and activity measures)

All too often a notion of a problem is attacked with a large outpouring of energy only to end up back at the starting point, because an immature issue formulation effort has led to solution of the wrong problem. There are a number of generating or issue formulation methods which may be used to aid a decision group in formulating or framing a problem or issue chosen for study. For this reason, these methods are known as *collective* enquiry methods. (See an article of the same title in Sage [1989] for a discussion of some of these.) They are, by no means, a panacea and should be called on only after simple conversational exchange of thoughts and ideas becomes inadequate, or is not possible for any of a variety of reasons.

Decision support systems [Keen and Scott Morton, 1978] are particularly useful support tools for framing environments. There have been a number of definitions of decision support and group decision support systems that often use these collective enquiry approaches, as well as evaluation approaches, such as multiattribute utility theory (MAUT). Simply stated, *a DSS is an interactive computer based system of hardware, software, and interfaces, that supports the decisionmaking process that involves resolution of unstructured problems.* A GDSS then is simply a DSS that supports a group of people or, more to the point, a group of decisionmakers.

It is possible to develop a taxonomy of GDSS based on the levels of support just discussed. From this perspective, a level I GDSS would simply be a medium for enhanced information interchange that might lead ultimately to a decision. Electronic mail, large video screen displays that can be viewed by a group, or a *decision room* that contains these features, could represent a level I GDSS. A level I GDSS provides only a mechanism for group interaction.

A level II GDSS would provide various decision structuring and other analytic tools that could act to reduce information imperfection. A decision room that contained software that could be used for problem solution would represent a level II GDSS. Thus, spreadsheets would represent a possible component in a level II DSS. To become a level II GDSS, there would also have to be some means of enabling group communication. A level II GDSS is simply a communications medium that has been augmented with some tools for problem structuring and solution with no prescribed management control of the use of these tools.

A level III GDSS also includes the notion of management control of the decision process. Thus, there is a notion of *facilitation* of the process, either through the direct intervention of a human in the process, or through some rule based specifications of the management control process that is inherent in a level III GDSS. Clearly, there is no sharp transition line between one level and the next and it may not always be easy to identify at what level a GDSS is operating.

Other relevant efforts and interest areas involving GDSS include group processes in computer mediated communications, the computer support for collaboration and problem-solving in meetings study of Stefik et.al.[1987], the organizational planning and computer-aided deliberation model study of Appelgate et. al.[1987] and Nunamaker et.al.[1988], and the knowledge management and intelligent information sharing systems study of Malone et.al.[1987].

There are other tools and methodologies for use in the framing environment that more specifically relate to the translation of identified requirements specification into software technical requirements specifications. These include the *software development system* (SDS) [Alford and Davis, 1981], the *dream realization, evaluation, and modeling system* (DREAM) [Riddle, 1981], and the *software lifecycle support environment* (SLCSE) system [Strelich, 1988]. The next section will discuss environmental management CASE tools. There will also be a brief discussion of some CASE tools that specifically support the macro-enhancement efforts in Chapter 8. Let us briefly discuss the ones mentioned here as they directly support integrated software developments.

The *software development system* is designed to be a support environment for complex real-time systems. There are four primary activities involved in using this methodology:

1. *Data processing systems engineering* (DPSE), which involves translation of the objectives of the system into a consistent and complete set of functional and performance requirements expressed in Petri net, finite-state machines, and graph theoretic representations
2. *Software requirements engineering methodology* (SREM), which enables the use of what is known as the *requirements engineering validation system* (REVS) to result in an expression of the functional and performance requirements for the software in a language known as the *requirements statement language*
3. *Process design engineering* (PDE), which results in the translation of these requirements into a *process design language* (PDL), verification of the design, and the production of source code
4. *Verification and validation* (V&V), which is accomplished throughout the SDS effort

The *DREAM system* is a software engineering design environment oriented to use of the *DREAM design notation* (DDN) for development of concurrent systems. The DDN language is potentially capable of modeling a total system, including software and hardware. The tools provided for use in the environment include a database core that is used to store DDN fragments, bookkeeping tools for entry and retrieval, and analysis tools for simulation and consistency checking.

The *SLCSE system* supports software system development throughout the lifecycle. It is asserted to be an *environmental framework* that can create a variety of environments, each of which is tailored to a particular software design and development project. A conceptual model of the SLCSE is presented in Figure 7.18. The *project database* of SLCSE is both an information repository and a medium for intertool information exchange. It is an entity-

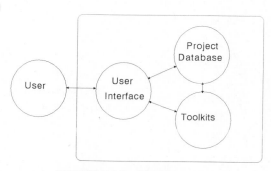

FIGURE 7.18   SLCSE structure

relationship model partitioned into nine submodels: contract, system requirements, software requirements, design, test, project management, configuration management, product evaluation, and environment. These correspond to the phases in the system lifecycle and a number of additional phases that extend across the basic phases. There are a number of tools that support each of the possible lifecycle phases in which the SLCSE may be used. In reality, then, the SLCSE is an integrated metalevel tool that does provide support throughout the framing, the production, and the evaluation environment.

7.6   REQUIREMENTS FOR AN INTEGRATED SOFTWARE SYSTEMS DESIGN ENVIRONMENT

Figure 7.19 illustrates the use of tools at different levels. Figure 7.20 shows an expanded conceptual model of the complete systems design engineering process that conceptually incorporates an awareness of the operational situation of the user. Thus, Figure 7.20 represents a conceptualization of an *environment for systems design engineering* in that it includes awareness of both the environment of designers and of users.

System integration concerns follow a path almost parallel and analogous to those discussed concerning system environment. It is possible, for example, to speak of an integrated design environment or an integrated set of system design methods. This may refer to a set of methods that have been integrated together in the sense that there is data interoperability across the inputs and outputs of several design packages. While integration at the level of the methods and tool needs of designers is very important, this alone will not

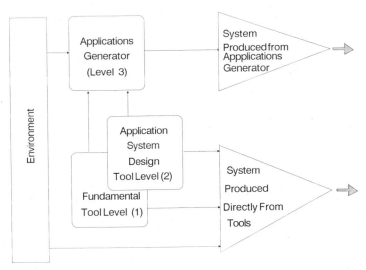

FIGURE 7.19   Three technology levels for software systems design

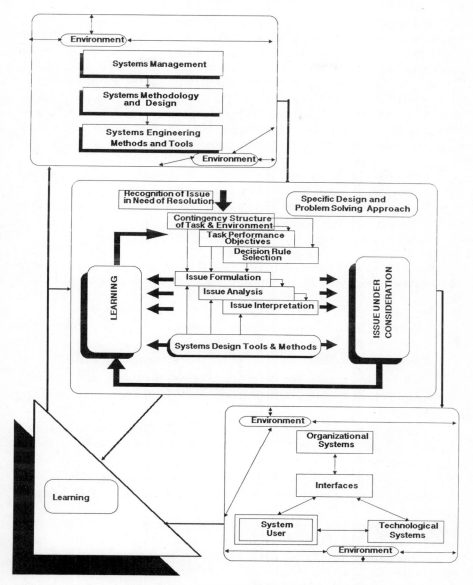

FIGURE 7.20   Integration of designer and client environment in the software systems engineering process

ensure that the resulting technical and management systems have been designed for successful human interaction with them, or that it will be possible to orchestrate together the technological systems or the management systems of different vendors.

Thus, an expanded view of system integration is needed and it, as previously mentioned, has many conceptual similarities to those just expressed for environmental issues. There are a number of objectives to be satisfied by an appropriate system design environment. These are intensively concerned with such fundamental needs as data and information interoperability for reliability, availability, maintainability, and the development of standards to ensure these. An appropriate environment must contain analytical techniques that allows us to explicitly consider human performance characteristics when making quantitatively based trade-offs that:

1. Support analysis and interpretation of performance and cost factors throughout the entire system lifecycle
2. Ensure consideration of all important technological and management system design variables and human interfaces throughout the lifecycle of a proposed system

Human concerns are especially important in the design of complex systems of large scale and scope. These concerns are needed in order that we be able to:

1. Convert human performance requirements into engineering specifications
2. Design to identified human cognitive requirements and needs
3. Access physiological and cognitive workload potentials to the fullest
4. Identify human error potential at very early stages of preliminary system design
5. Predict human-system performance capabilities and limitations early enough in the lifecycle such that these provide an input to design requirements
6. Explicitly quantify human performance factors such as to obtain system designs that are more appropriate for successful human interaction

The U.S. Army Research Institute's *Hardware Manpower* (HARDMAN) tools [Boorer, 1990] are designed to assist in this. These tools enable us to project manpower, personnel, and training requirements at an early phase in the system development lifecycle as a function of several potential design strategies that might be adopted. At this early point in the system lifecycle, the costs and other resources provided as inputs to a particular design can be analyzed to predict performance and insure that systems function as intended. While system integration needs occur at later portions of the lifecycle, attention to the four primary inputs at an early phase enables trade-offs between hardware and manpower when the cost involved is relatively low. It results in technological and management systems that enable machines to do what machines do well, and humans to do what humans do well.

There are, therefore, many requirements for an integrated systems design environment. From our preceding discussions, we see that some of these are: (1) the data and algorithmic processes that occur within the system, (2) a set of software tools that facilitates resolutions of the control and planning issues that occur in the planning of operations, and (3) a control structure that will create and execute the applications that are definable and solvable using the various system design environment that has been provided.

Our preceding discussions also indicate that control system design efforts can not be considered as independent of the other technology areas of concern, which include such software concerns as:

- Software design and analysis tools
- Command languages
- Operating systems
- Database tools
- Text processing systems
- Graphics protocols
- Network protocols

Taken together, these are components of the technological systems, or methods-based, design environment. Other components include elements associated with the environment of the user:

- The physical system or process that is to be controlled
- The user or customer with a need for the resulting system or process
- The associated human and organizational concerns

We can take a methods based view of *environment*. We can also take a *process* or systems management view. From this latter perspective, we would be concerned primarily with management of the overall systems design process, and with identifying and providing rules and procedures to govern the tasks performed within the environment. In this sense, the process view includes the methods or technological perspective.

There exists at least one process based effort for system design environments, the *Knowledge-Based Software Assistant* (KBSA) project funded by Rome Air Development Center. The primary goal in this in progress effort is to provide an automated software development environment comprised of seven *assistants*. Five of these are *framing, production,* or *evaluation* environment-based aids:

1. Project or Configuration Management Assistant (PMA)
2. Requirements Assistant (RA)
3. Specification Assistant (SA)

4. Implementation or Development Assistant (DA)
5. Testing or Performance Assistant (PA)

Two *generic environmental* aids are also provided:

1. Intelligent editors
2. Documentation aids

In the KBSA, new cost and schedule estimates for the system will be determined when a new system requirement is added. When possible, the information to enable this determination is obtained from the user of the KBSA. When the user does not desire to supply needed information, the KBSA will search through its knowledge base for the relevant information, use it to update estimates, and propagate these throughout the system. We will have some additional commentary concerning this system, as a software production tool, in Chapter 8.

The primary objectives of the development and use of a software systems engineering environment is to develop an integrated suite of analysis and design tools, methodologies, and systems management processes that support the efficient and effective design of complex systems of large scale and scope. The system design environment should have six major functional elements:

1. A system builder or system generator that selects appropriate algorithms and software packages
2. Data retrieval, entry, and editing capability to allow relevant design data and information to be used by the selected control system design algorithms
3. Exercise of the specific control design algorithm that is selected to be used for a particular application
4. Generation of output displays and reports, and presentation of these to the user
5. A user–system–designer interface to support human machine communication from both conceptual and linguistic points of view and to assist the system user in efficient and effective use of the resulting *prototype* system such as to enable iterative adjustments towards a *better* system
6. A knowledge based lifecycle assistant to determine the implications of design changes throughout the development lifecycle

Two general types of decision and development plan evaluation aids might be envisioned for most system development environments: *smart checklists* and *spreadsheets*. The smart checklist is a tree structured data base intended to alert the user to possible action options and outcomes at each step of the planning and design process. Effectively, the smart checklist is a decision or option tree. For cases of decisions under certainty, this sort of display can often be easily cognized. When there are many stages in the decision process, or when there are many chance nodes, then the display of information in a decision-tree-type format may not be especially easy to comprehend. The presence of incomplete, imprecise, contradictory, or otherwise imperfect information will also complicate this form of presentation.

The spreadsheet display is basically a two-dimensional array. As with decision trees, spreadsheets may become quite complex when there is imperfect information present. Aggregation of elements in a spreadsheet may pose some very interesting interface concerns with the knowledge bases and database management systems.

It may also turn out that decision trees and spreadsheets are very effective representations for analytic calculations but not for presentations to the system user. Graphic displays, and frame- and script-type presentations may well be more understandable. For example, the system user may find it much easier to select effective courses of action when domination digraphs of alternative courses of action are presented. A production rule type representation of implementation plans may well be more easily appreciated than the equivalent presentation in the form of decision-tree-type smart checklists. Thus it may be very appropriate to use these smart checklists and spreadsheets as aids for the analyst, and as convenient database representations of decisions and plans, but to use alternative representations for display to the system user.

Methods used to assist the system user in identifying alternative courses of action, or alternative designs may play a major role in enhancing the effectiveness of a design support system in an environment such as the one described here. Often the initial generation of alternative courses of action is in a very wholistic form and heavily based on experiential familiarity and perceptual feelings relative to the design task at hand. We see that these are very closely associated with the *evaluation environment* for system design and development that we have discussed in an earlier section of this chapter.

Generally, neither application system designers, software systems engineers, or users are each very knowledgeable about all characteristics of the end system under consideration. This is because they will not have sufficient experiential familiarity with the knowledge domains of the other group to enable full appreciation of the implications of system design and development decisions. This is one of the primary purposes of the *design support environment* and why one is quite needed. A purpose of this section is to specify some of the needed features for this environment.

One of the major environmental ingredients in supporting software productivity is the development of a *model base management* system (MBMS), which consists of a number of modules that support efficiency and effectiveness throughout the system development lifecycle. Prominent among these are software prototyping and software reusability approaches for what we have called "macro-enhancement of software productivity." Associated with this are other issues concerning knowledge representation and dialog management. An overarching question concerns cognitive issues associated with the ability of humans to cope with the requirements potentially imposed through introduction of information and knowledge support technologies for software productivity improvements.

An ideal software and systems engineering development environment is one in which the end user is able to identify system requirements [Davis, 1982] through an interactive human–machine interface that enables visualization of the impact of alternative requirements specifications. Through this, the user should be able to refine these requirements iteratively and throughout the process, so as to produce the software system closest to that required to fulfill identified needs. The ultimate operational goal of a software development environment is to enable automated production of requirements specifications and to be able to ultimately enable these to be translated into operational code that meets all of the operational functionality requirements of reliability, maintainability, availability, portability, interoperability, verifiability, validability, and trustability [Beam et al., 1987; Frenkel, 1985; Harrison, 1985]. This process implies the need to look beyond the conventional "waterfall lifecycle" [Boehm, 1981] and other production lifecycle models, to take advantage of the opportunities afforded by emerging information technology advances: expert systems, artificially intelligent interfaces, open systems architectures, distributed databases, graphic interfaces, and cognitive interfaces.

Progress is being made in the incremental development of such a software design and management environment, as indicated by the following advances:

1. The Common Ada Missile Packages (CAMP) project has developed an environment that demonstrates the ability to develop and use Ada parts that are reusable, tailorable, efficient, and protected [Czarnik, 1987]. This demonstrates the ability to provide automated assistance to the part user; and apply DoD-STD 2167 [U.S. DoD, 1985] to Ada and the parts selected.

2. Object-oriented language applications to identify requirements specifications have been implemented [Nordby, 1986] and produce full specifications according to DeMarco's [1982] rules including data flows, hierarchical structure, and data definition.

3. Fourth generation languages (4GL) and automatic program generators have been applied to the production of code [GSA, 1986]. These have proved to be able to produce code faster and with significantly fewer errors than coding in a high-level language. Problems with 4GL and automatic program generators generally are that the code so produced often requires longer run-time, and has more lines of code, although it does otherwise improve productivity [Balzer, 1985; Green, 1985].

There are other significant environment developments that involve the translation of user needs to detailed requirements specifications [Wasserman, 1986]. These latter advances are clearly precursors for the future total software systems engineering design and management environment, and are essential to the work necessary to produce this environment.

Important work continues in the explication of a coherent software development environment, especially through the development of reusability via libraries of parts, the development of intelligent interfaces for database management systems, direct translation to code of detailed specifications automatically developed, and implementation of validation and verification procedures early in the development process. These research and development programs will have significant impact on the utility of the software development environment of the future.

Absent from these research and development programs is the development of the interactive cognitive interface between the user and the system analyst that will enable the translation of the system requirements in an effective and efficient manner. The notion of the ideal software development environment would provide for a *model of the user,* and the interactions of the user across the interface, so that the system would be tailorable to meet the needs of the user. This would enable the transfer of information between the user and the system development processes in a continuous way, without serious penalty to the entire process, such as to facilitate system evolution and modification as user perception of these needs develop.

In order to model the user at the system interface and, as a result, tailor the interface to the capability of the user, it is necessary to know and understand better those cognitive issues that affect the interactive process of information elicitation and transfer.

7.7 SOME HYPOTHESES CONCERNING A SOFTWARE ENVIRONMENT SUPPORT FACILITY

The function and purpose of this design support facility is such that it will enable rapid and interactive cycling through the steps and lifecycle phases of a software design and management activity. The facility will enable and enhance application of the macro-enhancement approaches. It will enable these approaches to be imbedded into a methodology for systems design and systems management of trustworthy software.

Contemporary needs associated with the systems engineering design and management of software for enhanced productivity suggest that much benefit can be achieved through integration of systems engineering, cognitive science, and computer science approaches now made possible by developments in information technology. A principal goal of software systems engineering is the organization of knowledge for the realization of trustworthy software [Fairley, 1985; Somerville, 1985]. Human initiative and creativity are best enhanced when the user of a knowledge support system is able to self direct the system toward skill-based, rule-based, or formal-reasoning-based assistance rather than having to respond to the dictates of a behaviorally insensitive and inflexible paradigm that is often used as the basis for support system development.

We have presented an overview of our conceptual approach to design of a environmental support system for software productivity enhancement. This, as we have discussed, is basically a software repository consisting of reusable software modules and nonprocedural approaches that enable rapid system specification and evaluation in a prototype like fashion [Palmer and Nguyen, 1986]. A critical needed task to obtain a successful system design product is the integration of these findings into a cohesive whole that will enable the sought for system design principles to be evolved into the design of an operational knowledge support system. One of the major tasks associated with the design of a software systems engineering development environment is the determination of a set of information presentation principles and a resulting strategy for information presentation that enables judgment and choice in software productivity areas.

The hypotheses that follow relate to the cognitive aspects of group and individual interactive processes involving human–computer interfaces. One of the major goals of the interactive processes at the human–machine interface is the ability to elicit and transfer information from the user for implementation in the development of the software. One of the hoped for achievements in so doing is a better understanding of the important factors governing the effective, timely, and quality information transfer characteristics that influence the utilization of the software systems engineering development environment and the related tools and activities.

Many issues must be resolved during the course of design of the facility suggested here. These include the formulation of the methods and processes for information transfer, model definition within the model base management system, reusability trade-offs, tailoring of the processes, security and control access, interfaces, expert systems and the application of knowledge-based systems and controllers, interactive languages, configuration management, distributed systems architectures, automation of processes, and all management control areas. The evaluation methodology must address the goal formulation statements, estimation of appropriate metrics, planning, designing and performing tests, and analyzing the outcomes.

The basic scenario will be to provide the development environment, establish user goals in the formal sense, and supply data for the implementation process. The user will then tailor the interactive interface to the comfort level of the individual and utilize the generated internal model of the user for all interactive sessions. The process will be closely monitored to ascertain the selection of tools and methodologies with a trace provided through the expert system at the interface. Concurrently the expert system will trace the preferred tool and method selection as determined from the internal inference engine and knowledge base. These will be compared and the outcomes will be used to drive improvements on the continuing development of the interactive interface. The major goals will be to determine an assessment of the situation regarding the ease of interaction and the efficiency and effectiveness of the tool and methods selection process. Strategic and tactical assessment of the situation will be generated for evaluation purposes. The hypotheses that support design and use of a facility such as this are:

H1. The quality of the requirements phase of software development will improve markedly if the information presentation aids and other parts of the human-machine interface (HMI) affect a symbiosis between the user and the interactive interface.

H2. Productivity and quality will improve if the HMI models the user and tailors the interface to the user needs both intellectually and operationally.

H3. Small groups develop in a known (based on observations from small group dynamics studies) and prescriptive way to maximize individual contributions in a group situation if tailored HMIs are utilized.

H4. The use of an *advanced software systems engineering development environment* (ASSEDE) will increase the information available and enhance effectiveness and efficiency of the software design and management process.

H5. The use of an ASSEDE will increase the span of user control throughout the software lifecycle.

H6. The use of an ASSEDE will decrease the number of hierarchical levels needed in the approval process for identification of requirements specifications and system-level architectures.

H7. The use of an ASSEDE will increase the range of software and system decomposition levels (phases in the software lifecycle) at which design decisions can be made without increasing the costs that are caused by imperfect information about the problem situation.

H8. The use of an ASSEDE will enhance the efficiency and effectiveness of the information systems integration engineering efforts.

Figure 7.21 presents a conceptual view of this environmental support facility. This is very relevant to our discussions here and in the next three chapters.

As we have noted in our foregoing discussions on software environment characteristics, information needs abound in each of the activities of software development. We have presented the requirements for an ideal software systems engineering development environment as one in which: the end user is able to identify system requirements through an interactive human–machine interface that enables visualization of the impact of alternative requirements specifications; provides an extensive software toolkit that automates the development of specifications to include all data elements, data dictionary information, data flows, structured design, and similar; extends the concept of reusability through libraries of code, specifications, testing procedures, and so on; provides prototyping for early review and for code generation; incor-

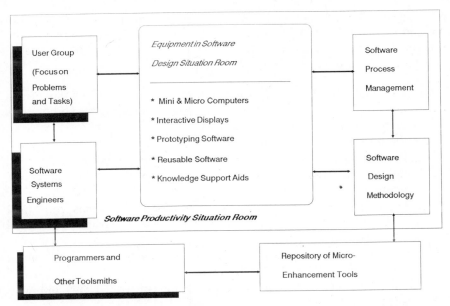

FIGURE 7.21 Environmental support through a software productivity situation room

porates the concepts of verification, validation, and maintenance; and takes advantage of all automated processes such as 4GL generators and documentation generators. The operational goal of the software development environment would be to enable:

1. Automated production of requirements and specifications
2. Translation of these into operational code that meets all the operational functionality requirements of performance, reliability, maintainability, availability, and portability
3. Full software performance verification and validation
4. Software modification over the entire useful life of the system

There are at least five issues that must be addressed in a software development environment in order to significantly improve software productivity. These major issues and their ingredients are:

1. Shorten the software development time.
2. Reduce the software development cost.
3. Achieve higher quality and reliability with software products.
4. Achieve predictability for software development in terms of cost, schedule, and performance.

5. Achieve better communication between the software developers and the end users.

7.8 CASE TOOLS FOR SOFTWARE SYSTEMS ENGINEERING ENVIRONMENTS

Currently available commercial software development environments are generally centered around a specific automation tool. Tools that implement various portions of the software development process have been available for many years. The so-called CASE tool concept is over 20 years old and is just now being realized through integrated toolkits. It is possible to classify tools according to such activities as application, data element, and functionality. The attributes or requirements of CASE tools that have been selected for discussion here are:

1. *Front-end design* and specification graphic support that will replace manual production of diagrams for requirements specification and design
2. *Design analysis*, including tracking and reporting of basic design flaws and detection of design inconsistencies in accordance with the rule set that has been implemented in the tool
3. *Automatic code generation*, including automatic translation of specifications that have been developed earlier in the process
4. A *data dictionary*, including a metadictionary which holds comprehensive entity models or views of the system
5. A *user-friendly workstation* that provides good interfaces, including menus and windows and the use of pointing devices such as a mouse
6. *Capability of being installed on a PC* that is user friendly and which has interfaces including windows and menus

It is essential that goals for a CASE environment be well articulated and understood prior to embarking on the acquisition of a software development lifecycle support environment. These goals ought to be independent of the tool functions and the analysis and design methodologies supported by the tools. Wasserman and Pircher, [1987] in conjunction with a discussion of their company's CASE product, have stated some of the goals which they believe to be essential in an integrated environment:

1. The user must have the ability to customize the environment.
2. Tools must be capable of being integrated and interfaced into the presently used development environment and the environment must be extendible.
3. Tools must have interchangeable data formats or store data in a common database accessible to other tools.

4. Tools must be compatible as well as interface easily.
5. Tools must be easy to learn and use.
6. Tools should communicate via a general database and be able to handle multiple projects and support version control and configuration management.
7. Tools should provide extensive mechanisms for checking completeness and consistency of outputs of the analysis and design tools for error detection early in the software development lifecycle.
8. There should be complete user control of the tools.

To be effective and efficient in addressing the needs of a software development lifecycle support environment, tools must reside in an integrated and interfaced software systems engineering environment. They should be available on a PC or micro-based workstation which is connected via a local area network (LAN) to other parts of the development network. The outputs are to be placed in a consolidated database with a standardized format while in the database. Tools must be able to access the database, extract needed information, and produce their product. We can easily see from our last few numbered listings of desirable features for a software development environment that there are a plethora of attributes with which to evaluate potential support tool sets. The use of conceptual and technical design aids are intended to provide the software system designer with an environment that will aid in the identification and translation of user-based requirements specifications to functional and trustworthy code. At this stage of development of environments, implementation of support environments across all the phases of any software development lifecycle is not feasible, as only some of the steps are covered by any single technique or methodology. Among the more important of the characteristics that we have discussed are

Ease of use by users unsophisticated in computer technology
Increased ease of access to existing information
Increased security
Ability of new software to be integrated in with existing application packages
Effectiveness in coping with user needs
Trustworthiness

Automated tools to support the various software development lifecycles and increase productivity have become increasingly available in the commercial marketplace over the past few years. There exist a great variety of tools that aid the analyst, designer, and programmer to better complete software development tasks. Many of the techniques and methodologies that have been automated provide for graphic capabilities that make the procedures of software development from conceptual design through automated code development and testing a reality. These include structured specifications and structured designs, program design language or pseudo-code formatters, 4GLs and applications generators for the coding phases of the software development lifecycle, to name only a few of the several hundred toolkits currently available. Commonly available CASE tools for the MicroSoft–Disk Operating System (MS-DOS) environment include those shown next. Here, we provide a three-entry listing in which the tool name is followed by its supplier, and a few key words that describe the principal function of the tool. There are new CASE tools appearing every day and so our list is necessarily incomplete.

Adagraph, The Analytic Sciences Corp.; code generation for Ada

Analyst/Designer Toolkit, Yourdon, Inc.; analysis, design, text formatting, standards

Cullinette Auto-Mate Plus and *IDMS/Architect,* Cullinet Software; entity-relationship, dataflow diagrams, logical data structures

Dan Bricklin's Demo II, Peter Norton, Inc.; screen painter demonstration and prototyping tool

Data Structured Systems Development, Ken Orr & Associates; CASE tool based on structured design

Design/l, Arthur Andersen & Co.; planning, design, requirements, data modeling, process design

Design Graphics System, Cadre Technologies, Inc.; menu building, screen design

Design Aid and CASE 2000, NASTEC; analysis, requirements, design, code generation, documentation

Design Machine, Ken Orr & Associates; requirements analysis

Developer Workstation, Asyst Technologies; application development

Excelerator; Excellerator for Real Time Systems, Index Technologies Corp.; analysis, design, data modeling, documentation, code generation

Higher Order Software (HOS), HOS, Inc.; structuring tool

Info Model, INFOMODEL Inc.; planning, application development, IRM

Information Engineering Workbench, KnowledgeWare; AI-based expert system for information systems

Information Resource Management, Arthur D. Little, Inc.; planning, data modeling, analysis

Lifecycle Manager, NASTEC; project manager workbench and analysis tool kit

Life-Cycle Productivity, American Management Systems; strategic planning, design, development, project management, maintenance

MANAGER, Manager Software; planning, analysis data modeling, data normalization, design, code generation, data dictionary

MicroStep, Syscorp,; program generation prototyping tool for database and information system design

Model-S, PC-Systems; menu building, screen design, execution flow modeling

MultiPro, Cap Gemini Software; development, project control, documentation

Natural, Software AG; 4GL for Adabase dictionary

POSE/PSR, Computer Systems Advisers Research; data modeling, database design, data flow, data dictionary

ProKit Workbench, McDonnell Douglas; planning, analysis, design

ProMod, Promod Inc.; integrated software development tool

PVCS, Polytron Corp.; library maintenance of reusable code

Structured Analysis and Technique (SADT), Softech, Inc.; general structuring tool

USE.IT, Higher Order Software; specification, analysis, design code generation

Visible Analyst, Visible Systems Corp.; graphics diagraming (Yourdon)

VS-Designer, Visible Software Inc.; family of tools

In general, software packages calling themselves "CASE tools" satisfy some, but not all, of the desirable characteristics noted earlier. Progress is being made in the development of CASE tools and several research efforts have been reported earlier that, if successful, will satisfy the requirements noted above. We will now examine several CASE, or CASE-like tools that might be useful in software systems engineering environments. We note other CASE-like tools elsewhere, particularly in our discussions of Chapters 8 and 9. Some of our discussions of the software development lifecycle in Chapter 2 also noted CASE tools, as did our discussions in Chapters 3 through 5.

7.8.1 THE ADA LANGUAGE ENVIRONMENT—APSE

The U.S. Department of Defense (DoD) initiated the development of Ada in the mid-1970s in response to the plethora of languages then commonly used in defense systems procurements, and the characteristics of those languages that worked against standardization and productivity improvements. Ada was designed to support realtime, embedded software for use in large weapon systems. The language was finally adopted in 1983 and was mandated for use in embedded systems in 1984.

Ada enforces the use of well structured design through the use of Ada Program Design Languages and the features of the language itself. It is able to reveal problems early through the use of strong typing, permits the use of software building blocks through the use of packages, and simplifies the design of real-time code through the use of tasking provisions. Ada also assumes the availability of powerful tools to support software developers who build weapons system software through its incorporation of optimized compilers, configuration control tools, and test and analysis tools.

Ada is based on the principles of abstraction, information hiding, and modularity. These facets of software engineering are all supported in Ada. In addition, Ada includes an *Ada programming support environment* (APSE), which is an integrated set of tools intended to support the development and support of Ada software throughout the software development lifecycle. The APSE environments are rehostable, retargetable, and extendible and the user interface provided is independent of the hardware and the host operating system.

APSE tools are intended to support the development of computer programs in Ada. These tools are needed to support such Ada features as separate compilation, to meet function needs, to insure potential system integration capability, and to provide compatibility with other languages and tools. The minimum set of APSE tools required for any implementation are:

Text Editor

Pretty Printer

Translator

Linkers

Loaders

Set-use Static Analyzer

Control Flow Static Analyzer

Dynamic Analysis Tool

Terminal Interface Routines

File Administrator

Command Interpreter

Configuration Manager

Ada incorporates several features that aid the process of development of requirements specifications. These include reusable software component libraries, rapid prototyping, operation of static analyzers for relational database representation to minimize debugging, and the use of the graphic input/output for increased and enhanced interface with the user. It is available in several PC-based versions that have been *validated* by the DoD. These include Ada compilers by *Meridian Software, Alsys,* and others.

7.8.2   Boeing Automated Software Engineering

Boeing Automated Software Engineering (BASE) has been developed by Boeing, to address mission-critical software development. The system covers the entire software development lifecycle and is implemented on Apollo, DEC

VAX, and microcomputer hardware. The system employs a user-friendly interface that leads to fewer operator errors and requires minimal training.

The system was developed with the cooperation of different tool vendors and features a common database of software requirements and design and test data available to all users via a LAN. There are on-line standards, automatically produced documentation in the required format, automatic generation of requirements traceability and allocation of matrices in the database, software problem reporting capabilities for change control, configuration management controls, and analysis and design tools that provide graphics-based system block diagrams, interface tables, DFDs, control flows and specifications. Boeing has built its own systems engineering modeling tool that features user-oriented, automated simulation modeling of hardware and software for performance evaluation. The cost of this development environment is undoubtedly quite high. The system is based on equipment vendors participating in the program (Apollo, DEC VAX, Cadre's Teamwork tool, etc.).

7.8.3   Software through Pictures

Another CASE tool example is *Software through Pictures* developed by Interactive Development Environments, Inc. The objectives were to meld hardware and system technology for the systems designer. The system highlights a high-resolution bit-mapped display, distributed file systems, laser printers, and sophisticated operating system support. A set of editors supports the various functions of the system. These include the following:

1. DFD editor supports structured analysis according to DeMarco or Gane and Sarson.
2. E-R editor supports the Chen E-R data modeling approach.
3. DS editor supports JSD notation according to Jackson.
4. SC editor supports structured design according to Yourdon and Constantine.
5. TD editor supports transition diagrams and USE (user support engineering) methodology for building interactive information systems.

This system resides on DEC VAX, Apollo, Sun workstations, and high-end PC based workstations using UNIX-based operating systems.

7.8.4   NASTEC CASE Lifecycle Manager Toolkit

Yet another CASE example is the NASTEC and DEC cooperative marketing agreement under which NASTEC develops tools that will operate within the parameters of VAX-based systems and interface with VAX layered products. The original effort was to establish a common development environment that encompassed the entire software development lifecycle. The intent was to increase productivity and quality. The basic tool in use is NASTEC's DesignAid running in a VAX/VMS environment and in an MS-DOS environment. NASTEC's DesignAid integrates DATATRIEVE, a DEC query language, RDB relational database management system, DEC word processing and DECpage, for formatting and printing.

7.8.5   Analyst Designer Toolkit

The *Analyst Designer Toolkit* employs structured analysis and is produced by Yourdon. Structured analysis uses graphic documentation tools to produce structured specifications. The basic tools include data flow diagrams, a data dictionary, data structure diagram capabilities, and structured English formats for reports. The structured specifications characteristics present a logical, partitioned, top-down system presentation in graphic display through this tool.

The Analyst Toolkit consists of packages that permit the user to create and edit data flow, entity relationships, and state transition diagrams. In addition, it includes the ability to create and maintain an extensive data dictionary. The other part of the package is called the *Designer Toolkit*. This tool adds the capability to create data structure diagrams for the system under consideration. The primary features of the Analyst Designer Toolkit are the following:

1. A comprehensive graphics editor that works with a mouse is included.
2. The system is able to create state transition diagrams in the design and analysis of real-time systems.
3. Data flow diagrams (DFD)s can be created and corresponding data may be entered into a data dictionary.
4. Diagrams can be checked and verified for proper connection. However, no rigorous checking is performed on connections between diagrams or between diagrams and related text specifications. Reports containing this information can be produced from the data dictionary.
5. Mini-specifications or pseudo-code relating to a diagram may be entered into the data dictionary.
6. Free-form sketching is supported: this allows using the graphic editor to create presentation diagrams, charts, or drawing without having to conform to the design rules or connection checks of the Analyst Toolkit.
7. No text editor is included, but access to an external one is supported.
8. Diagrams can be printed on external printers and plotters.
9. The open architecture facilitates access to data dictionary and diagrams created by the package. The data dictionary elements are dBASE III compatible.

10. The data dictionary offers the capability of report production.

11. An additional tool, called Compose, is available for the preparation of presentation documents. It allows text and graphics to be merged.

12. An optional Rule Tool is provided for those who use a method other than Yourdon. It allows changes in the symbols and connection rules.

13. The documentation is good and tutorials are provided. Both cover the basic package components and Compose.

7.8.6   DesignAid

DesignAid is a sophisticated, expensive, full-blown software engineering system offering a powerful tool for large and complex projects. It is designed for large teams of systems analysts and programmers who use the Yourdon method of system design and specification. The key features are as follows:

1. The documentation is very complete, professional, and exhaustive.

2. DesignAid is not easy to learn or even easy to put down and go back to. The most significant obstacles are the strange, nonstandard keyboard interface and the plethora of options that confront the user.

3. The user interface provides three ways to enter commands: with the keyboard or a mouse and pull-down menus, or with the keyboard in expert mode. Expert mode is aptly named; it is more difficult and sophisticated. For example, macros can be developed using expert mode command in a learn mode.

4. There is a sophisticated security system.

5. There are extensive capabilities for balancing, validating, and reporting on the structured specification dictionary.

6. There is a built-in word processor with a command set and design philosophy as unusual as the rest of the system commands.

Typical Yourdon diagrams, as we have discussed earlier, result from using DesignAid.

7.8.7   Excelerator

Excelerator is one of the more extensive CASE packages available for use on MS-DOS machines. It allows creation and editing of a multitude of systems charts and diagrams in a variety of formats, as well as generating reports and project documentation. Additionally, it facilitates functional prototyping to demonstrate operation and appearance of user interface screens. The following comments summarize the key features of the package.

1. The graphic editor allows the creation of data flow diagrams, structure charts, logical data model diagrams, entity relationship diagrams, struc-

ture diagrams, and presentation graphs. The data flow diagrams can be created using either Yourdon or Gane and Sarson formats.

2. An entry is made in the project dictionary for each drawing created.

3. Drawings can have hierarchical relationships with a maximum depth of 10 levels. The editor EXPLODE command allows examination of an object or connection in greater detail.

4. Graphs are checked for correct structure, connectivity, inputs and outputs, and correlation with data in the project dictionary.

5. XLDictionary allows access to and maintenance for project data. Several projects can be managed at once.

6. Data security is provided through user ID and optional password protection. Three privilege levels are available: user, project manager, and system manager.

7. Screens and reports can be designed and used for system documentation. Designed screens can be used to generate a functional prototype. A record of the screen can be generated in BASIC, C, COBOL, INFO, and PL/I or as part of an ASCII file.

8. Graphs, project dictionary information, and text can be integrated to form a document.

9. Excelerator supports the IBM PC/XT/AT and compatibles, as well as most common graphics adaptors, printers, and mice. Currently, it can be used with three LANs: IBM PC Network, 3Com EtherSeries, and the Banyan LAN with a 3Com EtherLink board.

7.8.8 PCSA

PCSA is a powerful and user-friendly CASE package intended for software systems analysts using the Yourdon analysis technique. The following is a list of key features.

1. A mouse is required: supported mice are the Mouse Systems PC-Mouse, VisiCorp VisioN Mouse, and Microsoft Mouse.

2. The only printer supported is the IBM/Epson graphics printer; however, a bit map file can be generated and uploaded to a mainframe to be printed on a laser printer.

3. It is an easy program to learn; it is mouse-driven and provides pop-up menus at the cursor position of the mouse. The menus are context-oriented; only those actions that can be performed on a given object at that time are active.

4. There is a scrollable window to show a virtual data flow diagram, one page at a time.

5. The vendor, *StructSoft*, claims that the system is capable of creating structured specifications with 15 levels and up to 32,000 data flow diagrams.

6. Child diagrams can be created from a parent diagram by pointing to a process symbol and clicking the zoom-in command. There are consistency checks and warnings of unused data flows and dangling processes that are available locally and globally.

7. The data element dictionary automatically creates definitions for objects that can be modified and further defined by users. An element in a definition can be further defined with its own definition, elements can be cross-referenced to other definitions, and the editor can locate recursive definitions.

8. Report capabilities of the data element dictionary are minimal; although with an ASCII file output option, a custom reporting and code-generation system could be built.

9. The documentation looks as if it were hastily developed by the programmers who developed the tool. It is printed on a dot-matrix printer and bound in one loose leaf notebook. It lacks an index for quick reference, has spelling errors, and includes a tutorial without a sample project to follow.

10. There is currently no save command, but one is promised. In the meanwhile, there are risks; for instance, power fluctuations could cause memory to be lost and all changes since the last exit or backup would have to be recreated. However, a toolkit of programs designed to help the user recover from disasters is provided.

7.8.9 Other Current CASE Packages

Most contemporary CASE packages attempt to provide for the desirable features and attributes we have noted. Typical of the claims for increased productivity are those for the products *Excelerator* and *Software System Support Environment* marketed by INTech and TRW, respectively, of 35 to 70% compared to similar development completed without the tools.

Current trends with CASE developers seem to be in the direction of interconnecting CASE tools with application code generators, and extending coverage to include entire lifecycle support. Developments on the horizon include the *TI Information Engineering Facility* (IEF), Cortex Software additions to its 4GL applications generator, and Cullinet's DBMS extension. Texas Instruments (TI), through IEF, has a product that is capable of applications development over the entire software development lifecycle. The primary application areas for this CASE tool are business objectives analysis and database generation. IEF purports to carry systems development through to a complete set of automatically generated COBOL programs. IEF runs on an IBM mainframe with DB2 and has a separate module that runs on MS-DOS microcomputers. IEF takes an AI based approach and is written in C for portability. Cortex software has opted to add CASE features to its established 4GL applications generator called the *Applications Factory*. This package runs in a DEC VAX environment. Cullinet has designed this package to support IBM's SQL and incorporate a CASE package so that programmers can design and prototype applications on a PC then store them in a mainframe dictionary for generation of code.

CASE tools are widely available and are being improved all the time. Opportunity for potential software productivity improvement abounds; however, CASE is not yet widely accepted nor in general use. Attitudinal changes by management and programmer–analysts are needed in order to realize the importance of requirements, systems management, design activities, and sound documentation on potential gains in productivity. CASE facilitates productivity improvement through provision of rapid prototyping of screens and reports, automated design that may be quickly and easily modified, and data dictionary facilities to document the design process and provide for integrity checks.

Extensive effort has been accomplished by the National Bureau of Standards (NBS—now National Institute of Standards and Technology (NIST) in developing software tool descriptions and placing these tools in a database. NBS has provided a taxonomy for classification of the tools included in its database. The U. S. Air Force Data & Analysis Center for Software (DACS) has taken the NBS model database and modified it to include more data elements, additional tool information, and more tools from vendors. The DACS database contained information on some 412 software development tools as of 1985 [DACS, 1985]. The tools included in this report are lifecycle support tools arranged in a classification scheme that contains the following categories:

1. Software management, control and maintenance
2. Software modeling and simulation
3. Requirements–design specification and analysis
4. Source program analysis and testing
5. Program construction and generation
6. Software support systems/programming environments

7.9 SUMMARY

We have covered quite a bit of territory in this chapter. We began our efforts with a discussion of system integration concerns associated with operational implementation of software systems. In this discussion, we saw that a critical need is to have a development environment that supports integration. This led to our discussion of software engineering environments, and the role of CASE tools in these environments.

7.10 Problems

7.1. There are two very popular word processing software packages in a large office, and the number of users of each package is approximately the same. Often, there is a need for a report that has been prepared in one format to be used in the other. The office management is concerned with whether to standardize on a single word processing package or to develop software that will allow data interoperability.

    a. Prepare a brief report outlining how an appropriate judgment could be reached concerning which alternative to adopt.

    b. Assume that the decision to provide for data exchange between the two formats has been made. Please discuss several possibilities for doing this and provide a cost benefit analysis of each of these alternatives.

7.2. Develop a checklist of activities to be accomplished when operational implementation of a software product is to be achieved. Discuss the relationships among the activities in your checklist. When in the development lifecycle should these activities have been identified?

7.3. Discuss the relationship between *implementation and integration* efforts and *maintenance* efforts.

7.4. In Chapter 6, we discussed bottom-up and top-down integration at the design level. Please prepare a discussion concerning *bottom-up* and *top-down* approaches to the integration of complete software packages.

7.5. Describe the cost influencers for system integration. Generally, development changes that change costs at one phase of the software lifecycle will have offsetting effects at other phases. Prepare a report indicating the trade-off concerns associated with changing the resources allocated to implementation and integration.

7.6. Please discuss the statement "A software development lifecycle with lower integration costs is always to be preferred to one with higher integration costs."

7.7. What trade-offs would you expect among *system integration and implementation* and *system maintenance*? Is it possible that lack of attention to integration will increase maintenance costs?

7.8. You have just selected new technical word processor software, *Mathwrite*, for your office. Write a plan for *integration* of this software into your office environment. This should include not only the technical features of integration but the human factors and management features as well.

7.9. You need to select spreadsheet software for use in your office. Three software packages are suggested. There are several other office automation software packages in use in your office. Please investigate and identify an attribute template for integratibility and/or usability of the three alternative packages and describe evaluation to enable selection of one of the packages.

7.10. Identify how design practices, design principles, and design perspectives were used to develop some software with which you are familiar.

7.11. How do the *framing*, *production*, and *evaluation* environments differ? What generic support tools would be most appropriate for each environment?

7.12. Characterize as many of the CASE tools discussed in this chapter as possible with respect to their usefulness in *framing*, *production*, and *evaluation* environments.

7.13. Develop a multiattribute utility-based evaluation appropriate for selection of an existing CASE tool for use in your organization.

7.14. What are potential roles for CASE tools in the *Software Productivity Situation Room* discussed in this chapter? How does their use effect other tools and methods, systems design and development methodologies, and systems management processes?

7.15. Contrast and compare features of CASE tools that might be appropriate for software development effort for:
   a. A university information system
   b. A real-time aircraft flight control system

7.16. How would you expect a typical software development lifecycle phased effort over-time chart (Gantt chart) to change as the toolset used is changed from manual tools to CASE tools and manual tools?

7.17. What are some of the *down-side* risks in using CASE tools? Are there any opportunities for worsening software productivity and what are they? On the basis of your responses to these, please develop an evaluation plan to determine whether a CASE tool should be used on a given application development.

7.18. An office automation system could be developed for a large corporation by purchasing hardware and then engaging a software development team to design appropriate software. Alternately, one could be developed by enforcing a contract requirement that no new software products be developed, except for small utility programs, and that all software satisfy an "in-production in-use" requirement that the software exist in the commercial market place a month or so before contract proposals are due. The purpose of this requirement would be to avoid *vaporware*. Please contrast and compare the two approaches.

7.19. Is the assumption in Problem 7.18 that the hardware be purchased before the software is developed, or procured, a good one? Please redo the problem using the requirement that hardware and software systems be developed or procured together.

Chapter **8**

Prototyping, Reusability, and Expert Systems

8.1 INTRODUCTION

In this chapter we will examine the potential macro-enhancement improvements to software productivity made possible through prototyping, reusability, and expert systems. We have previously considered several micro-enhancement techniques, such as structured design tools. The only macro-enhancement approach that we have examined up to this point has been the systems management approach to software development. Of the three macro-enhancement approaches we will examine here, prototyping is by far the most mature technology, followed by reusability, with expert systems for software productivity still being much in the developmental stage. Even though we note that prototyping is the most mature macro-enhancement technology, we must further note that reuse is the most pervasive macro-enhancement approach in use at this time. This is due to the current practice of experienced programmers who draw upon their repertoire of information concerning program parts that they have used elsewhere. This is "re-use-ability," although it is often not the organized systemic approach to reusability that promises the greatest potential return.

Prototyping was introduced in Chapters 4 and 5 as a micro-enhancement approach to improve software development. When used to test detailed design characteristics, prototyping becomes a micro-enhancement approach. When used in the evolutionary development environment, such as to enable evaluation and test of overall system level concepts and requirements, prototyping becomes a macro-enhancement approach for software productivity improvement. In this chapter, we view prototyping as a pervasive component of an advanced software development environment. The view of prototyping taken in Chapters 4 and 5 is very much that of *structural prototyping*. Here, we will discuss *functional prototyping* and *purposeful prototyping* as well.

Software reusability concerns the use of already constructed software "parts," perhaps even "conceptual parts," that are available from other software development programs, in new software development situations. The single most common contemporary form of reusability is one in which the individual programmer recollects a program that has been built, and which has a part contained within it that may work in the present effort. The programmer locates this part, modifies it in an appropriate way, and uses it over again in the new effort. Reuse efforts at this level may make significant contributions to software productivity. However, this reuse of software parts may not be systemic, as it depends solely on the memory of the individual to make reuse happen.

What is required here is the development of standardized approaches to regularize and systematize the reusability concept, thereby bringing it into productive usage for software process development. Concerted efforts are being undertaken to build libraries of software parts that may be accessed after gaining admission to a software reuse library.

Expert systems are in the embryonic stage for software development purposes. Some uses of expert systems have occurred in the areas of specification development and as computer aids to detailed design. The *Programmer's Apprentice* [Waters, 1985; Rich and Waters, 1988] is one very noteworthy computer aid for program design that is based on expert system concepts.

In essence, an expert system for software productivity would function as an expert manager of a software development process and would bring forth suggested implementations of any (or all) of the lifecycle development phases from its knowledge base in response to system user inputs. Many areas of artificial-intelligence-based support for software development are under investigation at this time. The introduction of expert systems offers significant prospects for improvement in software productivity.

Software development environments have been the subject of intense recent undertakings [Charette, 1986]. A conceptual view of an idealized software systems development environment is shown in Figure 8.1. Many of the present efforts have concentrated on development of automated programmer support tools. These range from automated code generators, to automated documentation generators, to automated specification development generators, to fourth- and fifth-generation languages. The key word in most computer-aided software development tools, or early generation *computer-aided software engineering* (CASE) tools, is "generate." We will comment on environments and CASE "generation" efforts in the concluding portions of this chapter.

Historical efforts to solve the "software crisis" have focused on improving the techniques and speed by which code is written by individual programmers. Early micro-enhancement approaches relied on standard programming languages and compilers as basic development tools to enhance productivity and

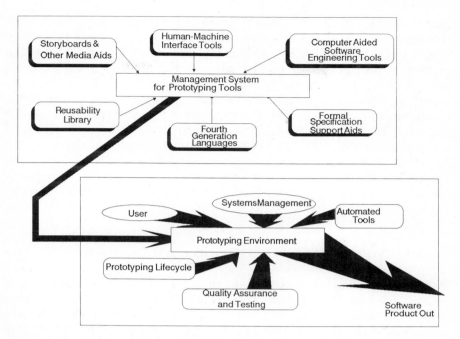

FIGURE 8.1   Conceptualization of prototyping environment for software development

quality. These focus on methods of providing coding solutions, rather than working on requirements, integration of the development process, or reusability of software parts. The results of these early efforts to enhance programmer productivity, often based on the use of structured analysis and programming, were discussed in Chapter 4. While they are certainly very useful, they have not enabled the truly significant improvement in software productivity that is needed, even though they represent a definite improvement over unstructured ad-hoc approaches. High personnel costs, extended time periods for development, and high maintenance expenses have still continued to plague many large scale software development programs.

Computer-aided software engineering tools are intended, ultimately, to integrate and automate the software development lifecycle and to specifically consider development environment concerns. The present-generation CASE tools are of great potential importance in resolving the problems of productivity at the micro-enhancement level of software development. However, many CASE tools usage do not address the larger issue of macro-enhancement of software development. There are some that do, however, and some that concentrate on the *front end* of the lifecycle. These are, perhaps euphemistically, called *upper* CASE tools in order to distinguish them from *lower* CASE tools that are intended for the conceptual and detailed design portions of the lifecycle. It has been claimed by Brooks [1987], Beam et al.[1987], and many others, that significant advances in both quality and productivity are unlikely to occur as a consequence of *only* better micro-enhancement procedures intended for programmer productivity improvement. Further, these studies often suggest that the place for real gains will be in the macro-enhancement areas of prototyping, reusability, and the application of knowledge-based or expert systems. It is these areas that will be emphasized in this chapter.

The macro-enhancement approaches to software productivity hold promise for significant improvements in both productivity and quality, especially if integrated into a software development environment that takes advantage of the substantial improvements that have been made in micro-enhancement approaches. A purpose of this chapter is also to explore software development environments necessary to support macro-enhancements to the software development process.

8.2   PROTOTYPING AND PROTOTYPING ENVIRONMENTS

Prototyping is a method for increasing the utility of user knowledge for purposes of software development. Prototyping has the capability of increasing software productivity through the modeling of the software development process. Some of the ways in which prototyping effects software productivity are by provision of support for:

1. The requirements process, in terms of identifying user needs and in transforming these to system specifications
2. Understanding the operational environment and modeling potential operational environment changes
3. Understanding the intended and desired system level functionality in terms of what the system should accomplish
4. Assisting the software designer examine various structural approaches to software design for the intended applications

Figure 8.2 illustrates these software development supports realized through prototyping.

Through the use of prototyping, the details of the software development lifecycle itself are modified to accommodate the potentials of this technique. Fundamentally, however, there are still three phases to the lifecycle, as shown in Figure 8.3. Feedback and interactive iteration is assumed to occur as shown in this figure. The three-phase model of the lifecycle shown here can be expanded to incorporate the (generally) seven-phase models identified in Chapter 2.

One of the more important uses, in some ways *the* most important use of prototyping, is to increase user awareness of the software product that is being developed, as the development is being carried on. Additionally, it is feasible to address uncertainties in the system-level and software-level requirements,

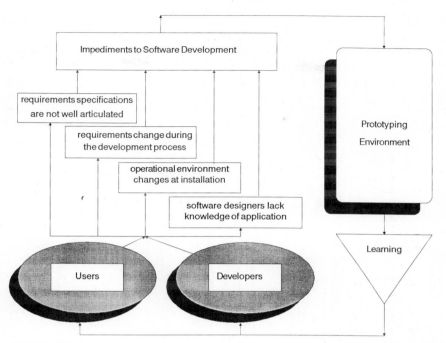

FIGURE 8.2 Some impediments to software productivity addressed by prototyping

and these uncertainties may be reduced or resolved through the use of prototypes that provide feedback to both the software developer and the user. Through this feedback, the user may participate in the software development as an integral part of the software development team. There are at least three ways in which the user may interact to aid in developing the original requirements specifications:

1. Becoming, in effect at least, a part of the requirements identification team, to better cope with both the initial identification of requirements as well as coping with requirements that change during the course of the development process
2. Being involved with the identification of operational functionality needs, including the environment changes that might potentially influence system installation and maintenance
3. Working with the software designers to assist in gaining a better mutual understanding of the actual application for the software product as it evolves over time

Doing this will ultimately act to insure that the operational system incorporates needed functionality. There are different types of *prototyping,* although each

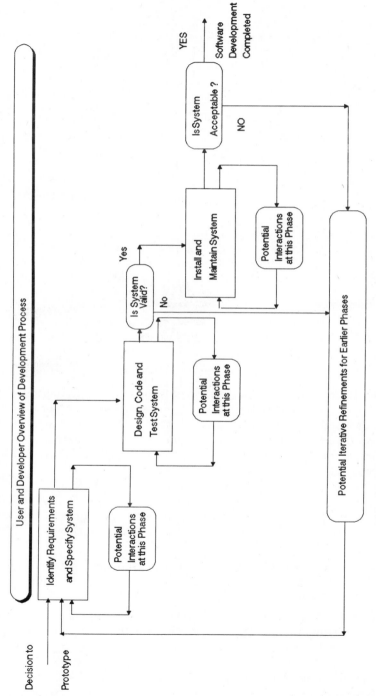

FIGURE 8.3 Generic software development lifecycle with prototyping

involves the production of functionally useful and trustworthy systems through experimentation with evolving systems. This is a not unreasonable definition of prototyping and the one that we will use here.

Prototype models may be classified in several ways. We shall present some of the more important of these in the material to come. One of the greatest uses of prototyping in contemporary systems development lies in the acquisition of useful information that affects many aspects of system development early in the development process. This information is important to software designers, management, and the user in order to identify issues and problems associated with the software development process. Through this it is possible to save considerable amounts of time and resource prior to the commitment of effort in nonproductive activities. Advanced software development environments will generally provide for provision of information to the user that will enable *rapid* determination of whether:

1. The particular design approach used is feasible and is evolving into production of appropriate software (*structural prototyping*)
2. The impacts of using the system are what the user wishes (*functional prototyping*)
3. The user requirements and software requirements are consistent and veridical to the satisfaction of user needs (*purposeful prototyping*)

One major problem in developing new computer applications is that of specifying the user's requirements in such a manner that the resulting requirements specification is clear, correct, complete, and unambiguous. Although prototyping is often considered too expensive relative to other approaches because of extensive, continual iteration on the requirements data and definitions, correcting ambiguities and misunderstandings at this specification stage is significantly cheaper than correcting a system after it has gone into production and deployment. This is possible with prototyping, and often not possible with other competing classical approaches. Requirements identification and specification are directly accessed through purposeful prototyping. However, functional and structural prototyping can also be used to identify and specify requirements, although these approaches would seldom be used only for this purpose.

8.2.1 A Taxonomy of Prototyping Approaches

As might be expected in any very new area of inquiry, various authors have adopted somewhat differing descriptions for the various types of prototyping. It is important to examine some of these and then to provide a summary description and taxonomy of these.

According to Church et al. [1986], a software prototype may be a functionally immature model of a proposed system, built to (1) explore potential requirements, (2) investigate alternatives, or (3) demonstrate feasibility. The model may, or may not evolve into a mature functionally useful system.

Riddle and Williams [1986] identify three kinds of prototyping.

1. *Evolutionary prototyping*, which is used for the iterative creation and evolution of a system. This represents a *structural* approach to creation of trustworthy software in which continued incremental iterations of the software, and augmentation with increased functional capabilities, allow and enhance convergence by the software developer and user to an appropriate software system.

2. *Experimental prototyping*, which is used for investigation of alternative solution approaches. As a result of *experimental prototyping*, the software developer and user will have conducted an exploratory *analysis* of various possible *functional* solutions to the issue under study and will *interpret* these such as to enable selection of a satisfying experimental prototype.

3. *Exploratory prototyping*, which is used for the purpose of problem or issue *formulation*. As a result of exploratory prototyping, the user will have *explored* major aspects of problem identification and will have identified, with assistance from the software development team and the *exploratory prototype*, the requirements for a *purposeful* solution to the problem.

Another classification of prototyping techniques is given by Carey and Mason [1987]. The authors identify three categories of prototyping techniques:

1. *Version 0 prototype*, which is a functionally limited system that is released to the customer for evaluation and indication of potentially needed refinements. Although it is specifically designed as a test or trial release only, it is expected to evolve into the final product through iterative refinements.

2. *Demonstration prototype*, which processes a limited range of user queries or data, using limited files. Frequently, some portion of the demonstration prototype is carried over to the production system. On the other hand, the entire demonstration prototype can be coded as a throwaway.

3. *Scenario or simulation prototype*, which presents to the user a scenario of the user interface. In a *simulation prototype*, the eventual functional, application-oriented, solution is not developed. Generally, only a demonstration or mock version of this is present. This user interface may be used in the actual production system, depending on the tool used to build the scenario.

Hekmatpour [1987] characterizes three prototyping approaches:

1. *Incremental prototypes*, which will be *evolving* prototypes based on iteration through the conventional lifecycle phases. Figure 8.4 illustrates the phase dependency of *incremental prototyping*. We will have more to say about *incremental* or *structural* prototyping very soon.

2. *Evolutionary prototyping*, which is said to be *prototyping as a software development paradigm*. Evolutionary prototyping involves multiple iterations of the overall lifecycle as contrasted with incrementing at each phase of the lifecycle. There is no explicit plan to throw away the prototype, although portions of it may be discarded when they are shown to be dysfunctional. The prime intent in evolutionary prototyping is to view software system development as an integrated, *evolutionary* series of design, implementation, and evaluation stages that are iterated until the prototype converges on something that the user will accept as an acceptable system. Figure 8.5 illustrates the lifecycle of evolutionary prototyping.

3. *Throw-away prototypes*, which are generally used for the user requirements and software requirements phase of the software development lifecycle. The prototype is generally built quickly so as to enable the user to rapidly interact with the requirements determination early and thoroughly. Since the prototype will ultimately be discarded, it need not necessarily be fast-operating or maintainable, nor need it have ex-

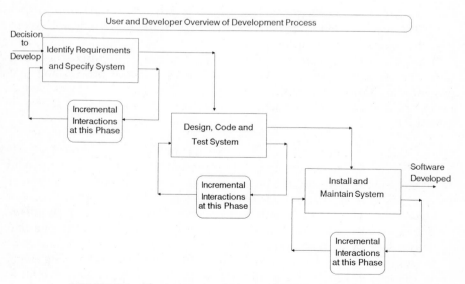

FIGURE 8.4 The incremental phase-wise prototyping process

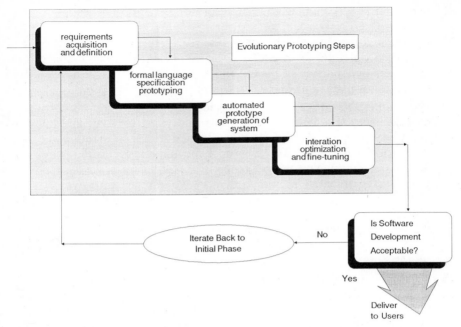

FIGURE 8.5 Evolutionary prototyping, with formal language specification and automatic code generation

tensive fault-tolerant capabilities. Generally, *throw-away-prototypes* will be developed using 4GLs. This approach to prototyping appears to be the most common, at this time.

Schneider [1987] conceptualizes prototyping methods into three stages that deal with differences in kind. He also discusses levels of prototyping that provide transitions between the prototyping stages. The three stages of prototyping are meant to be sequenced from the first to the last as shown in Figure 8.6.

1. *Concept prototyping* is the first stage in this scheme for prototype development. The object here is to represent the user requirements and the resulting software system in a way that will encourage user-developer dialog such as to encourage mutual agreement that a proposed concept will cope satisfactorily with user requirements. The *concept prototype* can vary from a totally static demonstration system model to one that considers system dynamics. The concept prototype may be a *throw-away* prototype, or may actually be used in the next prototyping stage. Either a *structural, functional,* or *purposeful prototype* could be built as a *concept prototype.*

2. *Laboratory prototyping* is begun as soon as the *concept prototype* is

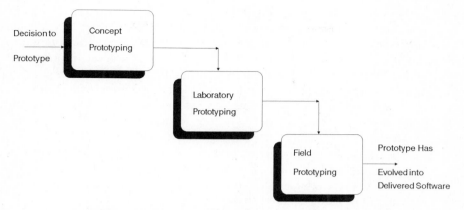

FIGURE 8.6 Prototyping through evolving prototype models

accepted. The object here is to create a real working model of the system using actual real-life data and algorithms. It appears that the primary difference between the laboratory prototype and the working system is that, as a laboratory model, advantage can be taken of a more friendly development environment and development tools that might not necessarily be available in the actual operating environment. It would not make sense to build a *purposeful prototype* or *exploratory prototype* as a laboratory prototype since these are not real working models. *Structural* (*incremental or evolutionary*) or *functional* (*experimental*) *prototyping* would be acceptably accomplished at this stage, however.

3. *Field prototyping* begins after the laboratory prototype is accepted and, typically, becomes the first unit to be installed in the field. Thus, this is a *Version 0 prototype*. It is possible to test and evaluate a *field prototype* under actual operating conditions. This is still regarded as a prototype since user feedback will result in modifications. It would not make sense to accomplish field prototyping using a purposeful or exploratory prototyping approach since this type of prototype does not actually produce real outputs, in contrast to an experimental or evolutionary approach. Either an experimental (functional) or evolutionary (incremental) approach to prototyping could be appropriate, although it may be quite difficult to evolve many functional prototypes into operationally useful products. Thus, a field prototype would usually be a structural prototype as neither the functional nor purposeful prototypes easily evolve into operational systems.

Freeman [1987a] also identifies three types of prototypes and three corresponding ways in which prototyping can be used in productive software development.

1. *Decision prototyping* is used at each stage of the software development lifecycle in order to obtain a decision concerning whether a particular *incremental* iteration is satisfactory. Once convergence to an acceptable solution at a particular phase of the development lifecycle is achieved, effort proceeds to the next phase. This incrementalism can be accomplished in parallel as it is always possible, although perhaps costly, to build several software solutions, say, at the algorithm design and implementation stage. The user can then select the implementation that performs "best." This is, in essence, a *structural prototype*.

2. *Preliminary prototyping* results in a traditional, functioning system that is substantially like the final system desired by the user. It is placed into operational or perhaps laboratory service and evaluated by the user. Changes are made by the software developer so as to improve on the evaluation of the system. This continues in an *experimental* manner until one of the iterations is accepted by the user as *functionally* acceptable. A preliminary prototype does not have all the functional capabilities, fault tolerance, and reliability provisions of the final system. However, functional capability is improved from iteration to iteration until the evolving system does become functionally useful. It would appear that *preliminary prototyping* would be done in an experimental (functional) manner primarily, although it could be done in an evolutionary (incremental or structural) manner.

3. *Concurrent prototyping* is an approach that can be used to quickly yield a restricted but *purposeful* version, generally a *throw-away* version of the software system. A parallel traditional software development process is used to construct the actual operational software from what is learned from this *exploratory prototype*. Thus, *concurrent prototyping* is, in essence, purposeful prototyping.

Our discussion of prototyping characterizations emphasizes the fact that each of these definitions of the types of prototyping are rather closely related as shown in Figure 8.7. The differences among them is relatively small, although each definition does shed somewhat different light on prototyping activities.

8.2.2   Explicit Phases Involved in Prototyping

Our previous discussions have indicated that prototyping efforts can generally be described as following the usual waterfall model of software development, with additions to allow for the iteration and feedback that are a part of the prototyping process. It is helpful to restate the essential phase descriptions in such a way that the explicit involvement of prototyping activities is evident. Our description of these prototyping phases is as follows:

1. *Identify and evaluate the request for software development services.* De-

Structural	Functional	Purposeful	Systems Characterization
Evolutionary	Experimental	Exploratory	Riddle's Characterization
Incremental	Evolutionary	Throw Away	Hekmatpour's Characterization
Concept			Schneider's Characterization
Laboratory			
Field			
Decision	Preliminary	Concurrent	Freeman's Characterization

FIGURE 8.7   Comparison of prototyping characterizations

termine preliminary information requirements concerning user needs. Determine preliminary user requirements and software requirements. Identify the most appropriate approach to software development and, in particular, whether a prototyping software development is appropriate. Among the factors that influence this are: application area and complexity, user experiential familiarity with the application area, and developer experience with prototyping. Assuming that the decision to prototype is favorable, proceed to phase 2.

2. *Identify the type of prototyping that is most appropriate,* which will be some form of *structural*, *functional*, or *purposeful* prototyping. We will address criteria for accomplishing this selection in a meaningful way in Section 8.2.3.

3. *Develop a set of user and software system requirements* appropriate for the prototyping approach selected and the resulting prototype.

4. *Identify a set of design specifications* for the prototype.

5. *Create the prototype, and test and refine it.*

6. *Involve the client or user in use of the prototype,* in an appropriate way, relative to accomplishment of prescribed prototyping tasks.

7. When directed to this phase from the primary software development lifecycle, *identify whether the prototype developed* up to this point *is acceptable.* If the answer is affirmative, proceed to the next phase in the primary lifecycle. If the answer is that further refinement of the prototype is needed, iterate back to prototyping phase 2 if it is believed that the initial judgment concerning prototyping type is flawed, or to phase 5 if refinement of the present prototype is appropriate.

There are necessarily a number of details to be filled in for each of the foregoing phases. These will depend on the particular prototyping approach selected and the characteristics of the application considered.

The prototyping notion is very appealing. In theory, software prototyping may be applied to any or all software development lifecycle phases, or across all phases. In principal, it may be applied to any application area. However, experience indicates that prototyping is a more useful approach for some types of systems than for others. There are several characteristics that we might consider.

Real-Time (Concurrent) versus Non-Real-Time Systems Many authors [Boar, 1984; Carey and Mason, 1986] suggest that a good candidate for prototyping should address well-structured problems that require a large amount of data and perhaps multiple data relationships, but only very limited algorithmic complexity. This suggests that information systems development is an appropriate area for prototyping , whereas real-time adaptive flight control system design would not be a good candidate. In an information system development, the major difficulties often concern poorly defined user interfaces and misunderstood user requirements. These non-real-time system areas are precisely those where purposeful prototyping is appropriate.

Real-time systems will have requirements that are real-time in nature or function. They will often have requirements that are *nonfunctional* and that do not have real-time requirements, although they may have concurrency requirements. Often, it will be possible to partition a real-time system into components that require real-time approaches and those that do not. For those components of the system in the latter category, purposeful prototyping is appropriate. For those portions of a system that are functional or that have real-time requirements, we will often find purposeful prototyping to be not appropriate.

For portions of a system with non-real-time or nonfunctional requirements, evolutionary or structural prototyping is appropriate in that the environments associated with information system development are often mature and relatively unchanging. The underlying complexity is low, and the tools used to develop a functional prototype can often also be used to develop the operational system. There is often little need for a *throw-away prototype* because of this environmental similarity. In this sense then, structural, functional, and purposeful prototyping can often be done simultaneously.

Large Systems versus Small Systems Software prototyping appears to apply well to small-scale systems in which the user interface is critical. In one experiment, Boehm et al. [1984] indicated that for small systems containing only a few thousand lines of code, prototyping teams were able to produce software systems that were considerably smaller in size, less complex, and easier to use than programs developed by conventional *specification* teams.

For large systems that must, of necessity, be decomposed into a number of smaller development projects, it is much less obvious that structural and functional prototyping are appropriate. In such situations Gomaa and Scott

[1981] suggest using purposeful prototyping only to identify user requirements, and to then switch to a traditional software development approach.

8.2.3 Observations Concerning Prototyping

In many system development projects, the first prototype system built is barely usable. It is usually too slow, too big, too awkward to use, or all three. Generally there is considerable lack of understanding of user requirements. There is no alternative but to start again, smarting at the setbacks, but perhaps smarter as a result of the experience, and build a redesigned version in which these problems are solved. When a new system concept or new technology is used, we generally plan to build an initial trial system to throw away, for even the best planning is not so omniscient as to get it right the first time. For obvious reasons, we would like to not spend great amounts of energy, time, and money in building something that is to be thrown away.

A prototyping software development approach for incremental development of subsystems was shown in Figure 8.4. Here, the prototyping environment provides for an incremental approach to rapid prototyping of subsystems development in which management oversight permeates the entire process to ensure that resource usage is effective and efficient. Product assurance is likewise implemented throughout the process to make certain that the prototype operation maintains the necessary awareness of the subsystem requirements. Here, incremental requirements analysis is prototyped and reviewed, then incremental specifications are developed and reviewed, followed by design of the approved specifications, and completed by implementation of the product assured part. This is the sort of structural programming environment discussed in Chapter 4.

The decision concerning whether a prototype should be refined into the complete system or be thrown away should be based on the costs and benefits of each alternative [Agresti, 1986]. Two of the key factors are:

1. How much functionality is already present in the developed prototype?
2. Will the prototype design support a maintainable system, or is the prototype really worth the investment of more effort and money?

The major potential advantages a general prototyping effort for software development are:

1. It enhances the descriptive power of the resulting lifecycle development process model.
2. It more closely resembles the reality of the development process, and allows for the usual iteration of a system to take place more naturally than in a software development lifecycle that does not contain prototyping.

3. It allows for control of the software development process by incorporating the aspects of resource management, configuration management, verification, and validation at early phases in the lifecycle.
4. It enables the construction of larger and more complex systems with smaller development teams, thus increasing overall developer communications and productivity.
5. It enables user feedback early in the system development process.

Of course, prototyping has some disadvantages as well. For prototyping to be effective, a prototype must be developed over a short period of time for review and concurrence of the user. In this way, an assessment of the fit of the identified requirements and the resulting software design leads to modifications resulting from the user review that are incorporated into the next iteration of the prototype. In order to be successful in producing a prototyping environment, there are at least three generic classes of tools and methods that should be available. These include (1) 4GL tools and techniques, (2) reusable software parts and components, and (3) an appropriate formal specification and prototyping environment. Figure 8.1 has indicated these ingredients in the software development environment for prototyping. Although 4GLs and related tools are available, much less has been done to date relative to provision of reusable software and formal specification and prototyping environments.

A 4GL encompasses a broad variety of database query and reporting languages, program and applications generators, and other very-high-level nonprocedural language capabilities. Contemporary 4GLs include a number of elements of a software development environment, including various structured design and programming tools. They are particularly useful in developing prototypes but are restricted primarily to financial and information system efforts. Application code generators are of particular value as well, although they are not, at this time, as versatile as 4GLs. An appropriate fourth generation language or applications code generator is a tool that will allow the prototype developer to easily and rapidly accomplish five specific activities.

1. Define the logical data model of the system, that is to say, the overall structure needed for a database.
2. Define interactive screens that would be used to prompt the user for data, and thereby allow the user to easily enter information into the system.
3. Create reports using a report generation capability that will allow users to view data in the database in such a format that they can easily comprehend it.
4. Use system graphical capabilities to create useful representations such as bar charts, histograms, and pie charts.

5. Provide a query language capability such that the users can easily interrogate the database.

Specification languages currently in use in prototyping environments include PSL, RSL, IORL, GYPSY, and OBJ. These are used to achieve an automated software engineering environment for employment in the early stages of the software project.

One potential approach to design of a prototype is to use the rapid code generation possibilities made possible through use of what is called the *operational model* [Zave, 1982, 1984]. This is basically a prototyping system in which the requirements specification is an executable model of the system to be developed as it interacts with its environment. It is based on the assumption that we cannot easily differentiate the *what*, or function, from the *how*, or structure, in discussing a system [Swartout and Balzer, 1982]. The operational model development system is shown in Figure 8.8. It is claimed to create executable specifications (called *operational specifications*) that are successively transformed into efficient implementations or realizations of these specifications in terms of code. There are three claimed advantages of the operational model:

1. It has descriptive power directed at solving a software system problem. The descriptions are to be formal, rigorous, and can be analyzed.
2. The user and developer each have an executable model, or prototype, from which to evaluate alternative solutions early in the system development.
3. The model is very suitable to computerization.

This is essentially a purposeful prototyping approach that has been combined

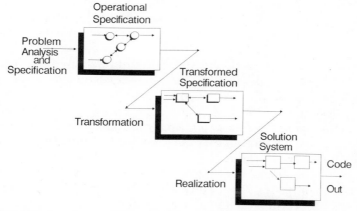

FIGURE 8.8   The operational model software development lifecycle

with a transformation mechanism and some form of automatic code generation that will also result in the equivalent of a structural prototype. By observing the responses of the system, the equivalent of a functional prototype is generated as well.

There have been a number of research efforts concerning the operational model. Most research efforts in this area are aimed at automating the transformations of the operational specifications [Agresti, 1986; Cameron, 1986; Charette, 1986; Smoliar, 1981] to realization of the solution system in terms of code.

This transformational paradigm is actually a knowledge-based model that is obtained from a combination of prototyping notions and expert system concepts [Bauer, 1982; Cheatham, 1984; Kant and Barstow, 1981]. It uses automated support to apply a series of transformations that change a specification into a concrete software system [Partsch and Steinbruggen, 1983]. The support system guides the developer through the process. Software engineering knowledge is separated from the application knowledge, and this knowledge along with the process paradigm is captured in a knowledge base. Rules based on accepted software engineering techniques are encoded into expert systems. These software engineering expert systems are used in conjunction with expert systems containing application knowledge rules to form a specific instance of a software system.

This paradigm really represents a normative goal that is being pursued by many research and development projects. The above description is *softproduct speculation,* since complete systems do not exist today [Charette, 1986]. In practice, this automated paradigm has been applied to very restricted application areas and at the level of individual programs [Balzer, 1981; Partsch and Steinbruggen, 1983; Wile, 1983]. Three products emerge from the transformational paradigm: (1) the formal specification, (2) the delivered system, and (3) the formal development record. Theoretically, the model's descriptive power, generality, and suitability for automation would allow the construction of systems orders of magnitude larger than those being conceived today. This indicates both the potential use for prototyping like approaches and their close linkage to other knowledge-based systems approaches that act as management controllers for this approach.*

Evolutionary or structural prototyping is most often used for operational versions of the software product and for instances where full implementation is not feasible because of resource constraints. Tools for evolutionary prototyping include libraries of code, subroutines, packaged modules, and other archived softproducts. The basic problems are to provide coherent designs, avoid problems of low functionality, and provide for sufficient robustness to avoid the "throw-away" status.

Experimental or functional prototyping is most appropriate for requirements and design phases of the software development lifecycle and is used to investigate tools, provide for tool integration and appropriate software

*We will discuss some other knowledge-based approaches in Section 8.4.

development environments for the development process, and to investigate alternative architectural structures for the software product. Some of the tools used in experimental prototyping include such expert systems as XCON by Xerox Corporation, simulation methodologies, and such flowchart methods as HIPO, Warnier-Orr, DFD, SREM, and SADT.

Exploratory or purposeful prototyping is most appropriate for use during software requirements development as it provides rapid feedback to the user and tends to reduce uncertainty in the communications processes while increasing the developer's knowledge of the user's environment. Some of the tools for exploratory prototyping include graphical analysis tools, storyboards, menu generators and report generators.

One exploratory prototyping technique is storyboarding. This approach [Andriole, 1987, 1989] uses an interactive mix of requirements analysis and simulation. Taylor and Standish [1982] indicate that through the use of this form of prototyping:

> potential users of the system could learn about whether the prototype satisfied their true user needs—i.e, the prototype was a fully effective means of accelerating the learning process about the true system requirements at a fraction of the cost of experimentation with real systems.

The availability of microcomputers enables the rapid construction of storyboard prototypes in the form of display screens and operational scenarios. Storyboard prototyping is one form of requirements validation and verification for the systems engineering process. This method provides a structured yet flexible design approach to the capturing of requirements and specifications for a system. A prototype may also be used as a vehicle for training users how to use the system. However, this requires that the prototype be kept up to date, rather than being retired when the system to which the prototype contributes becomes operational. The advantages of this approach to training must be weighed against the additional cost of maintaining the prototype for a longer period of time.

Previously, the circulation of a written statement containing proposed requirements specifications to process engineers, management personnel, facility operators, and supervisors yielded virtually no useful feedback. Unfortunately, the specifications for most systems have to be quite lengthy in order to be complete. Much past experience has indicated that prospective users often do not find available time to evaluate a written specification thoroughly [Gomaa, 1986]. Even if they have the time, the task of carefully scrutinizing a very large document is difficult and boring and is not therefore, performed with the enthusiasm that is most conducive to obtaining good results. Even if people wished to spend this time, they will doubtlessly not be sufficiently familiar with the details of sophisticated and technical specifications to understand well what they would read. Storyboard prototypes could help relative to fulfilling this major need, also.

Storyboards are but one of the purposeful prototyping approaches, the

,ose of which is identification of user requirements, or software
.nts. As we have discussed the general problem of requirements
.ation and specification in Chapter 3, there is little need for a detailed
.t this here. Fundamentally, two sublevels of requirements are necessary
t. determination of user requirements for a software system:

1. *Organizational level requirements*, which specify the system structure,
   portfolios of applications, and interface boundaries
2. *Application level requirements*, which determine specific system requirements to be implemented in a specific application in order to satisfy
   user needs

Although the uses of information at these two levels are different, the generic
procedures for determining user requirements are the same for each level.
There are four basic ways to identify requirements, as we have also indicated
in Chapter 3:

1. *Simply ask people for their requirements.* The appropriateness and completeness of the needs and requirements identified by this approach will
   be determined by the extent to which the people in question can define
   and structure their problem space and can compensate for their biases
   in order to provide a realistic description of needs and requirements.
   This approach can be further disaggregated into interacting group approaches to asking and nominal group* approaches to asking. The former is usually easier and more effective, but a number of group communication maladies may make the nominal group approaches more
   effective.
2. *Elicit information requirements from existing systems that are similar in
   nature and purpose to the one in question.* Properly executed anchoring
   and adjustment strategies or perhaps analogous reasoning strategies are
   useful here since a starting point can be determined from the existing
   system and extrapolation of this can then be made. Examination of
   existing plans and reports represents one approach of identifying user
   requirements from an existing, or conceptualized, system. In a similar
   way, software requirements can be identified from examination of existing software requirements for a similar system. This brings us to the
   notion of *reusable requirements specifications*, a subject that we shall
   explore in our next section.
3. *Synthesizing requirements from purposeful characteristics of the utilizing
   system.* This permits an analytic structure for the problem space to be
   defined, from which information requirements can be determined. This
   strategy would be appropriate when the needs or requirements in ques-

---

*Examples of the nominal group approach include *ideawriting* and the *nominal group technique*
[Sage, 1989].

tion have changed and thus cannot be easily and meaningfully identified from the ones that are present in an existing system. It is here that the need for sophisticated prototyping to determine requirements is first felt. The user exercises the prototype and purposeful evolutionary updates to the initial prototype are made. The prototyping process is such that it evolves into a purposeful representation of the needed system. From this identification of the needed system, the requirements follow.

4. *The fourth strategy consists of discovering requirements through experimentation.* Additional information can be requested as a functional version of the system is employed in an operational, or simulated operational, setting and problem areas are encountered. The initial set of requirements for the system provides an anchor point for the experimentation. This represents an expensive approach, but is often the only alternative when there does not exist the experience base to use one of the other approaches.

Enhancing the abilities of system users to specify requirements as well as the abilities of appropriate people on the software development team to elicit and evaluate requirements are *each* important. To this end, it is desirable to be able to select the best mix of these four strategies for requirements identification and specification. The method of selecting the most appropriate strategy is based primarily on determining the amount of information imperfection involved in the set of requirements that result from the use of each strategy. Five steps are potentially useful in selecting an appropriate requirements determination strategy in terms of the amount of information imperfection involved in a particular software development effort.

1. Identify those characteristics of the application needs of
   a. Elements of the utilizing system to be developed
   b. Elements of the application system to be developed
   c. User characteristics such as experiential familiarity with task and environment
   d. The capabilities and experience of the software development team as they relate to information imperfections in requirements identification.
2. Evaluate the effect of the characteristics of these four elements on three types of requirements identification imperfection:
   a. Availability of a set of requirements,
   b. Ability of users to specify requirements,
   c. Ability of the software development team to elicit and specify requirements.
3. Evaluate the combined effect of the requirements determination process imperfections on overall system development volatility.
4. Select a primary requirements determination strategy.
5. Select a set of specific methods, prototyping and others, to implement the primary requirements determination strategy.

Figure 8.9 illustrates the use of these steps to identify an appropriate mix of requirements identification strategies, and the role of the various types of prototyping in this.

The requirements determination process uncertainty, that is to say, the amount of information imperfection that exists in the environment for the particular task, influences the selection from among the four basic strategies in that simply asking for requirements is very appropriate when there is little or no information imperfection. As the amount of imperfection in available information increases, we move from asking, to examining an existing system, to synthesizing requirements from a purposeful system, to experimenting with a functional system.

In terms of the organizational level elements, the factors that primarily influence or effect information imperfection include:

1. Stability of the environment
2. Stability of user organization management
3. Experience with planning, design, and use of systems of the type to be developed
4. The extent to which the presently utilized system is appropriate

Identification of requirements specifications has also been a subject of much interest in software systems engineering [Boar, 1984; Mills, 1983; Peters,

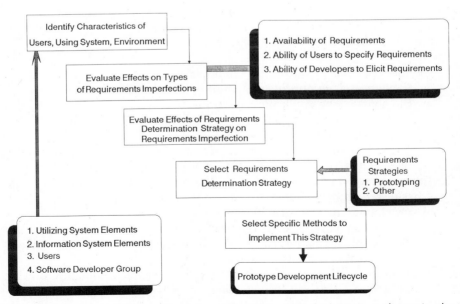

FIGURE 8.9   Identification of requirements determination strategy and use in the prototyping process

1980; Taggart and Tharp, 1977]. Researchers in this area have come to much the same conclusions as workers in human and organizational information processing [Sage, 1989] that humans have great difficulty in specifying requirements in terms of verbal discourse or unstructured paragraphs of natural language.

There has been some development of programming languages to assist in information requirements determination. The "Problem Statement Language/ Problem Statement Analyzer" language of Teichroew and Hershey [1977] is typical of several general purpose languages for specifying requirements even though it was developed some time ago. These identified requirements are translated into system inputs that are stored in a database for later recall and possible updating. Software tools produce a report directly from the identified database. A top-down approach is used and this allows development of criteria, and definition of system boundaries through examination of the internal and external problem environment. After this is accomplished, as many as 22 objects may be utilized to define the conceptual qualities of the proposed system. Relations between each of the identified objects are identified next. These are stored in a centralized database for later use in responding to queries.

A manual system can be developed to function in much the same manner as a computerized system for requirements determination. Heninger [1980] describes one such system used to describe the input, output, and functional relationships relating output to input for a particular software system for aircraft. The system requirements were determined through analysis of the completed forms. The objective of this was to develop a "software requirements document" that serves as a reference tool and provides formal documentation of initial wisdom concerning the system lifecycle. One purpose for a document such as this, as well as for formal statements of information requirements is that it then becomes possible to validate the requirements, at least in part, with respect to such important considerations as consistency, completeness, realism, and responsiveness to the needs of the system user.

In general, major emphasis is placed on rapid implementation and low development costs [Gomaa, 1987] in those aspects of the lifecycle that specifically relate to the prototype. Gomaa [1987] cites a number of factors that may assist in attaining these objectives:

Emphasis on the User Interface As an objective of the prototyping paradigm is to maximize user interaction with the system, the prototype should emphasize the user interface at the expense of lower level software that is not visible to the user.

Small Development Team Typically, a software development effort involving prototyping should be undertaken by a small development team, such as to minimize potential communication problems among users and developers.

Prototype Development Language A fourth-generation programming language that facilitates the rapid development of the prototype should be used. Emphasis is on reducing development time to obtain the prototype, and not on the performance of the finished product. An interpretive language is advantageous, since it can lead to rapid detection of a programming errors. A language with powerful data manipulation features is also an advantage.

Tools to Enhance Rapid Prototype Development   If prototyping is to be very useful, tools must exist that will enable rapid development of prototypes.

As noted earlier, a multiproject experiment has been conducted to compare an incremental prototyping approach to the conventional one of *specifying* user requirements. The experiment was conducted, in early 1982, as part of a one-quarter first-year graduate course in software engineering at UCLA [Boehm et al., 1984]. Fifteen students were divided into four "specifying teams" and three "prototyping teams." The students decided which type of team they wanted to belong to. Since a student's decision was made by taking their particular interests into consideration and, in addition, since their grade depended on this project, at least some aspects of their motivation were very high. Unfortunately, the project's user interface requirements were precisely defined. This is an unrealistic assumption, since prototyping seems to be a more appropriate approach than specifying in situations where there is uncertainty involved. The summarized results of the experiment, however, favored the particular prototyping approach used in that:

1. Prototyping yielded products with roughly equivalent performance, but with about 40% less code and 45% less effort.
2. The prototyped products rated somewhat lower on functionality and robustness, but higher on ease of use and ease of learning.
3. Specifying produced more coherent designs and software that was easier to integrate.

The assumptions noted, and other assumptions that are explicitly stated in the referenced paper, limit to some degree the validity of this experiment that concerned developing an interactive version of the COCOMO model for software cost estimation [Boehm, 1981].

From the experiment described above and a survey study described by Alavi [1984], we may conclude that prototyping does not always yield coherent designs, thus making the task of evolving the prototype into the complete system a difficult one. The question of whether to throw away the prototype after it has served its purpose, or to evolve it into the complete system is indeed a significant one. Generally, of course, only structured prototypes can be so evolved. Further research is needed to identify standards according to which it can be decided whether a prototype should be thrown away.

In a process where prototyping is being used for getting user feedback and for the investigation of alternatives, one of the requirements is that the developers be able to perform the prototyping process as fast as possible. Prototyping tools have been developed to assist in the rapid construction of prototypes. Further research should address not only the creation of more prototyping tools but also the creation of prototyping libraries. The problem of a classification of prototyping tools and the creation of libraries of prototypes is strongly associated with the more general problem of reusability, a topic to which we will next devote our efforts.

Prototyping has not been an everyday practice in the development of software even though it is called for in nearly all of the software development lifecycles that we have studied. Certainly, software prototyping does not enjoy the widespread use for software development that it does in hardware development. Software prototypes may sometimes cost more *initially* in terms of time and money than other approaches. However, proper use of prototypes will likely provide better results due to the interactions with the user. Prototyping requires a commitment on the part of the user to provide sufficient information throughout the development process so that the activities may proceed smoothly. It requires the developers to supply information to the user during the development process for any of the real benefits to be derived.

The benefits of doing this are potentially quite considerable. The following are among the primary benefits that may be achieved from an appropriately selected prototyping approach.

1. Potential disagreements between the software developers and users may be revealed, clarified, and ameliorated through use of a prototype.

2. Ambiguities, inconsistencies, incompleteness, and other forms of information imperfections are typically found in requirements specification. The prototype aids in identifying these, and in righting them.

3. Omissions extant in the requirements specification may be discovered when system users ask developers to exercise features that they consider essential for inclusion in system capabilities, but that are not available in the prototype.

4. Potential software errors in the prototype due to incorrect or missing requirements may be discovered. Had these requirements been transitioned into the operational system, they would be much more expensive and time consuming to correct.

5. Some functional capabilities, when implemented, do not provide the user with the information desired. These may be modified to provide an improved set of capabilities.

6. System users are able to furnish valuable information concerning the features of the system that they find difficult to understand or confusing to use. This enables improvement in the functional capabilities of the system, as well as improvements in terminology and operating procedures.

7. Often, users are unsure concerning how they wish to have needed functional capabilities implemented. Having a prototype encourages experimentation relative to this.

8. As users experiment through interaction with the system, needed modifications are made to the prototype, primarily in the areas of report formats and user prompts. This enables users to experience the results of implementing their suggestions quickly.

Selection of the fundamental software architectural design has such a significant effect on the ease with which prototyping may be implemented that a good understanding of the questions about the development project is essential to determining the best approach. In general, exploratory and experimental, or purposeful and functional, prototyping provide support for early phases of development, while evolutionary, or incremental or structural, prototypes support later phases. Of course, as inferred earlier, these are not mutually exclusive categorizations of prototyping approaches.

The particular prototyping approach used should be determined by the availability of information, accuracy required of the prototype process, specific properties to be investigated, and the analysis techniques to be used. Current prototyping environments support parser generators, attribute grammars, 4GLs, object-oriented design approaches, declarative descriptions, and various procedures to produce incomplete versions of software. There is indeed, much to be anticipated from this promising macro-enhancement approach to software productivity.

8.3 REUSABILITY AND REUSE

Software reuse notions provide one of the greatest possibilities for major enhancements in software productivity [Brooks, 1987]. There are many ways in which we can reuse software *products* or *processes*. Here, we use the word "softproduct" in a very generic sense to include lines of code or subroutines, and other software-related product items. We will use the term *softprocess* to refer to software application domain expertise, that is to say, the systems management wisdom that comes about through experiential familiarity with the development of software products, or *softproducts*. The greatest potential gains are doubtlessly associated with reusing sophisticated and expensive software process development knowledge, as contrasted with code. We have just delineated the two principal approaches to software reusability. These may be referred to as *constructive reusability* or *softproduct reusability,* referring to the reuse of the *constructed* parts of software such as code or documentation, and *generative reusability* or *softprocess reusability,* which will refer to the reuse of process knowledge or software development knowledge.

Reusability relates to the ability of a software product or process to be identified, acquired, classified, archived, and used again by the software de-

veloper. A definition of a software reusability environment is that of a system with the provisions necessary to support access to a variety of software soft-products through an interface. A conceptual view of such a system is shown in Figure 8.10. In this, the interface provides for access by the developer to the application domain reusability support environment. To make this sort of approach truly feasible, it will very likely be necessary to have an expert system that assists in the classification and retrieval of such softproducts as specifications, algorithms, tools, test plans, and documentation. This will facilitate reuse of softproducts and softprocesses for essentially all aspects of software development. Reusability promises greater economies in software production through the development of software with less routine coding. Software reusability also promises great effectiveness through the much enhanced possibilities for developing more reliable and maintainable software.

Systems engineering takes the lead in giving us tools to aid in the search for satisfactory reuse schemes through the use of approaches such as architectural blueprints. These architectural blueprints should include such information as design constraint modifications, choice of selection from among many possible softproducts, use of standard components to the greatest extent possible, and a classification scheme to describe the key functional characteristics of the softproduct to be reused. A reusability facility must address

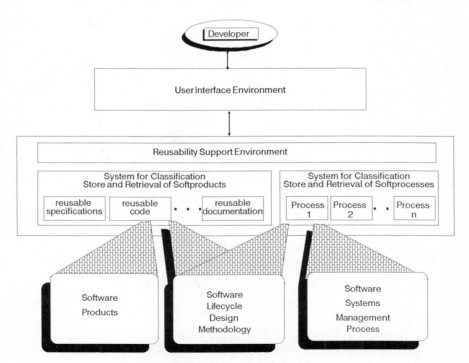

FIGURE 8.10   Software reusability elements

much more than code, as code in and of itself may be the least valuable of possible reusable softproducts, even though today code is clearly the reuse leader. We must also include software process management information and representation to complete the software reuse facility. Typical reusable components to be archived within such a facility are part shown as part of the conceptual software reuse scheme, as partially shown in Figure 8.11.

There are three *domains* that support the development of a software reuse facility:

1. The *application domain* provides the motivation for development of specific *softproducts* that will be of use in later software development efforts, perhaps in a totally different domain.
2. The *software lifecycle development process* provides the environmental setting in which *softproducts* are obtained.
3. The *software reuse process* provides for knowledge acquisition relative to *softproducts* and *softprocesses*.

A process model illustrating the reusability concept is shown in Figure 8.12. We note here the learning, through accumulation of *softproducts* and *softprocesses* due to the repeated use of software development lifecycle on specific applications and a reuse process that allows for accumulation of both a knowl-

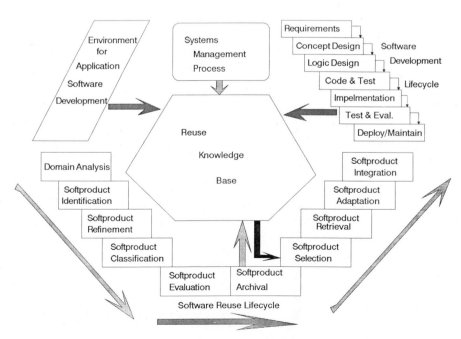

FIGURE 8.11 Conceptual model of software reuse process

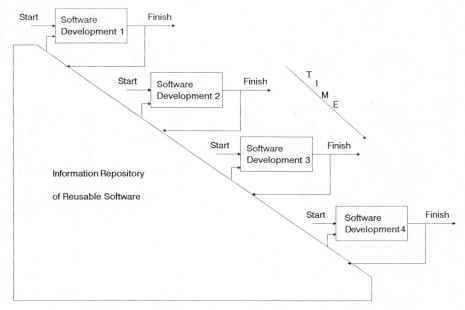

FIGURE 8.12 Reusable software process evolution over time

edge base that enables reuse as well as the "components" of reuse: *soft-products* and *softprocesses.*

We surely do not make the claim that we are anywhere near the possible state of development related to software reusability. It should also be noted that even the softproduct with the highest record for reuse, code, has significant reuse-associated problems. These include the initial cost to develop a library of softproducts, establishing suitable metrics for reuse, measuring any changes in productivity as a consequence of reuse, and technical aspects related to storage and retrieval processes. The major impediment here is that we really do not have an effective systemic method for code reuse. Nor do we know much about documentation of reusable code such that it can be efficiently and effectively integrated into existing operational situations.

There are new developments that encourage code reuse. For example, some languages, such as Ada, have specific features that are intended to facilitate and support reusability. The main feature of Ada that supports reusability is the concept of packages. Packages in Ada permit the designer to define logically related terms and account for the information available internally and externally to the package, and become the essential component of program modularity. Ada reusability is accounted for by the encapsulation provided by the packages. Control is brought about through a combination of features that include the *with* clause, *visible* and *private* softproducts, and nesting capability. The *with* clause provides access to entities within the *visible* softproduct package only, while the *private/visible* capabilities give access to either all modules in the package or none. Packages possess the capability of being compiled as a separate entity, thus permitting error determination to be performed on a package basis. These features give Ada advantages for reuse that are not common in other languages. These include:

Recompilation: An Ada program can be compiled at one time or in several separate compilations. This means that the whole program does not have to be recompiled when a compilation unit is modified or added.

Generics: Ada allows a single module to serve for all instances of the same implementation of a data structure, applied to any type of object. It complements the overloading construct.

Overloading: Ada allows two procedures or functions to have the same name in the same scope provided that the ordered list of formal parameters are different.

Modularity: Ada uses something called *Package,* a higher-level structuring facility rather than a single procedure. A Package contains procedures, together with declaration types, constants, and variables. A module may be exclusively devoted to an entire data structure through use of the "*with*" clause.

A caution should be provided. In spite of these specific features, the language alone is not sufficiently robust to capture commonality between groups of implementations of the same generic types of data structures. Thus an externally imposed library system must be provided.

In the case of reusable code, it was estimated by Jones [1984] that less than 15% of code generated is unique and specific to an application. Consequently, the opportunity for reuse of code as a *softproduct* is substantially greater than might be initially expected. In addition to lack of uniqueness in code, duplication of algorithmic structures is often found in the design of most large systems, even when the implementation of the algorithms is unique to the user system. Further, user and software development specifications, testing routines, maintenance guides, and the like are generally duplicated, at least in part, by large complex software systems. Today, most of these should be obtained from *softproduct* libraries rather than rewritten each time a new development is undertaken.

To implement reusable requirements, specifications, design, testing, maintenance documentation, and code, it is necessary to define a set of standards for reuse that can be used to create new systems from library modules. A classification scheme is an absolute necessity in order to store and retrieve *softproducts*. The classification scheme must preserve all the essential aspects of the *softproduct* to be archived and retrieved. The storage modules must preserve the functional elements and objects of the original *softproducts* in a readily accessible classification taxonometric scheme in order to be useful. The impact of size of the *softproduct* on reusability is significant. As the size of specific softproducts grows, the more difficult it is to reuse, hence the lower the potential value of the softproduct. At the other end of the scale, the smaller the size of the softproduct the more frequently it can be reused. However, as the softproduct approaches such a small number of lines of code that the cataloging job becomes overwhelming, the lower the reuse value. For larger software softproducts, the relationship between size of *softproduct* and reuse value would generically be expected to be as shown in Figure 8.13. For very small size *softproducts,* the nuisance value associated with cataloging, retrieval, and other necessary bookkeeping chores would be sufficiently great that there would be little value associated with these very small softproducts and very little likelihood of their use. From this figure, we see that the product of use probability and value, which indicates something analogous to expected value, is a maximum for some finite softproduct size. It is indeed plausible, perhaps even correct, that there is some *optimal size for reusable softproducts.* However, this optimal size, if it exists, would be very much a function of intended use, environment, and other elements of the *contingency task structure.* *

We have defined two levels of reuse, *softproduct* and *softprocess.* Actually, these can be viewed as the ends of a continuum and several other reuse entities used to fill in the space between the two. Freeman [1983] writes of five levels of reuse. We view these as emanating from the knowledge domains for reuse. Further, we view reuse knowledge as coming from three domains: *applications domain,* the *software lifecycle development process domain,* and

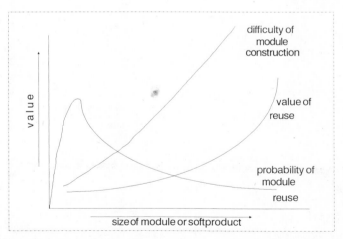

FIGURE 8.13 Module size and associated value and probability of reuse

*See our discussions concerning *contingency* task structure in Chapter 9. Briefly, the *contingency task structure* involves the characteristics of the user, the developer, the task, the environment into which the task is embedded, and the experiential familiarity of the user and the developer with the task and the environment.

the *software reuse process domain*. Figure 8.14 indicates this conceptualization.

In our taxonomy of the software reuse process, we will also identify three perspectives for reuse. In addition to *reuse level*, we also have *contingency task structure for development management* and *reuse attributes*. Each of these dimensions for reuse perspectives are related to the reuse domains, as also shown in Figure 8.14.

The *contingency task structure for development management* involves the characteristics of the user and developer organization, standards, economic considerations, and the present state of reuse technology. Since this is, at present, a relatively immature technology, there will be many elements of risk and information imperfection associated with reuse. There will also be a potentially large up-front investment required to develop libraries of reusable softproducts, and to introduce this new technology into a developer group potentially unfamiliar with it.

Primary management concerns with the potential application of reuse on a large scale lie in the extremely high initial costs and high risks associated with pioneering reusability efforts. At the present time there are no standards for library development, no metrics to ensure increased productivity and programmer effectiveness; no assurances that library softproducts will be used

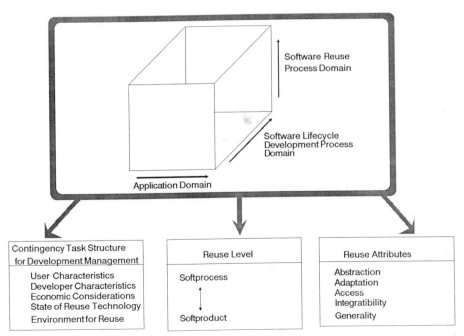

FIGURE 8.14 Software reuse perspectives as a result of software lifecycle, reuse and application domain

by programmers; and the potentially high cost of implementation of software reuse libraries, conversion of software softproducts for reusability, and retraining of software designers to take advantage of any reuse facilities, are but a few of the areas where much additional research is needed.

There are also *technical issues* associated with the *contingency task structure for development management* dimension. These involve such concerns as module interconnection languages (MILs) to provide formal grammars that describe the structure of a software system and that specify interfaces for assembly of softproducts, classification of softproducts, library schema and representations, and other tools and specification methods. There is much current interest in this area as evidenced by the work of Freeman [1987a], Kaiser and Garlan [1987], Prieto-Diaz and Neighbors [1986], and the recent edited monograph by Freeman [1987c] which presents reprints of many works concerning reusability.

There are human factors issues associated with the contingency task structure dimension as well. The primary concerns expressed by programmers and analysts relate to the perceived loss of control over the design and the need to become integrators rather than innovators. Specific concerns as a result of this translate into a general lack of confidence in the quality and capability of library softproducts, the loss of individual creativity, and feelings about becoming just another "softproduct assembler" in a software factory. This latter point is of particular (*softproducticular?*) concern to contemporary designers and programmers, as they would like to perceive and believe that their work is both original and creative.

In this regard, one of the most difficult obstacles to overcome may be the natural inclination of a programmer to feel that "better" program code can be written for a specific application than that contained in the library. This leads to a tendency of programmers to "reinvent the wheel" [Zvegintzov, 1984]. Programmers working with a reuse paradigm must come to understand that one of their functions will be to decide what reusable softproducts will fit, and that another will be to begin to depend on the system to provide alternatives to simply writing the code without considering the potential for reusability.

These issues, problems, and the associated needs relative to this contingency task structure dimension are very real. However, there is little to be gained in solving these problems until substantive changes, such as acceptance of standards for development and archiving software softproducts and general acceptance of macro-enhancement approaches to software development, occur. These changes in software systems engineering development environments that are intended to handle reusable software softproducts must be accomplished in order to have confidence that reusability is a viable approach.

The third perspective from which we can view reusability is that of *reuse attributes*. These are the *reuse dimensions* of Barnes et al. [1987]:

1. *Abstraction*—the degree to which a reused softproduct is logically re-

moved from implementation of the software (e.g. conceptual design specifications are more abstract than source code, and therefore potentially are associated with relatively higher productivity gains)

2. *Adaptation*—the degree to which the softproduct is pliable such that it can be modified or *transitioned* to meet a somewhat different use from that for which it was initially intended

3. *Access*—the extent of availability of a softproduct

4. *Integratibility*—the extent to which one softproduct can be interfaced, *directly* through building software systems that constitute the interfaces of the individual workproducts, or *indirectly* through use of an automatic program generator that instantiates a particular software application in terms of the softproducts that are used

5. *Generality*—the extent to which a softproduct has a broad range of applicability (e.g. one softproduct may be very useful and appropriate only for an applications domain that is seldom used whereas another may be equally useful but for very general purpose use)

Here, we have the beginnings of a set of attributes for reusability softproducts. A list such as this needs to be extended to include other attributes of reuse. Attribute measures, or metrics, can be developed and the multiattribute utility theory (MAUT) approach of Chapter 6 used to develop an analytical base for trade-offs among softproduct candidates. This would enable selection of the most appropriate softproducts for use in a reuse library.

These three dimensions provide us with a reasonably complete view of the perspectives from which software reuse must be considered. Figure 8.15 illustrates this three-dimensional perspective on software reusability.

As we have noted, the major issues to be resolved relative to softproduct reusability are technical and include closely related developments that involve standards and macro-enhancement processes of prototyping and expert systems uses. These advances should be made in order to moderate the extent to which software development management and personnel are overly burdened at this time.

As we have also noted, there is much need also for softprocess reusability. This area is very understudied at present and it is where the greatest potential payoff, in terms of increased productivity, may be found.

There have been a number of approaches to reusability suggested. We will now examine some of these.

8.3.1 Approaches to Softproduct Reusability

There have been a number of approaches to softproduct reusability. In general, softproduct reusability can be further disaggregated into three primary approaches:

1. Subroutine libraries of reusable softproducts

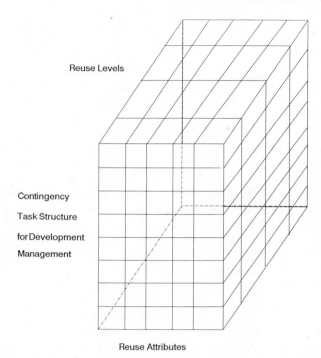

FIGURE 8.15 Three dimensional taxonomy of reuse perspectives

2. Software application softproduct (program) generators
3. Object oriented programming approaches

We will examine each of these categories.

Subroutine libraries may consist of libraries of object modules, or they may consist of very generic parametrized softproducts. These have had a very significant effect in such application domains as those which require mathematical software. This approach has also been useful in small-scale programming environments, but has not produced a very significant productivity improvement in other than large-scale mathematical software intensive areas. There may be a variety of reasons for this. Perhaps individual subroutines are either too small or too large. In the first case, the effort associated with reusability processing may simply be too large. In the latter case, the probability of reuse may be so small that the overall expected return from a piece of reusable code is too small to justify the effort.

A major need relative to developing subroutine libraries of reusable softproducts is to make the library as language independent as possible. Further, they should not be restricted to particular data types or data representation constructs or linking strategies. It should be possible to automatically change the number and type of parameters involved in a subroutine, as well as their range of values. It should also be possible to automatically bind together two or more softproducts. Two major needs relative to reuse libraries are approaches for classification and for retrieval. We will now examine each of these.

Software product classification schemes support the archival and retrieval of reusable software products, much in the same way as written or other recorded materials are maintained and distributed from traditional libraries. Software library classification schemes may be implemented at several different levels depending on the degree of sophistication and abstraction of the user and the software. For example, if the degree of abstraction is confined to be at a single location within a specific domain, then the level of a classification scheme may be termed to be at the lowest level of abstraction and given the designation of level 1. Level 2 in this example might consist of several locations, but remaining within the same specific domain. Level 3 might be broadened to include several of the domains of level 2; thus, it would include several libraries of this category. The next level could include all the libraries located at a single physical site, and the nth level would include all general distributed libraries covering all domains. This model is exactly parallel to traditional library models, which provide for search of the local library, interlibrary search, retrieval, and loan. Softproduct reuse libraries could be used in much the same way. Softproducts would be classified according to accepted standards, archived in a software library that is electronically connected to a network of software libraries, and be able to be retrieved and evaluated for other uses by those with permission to use the facility. The key factors in this are the development and acceptance of suitable standards for classification purposes, so that the resulting softproducts may be archived, retrieved, and evaluated for future use.

Classification schemes must be able to handle expressions to define both syntax and hierarchical forms [Prieto-Diaz and Freeman, 1987]. Syntactical relationships are those that take place between classes that occur together in statements that represent subjects of documents. Hierarchical relationships fall into two facets; generic and nongeneric. A "generic" relationship is an absolute one that does not depend on the existence of related subjects, while "nongeneric" relationships exist only because of a specific relationship. No matter which softproduct development scheme is used, it becomes central to the archival and retrieval process.

Characteristics of reusability products such as size, complexity, and documentation are key to the development of any facility capable of supporting reusability of softproducts. In code reuse, for example, the issues may be decomposed into three major steps: accessing the code, understanding the code, and adapting the code to the new use, all of which depend on the characteristics of size, complexity, and documentation. The same factors must be specified for reuse of products such as specifications, documentation, or testing plans.

Two classification methods have been recently considered for software reuse and are considered as being generally capable of representing software [Prieto-Diaz and Freeman, 1987]. These are called *enumerative* and *faceted* methods. The enumerative method is that used by the Dewey decimal classification. The faceted method is used in contemporary library science classification schemes to break subject matter into its most elemental form and then use these terms to search for specific topics. When using the faceted approach to search for subjects requiring more than one elemental term, two or more facets are combined to form compound search terms.

The enumerative representation method is the more traditional method of information organization. It is a top-down approach that tackles a body of knowledge and successively decomposes this body of knowledge into lower and lower levels until all the information is grouped at its least level of abstraction. For the Dewey decimal classification scheme, the number of decomposition levels is set to 10, as being sufficient to describe any area. This is the traditional approach used to organize libraries of books, libraries of automotive softproducts, or libraries of classes of objects. As in traditional library classification approaches, material is indexed using key words that describe the general topic, specific items covered by the material, and cross-index connections to related topics. For example, we might have the general category structured analysis with specific items such as domain, guidance, media, and viewpoint followed by cross-indexed terms such as *structured analysis and design technique* (SADT). The enumerative approach is limited in user value, as it requires availability on the subject area to be searched, predefined, and listed. This limits the search space to those topics predetermined and classified. As we will see, the faceted approach is not limited in this manner, but rather on the range of elemental facets used to describe basic components.

The faceted method takes a bottom-up approach to the classification problem by beginning with the most elemental class, which should be immediately recognizable, then moving to successively higher levels of abstraction. In this classification scheme information is extracted from the subject statements only for the classes listed in the schema, which defines a component from an elemental class. To extend a search beyond elemental components, it is necessary to combine two or more elemental components. Thus, synthesis of elemental classes of information is used to express superimposed, compound, or complex assemblies of classes that include multielement values to be archived. When using this approach to archive and retrieve components such as code, the search space can be very large. This approach should take into account the facts that:

1. There are potentially thousands of subprograms contained in a sophisticated program at the source code level.
2. There are potentially many groupings of existing softproducts that will perform the same function.

3. Generally, users will prefer to classify their own work rather than depend on software librarians to do this chore.

These realities, separately or in combination, lead to great difficulties; especially when there is a lack of standards for classification.

Both the enumerative and faceted methods will accommodate the necessary requirements to be successful as software classification schemes. As an example, both the faceted and the enumerative approaches provide flexibility, extensibility, and precision within the classification process. Both of these approaches can be used within a single reuse facility in the same way more than one classification scheme is utilized for traditional library holdings. Each classification scheme has its positive and negative features. However, faceted systems appear to be more robust from the perspective of being able to add new items, of accommodating large-scale systems, and retaining flexibility while being modified. On the basis of these observations, the faceted classification approach appears to hold the greatest promise for future development of classification schemes and standards for reusability.

As an example of how we may make use of the faceted approach, we will present a classification scheme with sample facets for software product components. Component descriptions may be based on standard vocabularies of terms supplemented by a thesaurus of terms containing synonyms of all terms, as appropriate. The thesaurus may be extended and tailored to meet the softproduct needs of a user. A citation order may be described and used. A conceptual metric may also be defined in order to measure the conceptual distance between terms in each facet. All of these will aid in discrimination. The ordering and distance measurements of the facets is maintained in a separate classification scheme so as to permit a high degree of customization. Decision support tools are available to assist in the evaluation of similarity of items for optimum selection capability. Facets that may be used to provide a classification scheme for use in this approach [Prieto-Diaz and Freeman, 1987] are:

1. *Function*—specific primitive or action performed (input, compare, search, etc.)
2. *Objects*—such as characters, root, and variables
3. *Medium*—entities that serve as locale where action is executed (files, binary tree, input buffer, etc.)
4. *System type*—much may be a functionally independent module, application independent module, a unit larger than a single component, a group of components that perform identifiable functions (report formatter, scheduler, retriever, etc.)
5. *Functional area*—describes a softproducticular identifiable function performed in an application area and is application-independent (cost control, operation system, aeronautical guidance, etc.)

6. *Setting*—describes the location where application is exercised, captures the details of how to conduct certain operations (e.g., aeronautical guidance and control program for a guided missile)

Combining these facets gives the vector $[F_1, F_2, F_3, F_4, F_5, F_6]$, which is sufficient to both classify a component and to initiate a search for that component.

One approach that we can use to achieve this would be one in which we look at software products from the perspectives of system definition and software design. We could use an approach such as *structured analysis and design technique* (SADT) to organize our software products. The SADT operation utilizes the structure and approach introduced and discussed in Chapter 4. The level 0 model may be used as a means to identify each of the operational inputs to the system. Through this identification, the faceted representation may be used to implement the classification scheme and identify the optimum term to select for each facet, thereby enhancing the search vector information. SADT guides the analyst in the decomposition of software into various functions such as graphic notations, modeling principles, and review procedures that are candidates for software reuse products. If we are using software components that represent code softproducts, we can use the just delineated candidate list of faceted classifications.

Many schemes have been developed to organize software products for reusability, such as the *IBM Software Catalog,* the *Microsoft Software Catalog,* the *Sun Third Party Software Catalog,* and the *Apple Book.* Other classification schemes that may be used in place of SADT include *data flow diagram* (DFD) notation, *data structure diagram* (DSD) notation, or *Jackson structure program* (JSP) notation, to name some of the structured approaches to classification. These diagrams have been discussed in Chapter 4.

Softproduct retrieval is substantively different from data and document retrieval. Data retrieval systems are deterministic and as such are completely defined by the data itself. Document retrieval systems may be deterministic. Alternately, they may be based upon abstract descriptions that tend to be non-deterministic in that the user cannot be assured of the content until the document is perused. Softproduct retrieval falls between these extremes. For example, if a specific segment of code is to be retrieved, the representation scheme is nearly deterministic. For softproducts that have only abstract definitions, the retrieval scheme tends to be possibilistic and will generally require the use of methods for imperfect information processing. It is in the latter area that the greatest technological advances are required.

A best pattern match search may increase the potential for retrieval of a usable softproduct. Conditions to enable this are that the storage classification scheme and the search algorithms are reasonably compatible, relevant to the user needs, and available as attributes of objects in the library. For ease of search, the classification approach should provide both enumeration and faceted schemes. This enables the user to approach the problem from a top-down and a bottom-up perspective, as the information at hand dictates. In either event it is desirable to have a domain as narrow as possible. This reduces the search time and enables the user to examine relevant software products in less time. It is also desirable to be able to provide a means of evaluation and assessment of the nature and applicability of the software softproduct in order to ascertain the value of the software product to the intended reuse. Thus, a software library must be associated with documentation appropriate to the domain searcher of the library. It must be able to match user interest with search algorithms and provide a means of exploration of the documentation scheme.

One way to realize this is through use of an *expert system* (ES) or *knowledge support system* (KSS). Figure 8.16 indicates some of the subsystems that would have to act together in order to yield an appropriate knowledge base. This knowledge base supports such software products as code softproducts, specifications testing softproducts, and documentation softproducts. A support facility such as this is a most needed and desirable feature for retrieval of complex software softproducts. Ideally, the KSS would be a routinely available and useful component of the software systems engineering development environment. This approach would provide for linkages to the user that would enable human–machine interface tailoring to meet user needs and expectations. An additional feature would be to have a large selection of inquiry tools, such as query tools that provide templates to format the query, that would enable the user to select the sets of most value for the particular

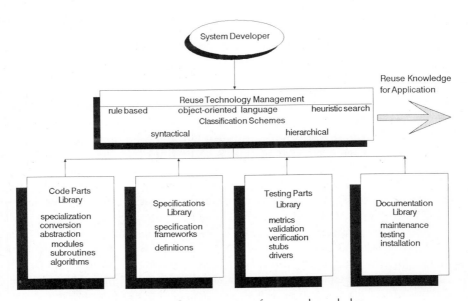

FIGURE 8.16 Support system for reuse knowledge

application at hand. This shows the close relationship of approaches that produce *softproducts* with *softprocess* notions.

As we have noted, the Ada programming language environment represents a significant step forward with respect to its provision of softproduct reuse of *building blocks* [Gargaro and Pappas, 1987; Burton et al., 1987]. We will discuss the *Reusable Software Library* (RSL) feature of Ada as an example of (currently) advanced reuse technology. The RSL* is intended to be a library of softproducts and associated information that enables their use in system design. The RSL has a user interface designed for ease of access by software developers. One of the principal initial uses of the interface is to encourage establishment of softproducts within the RSL itself, as well as to support the classification, evaluation, and archiving of these. There are four subsystems that support the reuse of softproducts:

1. *Library Management Subsystem,* which extracts pertinent reuse information from either design files or source code files, enables softproduct quality assurance, and enters softproducts into and maintains the RSL database

2. *User Query Subsystem,* which contains a fast-acting query language interface and an easy to use natural language interface and provides a menu driven interface that enables the search for softproducts with specified attributes and generates associated reports

3. *Software Component Retrieval and Evaluation* (SCORE) *Subsystem,* which assists the user to select appropriate softproducts through its provision of selection and evaluation methods that help reduce the time and effort that would be required to manually browse the RSL database

4. *Software Computer Aided Design* (SoftCad) *Subsystem,* which provides software design capability in terms of a graphical design and documentation tool that supports object oriented design diagrams and Ada PDL (program development language)

The RSL supports the softproduct archival process through the SCORE subsystem, which provides an ordered list of evaluated softproducts in terms of various attributes, functions, and constraints. This subsystem is predicted to not be adequate as the number of softproducts in the RSL increases. To cope with this, classification schemes are being developed that will organize and structure softproducts by such reusability attributes as function, objects, medium, system type, functional area, and environmental setting [Prieto-Diaz and Freeman, 1987].

The second softproduct reuse approach is based on *automatic softproduct (program) generation.* There are three possible approaches to this. The first approach would be based on the use of very-high-level, or fourth-generation (4GL) languages. We can approach automatic softproduct generation needs with a *pattern-oriented* code generator. The 4GL approach could be considered as a separate category. In a real sense, it does generate softproducts in

*Not to be confused with the RSL that stands for *Requirements Specification Language.*

that a few problem-oriented statements are sufficient to allow resolution of a complex problem that would take many more lines of code to accomplish if it were written in a lower-level language. The *operational transformation* approach that we described in our last section as a prototyping approach, which starts with an abstract specification and generates code after a number of transformations, could also be used in a pattern like production of reusable softproducts. This leads to an important conclusion concerning the closely related approaches of this section: *Macro-enhancement approaches are fundamentally* normative *perspectives on how software development can be conducted and managed. It will not always be possible, or even desirable, to examine a specific approach in use and characterize it exclusively as one of the macro-enhancement approaches.* We will conclude our discussions concerning reusability by briefly describing three currently available reuse methods based on this conclusion:

Refine—a LISP-like declarative language [Smith et al. 1985] that is both a transformational system and a programming environment. The language supports set-theoretic, first-order predicate calculus, and rule-based, symbolic, and procedural statements. The combination of the Refine language, a knowledge base of transformational rules, and software engineering rules enables the development of system specifications that will later be transformed into LISP code

Module Description Language (MODEL) [Prywes et al., 1986]—a declarative language that will translate algebraic system specification equations into either Ada or C. There are only two statement forms. One of these describes data, and the other describes the relationships between variables. An important need for a highly algorithmically based system such as this is support in preparation of the system specifications in terms of equations, and in the interpretation of the resulting equations. MODEL provides little support in this regard.

Draco—an approach to software development [Neighbors, 1984] based on both the reuse of software design information as well as specific source code. It also involves the use of expert system technology to capture application-domain-specific information. It also involves transformational techniques that use reusable softproducts as input and produce similar software system comprised, in part, of reused softproducts. Freeman [1987b] has developed an augmentation of the Draco approach through the development of a code generation system that is comprised of an extensible set of interrelated domains, each supported by five specification parts: (1) a *parser* to cope with internal and external domain syntax, (2) a *set of transformations* that iteratively evolve domain language system specifications into computer source code, (3) *rules* for using the transformations, (4) a *pretty-printer* that is responsible for production of the external domain representation, and (5) *predefined components* that can represent domain objects and operations. This augmentation provides for automation of some of the many techniques conceptualized in the Draco approach.

Our third approach for the creation of softproducts is that of *object-oriented programming*. We discussed object-oriented programming briefly in Chapter 4, and our comments here will be restricted to those characteristics of object-oriented programming that support softproduct reuse. In principal, object-oriented programming provides a very flexible approach for the identification, definition, and composition of potentially reusable building blocks as softproducts [Meyer, 1987].

Through use of this approach, potentially reusable softproducts yet to be instantiated are associated with the attributes of existing softproducts, in terms of the structure, function, and purpose of the existing softproducts. The object-oriented programming environment also provides potentially useful vehicles for administering such libraries of reusable softproducts as library browsers and search facilities.

The earliest successful illustration of a reuse strategy based on object oriented programming is given by *Smalltalk 80* applications. *Smalltalk 80* [Golberg, 1984] is a very productive software development environment that supports object-oriented programming. It supports softproduct reuse in the form of source code only. It includes such features as abstraction and information hiding, component or class libraries, library search and browsing, and module interfaces.

This reuse occurs both when a software developer chooses a softproduct (code module) to use from the library, and when the object or module inherits the functional methods of parent classes. *When we wish to reuse a softproduct, we must be able to access them.* This seems a simple enough statement, but it is not necessarily an easy accomplishment when there are many nearly identical copies of essentially the same module, with different names and stated functions. It turns out [Cox, 1986] that there are over 250 classes or high-level modules in the Smalltalk 80 environment and over 2000 methods.

8.3.2   Approaches to Softprocess Reusability

Sadly, this subsection is necessarily brief, but only because so very little is known about this subject at this time. Basically, this approach uses the notions of systems management of reusable patterns of software reuse and emphasizes activities involved in reuse. The approaches to *softproduct* reusability that we have discussed all support the hypothesis that full use of *softproduct* approaches will require efforts at *softprocess* reuse. This occurs simply because *softprocess* reuse is a meta-level activity that supports *softproduct* reuse. Automation and support of human cognitive processes are the goals of *softprocess* reuse. Figures 8.14 and 8.15 each place emphasis on the logical transition between *softproduct reuse* and *softprocess reuse*. Our work to follow, in Chapter 9, will emphasize some of the meta-level concerns that are appropriate for development of efficacious *softproduct support*. Tracz [1988] suggests nine myths about software reuse. Many of these suggest that software reuse will ultimately occur only when we are able to successfully address *softprocess reuse* concerns.

8.3.3 Characteristics of a Software Development Environment for Reusability

In an ideal software systems engineering development environment, standards will be developed so that reference sources will be available to the user such that systems and programs of common application types may be created with relative ease. These standards must include items such as the documentation of methodologies for application fields, documentation of testing routines, codification of algorithms, documentation of specifications, and other similar software softproducts. These systems or modules must be clearly documented. For example, the methods potentially useful for sorting data have been well researched and are readily accessible. Documentation is essential for efficiency and effectiveness in the use of the library of software softproducts that might contain reusable sorting algorithm software. Without this, the user would be not be able to determine the applicability of a specific sort algorithm and would have to move to lower levels of the software characteristic identification scheme than necessary before identifying an appropriate reuse softproduct.

The reference sources contained in the software development environment will permit the user to carry on operations on either the design or implementation level, however the user must exercise great care when selecting modules. In an ideal environment, all library modules would be compatible. However, a common problem of implementation that usually arises relative to the actual code generation that is contained in the library module is the lack of compatibility in both data formats and control functions. This issue would exclude many existing tools and code packages, as these are based on different codes. Therefore, an interim approach in moving toward a full library of reusable modules would be to utilize the reuse of design aspects of software development as the initial activity in realizing the goal of reusability.

The construction of new softproducts from building blocks of reusable modules is sure to become more common with the continued development of system resources, and fully articulated software development environments; such as, the Ada programming environment, the Unix operating system environment, object-oriented programming languages, or other environment oriented resources. However, the generality necessary to ensure reuse potential can result in large and sometimes unwieldy systems. An ideal environment may be forced to accept a tradeoff between specificity and application efficiency.

There are several views that we might take in examining how a reuse facility fits into a software systems engineering development environment. We will look at two of these, a technology transfer model that depicts a functional approach to a reuse environment and a classification scheme that has as its major objective the reuse of softproducts to produce code.

Our conceptual model for software reuse that is depicted in Figure 8.11 is a functional model that envisions reusability products at each of the several levels supported by a single knowledge base. We begin with software development knowledge that leads us to a framework for generic systems, function collections, software architectures, and finally code. The other input to these is derived from applications knowledge that is domain-specific. Domain-specific applications knowledge may consist of functional architectures, logical structures, and code segments. Domain applications contribute to the rounding out of the necessary and sufficient information to provide reusability products from each stage of the model: generic systems, functional collections, software architecture, and code. This learning process is also depicted in Figure 8.12.

We also need a classification schema to denote *reuse structure, reuse function,* and *reuse purpose.* At the highest level, the user will select an application. After selection of the application, the user will move to the next level, which enumerates functions within the application. Functions are operations such as the control exercised by the system, updating databases, sorting files, and report generation. A menu-driven tool selector will extract the necessary information from the user and support user selection of desirable functional capabilities of the system. The output of this selection may be a collection of well-documented design paradigms, each of which contains pointers to code generation modules on the next level. An important aspect of the system is that at each level the user is able to modify the selection after a review of requirements and system specifications. The environment uses an iterative process that can be controlled at each level of software system development.

An obvious requirement for reusability is that of devising an efficient way to store and retrieve modules from the tool catalog. Expert systems are potentially able to guide the user in the selection of those tools that are most applicable to the requirements of the project. The functional architecture, logical structure, and code generation databases must contain sufficient specification to describe the relevant characteristics of each module. Further research is needed to determine what specifications are of interest and how detailed these specifications can be without causing degradation of the system due to excessive search time. A conceptual chart showing an expert support system for reusability was shown in Figure 8.16.

The effect of improvements in software reuse technology is felt at each level in the reuse strategy selected. This strategy will involve use of generic systems, functional architectures, logical structures, and code generation. For example, developments in design technology could force restructuring of system development due to application of a new approach. Such a change could be moving from a structured design paradigm to an evolutionary paradigm. Thus, additional software development approaches must be able to be added to the reuse library, as they are developed or implemented in a softproduct operational situation. Hardware developments may require revision of code generation modules. Controls are necessary to ensure appropriate management of existing systems in order to be able to handle the possibility of adding new or different approaches that may not be compatible with the other versions of the system. To be successful, the software development environment that will include the capability of incorporation reuse paradigms must be flexible and able to respond to changes in various aspects of system development and implementation.

One key to reusability is the accessibility of software products that have been archived in a library. Reusable products must include more than code; indeed, the reuse of archived code in and of itself has little intrinsic value. The greater value and need lies in software design and analysis information, which has considerable value and makes code much more valuable. Thus, any reusability facility must be designed and constructed so as to take advantage of software products for all phases of the lifecycle development process, especially design and analysis information.

A summary of the requirements for the implementation of the reusability concept is:

1. Provide a well-defined scope for the reusability constructs that are being considered that incorporates both *softproducts* and *softprocesses*.
2. Incorporate standards for reusable *softproducts* and *softprocesses*.
3. Provide adequate documentation for *softproducts* and how to retrieve them in a way that is efficient, effective, and explicable.
4. Provide sufficiently complete representation of information describing any reusability product.
5. Provide modification procedures that enable adaptation and transitioning of a *softproduct* to meet new demands.
6. Incorporate a *softprocess* management philosophy that encourages reuse

There are major cognitive concerns to be overcome before we are able to see reusability come into its own. A reuse facility must be well supported in the use of those software development lifecycles that give maximum support to reusability concepts. A conceptual framework for software development must support reuse of softproducts and be strongly guided by definition and classification systems for reuse. An environment that provides support to users in retrieving and evaluating softproducts is essential. Finally, it is essential to know the way in which the retrieved softproduct behaves if this product is to be useful in the new software development effort. None of these concerns is trivial, and each are needed in order to obtain a reuse capability that will support effective and efficient *softproduct and softprocess reusability*.

8.3.4   Reusability and Software Productivity

Reusability represents one of the opportunities to realize a significant gain in software productivity. Reuse was proposed as a formal process to aid in improving software development productivity over 20 years ago. However, real progress has been very limited. Conceptual, technological, management, and institutional reasons thwart institution of productivity programs involving reusability. The need to define the type and structure of software softproducts together with classification and retrieval schemes have been identified as essential elements for a successful reusability facility. This means that future software should be constructed so that understanding, modification, and component integration are feasible, if we are to realize any of the potential of improved productivity. To do this requires attention to softprocess reuse!

Definition of productivity over the software lifecycle is a difficult and complex activity, as we will see in Chapter 10. In economic terms, productivity means the creation of economic value or producing goods and services of economic value. Software productivity is defined in the same manner as productivity in any area is defined, namely, as the value of the output produced ($output_{value}$) divided by the input cost ($input_{cost}$), or

$$\text{Productivity} = \frac{output_{value}}{input_{cost}}$$

The output value is measured on the basis of the user satisfaction, unit cost of the product, source lines of code delivered, or other similar values. The input cost is determined by summing the costs of labor, capital, material, and energy required to produce a software product. The determination of the input cost is relatively well defined and lends itself to calculation following software delivery. While calculation of input cost is not without difficulty, this is insignificant when compared to measuring the value of the output. Even though we are provided with a relatively straightforward metric, such as source lines of code, it is not a simple matter to determine output value. While the source line of code appears to be a straightforward metric, it is not. It is not a uniform metric and resists precise definition [Boehm, 1987], which makes software productivity a difficult activity to measure and renders reusability contributions to software productivity constructs even more difficult to ascertain. The parameter, source lines of code, is the primary metric used for calculation of software productivity because it represents virtually the only item related to output that may be quantitatively measured.

It is commonly held that a substantial reduction in manpower applied to a software development project, with corresponding increases in productivity, may be achieved through introduction of modern programming practices, such as those presented in Chapters 4 and 5. This has generally been observed to be true. Costs for developing software in a 4GL will be generally a fraction of the costs to do the same program in assembly code. Boehm [1981] has collected much data on the impact on software productivity for a variety of factors and in comparative tests completed using the COCOMO model and has shown the impact of these factors on software productivity. The findings relevant to software productivity and reusability show that potential gains from software reusability alone are almost as great as from all others combined.

In an earlier call for increased software productivity through reusability, McIlroy conceived of a software factory in 1968 [McIlroy, 1976] with inter-changeable components much as that of a hardware components factory. Such a software factory was built by Toshiba in 1977 and is described by Matsumoto [1987]. The total amount of software shipped to customers as of 1987 was 7.2 million *equivalent assembler source lines* (EASLs) of code. The achieved production rates for code has gone from 1900 EASLs per-person month including reused code in 1977 to 3100 EASLs per person-month in 1985. This gives an annual increase in productivity of nearly 8%. Productivity increases without reuse of code has gone from 1000 EASLs per person-month in 1977, to 1600 EASL per person-month in 1985, which gives an average productivity growth of approximately 7.5% per year. Most important, however, is the productivity comparison between programmers who reused code and those who did not. The productivity for code reusers was 90% in 1977 and almost 94% in 1985. In this case at least, reusability provided a substantial improve-ment in software productivity over no reuse of code and, in addition, a marginal improvement in overall software productivity occurred over the same period.

On the basis of these outcomes of significant improvements in software productivity for those who are engaged in reusability, it is worthwhile to examine the structure of the Fuchu Software Factory. This software factory utilizes software development environments that support programming, as-sembling, compiling, and debugging at the source code level, support for tests, support for maintenance, support for program management, and sup-port for quality assurance. Methodologies supported in these environments include SADT, HIPO, and various structured design constructs and the ap-proach taken uses the classical waterfall software development lifecycle. A schematic configuration of the Toshiba Software Fuchu Works is depicted in Figure 8.17 [Davis, 1988]. The software workbench system provides integrated support for all users within the factory. The central feature of this system is the software engineering database, which stores all information related to system configuration management.

As seen in Figure 8.17, SWB-I provides support for all aspects of the programming effort, including program generation and program reuse; SWB-II provides support for all test procedures; SWB-III provides support for requirements specification descriptions, specification verification, and per-formance evaluation; SWB-IV provides support for project maintenance, troubleshooting, and maintenance of software at the customer site; SWB-P

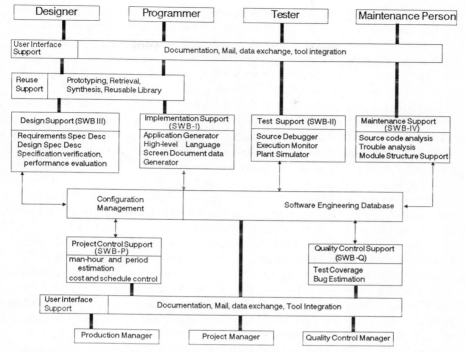

FIGURE 8.17   Software workbench configuration for the Toshiba Fuchu works

provides support for project management; and SWB-Q provides support for quality assurance. In operation, interactions by designers, programmers, testers, and maintenance personnel are through the user interface. This interface also provides support for mail, data exchange, tool integration, and documentation. Project management also has access to the same information through its user interface. Each SWB is identified as to the function supported. The flow of development for an individual project begins with management guidance, moves to design, and then moves to programming, testing, and maintenance, with management oversight and consultation as an ongoing function. Reusable software products that contribute to the significant improvements noted in programmer productivity in this software factory include documentation, specifications, and programs that satisfy characteristics for defined applications criteria. Reusable softproducts are maintained in the database and have an attached checklist that contains the evaluation of the component for reusability.

8.4   KNOWLEDGE-BASED SYSTEMS FOR SOFTWARE PRODUCTIVITY

We have seen how prototyping and reusability notions provide aid for potentially major improvements in software productivity. We have also seen that the use of prototyping alone does not guarantee such an improvement. With respect to reusability, much additional work is required before we will be able to assert that this approach is an unqualified success in improving software productivity. One major need relative to each of these is for some automated approaches that will provide the needed management of the many activities needed to successfully use these macro-enhancement approaches.

The general area of knowledge based systems provides us with many possibilities to fulfill this management need. What is now needed is an approach that will enable us to effectively and efficiently use various enhancement tools for the development of productive software. Figure 8.18 indicates the potentially central role of *knowledge-based systems* in this. One of the needs, for instance, is to make an initial determination of whether a structural, functional, or purposeful approach to prototyping is needed. After that is done, some management controls must be applied to the various interactive iterations as an initial prototype evolves into a final prototype and, potentially, a final set of requirements specifications if this is the lifecycle phase that is being prototyped. Figures 8.19 and 8.20 illustrate these efforts. While there is no question but that the various systems management functions required to accomplish the flows indicated in these figures can be accomplished manually, there is also no question but that the manual approach may involve sufficient time and complexity that an automated approach will very likely be preferable to a manual one.

As already noted, the major thrust of this book is to outline systems engineering approaches to increasing software productivity. Here, we cite the need for knowledge support systems used in conjunction with various library modules containing access to micro-enhancement tools: high- and very-high-level languages, compilers and automatic program generators, and macro-enhancement tools. We also discuss the need for macro-productivity tools

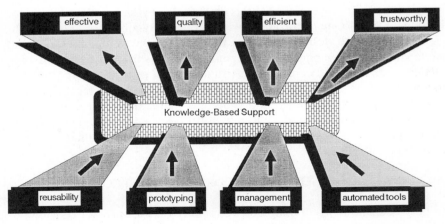

FIGURE 8.18 Knowledge based support for software productivity

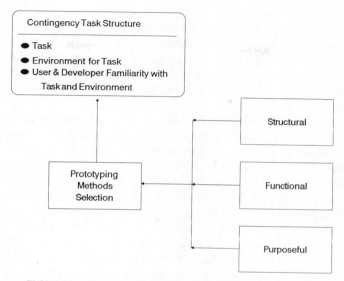

FIGURE 8.19   Selection from prototyping approaches

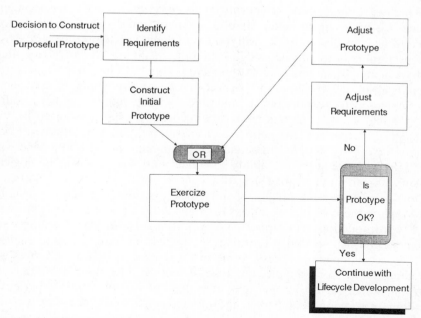

FIGURE 8.20   Flow diagram for early lifecycle phases with purposeful prototyping

such as rapid prototyping, reusability constructs, and an interactive support system environment that involves the systems engineer, the manager and the software engineer. Thus, our discussions in this section are very closely related to, and to some extent depend on, related discussions in other chapters. This is especially the case relative to the discussion of environments in Chapter 7 and those to come in Chapter 9 concerning management of the software development process.

There are a number of human abilities that a *knowledge support system* (KSS), which is a generic term describing a computerized system that supports knowledge workers in performing cognitive tasks, should augment. It should support the software developer and the software user in the formulation or framing of the software development situation in the sense of recognizing needs, identifying appropriate objectives by which to measure successful resolution of an issue, and generating alternative development strategies that will resolve needs and satisfy objectives. It should also provide support in enhancing the abilities of the developer and user group to obtain the possible impacts on needs of the alternative courses of software development action. This analysis capability must be associated with provision of capability to enhance the ability of the developers and users to provide an interpretation of these impacts in terms of objectives. This interpretation capability will lead to evaluation of the alternatives and selection of a preferred alternative development option. Associated with all of these must be the ability to acquire, represent, and utilize information or knowledge, and the ability to implement the chosen alternative course of development action.

This is a *formal, rational systems engineering approach* to development. While it is often appropriate, there are many instances where other factors need to be considered. As we will discuss in detail in Chapter 9, there exists a considerable body of knowledge, generally qualitative, relative to human judgment and decisionmaking. Although this applies to judgments in general, there is absolutely no reason to suggest that this massive body of knowledge does not apply to software development as well. The majority of these studies suggest that a bounded rationality or satisficing perspective, often heavily influenced by bureaucratic political considerations, will generally be the decision perspective adopted in actual decisionmaking practice. To cope with this effectively requires the ability to concurrently deal with technological, organizational, and cognitive structural concerns as they each, separately and collectively, motivate problem-solving issues. The intent of our next chapter is to explore these in some detail as they apply to the development of software.

The introduction of a support system into a software development environment in which one did not formally exist will bring about dynamic changes in the decisionmaking process. Some of these may be desirable; others will be undesirable. For example, one type of support now made possible is the introduction of expert system capabilities that potentially capture experiential wisdom for decisions that involve unconflicted adherence to an original course of action or unconflicted change.* These may be encoded in the form of rules, or other representations, to enable novices to use the system in the hopes of performing as if they were experts. Doubtlessly, the performance of the people using an expert system will differ from the performance of unaided experts. Further, the introduction of such a system presumably means that the time and effort mix of the top-level managers has been altered. These changes need to be given due consideration in support system design.

8.4.1 Types of Knowledge Support Systems

There are two generic types of knowledge support systems: the *decision support system* (DSS) and the *expert system* (ES). There are a number of variants of these terms, such as *executive support system*. In very general terms, a decision support system is a systems that supports decisionmaking by assisting in the organization of knowledge about ill-structured issues. The emphasis is on effectiveness of decisionmaking as this involves formulation of alternatives, analysis of their impacts, and interpretation and selection of appropriate options for implementation. Efficiency, while important, is secondary to effectiveness. There are many application areas where the use of a decision support system is potentially promising. These include essentially any area in which a decisionmaker has to cope with semistructured or unstructured decision situations.

The three principal components of a decision support system are shown in Figure 8.21. The "knowledge" in a decision support system is expected to come, at least in part, from the ultimate user of the system. Also, there are three technology levels at which a DSS may be considered. The first of these is the level of DSS tools themselves. This level would contain the hardware and software elements and those system science and operations research methods that would be needed to design a specific decision support system. The purpose of these DSS tools is to enable design of a specific DSS that would be responsive to a particular task or issue. Development and use of effective DSS generators to automate this process is an attractive possibility.

An expert system is a system that is able to assist the system user to use the expert knowledge of others, typically stored in the form of what are generally called *inference procedures* within the knowledge base of a computer, in order to resolve complex issues. The knowledge of an expert will consist, in part, of what are often called *fact files* and *knowledge sources*. The fact file will consist of data and information that are generally believed to characterize the domain under consideration. The knowledge sources will consist of a large number of skill- and rule-based forms of knowledge that an expert may be expected to bring to bear on a particular familiar issue. There will also exist a control structure or system, also known as an *inference* or

---

*These terms are defined and elaborated on in Chapter 9.

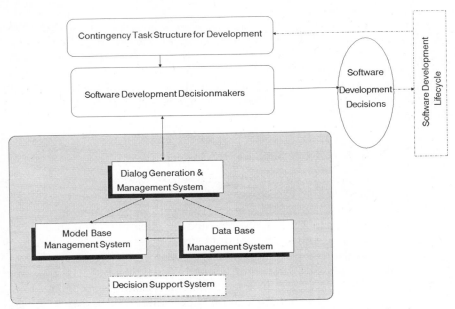

FIGURE 8.21 The generic role of decision support systems in software development

cognitive engine, that organizes and directs the steps that are actually taken to resolve a problem. The principal task of the cognitive engine is to act as an intelligent interpreter in the selection of those portions of the knowledge base that are most applicable to resolution of a given issue. There must be interfaces between the two principal components of an expert system: the knowledge base and the cognitive engine. Interfaces must also exist between these subsystems and the expert whose knowledge is captured in the system, and the ultimate users of the system.

An expert system is designed to assist users that are generally not experts in exercising judgment in situations that are familiar to, and therefore capable of being structured by, experts in the specific problem area of concern. The interrelationships among the subsystems of an expert system are many, and only a few are here described and illustrated. Figure 8.22 presents the conceptual structure of an expert system. While it appears very similar to that of a decision support system, as shown in Figure 8.21, it should be again noted that the types of users for whom the systems are most appropriate are really quite different. A software developer, for example, who is experientially somewhat familiar with the application domain in which a software system is to operate, would typically wish to use a DSS to assist in the evaluation of courses of action and, in this process, would supply knowledge to or for the system.

In the case of an expert system, however, the knowledge base is presumably supplied by a person with much greater domain expertise than possessed by

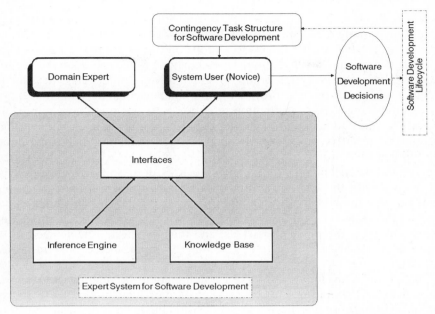

FIGURE 8.22   The generic role of expert systems in software development

the system user. The expert system would generally be used by those who are *novices* relative to some aspects of the system being developed. (Again, terms such as these are defined and discussed in Chapter 9.)

There are dangers in use of either type of support system. A potential danger in use of an expert system is that the environmental context in which certain rules are valid may change and the system user does not recognize this. This precise situation can, of course, exist with respect to an *expert* human who attempts to use intuitive or affective or wholistic reasoning in situations in which environmental changes have made this type of reasoning inappropriate. Thus, we see that an important need in support system design is one in which environmental awareness monitoring is considered as a need. Even in cases in which a human is acting without computerized support, there exists the possibility of need for alerts to potential environmental changes that would alter the value of experiential wisdom.

8.4.2   Generic Software Development Support Systems

Much of the discussion to be found in the software engineering literature relative to both software design and the use of knowledge-based systems concentrates on what may be called *formal reasoning* and decision enactment efforts that involve the issue resolution efforts that follow as part of the problem-solving efforts of issue formulation, analysis, and interpretation that we have discussed. There are other decisionmaking activities as well. Very important among these are activities that allow perception, framing, editing, and interpretation of the effects of actions on the internal and external environments of a decision situation. These might be called *information selection activities;* they are very important to software development as they are to other areas of information processing and human judgment and choice.

There will also exist information retention activities that allow admission, rejection, and modification of the set of selected information or knowledge such as to result in short-term learning through reduction of incongruities, and long-term learning through the acquisition of new schemata that reflect enhanced understanding. Although basic KSS design efforts may well be concerned with the short-term effects of various problem solving, decision-making, and information presentation formats, the actual knowledge that a person brings to bear on a given problem is a function of the accumulated experience that the person possesses, and thus long-term effects need to be considered, at least as a matter of secondary importance in system design efforts.

A software development support system should be adaptive to user requirements. It should not force users into a particular mode of thought or force them into using a specific set of decision algorithms or paradigms; nor should it force them into a prescribed protocol or procedure. Above all, the process should yield results that are of value in and of themselves at the moment they are obtained, as contrasted with having to wait until the end of the process to obtain any useful results at all.

Many features of a decision support system should be user-modifiable, or adaptive *to* the user, to accommodate the abilities and experiences of its users such as to enable them to be more efficient and effective. It must be adaptive *for* the user in the sense of providing gentle encouragement to the user to modify the initially suggested user approach to the system to enable greater user effectiveness and efficiency. It is also important that these approaches be specifically designed to encourage users to avoid poor cognitive heuristics and biases in their expressions of software-development-relevant knowledge. These represent some of the many points that should be addressed when developing software, as well as when developing software evaluation metrics for these systems, and also when conducting evaluations of existing software systems.

We espouse a three-layer approach to software systems engineering, as shown in Figure 8.23, in order to integrate together the technology for software production within an appropriate design approach that is matched to the organization and environment in which the software must function. From this perspective, software production truly becomes a systems engineering activity. It, like systems engineering, is a *management technology* in that it involves *technology,* which is the organization and delivery science for the betterment of humankind, and *management,* which is the art and science of enabling an organization to function in an environment such as to achieve objectives.

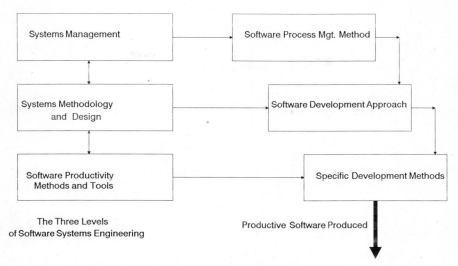

FIGURE 8.23 Another view of the framework for software systems engineering

Figure 8.24 illustrates this view of software systems engineering. Through use of this three-level approach to software engineering, we hope to provide symbiotic relationships between individual members of a programming team to enable successful completion of projects that enable better performance of organizations in operational environments. Figure 8.25 indicates this symbiotic embedding. Successful efforts in software systems engineering must be concerned with productivity across each of these entities. Here, programs, or program modules, lead to programming products. Collections of these lead to programming systems and programming system products. It is at these levels that the micro-enhancement and macro-enhancement efforts of software engineering can be applied.

All of this suggests development and use of KSS to aid in software development. In the requirements specifications processes, for example, a major need is to be able to transfer knowledge from system users to specifications in an appropriate manner. Better ideas and better problem resolution will potentially occur because individuals working interactively with the KSS will be working from a well-documented knowledge base. The goal is to make knowledge accessible, intelligible, and malleable so that the KSS may be adaptable to change and to feedback for error detection, and ultimately to meta-level learning on the part of the software design team.

8.4.3 Software Development Support Systems

There have been a number of important developments relative to the use of KSS technology in software development. We will examine some of these here. It is difficult, however, to make a precise determination concerning

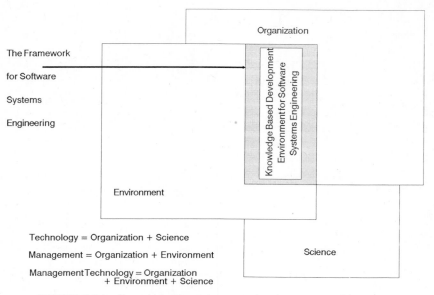

Technology = Organization + Science

Management = Organization + Environment

Management Technology = Organization
+ Environment + Science

FIGURE 8.24 Knowledge based system development environment

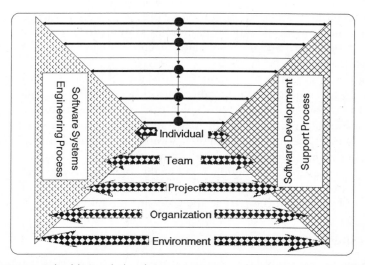

FIGURE 8.25 Imbedding of development process, development support process, individuals and environment through integrated support

what qualifies as a knowledge-based support aid and what does not. We do not include *automatic programming* aids within our categorization. However, transformational approaches such as we have described in our prototyping discussions would be included. As with many categorizations, the notion of purpose and process need to be considered in determining whether a specific approach fits into a given categorization. The transformational approach involves *pattern matching* to determine where to apply a transformation, a *set of applicability conditions* that determines the appropriate transformation to use, and *procedural action* that creates program code as tranformationally equivalent to the pattern or initial requirements that were identified. From this perspective, we could categorize this as a knowledge-based approach.

Our interest here is more in systems that assist and support in the development of software, as contrasted with approaches that automate and perhaps replace one of the lifecycle phases by an automated product. In this connection, there are several important questions:

1. What is the appropriate division of *cognitive* effort between human developer, perhaps individual programmer, and the machine?
2. How are the software developers, users, and the machine going to communicate and cooperate with respect to this division of effort?
3. What is the knowledge that system developers know and how can it be effectively represented by a machine.

We will describe the *Programmer's Apprentice* and the *Knowledge-Based Software Assistant* research and some of the extensions as prototypical of efforts in this area. Much more detailed overviews can be found in Rich and Waters [1986, 1988].

The long-term goal of the *Programmer's Apprentice* development effort is a theory of how expert programmers analyze, synthesize, modify, explain, specify, verify, and document programs. The hope for the Programmer's Apprentice is that it will provide programming support for the fundamental programming phases of *requirements, testing,* and *implementation.* Two formative principles supporting the development are the *assistant approach* and *inspection methods.* There are two technical advances, the *Plan Calculus* and a *hybrid reasoning* system, that result from these.

The fundamental assistant approach is that of eliminating programmer involvement in constructing specific application programs through automatic programming. In this, the end user of the software would write a complete requirements specification for what is desired and the automatic program generation system would generate functionally useful source code.

A major problem with this notion is that the specification languages that might be appropriate to enable this will be very restricted in terms of domain of applicability, and perhaps very difficult to use as well. For this reason, and to enable development of wide scope support, the notion of *programmer replacement* is replaced by that of *programmer support.* The apprentice is intended to be an agent in the software development process that has access to all the tools in the programming environment. Initially, it takes on only the simplest and most routine tasks but, as the design of the associate improves over time, will be able to take on greater responsibilities.

Given sufficient experience and a library of familiar roles and constraints for program development, it becomes possible to accomplish many programming tasks by *inspection*, that is to say, through wholistic or skill based intuitive reasoning, rather than only through the use of formal analytically based reasoning, or holistic reasoning.

The notion of inspection, or skill-based reasoning, is theoretical. There needs to be some specific, concrete, machine-usable implementation in order for this theoretical construct to be used. The *Plan Calculus* is one such implementation. It combines the representation properties of flowcharts, schemas, frames, and other abstract knowledge representation types into a hierarchical graph structure consisting of *boxes,* denoting tests and operations; and *arrows,* denoting control and data flow. This provides the apprentice with a wide-spectrum formalism that can represent inspections.

The *hybrid reasoning* system has a layered architecture that enables successive transformations from Plan Calculus to propositional logic as shown in Figure 8.26. Thus, there is a combination of special-purpose representations and general-purpose logical reasoning.

The *Knowledge-Based Editor in Emacs* (KBEmacs) is a part of the apprentice that demonstrates the usefulness of the *assistant approach* and *interpretations* in the implementation phase of the software lifecycle. In essence, it provides a high level of editing commands that allows changes in the al-

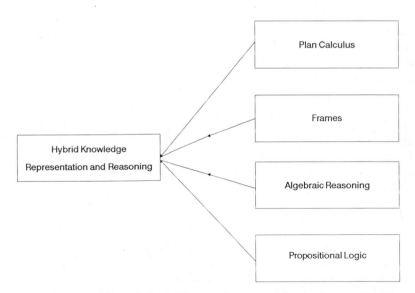

FIGURE 8.26 Hybrid knowledge and reasoning system for programmer's apprentice

gorithmic structure of programs to be made very easily, even when these require very large textual changes in the program code itself. Automatic generation of program documentation is a by-product of using KBEmacs, which is independent of programming language.

The KBEmacs concept has been extended into the realm of design, and the resulting product is known as the *Designer's Apprentice*. Three additional capabilities are incorporated: (1) a declarative, specification-like, input language; (2) detection and explanation of many programmer errors; and (3) automatic selection of reasonable choices. The knowledge of the Design Apprentice is based on typical illustrations, designs, and hardware configurations. (Typical hardware configurations include the types of printer, serial and parallel ports, and interactive display devices.)

Another prototype of a portion of the Programmer's Apprentice is known as the *Requirements Apprentice*. This supports the requirements phase of the lifecycle through:

1. A transition mechanism to enable transfer from informal user specifications to formal software specifications
2. A *repository system, information system,* and *tracking system* for requirements illustration
3. A *target scenario* display for requirements

The interconnection of the Design Apprentice with the Requirements Apprentice will result in a first demonstration of the complete Programmer's Apprentice concept. As of this writing, this is yet to be accomplished.

Sander's Associates has utilized and extended the Programmer's Apprentice concept in their *Knowledge-Based Requirements Assistant* effort. As we have noted, expert system technology can be brought to bear on rapid prototyping, such as to automate the execution of the conceptual prototyping model of Figure 8.20. Reusable software would generally be needed in order to enable *rapid* construction of the prototype. The *Knowledge-Based Requirements Assistant* (KBRA) [Czuchry and Harris, 1988] is a component of the *Knowledge-Based Software Assistant* (KBSA) being developed by the Rome Air Development Center [Green et.al., 1986]. It has several roles in managing the processing of requirements information as well as provision of support throughout the lifecycle, as shown in Figure 8.27. Support for project management is also provided, as shown in the figure.

In the KBSA, the reusable modules can be used:

1. For incorporation into the actual evolving prototype, or software system if appropriate, in a *cut-and-paste*-like fashion
2. As stimulants to further thought concerning requirements

There is also a multipresentation mechanism that enables people to enter information into the system using a representation and perspective that is

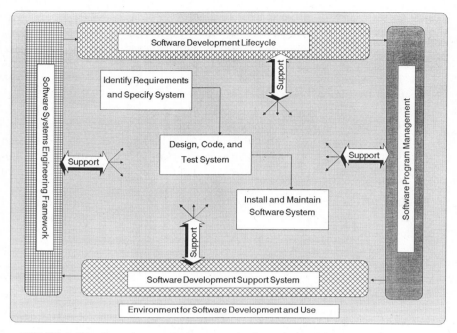

FIGURE 8.27   Generic support structure for knowledge based software assistant

appropriate for them. Knowledge concerning requirements decisions is incorporated into a central knowledge base of requirements statements and knowledge. This is associated with analysis capabilities that can determine the impacts of requirements decisions and also check for consistency of results. These features are accomplished through *inheritance of properties* from generic object types, *automatic classification* based on discriminators that indicate how to specialize instances, and *constraint propagation* that allows processing of the impacts of requirements decisions as well as the effects of changes in inputs to the system that alter previous assumptions.

A software systems engineering design issue can be viewed from the perspectives of the three principal actors involved. At one level are the users who are concerned primarily with what the specific, to-be-developed, system can do for them. Their natural, and almost exclusive focus, is on the problem-solving tasks that they face in a particular environmental context. It is the interaction of these variables and their experiential familiarity with task and environment that determines their problem-solving needs. The perspective of the system designer, or system architect or system builder, is that of assisting the user in terms of specifying architecture to accomplish the task or evaluating an existing system to determine the extent to which it fulfills needs and is operationally functional. At the level of tools, programmers are responsible for converting these architectural specifications into working code. What we are suggesting is that a principal role of the software systems engineer is to interact with the user to assist the user in organizing information.

This suggests the strong need for the development of a robust set of task, functions, and methods taxonomies within meaningful operational settings. What is needed is not a set of abstract listings of methods, but rather a set of application related taxonomies, developed to include methods and methods characteristics as well as tasks and functions, that will permit assessment of the benefits and costs of particular approaches. The primary benefits associated with development of a set of matching protocols, which will allow us to interrelate functions tasks and methods, is that we will be able to specify software productivity design protocols that result in the production of trustworthy operational software. This software must necessarily be compatible with the problems desirous of solution and the cognitive perspectives of the humans who ultimately serve as user and client for the software. These needs are not unlike the needs in the KBSA.

The developed software systems engineering methodology would enable users and clients to input problem characteristics into a *software design aid* and receive recommendations about appropriate software design strategies and protocols. An initial version of this software design aid and associated environment was presented in Figure 7.21 and has also been discussed in the concluding portions of our last chapter. It involves use of both the micro-enhancement-based approaches and the macro-enhancement-based approaches, together with appropriate systems design methodologies and systems management processes. This situation room for software productivity is potentially appropriate for the design and management of productive and trustworthy software. We have described it as an *advanced software systems engineering development environment* (ASSEDE) [Palmer and Sage, 1987].

There are several expert systems currently available that purport to perform a variety of operations relative to the development of software products. Those mentioned earlier in this book include XCON, a hardware configuration program for customized assembly of VAX computers developed by DEC, as well as CASE tools, such as Knowledgeware's Information Engineering Workbench/Workstation (IEW/ES), that have expert system capability. Another expert system that aids in the automated development of software is KnowledgeBUILD, offered by Cullinet Software, Inc. KnowledgeBUILD provides an application generator that operates in the VAX environment to provide nonprocedural application definition, generation of complete applications, easy-to-use tools, and is stand-alone. The system supports interactive development of customized user interfaces, report layout, and screen layout for use in COBOL, FORTRAN, or BASIC applications.

8.5 SUMMARY

In this chapter we have attempted to provide an overview of macro-enhancement approaches to increase software productivity. We have seen that of the approaches examined, prototyping is the furthermost along in development, while expert systems and reusability constructs require much additional work before these concepts are translated into standard software development environments.

One particularly interesting need associated with reusable software is that of *reverse engineering*, which may be described as the process of examining existing software such as to enable the translation of softproducts, perhaps even softprocesses (some day) from one environment to another such that it can be readily reused. An ideal in this regard might be a CASE tool in the form of an applications generator that would automatically examine software and attempt to extract reusable components [Cleaveland and Kintala, 1988].

The common threads running through this and other macro-enhancement approaches is the construction of advanced software development environments that support multiple views of the software, provide graphic representation, and take into account the cognitive aspects of interface design. The systems engineering approach supports macro-enhancement technologies, particularly from the overall perspective of software development, and emphasizes the need to obtain correct requirements prior to making a significant investment in writing code. In this way systems engineering design constructs of establishing the importance of system conceptualization, formalization of needs into requirements, and then following through with application of appropriate tools and management techniques give us appropriate tools to enhance software productivity.

8.6 PROBLEMS

8.1 Please prepare a discussion of *Storyboard Prototyping* for use as functional or structural prototype. You might wish to consult Andriole [1987] for an excellent discussion of the rapid prototyping process.

8.2. Please comment on the statement *The term "throw-away prototype" is inappropriate in that these prototypes expand and enhance the knowledge base that is retained and incorporated in the final prototype; therefore they are not disposed of or "thrown away at all!"*

8.3. Please write a paper concerning the extent to which *structural, functional,* and *purposeful* prototyping satisfies the four support requirements for software development discussed at the beginning of Section 8.2.

8.4. Please write a paper concerning the extent to which *structural, functional,* and *purposeful* prototyping are useful for the development of
   a. Real-time software, or
   b. Embedded software

8.5. Prepare a paper outlining the roles for *structural, functional,* and *purposeful* prototyping in reusability. Be sure to consider the several types of reusability and develop your report in terms of these.

8.6. Identify five software development situations appropriate for the use of prototyping. Describe each situation and also identify the most appropriate form of prototyping to use. Discuss an appropriate software development lifecycle for each situation.

8.7. For the software development situations described in the foregoing problem, comment on the use of reusability for each situation. What opportunities for combined prototyping and reusability are there?

8.8. Prepare plans to identify customer requirements for:
   a. An office automation system
   b. A real time air traffic control system
   and discuss how you would implement the plan.

8.9. Consult a few contemporary references and prepare a discussion of automated CASE tools to support requirements identification and system specification development.

8.10. Prepare a written report on the use of prototyping to accomplish the installation and maintenance phases of the software lifecycle.

8.11. Prepare a written report on the use of expert systems to accomplish the installation and maintenance phases of the software lifecycle.

8.12. *A prototype can be dangerous in that it is certainly possible to build a model of something that can be built in the prototyping environment but not in the operational environment.* Please comment on this and write a report concerning the extent to which the various types of prototyping are susceptible to this problem. How could you go about minimizing this potential difficulty?

8.13. Write a brief paper concerning how you would deal with *imprecise information* and *requirements volatility* in the requirements specification process.

8.14. Most real-time systems really contain a portion of the system, such as a flight control system, which is subject to real-time requirements and a portion, such as an information or database management system, which does not. Please write a paper concerning how you might partition the development effort about these two, real-time and non-real-time, requirements. Discuss prototyping and reusability for the development of operational software.

8.15. Augmented by a reading of recent literature, prepare a report discussing the use of expert systems and knowledge-based system technology for software development. What types of systems are appropriate for each of the three fundamental phases of the software lifecycle?

8.16. Augmented by a reading of recent literature, prepare a report on expert system tools available for software development.

8.17. Compare the enumerative and faceted methods for classifying software part for reusability.

8.18. Using a program fragment that you have developed for other purposes, apply the faceted classification scheme and determine the facet vector.

8.19. Explain how the SADT approach is used to foster reuse of software parts.

8.20. Show how an expert system may be used to retrieve software parts from a reuse library that classifies software parts according to the faceted method. Give a sample set of rules.

8.21. Show how an expert system may be used to retrieve software parts from a reuse library that classifies software parts according to the enumerative method. Give a sample set of rules.

8.22. Explain the differences between macro-enhancement and micro-enhancement approaches to reuse.

8.23. Explain the use of the Draco approach to reusability, and contrast and compare it with the faceted and enumerative approaches.

8.24. Object-oriented languages are purported to support reuse of software parts. Explain how reuse is implemented using object-oriented languages.

8.25. Characterize the desirable components of a software reuse environment and show where it fits in a general software development environment as presented in Chapter 7.

8.26. Explain how software reuse enhances software productivity. Under what circumstances would software reuse reduce software productivity?

8.27. How would you incorporate reusability, prototyping, and knowledge-based system development concerns in user (system) and software requirements specification?

8.28. Do you suspect that use of knowledge-based systems will lead to a reorganization of the software life-cycle [Kerschberg and Weitzel, 1989]?

Chapter **9**

Management of the Software Systems Engineering Process

In this chapter, we will discuss management of software engineering processes. There are two fundamental goals for our efforts here. We wish to describe management activities directed at the ultimate production of trustworthy software. As an essential part of this, we wish to be able to specify costs for the production of software, typically as a function of the benefits that might be obtained from alternative levels of realization of client needs. We will begin our discussions with a discourse on topics relevant to software process management, first from a somewhat philosophical perspective and then from a much more pragmatic perspective. Our next chapter will discuss costing in some detail.

9.1 INTRODUCTION

There are many definitions that could be provided for the term "management" and the related term "project management." For our purposes, appropriate definitions are:

Management consists of all of the activities undertaken to enable an *organization* to cope effectively and efficiently within its *environment*. This will generally involve planning, organizing, staffing, directing, coordinating, reporting, and budgeting activities in order to achieve identified objectives.

Project management is the organized and integrated set of procedures, practices, technologies, and processes that will contribute to efficient and effective accomplishment of management subgoals that lead to achievement of the overall plans or objectives of an organization.

The word "organization" appears several times in these definitions, as does the word "plan." It is important to note that a given business will, or at least should, have a plan, very likely a set of plans, to achieve the overall objectives of the organization. Many of these will relate to the way in which the organization provides products and services to its customers or clients. With respect to this, a plan will generally be identified that satisfies both general and specific needs. The general needs relate to the way in which the organizational units have been structured to achieve success in coping with the business environment at hand. Out of these high-level plans and policies will evolve a framework that will enable identification of plans that will fulfill the needs of a specific client and within the general objectives of the unit.

Far more often than not, specific software systems engineering projects will be part of a larger comprehensive systems engineering effort that will include identification of a client's needs; development of technical specifications for hardware, software, and systems management processes that will fulfill these; and the resulting system design, implementation, and operational test and evaluation. It is important here to provide some notions concerning each of these *management* efforts, even though our primary focus is on software management. This we will do in our discussions to follow in this chapter.

9.2   ORGANIZATIONAL MANAGEMENT—PHILOSOPHICAL PERSPECTIVES

There are a variety of definitions of an organization. Some of those that are relevant to our discussions here are:

- A system of consciously coordinated activities of two or more people [Bass, 1981]
- Social units deliberately constructed to seek specific goals [Etzioni, 1964]
- Collectives that have been established on a relatively continuous basis in an environment, with relatively fixed boundaries, a normative order, authority ranks, communication systems, and an incentive system designed to enable participants to engage in activities in general pursuit of a common set of goals [Hall, 1977]
- A set of individuals, with bounded rationality, who are engaged in the decisionmaking process [Mintzberg, 1973]

Organizations can be viewed from a *closed-system perspective,* which views an organization as an instrument designed to enable pursuit of well-defined specified objectives. In this view, an organization will be concerned primarily with four objectives: efficiency, effectiveness, flexibility or adaptability to external environmental influences, and job satisfaction. Four organizational means or activities follow from this: complexity and specialization, centralization or hierarchy of authority, formalization or standardization of jobs, and stratification of employment levels [Hayre, 1965]. In this view, everything is functional and tuned such that all resource inputs are optimum and the associated responses fit into a well-defined master plan.

March and Simon [1958], among others, discuss the inherent shortcomings associated with this closed-system model of humans as machines. Not only is the human as machine view inappropriate, but there are pitfalls associated with viewing environmental influences as "noise," as must necessarily be done in the closed-system perspective. March and Simon's broadened view of an organization is known as the *open-systems view*. In the open systems view of an organization, concern is not only with objectives but also with appropriate responses to a number of internal and external influences. Others authors have expanded upon these views. For example, Weick [1979] describes organizational activities of *enactment, selection,* and *retention,* which assist in the processing of ambiguous information that results from an organization's interactions with ecological changes in the environment. The overall result of this process is the minimization of information equivocality such that the organization is able to understand its environment, recognize problems, diagnose causes, identify policies to potentially resolve problems, evaluate efficacy of these policies, and select a priority order for problem resolution.

The result of the activities of the organization is the enacted environment of the organization. This enacted environment contains an external part, which represents the activities of the organization in product markets, and an internal part, which is the result of organizing people into a structure to achieve organizational goals. This relates to the general and specific organizational planning that we have already discussed. Each of these environments is subject to uncontrollable exogenous influences due to economic, social, and other changes. Selection activities allow perception framing, editing, and interpretation of the effects of the organization's actions on the external and internal environments. From this will generally follow identification of a set of relationships believed of importance. Retention activities allow admission, rejection, and modification of the set of selected knowledge in accordance with existing retained knowledge, and integration of previously retained organizational knowledge with new knowledge. There are a potentially large number of cycles that may be associated with enactment, selection, and retention. These cycles generally minimize informational equivocality and allow for organizational learning such that the organization is able to cope with very complex and changing environments.

A very important feature of most realistic contemporary organizational models is that of *organizational learning*. Much of this organizational learning is not necessarily beneficial nor appropriate in a descriptive sense. For example, there is much literature [Kahneman et al., 1982; Sage, 1981a] showing that organizations and individuals use improperly simplified and often distorted models of causal and diagnostic inferences, and improperly simplified and distorted models of the contingency structure of environment and task in which these realities are embedded. Individuals often join "groups" to enhance survival possibilities and to enable pursuit of career and other objectives. These coalitions of like-minded people pursue interests that result in emotional and intellectual fulfillment and pleasure. The activities that are perceived to result in need fulfillment become objectives for the group. Group cohesion, conformity, and reinforcing beliefs often lead to what has been called "groupthink" [Janis and Mann, 1977], and an information acquisition and analysis structure that enables processing only in accordance with the belief structure of the group. The resulting selective perceptions and neglect of potentially disconfirming information preclude change of beliefs and of adoption of appropriate strategies to achieve the task at hand. There is no evidence whatever that suggests that software development organizations are any less vulnerable to these difficulties than other types of business.

An important aspect of the study of organizations is the role of management and management decisionmaking. In an extraordinarily insightful work, Mintzberg [1973] identifies a three-dimensional taxonomy that characterizes managerial paradigms. These paradigms are described in Table 9.1. The *content roles, characteristic roles,* and *contingencies* that influence variations in managerial efforts are obtained from the results of the decisionmaking and

Table 9.1   A Taxonomy of Management Paradigms

Content roles of the manager
   Interpersonal roles
      Figurehead
      Leader
      Liaison
   Informational roles
      Monitor
      Disseminator
      Spokesperson
   Decisional roles
      Entrepreneur
      Disturbance handler
      Resource allocator
      Negotiator
Contingency task variations of management effort
   Environmental variables
   Task variables
   Person variables
   Situational (experiential) variables
Characteristic roles of the manager
   Much work at unrelenting pace
   Activities denoted by brevity, variety, and fragmentation
   Preference for live action
   Attraction to verbal media
   Contacts with subordinates, superiors, external stakeholder
   Initial decisions define long-term commitments
   Control of activities in which manager must engage

leadership schools of thought concerning managerial behavior. Mintzberg has identified eight schools of thought concerning management, as indicated in Table 9.2. The information roles and the decision roles of the manager are of particular interest here as well as the contingency task structure variables that influence these roles. Especially relevant to efforts that involve technical management is Mintzberg's discussion of several studies of managerial activities as a programmed system.

Many management studies show that, in practice, plans and decisions are the result of interpretation of standard operating procedures. Improvements are obtained by careful identification of existing standard operating procedures and associated organizational structures and determination of improvements in these procedures and structures. The *organizational process model,* originally due to Cyert and March [1963], functions by relying on standard operating procedures that constitute the memory or intelligence bank of the organization. Only if the standard operating procedures fail will the organization attempt to develop new standard operating procedures.

The organizational process model may be viewed as an extension of the concept of bounded rationality to choicemaking in organizations. It is clearly an application of reasoning and rationality, in terms of rather pragmatic discovery and application of rules, to actual cases as they occur. There are four main concepts of the behavioral theory of the firm that are suggested as descriptive models of actual choice-making in organizations:

1. Quasi-Resolution of Conflict

Decisionmakers avoid conflicts arising from noncommensurate and conflicting goals. Major problems are disaggregated and each subproblem is

Table 9.2   Management Schools of Thought

- *Classical* (managerial functions: planning, organizing, staffing, directing, coordinating, reporting, budgeting—POSDCORB)
- *Great managers* (biographical and autobiographical literature)
- *Entrepreneurship* (innovation in structured situations and economic rationality)
- *Decision theory* (unprogrammed behavior in unstructured situations—satisficing,[a] and muddling through)
- Leader effectiveness (interpersonal behavior—personality traits and managerial styles for effective performance)
- *Work activity* (inductive research and empirical studies of the characteristics of managerial work)

[a]"Satisficing," or bounded rationality, is a decisionmaking process necessitated by most complicated decision situations. It amounts to selecting an option that is satisfactory, or good enough.(This term is defined in further detail in Section 9.4.)

attacked locally by a department. An acceptable conflict resolution between the efforts of different departments is reached through sequential attention to departmental goals and through the formulation of coalitions that seek power and status. When resources are scarce and there must then be unsatisfied objectives, decisions concerning allocations will be met largely on political grounds.

2. Uncertainty Avoidance

This is achieved by reacting to external feedback, by emphasizing short-term choices, and by advocating negotiated futures. Generally there will exist uncertainties about the future, uncertainties associated with future impacts of alternatives and, uncertainties associated with future preferences. Generally, deficient information processing heuristics and cognitive biases are used in an unsuccesful attempt to avoid uncertainties. The effects are, of course, suboptimal.

3. Problem Search

This is stimulated by encountering issues, but in a reactive manner and not before issues are surfaced. A form of "satisficing" is used as a decision rule. Search in the neighborhood of the status quo only is attempted, and only incremental solutions are considered.

4. Organization Learning

Organizations adapt on the basis of experience. They often pay considerable attention to one part of their environment at the expense of another.

The organizational process model may be viewed as suggesting that decisions at time t may be forecast with almost complete certainty, from knowledge of decisions at time $t - T$, where T is the planning or forecasting period. Standard operating procedures or "programs" and education, motivation, and experience or "programming" of management are the critical determinants of behavior for the organizational process model. A strategy of management leadership is needed, primarily to cope with organizational process realities. Managers are encouraged to be intimately involved in organizations such that they will be able to strongly influence decisions, to become widely informed such that they will be highly valued in the information-poor organization, to be extraordinarily persistent since unmitigated chutzpah will often have entirely undeserved rewards, to encourage those with opposing views to participate, and to overload organizational systems such as to make themselves more necessary. In this view, the descriptive characteristics of the organization are seen as performance inhibiting factors. They are factors not to be overcome, but to be understood and used to the advantage of the manager.

Organizational learning results when members of the organization react to changes in the internal or external environment of the organization by detection and correction of errors [Argyris and Schon, 1974, 1978; Argyris, 1982]. An error is a feature of knowledge that makes action ineffective, and detection and correction of error produces learning. Individuals in an organization are agents of organizational action and organizational learning. Argyris cites two information related factors that inhibit organizational learning: the degree to which information is distorted such that its value in influencing quality decisions is lessened and lack of receptivity to corrective feedback.

Two types of organizational learning are defined. *Single-loop learning is learning that does not question the fundamental objectives or actions of an organization.* Members of the organization discover sources of error and identify new strategic activities that might correct the error. The activities are analyzed and evaluated and one or more selected for implementation. Environmental control and self-protection through control over others, primarily by imposition of power, are typical strategies. The consequences of this approach include defensive group dynamics and low production of valid information. The lack of information does not result in disturbances to prevailing values. The resulting inefficiencies in decisionmaking encourage frustration and an increase in secrecy and loyalty demands from decisionmakers. All of this is mutually self-reinforcing. It results in a stable autocratic state and a self-fulfilling prophecy with respect to the need for organizational control.

Double-loop learning involves identification of potential changes in organizational goals and of the particular approach to inquiry that allows confrontation with and resolution of conflict rather than the translation of incompatible objectives into intergroup conflict. Not all conflict resolution is the result of double-loop learning, however. Good examples of this are conflicts settled through imposition of power rather than inquiry. Thus, double-loop learning is seen to be the result of that organizational inquiry that resolves initially perceived incompatible organizational objectives through the restructuring and setting of new priorities and objectives. New understandings are developed that result in updated cognitive maps and scripts of organizational behavior.

Organizations are claimed to learn primarily on the basis of single-loop learning and, typically, do not engage in a double-loop learning. Individuals act as agents of organizational learning through the processing of initially inaccessible and obscure information and by resolving potential inadequacies associated with individual and organizational theories of action. In this *organizational learning* model of Argyris, all human action is viewed as if it were based on *theories of action*. There are two types:

- *Espoused theories of action,* which are the "official" theories that people claim as a basis for action
- *Theories in use,* which are the descriptive theories of action that may be inferred from actual behavior

While people are often adept at identifying those discrepancies between espoused theories of action and theories in use that are associated with the behavior of others, they are not equally capable at self-diagnosis. However, people are generally programmed with theories in use that suggest that this observed inconsistent behavior in others should not be reported to them by those who detect it. So we see again the presence of social exchanges and customs that inhibit double-loop learning.

There are several dilemmas associated with this *theory of action building* [Argyris and Schon, 1974]. Among these non-mutually exclusive dilemmas, which aggregate together to result in conflicting and intolerable pressures, are:

1. *Incongruity* between espoused theory and theory in use, which are recognized but not corrected
2. *Inconsistency* between theories in use
3. *Ineffectiveness* as objectives associated with theories in use become less and less achievable over time
4. *Disutility* as theories in use become less valued over time
5. *Unobservability* as theories in use result in suppression of information by others such that evaluation of effectiveness becomes impossible.

Detection and correction of inappropriate espoused theories of action and theories in use are suggested as potentially leading to a reduction in those factors that inhibit double-loop learning. Of course, single-loop learning often will be appropriate and is encouraged. The result of double-loop learning, however, is a *new* set of goals and standard operating policies that become part of the organization's knowledge base. It is when the environment, or more generally the contingency task structure, changes that *double-loop learning* is called for. Inability to accommodate double-loop learning is a flaw. Ability to successfully integrate and utilize the appropriate blend of single- and double-loop learning is called *deutero*, or *dialectic, learning*. Figure 9.1*a* presents a systems engineering conceptualization of this model, whereas Figure 9.1*b* illustrates a blending of the two types of learning.

Several intervention models, or approaches, are suggested to encourage organizations to adopt a capability for double-loop learning. These include:

1. Comprehensive intervention
2. Limited intervention through structural mapping of the issue
3. Internalization of a cognitive *map* or image of this issue
4. Attempts at validation of the map
5. Simulation and analysis of impacts using the map
6. Generation of knowledge using the map for use in future designs
7. Several partial models of intervention

Of particular interest in this seminal work are the several caveats given con-

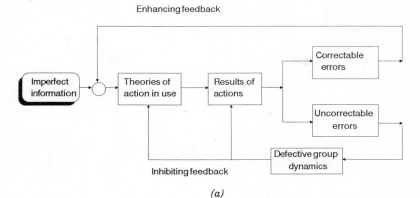

FIGURE 9.1a   Interpretation of single loop learning

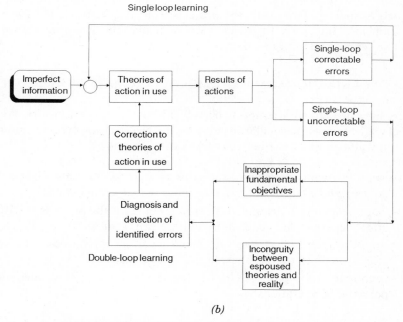

FIGURE 9.1b   Interpretation of double loop learning

cerning difficulties in the design of management information and decision support systems such that they support model II (i.e., double-loop learning) rather than model I (single-loop) learning.

We have just presented a description and interpretation of some recent results in behavioral and organizational theory that have direct relevance to information processing in systems and organizations. The primary organizing principles in organizations include:

- Division of labor and task assignment
- Identifying standard operating principles
- Top-down flow of decisions
- Formal and informal channels of communication in all directions
- The multiple uses of information
- Organizational learning

We must be conscious of these descriptive principles in order that we be able to produce systems management and technical direction perspectives that are realistically grounded in the realities of human desires and capabilities for growth and self-actualization.

Much of our discussion to this point may seem oriented more toward *management philosophy* than toward *management practice*. Doubtlessly, this is correct. We strongly maintain that successful management practice will embody these perspectives and philosophies. This management philosophy is needed to manage large software projects well. It is also needed for incorporation into the software we develop such that the resulting software is suitable for human interaction.

9.3   ORGANIZATIONAL MANAGEMENT—PRAGMATIC PERSPECTIVES

There have been many attempts to classify different types of decisions. Among the classifications of particular interest here is the decision-type taxonomy of Anthony [1965]. He describes four types of decisions:

Strategic planning decisions—decisions related to choosing highest level policies and objectives, and associated resource allocations

Management control decisions—decisions made for the purpose of assuring effectiveness in the acquisition and use of resources

Operational control decisions—decisions made for the purpose of assuring effectiveness in the performance of operations

Operational performance decisions—the day-to-day decisions made while performing operations

Simon [1976] has described decisions as structured or unstructured depending on whether the decisionmaking process can be explicitly described prior to the time when it is necessary to make a decision. This taxonomy would seem to lead directly to that in which expert skills [wholistic reasoning], rules [heuristics], or formal analytical reasoning [holistic evaluation] are normatively used for judgment.* Generally, operational performance decisions are more likely than strategic planning decisions to be prestructured.

---

*There is considerable difference in the way in which these terms are used in the literature. Some writers use wholistic as a variant of, and synonym for holistic. Some writers use holistic

Other discussions of organizational management will concentrate on activities of a management team, as contrasted with the decisions that they make. It is not unusual to find seven identified management functions or tasks:

1. *Planning,* which relates to the identification of alternative courses of action that will achieve organizational goals
2. *Organizing,* which relates to the structuring of tasks that will lead to the achievement of organizational plans, and the granting of authority and responsibility to obtain these
3. *Staffing,* which relates to the selection and training of people to fit various roles in the organization
4. *Directing,* which refers to the creation of an environment and an atmosphere that will motivate and assist people to accomplish assigned tasks
5. *Coordinating,* which relates to the integration and synchronization of performance, including the needed measurements and corrective actions, such as to lead to goal achievement
6. *Reporting,* such as to ensure proper information flow in the organization
7. *Budgeting,* such as to ensure appropriate distribution of economic resources needed for goal achievement

This POSDCORB theory of management is a very common one and is described in almost all classical management texts.

Planning is a prominent word in the foregoing. We have already noted the fact that there are three basic types of plans: organizational, program, and project plans. There will also exist the need for *contingency or crisis management plans,* which will be implemented if the initially intended plans prove unworkable. A severe form of contingency is that of a crisis situation, and it is to this that we now turn briefly. First, we remark that planning is, of course, only one of several phases in the system lifecycle, as we have noted in Chapters 1 and 2. There are several ways in which we can describe the typical lifecycle. At a minimal level, there are three phases in every lifecycle. These correspond to the issue *definition* or "formulation," solution *development* or "analysis," and the resulting *implementation and maintenance,* or "interpretation," as the user needs evolve over time. Figure 9.2 illustrates this three-phase view of the software systems engineering lifecycle.

9.4   ORGANIZATIONAL MANAGEMENT—CRISIS PERSPECTIVES

A management crisis exists whenever there is an extensive and consequential difference between the results that an organization is able to obtain from

---

to indicate skill based cognition and others use it to indicate analytical cognition. Our usage is internally consistent even though it cannot possibly agree with all uses of the term.

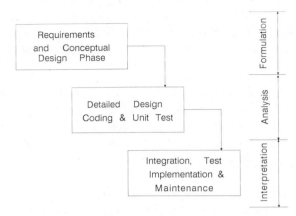

FIGURE 9.2 A three phase interpretation of the system lifecycle

implementation of a strategic plan and what it actually does obtain. This difference may have a variety of causes. A common element in all of these is that the corporation has, somehow, misjudged either the environment in which it is operating, or the impacts of its chosen alternative courses of action on the environment. A crisis may occur because of failure to identify a potentially challenging opportunity, or one may occur as a result of an existing situation that is threatening to the healthy survival of the corporation. The preferred solution to this difficulty is that of crisis avoidance. An acceptable, but somewhat less preferred, solution is that of extrication from an existing crisis situation. The key to each of these "solutions" to a crisis is effective management of the corporate environment.

Three fundamental activities are involved in crisis management. These are precisely the steps of the problem-solving or systems engineering process [Sage, 1977, 1982] that we have emphasized in our studies of software systems engineering:

1. *Formulation* of issues
2. *Analysis* of alternatives
3. *Interpretation* of the impacts of the alternatives

These steps are encountered at several levels of organizational management activities. They begin at the strategic level and result in the identification of strategic plans, which are then converted into tactical and operational plans and courses of action through an effective planning process.

At this highly aggregated level, it may be difficult to envision specific management activities. While there are many substeps into which the aforementioned three steps may be partitioned, the three upper- and nine lower-level distinguishable activities of Table 9.3 appear especially important. Managers perform each of the activities that we have indicated in Table 9.3. They

Table 9.3   Steps in Systems Management

1. Issue formulation
    1.1. Environmental monitoring
    1.2. Environmental understanding
    1.3. Identification of information needs
    1.4. Identification of alternative courses of action
2. Issue analysis
    2.1. Identification of the impacts of alternatives
    2.2. Fine tuning the alternatives for effectiveness
3. Issue interpretation
    3.1. Evaluation of each alternative
    3.2. Selection of a "best" alternative
    3.3. Implementing the selected alternative

are appropriate at each phase in a systems management effort as well as being appropriate in the special case of development of crisis management plans. Some of them may be performed at an intuitive level which is made possible because of much experiential familiarity with particular task requirements. Some should be performed in a formal analytical manner because they are initially unstructured and unfamiliar.

We could now proceed to describe each of these nine activities in considerable detail. Each of the descriptions would provide ample testimony to the critical importance of information in all of them. Information is needed about the external environment such as to enable understanding of the environment. This leads to identification of a set of information needs relative to already identified corporate objectives. In parallel with much of this, some preliminary identification of potential alternative courses of action are identified, and these further act to frame the information needs for proper analysis and evaluation of these alternatives. All of these are accomplished as part of issue formulation. The issue analysis and issue interpretation steps are equally rich in terms of their need for information.

9.5   IMPLICATIONS FOR ORGANIZATIONAL DESIGN *AND* SOFTWARE DESIGN

As we have noted, there have been many definitions of an organization. Most of them infer a *group of individuals, established on a relatively continuous and stable basis, in an environment with changing characteristics.* The organization contains *relatively fixed boundaries, a normative order for management and authority, a communication system, and a set of incentives that encourage engagement in activities that are in general pursuit of a common and accepted set of goals* [Hall, 1977]. From this definition of an organization, it follows that four top-level attributes or success factors are critical to the functionality of an organization. These are, as we have already noted: efficiency, effectiveness, adaptability to external environmental changes, and job satisfaction.

Management is vitally concerned with the processing (broadly defined to include acquisition, representation, transmission, and use) of information in the organization. Generally, information is recognized as a vital strategic resource. A simple three-step reasoning process leads to this conclusion:

1. Organizational success depends on management quality.
2. Management quality depends on decision quality.
3. Decision quality depends on information quality.

One of the major tasks of management is that of minimizing the equivocality or ambiguity of the information that results from the organization's interaction with the external environment. This is accomplished in order:

1. To better enable the organization to understand its environment
2. To detect or identify problems in need of resolution
3. To diagnose the causes of these problems
4. To identify alternative courses of action or policies to correct or resolve problems
5. To analyze and evaluate the potential efficacy of these policies
6. To interpret these in accordance with the organizational culture and value system
7. To select an appropriate priority order for problem resolution
8. To select appropriate policies for implementation
9. To augment existing knowledge with the new knowledge obtained in this implementation such that organizational learning occurs

The majority of human and organizational decisionmaking studies suggest that a bounded rationality or satisficing perspective, often heavily influenced by bureaucratic political considerations, will generally be the decision perspective adopted in actual decisionmaking practice in organizations. To cope with this effectively requires the ability to concurrently deal with technological, organizational, and cognitive structural concerns as they each, separately and collectively, motivate problem-solving issues.

Satisficing, or bounded rationality, results from a complex decision situation, for either an individual or a group, in which it is either (1) not possible or not needed to identify *all* alternative courses of action in advance of the time when an alternative must be selected or (2) not possible to predict, with the needed degree of precision, all consequences of implementing a specified alternative. In situations such as these, humans will typically attempt to "satisfice," that is to say, pick a readily identifiable course of action that has been known to yield satisfactory performance in the past and perhaps make minor refinements in this alternative to render it more suitable for the given situation. Humans learn over time to better adapt these previous solutions to new problems such that they are able to raise their aspiration levels. This bounded rationality model of choice is roughly equivalent to the *unconflicted adherence* to an original course of action or *unconflicted change* to a new course of action in the *stress-based model,* or *contingency structure model* of judgment and choice due to Janis and Mann [1977], which we have summarized in Figure 9.3. The realization that humans adopt various problem-solving styles as a function of experience, as contrasted with adopting stereotypical response patterns that are invariant across experiential familiarity with task and environment, is now fairly widely recognized. In Figure 9.4, we illustrate a model due to Dreyfus and Dreyfus [1986] that shows how expertise levels influence various problem solving characteristics.

In these two models of judgment and choice, we see that the types of judgment needed vary from the use of simple heuristics for easily structured issues, based on the intuitive and affective skills that come with experience, to formal reasoning in situations in which the problem to be solved is initially unstructured and where there is likely to be very imperfect information available.

These models illustrate many, but by no means all, of the same features. Neither of them illustrate the results that follow from making a decision, observing the results, and the learning (good or bad) that follows from this. In other words, they are primarily static models of decision and problem-solving situations. In reality, dynamic models are needed. Figure 9.5 presents a very simple conceptual model of a dynamic decisionmaking and problem-solving situation. Successful management systems will often be those that support this decision-style evolution over time.

These observations have major implications for the design and implementation of software systems in general, and especially for purposes that support various judgment and choice activities. The introduction of a support system into a managerial environment in which one did not formally exist will bring about dynamic changes in the decisionmaking process. Some of these may be desirable; others will be undesirable. For example, one type of support now made possible is the introduction of expert system capabilities that potentially capture experiential wisdom for decisions that involve unconflicted adherence to an original course of action or unconflicted change. These may be encoded in the form of rules, or other representations, to enable novices to use the system in the hopes of performing as if they were experts. Doubtlessly, the performance of the people using an expert system will differ from the performance of unaided experts. Further, the introduction of such a system presumably means that the time and effort mix of the top-level managers has been altered. These changes need to be given due consideration in software system design, or it is very likely that the resulting system will not meet the real need of the users.

There are a number of abilities that a typical software system should augment. It should support the decisionmaker in the formulation or framing of the decision situation in the sense of recognizing needs, identifying appro-

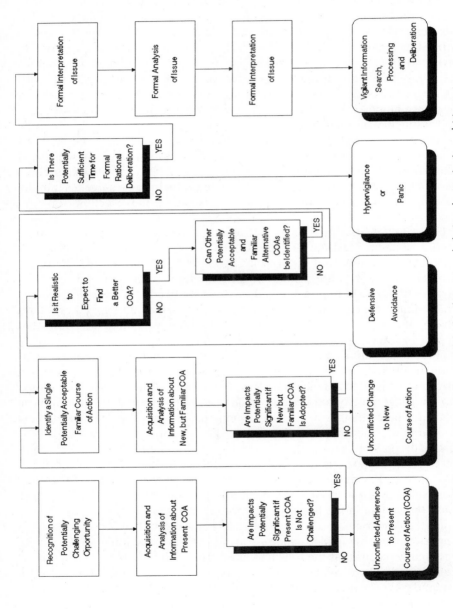

FIGURE 9.3 Contingency model of judgment and choice due to Janis and Mann

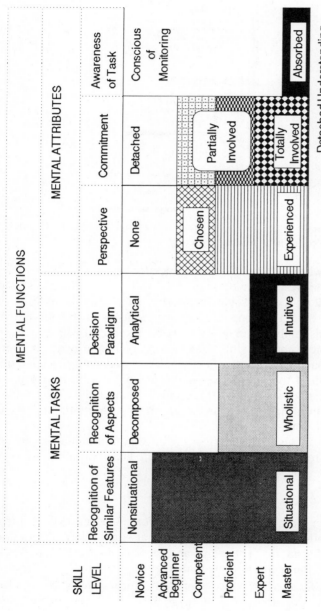

FIGURE 9.4 Interpretation of the Dreyfus decision style model

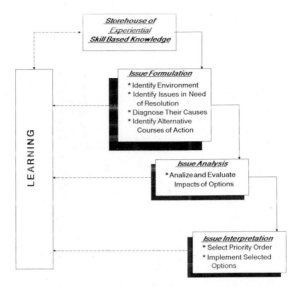

FIGURE 9.5 Illustration of the three formal steps in problem solving and decision making with learning to result in a dynamic process

priate objectives by which to measure the successful resolution of an issue, and generating alternative courses of action that will resolve the needs and satisfy objectives. It should also provide support in enhancing the abilities of the decisionmaker to obtain the possible impacts on needs of the alternative courses of action. This analysis capability must be associated with provision of capability to enhance the ability of the decisionmaker to provide an interpretation of these impacts in terms of objectives. This interpretation capability will lead to evaluation of the alternatives and selection of a preferred alternative option. Associated with all of these must be the ability to acquire, represent and utilize information or knowledge, and the ability to implement the chosen alternative course of action.

There are many variables that will affect the information that is, or should be, obtained relative to any given decision situation. These variables are very clearly task-dependent. Keen and Scott Morton [1978] identify eight such variables:

Inherent Accuracy of Available Information Operational control situations will often deal with information that is relatively certain and precise. The information in strategic and tactical planning situations is often uncertain, imprecise and incomplete.

Needed Level of Detail Often very detailed information is needed for operational-type decisions. Highly aggregated information is often desired for strategic decisions. There are many difficulties associated with information summarization that need attention.

Time Horizon for Information Needed   Operational decisions are typically based on information over a short time horizon, and the nature of the control may be changed very frequently. Strategic decisions are based on information and predictions based on a long time horizon.

Frequency of Use   Strategic decisions are made infrequently, although they are perhaps refined fairly often. Operational decisions are made quite frequently and are relatively easily changed.

Internal or External Information Source   Operational decisions are often based on information that is available internal to the organization, whereas strategic decisions are much more likely to be dependent on information content that can only be obtained external to the organization.

Information Scope   Generally operational decisions are made on the basis of narrow-scope information related to well-defined events internal to the organization. Strategic decisions are based on broad-scope information and a wide range of factors that often cannot be fully anticipated prior to the need for the decision.

Information Quantifiability   In strategic planning, information is very likely to be highly qualitative, at least initially. For operational decisions, the available information is often highly quantified.

Information Currency   In strategic planning, information is often rather old, and it is often difficult to obtain current information. For operational control decisions, very current information is often needed.

All of this suggests some ingredients for an *information value theory* as a real need in systems management and in the systems management of software.

This is particularly the case since the central result of a majority of studies of the process of human problem-solving is that there is no single unique judgment and decision style that is adopted independently of the contingency task structural variables of issue, environment, and problem-solver familiarity with task and environment. Rather, the style of decision behavior adopted is a function of these three ingredients.

Critical to success in the design of software systems to aid humans in tasks is an understanding of the way in which humans formulate issues, identify possible alternative courses of action, analyze the impacts of these alternatives, and integrate these impacts in accordance with a value system. It is now generally recognized that experiential familiarity with the perceived task at hand is the dominant influence on the way in which task requirements are cognized, and the way in which problem-solving activities proceed. This creates many challenges for the successful design of "*user-friendly*" software.

Judgments, at least prudent judgments in important situations, are seldom made without information. Information is often defined as data of value for decisionmaking. Activities associated with acquisition, representation, storage, transmission, and use of pertinent data are generally associated with information processing. The task of information requirements determination is associated with each of these. Initially, it might appear that this would be associated only with an information acquisition effort. But since information acquisition is necessarily related to other activities associated with information processing, so also is information requirements determination.

There are many ways in which we can characterize information. Attributes that we might use include: accuracy, precision, completeness, sufficiency, understandability, relevancy, reliability, redundancy, verifiability, consistency, freedom from bias, frequency of use, age, timeliness, and uncertainty. It is also possible to define information at several levels. At the *technical level,* information and associated measures are concerned with transmission quality over a channel. At the *semantic level,* concern is with the meaning and efficiency of messages. At the *pragmatic level,* information is valued in terms of effectiveness in accomplishing an intended purpose. From the viewpoint of design, we are clearly concerned more with pragmatic and semantic issues than we are with technical level issues. At the pragmatic and semantic levels, our concerns with information for design purposes are fivefold:

1. Information should be presented in very clear and very familiar ways, such as to enable rapid comprehension.
2. Information should be such as to improve the precision of understanding of the task situation.
3. Information that contains an advice or decision recommendation component should contain an explication facility that enables the user to determine how and why results and advice are obtained.
4. Information needs should be based on identification of the information requirements for the particular situation.
5. Information presentations and all other associated management control aspects of the software process should be such that the user, rather than a computerized support system, guides the process of judgment and choice.

Clearly, this relates directly to the concept of *value of information* and indicates that this concept is very dependent on the contingency task structure. The mix of task at hand, the environment into which the task is embedded, and the problem-solver's familiarity with these interact to determine both the perceptions and the intentions of the problem-solver.

There are at least three human limitations associated with information processing that may significantly affect the requirements for information that are likely to be identified: limited information processing capability, potential bias effects in the selection and use of information, and limited knowledge of appropriate problem-solving behavior that results in incorrect assessment of the contingency task structure associated with a given issue.

Davis [1982] suggests four strategies for determination of information requirements, as we have noted in both Chapters 3 and 8. The first of these is simply to ask people for their requirements. The appropriateness and completeness of the information needs determined by this approach will depend on the extent to which the people questioned can define and structure their problem space and can compensate for their biases. This approach can be further subdivided into the use of interacting and nominal group approaches to inquiry. The second strategy is to elicit information requirements from existing systems that are similar in nature and purpose to the issue or design task under consideration. Properly executed anchoring and adjustment strategies, or analogous reasoning strategies, are potentially useful here since a starting point can be determined from the existing system and extrapolation of this can be made. Examining existing plans or reports represents one approach of identifying information requirements from an existing or conceptualized system or previous design. The third approach consists of synthesizing information requirements from characteristics of the utilizing system or individuals. This permits definition of an analytical structure for the problem space and will often allow use of formal analytical procedures, such as input/output analysis or decision analysis. The fourth strategy consists of determining information requirements through experimentation on an actual system, perhaps a *prototype* specifically constructed for this purpose. Figure 9.6 illustrates how these strategies are called for as a function of system elements, users, and analysts; and the availability of present system information, the ability of users to specify needs, and the ability of analysts to identify needs.

Generally the first-mentioned approaches are simpler and more economic than the latter approaches. There are three primary elements affecting cer-

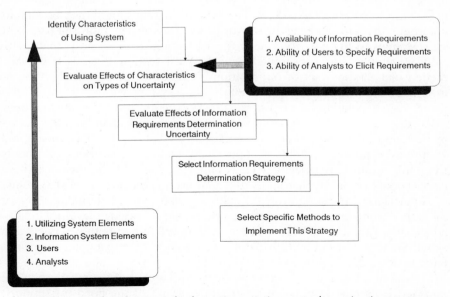

FIGURE 9.6   Identification of information requirements determination strategy

tainty of determined information requirements. The first of these is the *utilizing system and the application system.* The major determinant of certainty here is the existence and stability of a set of usable system information requirements. The second element is the intended system *users.* The ability of the users to specify information and system requirements is a major determinant of certainty of the resulting requirements. The final element affecting information imperfection, or uncertainty, in the requirements is the systems *analysts* who attempt to obtain requirements and their ability to elicit, identify, and evaluate these requirements. Where the information obtained is of high precision, simply asking users is an appropriate strategy. When the degree of information imperfection is high, discovery through experimentation or prototyping is the preferred approach. Of course, prototyping a system and having the user interact with the prototype is *initially* a more expensive approach than simply asking the users for their requirements. In the long run, it may well not be more expensive than developing a very sound implementation of a system designed to solve the wrong problem. These errors of the *fourth kind* are very common in systems engineering practice. In many instances, a hybrid approach is desirable. These approaches can certainly be combined, and it would be desirable to be able to determine which approach is best in a given situation. Sage et al. [1983] have discussed some of these needs.

Information obtained from any, or a combination, of the several possible approaches must be capable of representation in a support system to properly aid the system user. A purpose of a support system should be to determine possibilities of insufficient and/or inappropriate information, that is, information that is sufficiently imperfect such as to make the likelihood of success in the task to be undertaken low. The support system should then be able to determine the nature of the missing or otherwise imperfect information, and suggest steps to the user to remedy this deficiency. This suggests that many software support systems should be capable of detection, diagnosis, and correction of faults in a set of information obtained for an issue. The type of information that the user of a particular support system will wish to, or should, use is very dependent on contingency task structure. Another information-associated requirement for a support system is that of identifying the information, and judgment and choice, perspectives that the user will and should wish to use, and to be capable of coping with requirements for design support from this multiple perspectives viewpoint. Satisfactorily coping with these needs should result in truly innovative and useful software support systems.

A particularly important role for many software systems should be to assist the user in minimizing errors between perceived knowledge level relative to a particular task and their actual knowledge level. When both perceived and actual knowledge level are at the level of "master," for example, then skill-based knowledge is generally appropriate for judgment and choice tasks. When the perceived and actual knowledge level is that of "novice," then the knowledge support system user is generally aware of the need for support.

When the perceived knowledge level is that of "master" and the actual knowledge is that of "novice," perhaps due to an unrecognized change in environment, then it is very likely that acts of judgment and choice will be associated with self-deception. In this regard, it would be very important to alert the decisionmaker to the potential difficulties of skill-based behavior in an appropriate manner. A very important role, also, is that of alerting users of the system to the information requirements appropriate to the task at hand and the environment surrounding the task and task requirements.

9.6 SOFTWARE SYSTEMS MANAGEMENT PLANNING

Let us examine some specific implications of management planning to the production of trustworthy software. Regardless of the hierarchical level at which planning is considered: *A plan is a statement of what ought to be, together with a set of actions that are designed to cause this to occur.* Of course, the interpretation of "ought" may vary considerably as a function of the level at which planning is accomplished. Also, there may be a number of uncertainties that may act to prevent a normally useful set of activities from achieving the objectives that they should achieve. Independent of these levels, planning involves in part:

1. *Identification of goals* to be realized, some of which may already be fulfilled to some extent, at the particular level of planning under consideration

2. *Identification of current position relative to the goals* such that it becomes possible to specify a set of needs that, when fulfilled, will lead to goal realization

3. *Identification of past, present and future environment* such that it becomes possible to embed the issue resolution effort in a contextual reality that leads to a knowledge of the *constraints* and *alterables* that affect realistic alternative courses of action

4. *Identification of suitable alternative courses of action* that are, at this point, only options that could lead to need fulfillment and goal attainment

As a result of this, we will have identified a number of planning elements. These are associated with the internal organization and the external environment. We also need to identify *measures* or *metrics* such that we can determine success in need satisfaction, goal attainment, and activity accomplishment. These should be linked together such that we have a number of cross- and self-interaction matrices that show the relationship among the elements of planning illustrated in Table 9.4.

Implied in the identification of planning options presented in Table 9.4 is:

Table 9.4   Planning Element Linkages

Issue definition elements
   Needs
   Constraints
   Alterables
   Organizational Culture
   Environmental Realities and Futures
Value system elements
   Objectives
   Objectives Measures
Alternative action elements
   Alternative Courses of Action
   Alternative Measures

1. An *external environment analysis* to identify the present context in which the issue being considered is embedded and to forecast possible future situations
2. An *internal environment analysis* (of the organization and at the level where planning is being accomplished) to determine available resources and to identify the organizational culture

We can disaggregate this still further. We can speak, for example, of a *general environment* as those planning elements that affect all organizations within a specific domain: cultural, demographic, technological, and so on. Also, we can speak of a *task environment* as those elements specifically effected by, and effecting, the particular organization and alternative course of action in question.

At this point in a planning effort, we have outscoped the issue considerably and identified a number of possible courses of action. Up to this point, we have accomplished *formulation* of the issue. The major planning ingredients needed for a complete and useful plan are: (1) *realistic objectives*, and (2) *identification of a suitable alternative course of action in terms of observable activities measures*. To achieve these, we need to analyze the options that have been generated to determine their impacts on needs. In dealing with a large and complex issue, a variety of systems *analysis* tools may need to be used to facilitate this. After this analysis effort, we need to obtain an *interpretation* of these in terms of the value system of the clients for whom the potential development will be undertaken. This interpretation will include evaluation of these impacts and selection of an alternative course of action. This does not quite complete the interpretation step of planning, however. We will need to accomplish some planning for action or for implementation of the next phase in the systems engineering lifecycle.

If the planning study at hand involves program planning for example, it will be necessary to next accomplish project planning. In any large and complex effort, it will be necessary to break a program down into several projects plans. A successful project plan must identify and detail: *what is to be done, who will do it, with what resources, and in what time period.* Although not explicitly mentioned in this, what is done must meet the needs of the client and must possess *sufficient* quality and functionality. *Sufficient* is a typically very subjective term that depends on the client's needs, priorities, and available resources to meet these. There are a number of systems engineering approaches that assist in the formulation, analysis, and interpretation stages of planning. Many of them are described in Sage [1977, 1987a, 1989] and the references contained therein.

9.7 SOFTWARE ENGINEERING PROJECT MANAGEMENT

As we have seen, there are several ways in which we could describe and learn about software engineering management activities. These involve the several management schools of thought that we identified in Table 9.2. Regardless of the approach that is taken to management, at some point the *classical management POSDCORB functions* of

Planning

  Organizing

    Staffing

      Directing

        Coordinating

          Reporting

            Budgeting

must be undertaken. We have discussed the first of these functions, planning to some extent in our efforts thus far. For completeness, less us define all of these classical management functions:

Planning

This involves identifying the environment for the organization, identifying objectives or goals, developing policies, determining courses of action, making decisions, setting standard operating procedures and rules, developing programs, forecasting future situations, preparing budgets, and documenting project plans.

Organizing

This involves identifying and structuring required tasks, selecting and establishing organizational structures, creating organizational positions, defining responsibilities and authority, establishing position qualifications, and documenting organizational structures.

Staffing

This involves filling organizational positions, assimilating newly assigned personnel, educating and training personnel, providing for general development, evaluating and appraising personnel, and making and documenting staffing decisions.

Directing

This involves providing leadership, supervising personnel, delegating authority, motivating personnel, developing standards of performance, establishing monitoring and reporting systems, measuring results, initiating corrective actions, and documenting these.

Coordinating

This involves coordinating activities, facilitating communications, resolving conflicts, and managing changes.

Reporting

This involves documenting decisions and preparation of informational reports such that there is appropriate awareness of the organizations activities. In a more general context, it involves developing information resource management capabilities and implementing these in the organization.

Budgeting

This involves the determination of financial and accounting strategies to ensure that the organization has the ability to carry out its mission.

It is quite clear that these functions are not at all independent. As details of these functions are provided in essentially any introductory management guide, we will not pursue these in any further detail here.

There are many identified causes of management failure. Among these, some which often cause projects to be unable to finish their scheduled activities on time and within costs are:

1. Difficulty of defining work in sufficient detail for the level of skills available.
2. Problems with organizing and building the project team.
3. Project staff is reassigned prior to project completion.
4. Clients did not review requirements specifications.
5. No firm agreement on program plan or project plans by management.
6. Insufficiently defined project team organization.
7. There was no adequate set of standards.
8. No quality assurance plans were developed.

9. No clear role or responsibilities defined for project personnel.
10. Project perceived as not important for individuals or organization.
11. No contingency or risk management, or crisis management provisions.
12. Inability to measure true project performance.
13. Poor communications between management and members of the organization.
14. Poor communications with customer or client, or sponsor.
15. Difficulty in working across functional lines within the organization.
16. Improper relations between program and project performance and reward systems.
17. Poor program and project leadership.
18. Lack of attention to early warning signals and feedback.
19. Poor ability to manage conflict.
20. Difficulties in assessing costs, benefits, and risks.
21. Insensitivity to organizational cultures.
22. Insufficient formal program and project guidelines at the level of procedures.
23. Apathy or indifference by program or project teams, or management.
24. Little involvement of project personnel during program planning.
25. Rush into project initiation before adequate definition of key tasks.
26. Poor understanding of inter-organizational interfaces.
27. Poor understanding of intra-organizational interfaces.
28. Weak assistance and support from upper management.
29. Project leader not involved with team.
30. Credibility problems with task leaders.
31. No mutual trust among team leaders.
32. Too much unresolved conflict.
33. Power struggles at various levels in the organization.
34. Too much reliance on established procedures that are inappropriate for the task.

There is often disagreement within various groups concerning which of these factors are most important, and which is likely to be responsible for general failure of projects, including software projects. For example, top-level managers will generally indicate that front end planning, including identification of system-level requirements, is very important; project engineers will usually consider this to be less important. On the other hand, project engineers will likely perceive technical complexities of a project as very important and wish to devote significant effort to understanding these. Program management will often consider this relatively less important than such factors as identification of requirements and establishment of requirements specifications. Both groups will generally identify customer changes in specifications during project completion as being a major factor in time slippage and cost overruns. On the other hand, clients will doubtlessly not perceive their requirements as changing. They will doubtlessly perceive that these were very poorly identified inititially, and potentially very poorly translated to specifications and implemented, as well. We believe that these differences in perceptions strongly support the use of prototyping techniques and the use of situation rooms for issue exploration and judgment so as to enable full understanding of tasks to be undertaken.

In general, three types of project organizations can be considered. The first and most often used is the *functional organization.* In this conventional functional or *line organization,* one particular group is asked to perform the entire set of activities associated with developing a software product. This does not suggest that one person is necessarily asked to perform all phases of a software development effort. Rather, it suggests that a team of people within a fixed structure are asked to do this. Each manager of a "section" in the organization is given a set of requirements to be met. Each manager is able to exercise more or less complete authority over the activities going on within that particular "section."

The functional organization structure is depicted in Figure 9.7. We note that this is a typical hierarchical structure in which management authority for a specific software development program is vested in the management at the

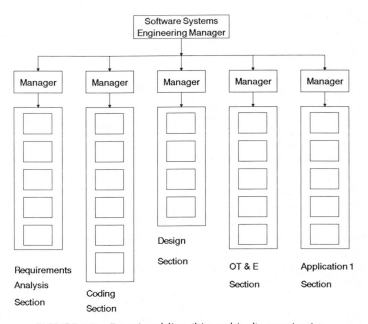

FIGURE 9.7   Functional line (hierarchical) organization

top of the hierarchy. The various line supervisors are given tasks and report to the software systems engineering management office at the top of the hierarchy.

There are some advantages to this type of program management:

1. The organization is already in existence prior to the start of a given project and this enables quick start-up and phase-down of projects.
2. The recruiting, training, and retention of professional people is easier as they generally remain with one, often relatively small, unit throughout much of their career. For this reason, functional projects are very people-oriented.
3. Standards, metrics, operating procedures, and management authority are already established.

Of course, there are a number of readily identified limitations also.

1. No one person has complete responsibility or authority for the program, except at a very high management level. That person will often be in charge of several development programs.
2. Interface problems within the organization are difficult to identify and solve.
3. The program is often very difficult to monitor and control.
4. Functions will tend to perpetuate themselves long after there is any real need for them.

The *program organization* is one possible remedy for this. In a program organization, or project organizations within a given program, one person is vested with overall responsibility to see to it that one specific program is accomplished in a timely and trustworthy manner. In a program management organization, people are, in effect, excised from a perhaps initially existing functional organization and wedded together under the management of the program, or project, manager.

Figure 9.8 illustrates some of the features of this superposition of program authority on a line organization. Figure 9.9 illustrates the resulting program organization, which may and generally will include hardware and other projects within a given program. There are several advantages to a program or project structure:

1. There is one person in a central position of responsibility and authority for the program, the program manager.
2. That person, or a designee, will generally have authority over all system-level interfaces, especially those that cut across the phases of the development effort and projects within those phases.
3. Decisions can generally be made very quickly at the program level

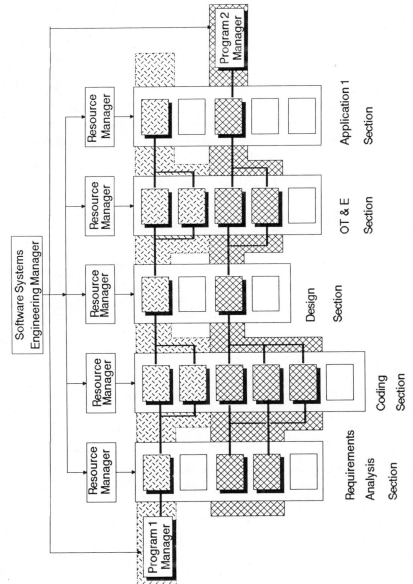

FIGURE 9.8 Project management (obtaining staff from resource managers)

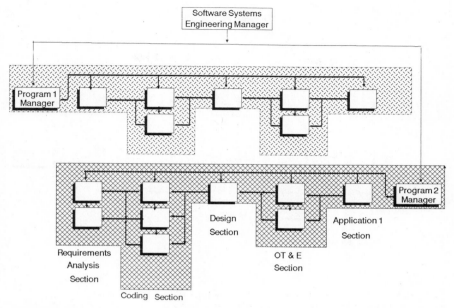

FIGURE 9.9   Project management (after obtaining staff from resource managers)

because of the new centralized organization, shown in Figure 9.9, which puts the program at a central management level in the organization.

The limitations to program and project organizations are allied with their strengths.

1. The project organization must be formed from the existing line organization.
2. Recruiting, training, and retention of people to work in a program office is more difficult than in a functional organization, as projects are product-oriented rather than people-oriented.
3. The benefits of economy of scale cannot be achieved for other than very large programs, as there will often be only one or two people in a given specialty area associated with a program or project.
4. Programs tend to perpetuate themselves, just as a given functional line will tend to perpetuate itself in a strictly functional organization.
5. Often, it will be necessary to develop standards, metrics, techniques, and procedures for each program undertaken. This will make comparison of efforts across programs very difficult.

The *matrix program*, and project, organization has been proposed as a way to, hopefully, combine the strengths and minimize the weaknesses of the

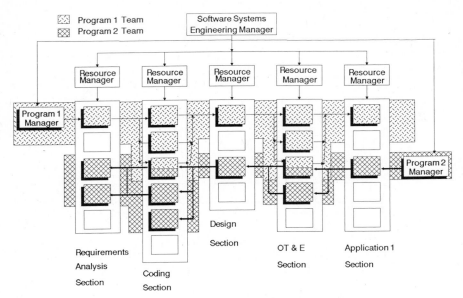

FIGURE 9.10   Matrix management of programs

functional organization and the program organization. Figure 9.10 illustrates how people in a matrix organization are managed both by functional line-type supervisors, often called *resource managers,* and by program or project managers. In this management structure, any given person in the functional line may be working on more than one program or project at a given time.

In this sort of management structure, the program and project managers have responsibility for short-term supervision of the people working for them on various programs. The resource manager would be responsible for longer-term management of these same people, in such areas as professional education and training. As with the other two management types, there are advantages and limitations to this form of management. Some of the advantages are:

1. There is an improved central position of responsibility and authority over the program being undertaken, as contrasted with that in line functional management.
2. The interfaces between the various specialty functions can be controlled more easily than in line functional programs.
3. It is usually easier to start and terminate a program than in program management organizations.
4. Standard operating policies, technical standards, metrics, and procedures are generally already established, unlike program organization, as these are the responsibility of the typically longer term functional line management.

5. Professional staffing, recruiting, education, and training are easier and retention of the best staff members is higher than is typically the case in program management organizations.
6. It is potentially possible to have more efficient and more effective use of people, through its greater flexibility, than functional line or program management.

There are also potential weaknesses:

1. Responsibility and authority for human resources is shared between the line resource manager and one or more program or project managers.
2. It is sometimes too easy to move people from one project to another, especially compared with the project management organization.
3. Because of its complexity, greater organizational understanding and cooperation are required than in the program or functional line organization.
4. There is often greater internal competition for resources than in either the program management or functional line organization.

There are many responsibilities of top-level systems engineering management. These include:

1. Coordination of issue identification with the client and translation of user needs into system specifications
2. Identification of the resources required for trustworthy development of a software system
3. Definition and coordination of software and hardware identification, design, integration, and implementation
4. Interfaces with top level management of both the client and system developer

There will be a number of front-end problems facing the typical systems engineering program management team. Generally the most difficult of these involve human communications and interactions, system requirements that change over time, and where understanding of the requirements will change over time even if the requirements do not so change, sociopolitical problems, and a lack of truly useful automated planning and management tools.

It may appear by now that the critical success factors affecting a software project, and its management and technical direction, need to be identified and resolved at the initial phases of system development. *This is, indeed, correct.* Effective systems management not only demands the generation of plans but also requires communicating them. There are many reasons that support preparation of written plans. This should be done at both the program and project levels. Table 9.5 presents the generic components of a typical project plan.

Table 9.5   Table of Contents of a Typical Project Plan

Specific goals for a project plan, and the written documentation concerning it, include sufficient details to indicate that the project plan is satisfactory. As a minimum, this must include evidence that the following are present:

1. There exists an understanding of the problem.

2. There exists an understanding of the proposed solution.
3. The project is feasible from all perspectives.
4. The project benefits the program.
5. The project risks are tolerable.
6. There exists an understanding of project integration needs.

We have discussed most of these needs and how to determine their possible fulfillment. Our efforts in the next chapter will expand on our earlier discussion concerning these through the use of some specific models for cost estimation for software projects. One of the major needs in program and project management is monitoring and control. It is necessary to monitor progress of the program and projects associated with the program in order to know how well the effort, at any specified instant of time, is proceeding according to the schedule that has been set for it. We will attempt change, if and as needed, to ensure that the actual project schedule and performance is as close as possible, or needed, to that planned.

Figure 9.11 illustrates the necessary feedback and iteration in monitoring and controlling. An appropriate sequence of steps is shown in Table 9.6.

If monitoring and controlling are not performed effectively, it is very likely that project and program progress will suffer, and this will not be noticed until it is too late to effectively deal with this slippage.

Another important need relative to this is the need for organizing and scheduling the technical details to be performed on the identified projects. The first step in this is to identify the key tasks to be accomplished in terms of:

1. The software system itself
2. Documentation for the software system
3. Software tests, reviews, and evaluations
4. Needed project management functions
5. Software installation and training requirements

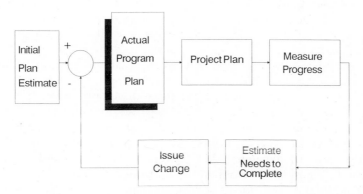

FIGURE 9.11   Monitoring and control as a feedback and iterative process

Table 9.6 Steps in Monitoring and Controlling of Projects

1. Monitor progress of the program and projects
2. Compare actual progress with that contained in the plan
3. Monitor quality of evolving software
4. Revise the plan as needed
5. Define and utilize metrics for evaluation in terms of
    5.1. *Audits*—formal examination, generally by an external team, of project management and development
    5.2. *Reviews*—formal examination, generally by internal project management, of plan and project documents, people, and products
    5.3. *Inspections*—formal examination, generally by an internal peer group, of deliverable parts of the projects
6. Establish procedures for
    6.1. Understanding of required functions
    6.2. Identification of critical milestones
    6.3. Identification of task responsibility
    6.4. Crisis management

The principal task here is to identify schedules for people and resources such that there will be no unpleasant *surprises* as the software effort progresses. Essential in this is the need to *communicate* these key tasks and requirements to all concerned.

Staffing is a very important need for project success. Organizations are no better than the people who belong to them. This is as true of software productivity organizations as it is of any other type. One fundamental and often overlooked notion is productive staffing in what we choose to call *the staffing quality principle.* In its simplest form, this states that six people who can each jump one foot does not equal one person who can jump 6 feet. Few would disagree with this notion as stated. Yet, it is not at all uncommon to find that it is very hard to apply this principle to projects where a few good people are really needed for project success, and where a larger number of those with lesser talents will not contribute to project success.

In Chapter 7, we presented an extensive discussion of software systems engineering environments. There is a major role for software systems engineering management in this, as shown in Figures 9.12 and 9.13. As with almost all constructs in a *top-down* systems approach, all of the dimensions of elements can be expanded. For example, we can expand the methods dimension in Figure 9.13 to obtain the four disaggregate elements shown in Figure 9.14. In our discussion of program planning, for example, we indicated that several projects would likely be identified and plans for each of them

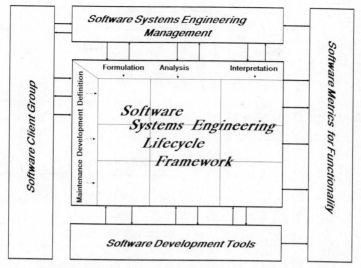

FIGURE 9.12   Interrelationships with the SSE lifecycle

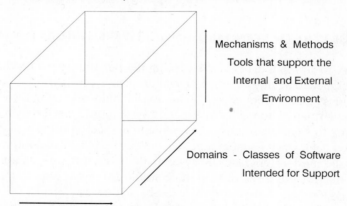

FIGURE 9.13   Multiple dimensions of software engineering environments

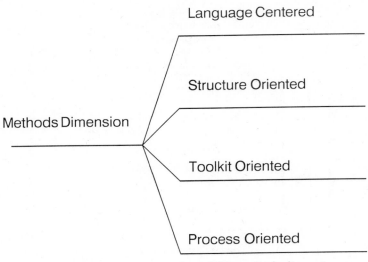

FIGURE 9.14   Disaggregation of the methods dimension

obtained. At a very high level of aggregation, we might have one software project and one hardware project. Figure 9.15 illustrates a realization of this and is also an adaptation of the U.S. Department of Defense Software Standard 2167.

9.8   THE ROLE OF STANDARDS IN SOFTWARE SYSTEMS ENGINEERING

It is easy to set up a dialectic concerning the benefits of *standards*. It can be easily argued that any attempt at standardization will bring about unwise restrictions on management and technological innovation. On the other hand, it will be virtually impossible to integrate system products if they are not built according to some reasonably common and agreed-on official specifications. Not even cables will connect together unless the plugs are compatible. Very few of the modern engineering systems that we enjoy in our home, or use for productive purposes in the office would be anywhere near as useful if their development were not influenced by standards.

We are strongly on the side of standards development and believe that it is possible to develop appropriate standards whose use enhances the efficiency, effectiveness, and other usability attributes of systems. The simple reason for this is that a common base of understanding is an absolute need for such essential engineering accomplishments as management controls over development and technological trustworthiness.

Standards may be of at least two types: *personal or organizational internal standards* that are unique only for a given individual or organization and *external standards*, which are promulgated by industry or national or inter-

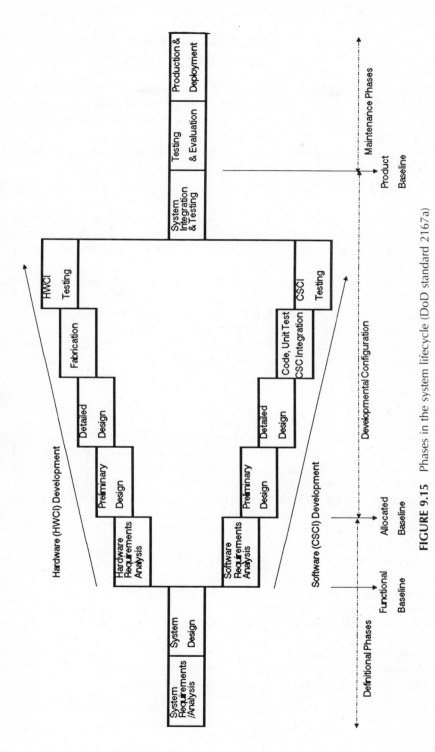

FIGURE 9.15 Phases in the system lifecycle (DoD standard 2167a)

national organizations and are intended to be adhered to by many, ideally all, organizations. Any standard should satisfy certain essential properties:

1. There should be reasons supporting every standard, or component of it, and these should be explicated such that the standard *and* the rationale behind it can be understood and appreciated by those who are obligated to follow it.
2. Illustrations should be provided of the benefits associated with following a standard and the disbenefits associated with not following it.
3. Standards should be kept up to date and abreast of contemporary society.
4. Standards should be introduced to increase the common good and to encourage competition for this common good, and never to bar potential competition from entering a market with an otherwise good product or service.
5. Standards that are unenforceable should not be established.

In the United States, standards for software are established by the Institute of Electrical and Electronics Engineers, the National Institute Standards and Technology, and the Department of Defense. Our Figure 9.15 is an adaptation of a portion of the very comprehensive and evolving DoD Standard 2167.

9.9   SUMMARY

We have examined some philosophical and pragmatic concepts relative to the systems engineering management of software development programs and projects. An essential ingredient in the systems management and technical direction of software projects is that of understanding and managing software program costs and benefits, through all phases of system development. We will now turn our attention to this topic.

9.10   PROBLEMS

9.1. In one recent survey, general management and programming management were asked to evaluate causative factors leading to software development failures. The results of such a survey might be:

Rank by General Managers	Rank by Programming Managers	Reason or Problem
1	10	Insufficient front-end planning
2	3	Unrealistic project plan

Rank by General Managers	Rank by Programming Managers	Reason or Problem
3	8	Project scope underestimated
4	1	Customer/management changes
5	14	Insufficient contingency planning
6	13	Inability to track progress
7	5	Inability to detect problems early
8	9	Insufficient number of checkpoints
9	4	Staffing problems
10	2	Technical complexities
11	6	Priority shifts
12	10	No commitment by personnel to plan
13	12	Uncooperative support groups
14	7	Sinking team spirit
15	15	Unqualified project personnel

How could you work to ameliorate the effects of these differences? Is it possible that both groups over- or underestimate the same factors, even though they might be in agreement on them, for political or social purposes?

9.2. How would you expect a software user group, that contracts externally for software development, to evaluate these factors? How would you work as a software systems engineer with all three types of reactions to development problems?

9.3. Discuss the integrated role of program management and technology management in software development.

9.4. How would you expect to solicit requirements specifications from people in each of the Dreyfus expertise categories?

9.5. How would you expect to solicit requirements specifications from people in each of the Janis–Mann expertise categories?

9.6. What sort of an applications software system would you expect to design for people in each of the Dreyfus expertise categories?

9.7. What sort of an applications software system would you expect to design for people in each of the Janis–Mann expertise categories?

Chapter **10**

Software Cost and Value Models

In the preceeding chapter, we discussed philosophic and pragmatic issues of importance in management of the software systems engineering process. Here, we will turn to issues associated with identifying the value and cost of software production efforts.

We immediately see that we need to provide greater specificity if we are to cope with terms such as "value" and "cost." In particular, we need to talk about *cost to whom* and *value to whom*. For our purposes, we will use the term "value" to infer *value to the user* or client who potentially desires the software product. We will use the term "cost" to infer *cost to the software producing unit*. Most of our effort will be associated with cost. In the concluding sections of the chapter, we will discuss some aspects of software benefit, effectiveness, or value. We will first describe a general approach to modeling, including software production cost modeling. We will then examine the types of cost included in several well-known cost models and some features concerning the derivations of these models. Our goal in this is understanding the supporting constructs and their influences on model usefulness and validity.

10.1 INTRODUCTION TO SOFTWARE COST AND VALUE

Many elements influence the cost of producing software. Among the major cost ingredients are the following:

Software Type or Purpose The ultimate purpose to which software will be put will surely be a major influence on how much it will cost to produce the software. Factors influencing this include such features as:

real time, scientific, process control, accounting, decision support, distributed or decentralized software.

Machine Configuration The specific type of processor, the type and amount of memory available, the operating system, and other factors associated with the machine(s) on which the software is to run will influence cost.

Requirements Specification and Analysis Effort The effort required to identify system-level specifications and to translate these into software specifications will influence the cost to produce the software. Included in this category also will be the extent to which the requirements are likely to be misidentified initially and modified after initial software development has begun. The experiential capabilities of the users will influence the most appropriate software requirements, and ultimately the costs of producing the software. However, this cost will be reflected in costs associated with software type or purpose. Thus, we see that these ingredients are not independent.

Integration and Maintenance Efforts The extent to which it will be easy or difficult to implement and integrate the software into the operational environment of the client will influence costs, as will potential needs to maintain the software and transition it to a new environment, or produce software that is capable of being maintained and transitioned.

Major Needed Functionality The requirements specifications will ultimately be translated into a number of needs in various function categories such as database, input/output, terminal, distributed facilities, appropriate programming language, and other functional resources required to produce a software product.

Experiential Familiarity of Software Developers The extent to which the software development unit is familiar with the applications area in which the software is being developed will be a major influence on the costs of producing the software. For commercial products, the extent to which the software development unit is familiar with the market for the software being developed will influence overall costs associated with delivery of the software to ultimate consumers. Since expertise can be acquired from outside units, the extent to which the user group and the software development community is familiar with the software product will also influence costs. (See our discussions concerning experiential familiarity in Chapter 9.)

Experiential Familiarity of Software User Group The extent to which the user group is familiar both with the tasks to be performed and the environment into which these tasks are embedded, as well as with the computer software and hardware that will ultimately form a new or modified process for task accomplishment, influences what can and will be done. There are a number of observation on this point in Chapter 9.

Figure 10.1 illustrates a structural model of these cost influencers. In a real physical sense, it is the program code, source or executable as the case may be, that is delivered to the client together with appropriate documentation, training and other items that lead to a complete software system. It appears, therefore, not unreasonable to base an initial cost estimate on the amount of code that is to be delivered. This initial estimate could be modified by several complexity factors, such as the six ingredients just noted. This approach is the basis for most software cost models in use today.

There are three basic ways in which we can estimate the cost, perhaps even the value, of a product:

1. *Wholistic*—whereby we base an estimate of the cost or value of a product in an affective, or gestalt or experientially based intuitive, fashion by examining the product as a *whole* and without detailed examination of the micro-level ingredients that comprise the product
2. *Heuristic*—whereby we base an estimate on one or more established and agreed-on *rules of thumb*
3. *Holistic*—whereby we determine the micro-level ingredients that make up the product, determine the cost or value of each of these, and sum these to determine the overall value

Each of these approaches has merit and is commonly used, and the results are often combined. The type of appraisal nature of value that is appropriate is very much a function of the type of product that is being examined.

Let us consider some illustrations of this. Suppose, for example, that we wish to obtain an estimate of the cost or value of a piece of real estate—say,

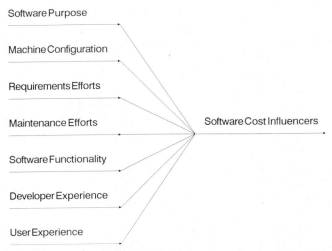

FIGURE 10.1   Some cost influencers for software production

a home or office building. We assume that the structure is not in existence. It would be possible for an architect to obtain the user requirements for the structure and to translate these into the number and size of rooms, and various finishings and fixtures associated with these. It would certainly be possible to total the costs associated with the physical construction materials needed and the cost of the labor required to build the structure. A construction management and architect's fee, perhaps calculated as overhead on the basic labor and materials, could then be determined and a total price for the structure obtained. If the site is already under the ownership of the client, and no site cost estimates are needed, this completes the cost estimate in a holistic fashion.

Alternately, the user might need to specify and then purchase a location for the structure. Here, we have a problem with our holistic appraisal approach. There is no way that we can easily decompose a physical site location into a number of components and determine the price of each of these. A heuristic approach might be used, however. There exists a variety of models, based mostly on center-of-gravity concepts, that project the price of land in terms of its distance from the center of a city and other related factors. One of these might be used to project site costs in terms of client desires in terms of distance from city center, availability of transportation, and other factors. This would represent a heuristic approach to site evaluation. Of course, an alternate approach would be to find the specific price for several available locations and ask the client which is the most desired in terms of costs and benefits associated with the specific site locations. Clearly, these estimates could be combined such that we obtain a *composite estimate*.

As another illustration, suppose that we wish to establish the value of a diamond. We might just look at it and attempt to put a price at which we might buy, or be willing to sell, the diamond. One possible problem with this approach is that our personal estimate of the value of the diamond might be so vastly different from that of most of the rest of the world that we might set a purchase price so low that no one would sell it to us at that price or so high that we would find out that we had a foolish purchase if ever we try to sell the diamond. In a similar way, we might establish a selling price that is so high that no one would purchase it, or one so low that we would really be giving a valuable asset away.

We might attempt to establish a value for the diamond by finding out what a *reasonable person* should be willing to pay for it. We would find that there is a generally established heuristic that says that the Value of a diamond is a function of four attributes or Cs: cut, clarity, carat, and color

$$V = f\,(\text{cu, cl, ca, co})$$

A little further search would indicate that these are *attribute measures* or *metrics* that a trained gemologist can easily use to characterize a given diamond. Further, there would be general agreement among gemologists concerning the value of these metrics as applied to a given diamond. Armed with this functional relation, which is surely heuristic, it is possible to establish the value of a given diamond. This is generally quite correct subject primarily to the difference that we might expect from wholesale and retail-type considerations.

But what about the value of an oil painting, or an ivory carving, or a bronze statue? No reasonable person would say that it would or should be equal to the cost of the materials involved plus an amount for labor. We would generally say that the value of a piece of art, such as one of the above, would be what a willing and uninvolved buyer would be willing to pay for it, or the price for which an uninvolved seller would be willing to sell it. But how could these be determined? We might go to an auction to attempt to find out. This would help, doubtlessly. The real answer is that we would need to determine the functional ingredients that influence value. For these items, it turns out that some of them are: the reputation of the artist; the age, condition, size, and beauty of the item; the provenance (or record of past ownership) of the item; and the present marketability and desirability of the item (with some projection of this to the future). Clearly, very little of this is holistic. Much of an appraisal of a piece of art would necessarily be heuristic or wholistic.

We could continue with this and examine the appraisal, or costing or valuing, of other items. A book, or an opera, might represent interesting items for discussion. But our real interest here is in software. So, what does all of this have to do with software?

To answer this, perhaps we might pose another question: *Is appraising, costing, and valuing software more like valuing: a building structure, a diamond, a work of fine art, or a book or opera?* Surely, costing a software product is very unlike costing a building, or a washing machine. We might be tempted to say that these are hardware items. But that is not the answer. A person with the requisite knowledge could doubtlessly cost out the design of a supersonic airplane, or an aircraft carrier, or a large building. The primary reason for this is not that all of these are primarily hardware but because known design practices are brought to bear on them *and* they are generally constructed from *off-the-shelf* items whose cost is easily determined. The initial estimates for the first supersonic airplane or aircraft carrier were doubtlessly in significant error. There were cost overruns and late product deliveries as well! *Just like with software.*

It appears to us that there is one primary reason for this, and it has little to do with whether the product, or process is hardware or software:

The uncertainties and error variance associated with costing the design of products and services will increase dramatically with increases in the formal intellectual content in the effort and with increasing lack of standardized design practices. It will be reduced with increases in understanding of the needs of the client, experiential familiarity with past similar successful developments, availability of "off-the shelf" subsystems and standardized practices.

Three *correlates* result from this observation:

1. Development of standardized design and development approaches is a real need.
2. The macro-enhancement approaches of reusable software, prototyping, automatic program generation, and expert system use could potentially have much to do with increasing software productivity.
3. There is bound to be much uncertainty and error variance associated with developments that involve new and previously untried subsystems and the cost estimates associated with these.

It goes almost without saying that it is necessary to be able to obtain reliable estimates of costs and other resources required for software development efforts. These costs will invariably be a function of the benefits that are proposed for achievement. A major goal in software productivity efforts is to achieve the maximum benefit-to-cost ratio for software development efforts, or to be able to produce software that has a given benefit for the minimum cost. At first glance, it might appear that these are equivalent statements. This is, however, not usually the case. To examine this now would be getting just a bit ahead of ourselves.

From this discussion, we see that we will often need to develop *several costs* to produce software that will satisfy the client's needs to varying degrees. A professional-level presentation to the client of these would also include any contingencies associated with the estimates, especially if these are to be the responsibility of the client.

Software cost and value estimates are intimately related with notions of software productivity. Definitions of software productivity are, therefore, of much interest. First, we will offer a rather simple definition. *Software productivity is equivalent to the number of lines of source code that are delivered to the client per person month of effort.* But what is a line of code? Here, a line of code might represent a high-order language line of source code. Even here, we must be concerned with whether we include retainable lines of code in the resulting compiled code only, or whether we also include nonretainable lines of code.

There are many concerns with either approach. An object line of code is a single machine language instruction either written as a machine language instruction or generated through some translation process from a different language. Immediately, we see a problem. Lines of code can be meaningful only at the end of a project after operational executable code is delivered and accepted by the client. Surely, delivered lines of code is not an unmeaningful measure of productivity. However, it does assume that *one line of code is equal to and has precisely the same value as any other line of code.* Clearly, there is no reason whatever to accept this assertion.

Yet, *source lines of code* (SLOC) is often used as the primary driver of software cost estimation models. Often, this is modified to *delivered SLOC*

(DSLOC) through the simple artifice of multiplying the estimate of SLOC by some fraction, which would generally depend on programmer experience and other variables. Boehm [1987] delineates some of the difficulties:

1. Complex instructions, and complex combinations of instructions, will receive the same weight as a similarly long sequence of very simple statements.
2. This is not a uniform metric in the sense that similar length lines of machine-oriented language statements, higher-order language statements, and very-high-order language statements will be given the same weight.
3. It may be a demotivator of truly productive work if programming teams learn that their productivity is measured in terms of the number of lines of code they write per unit time and then artificially increase this *productivity* through writing many simple and near useless lines of code.
4. It may encourage poor-quality code by encouraging rapid production of many sloppily structured lines of code.

We could continue on with this to also note that maintenance costs may well increase through the implied encouragement to produce many lines of code without regard to maintainability. Transitioning to a new environment is especially difficult when many lines of carelessly structured code are involved.

Even if we could agree that SLOC or DSLOC is a worthwhile driver of costs, there would still remain a major problem in effectively estimating either quantity prior to the start of a software development effort. Further, neither term gives explicit or implicit consideration to such important macro-enhancement efforts as prototyping, reusable software, or the use of expert systems technology.

Productivity could also be defined in terms of an importance-weighted sum of delivered functional units. This would allow us to consider the obvious reality that different lines of code and different software functional units have different value. This is the basis for the "Function Points" measurement method of Allan Albrecht [1979]. It leads, as we will see, to an approach where software costs are measured in terms of such quantities as input transactions, outputs, inquiries, files, and output reports. These are software product quantities that can be estimated when the requirements definition document is developed. Such an approach will enable us to estimate the size of the program in terms of:

1. The *purpose to be accomplished,* in terms of such operational software characteristics as the operating system used and application for which the software was developed, and development and test requirements for support software
2. The *function to be accomplished* in terms of amount or size, complexity, clarity, and interrelation with other programs and computers

3. *Use factors* such as the number of users of code, sophistication or u... number of times code will execute, number of machines on which code will run, and hardware power

4. *Development factors* such as the operating system to be accommodated, development time available, development tools available, experiential familiarity of software development team, and the number of software modules

Other taxonomies of factors are possible. We have already developed one of these, in which we identified six cost-influencing ingredients; we will examine a number of those now available in our efforts in later sections of this chapter. In general, the important factors will include the people, process, environment, product, and computer system to be used. The major requirement is that the factors be significant, general, measurable, observable, and independent. This poses major requirements, as we shall soon see.

As we have noted, there are three basic approaches to modeling a software system. The first is derived from the experience of those who have developed similar systems and is based upon wholistic or gestalt reasoning. For this reason, these models are also called *experiential models.*

The second approach is that of *heuristic,* or *approximate, reasoning.* The third approach, which would be based on establishing micro-level details for all aspects of software construction, is really not feasible, at least at this point in time, since there is no way to obtain the detailed micro-level estimates needed in a way that this could be done for well-understood physical systems with standardized design practices. While it is not at all difficult to determine the source lines of code delivered to the client for completed projects, there is no known present way to obtain trustworthy estimates of code size for projects yet to be undertaken!

10.2   MODEL CONSTRUCTION

It is very characteristic of everyone that they always want to know how much an item that they might want to purchase will cost. Often, particularly for major items, we also find out the cost of essentially equivalent items and then select the one for purchase that is within our resources and that *seems best.* This is also true relative to software purchase. As we have already noted, initial estimates of software development costs are seldom very close to the actual final costs. This is especially the case for projects of large scale and/ or scope.

One of the ways to understand a complex situation is to build a *model* of it. Models are usually developed for two reasons [Sage, 1977]: (1) to explain how some system or process works, or (2) to predict some characteristic of the system or process. The construction of a model is initiated by first identifying a theory of how the components of the process or system relate to one another. In the physical and engineering sciences, this is often accomplished by building a differential equation model of the process, system, or physical phenomenon. In more general terms, some theoretical or empirical knowledge is used to establish a structural framework for the item to be modeled. Often, there are a number of unspecified parameters within this structure, and data and observation are used to adjust these unspecified parameters such that the response of the model to a given input is as much like the response of the real system as possible. This is usually known as *system identification* [Sage and Melsa, 1971] and provides a basis for the modeling of systems.

There are two primary steps in the process of constructing a model:

1. Identify a structural framework for the proposed model in terms of behavioral or physical observations or hypotheses.
2. Identify unspecified parameters within this structure such that the model replicates reality in some *best,* or at least *satisfactory*, sense.

A third step really should be included:

3. Estimate the *worth* of the model by determining how well the model is able to forecast or predict phenomena of interest.

Software cost models have provided software engineers, in particular those associated with management of the software engineering process, that is to say, software systems engineers, with the ability to better understand the software development process and how costs are related to it. Many cost models have been identified. The purpose of all of these is to aid in understanding how costs are related to the software product produced, and to estimate the cost of the software to be produced in terms of the requirements specifications for the software. Software production cost models attempt to capture the relationships among the lifecycle components in an equation, generally an heuristic algorithm, that allows determination of the effort and cost required to build a software system.

The accuracy of the cost estimates, and other estimates such as lifecycle effort, generated by these models can be compared with what actually occurs. This provides a test of how well the model reflects the actual relationships among cost factors. We must be able to demonstrate that a proposed model of the software production process is valid. We can speak of several types of validity:

Structural Validity   This means that there is a one to one correspondence between nodes, or elements, in the structure and nodes in the actual system or process.

Parametric Validity   This means that the unspecified parameters have been identified accurately and that they correspond closely to equivalent parameters in the actual system or process.

Forecast or Prediction Validity   This means that the model is able to project future events, or costs and schedules in the case of software, within acceptable error tolerances.

There are numerous occasions when humans wish to make a forecast of possible future states and events. Any of several methods might be used to accomplish this. Some of these are very crude, and some are sophisticated. Some are based on the information that constitutes the expert judgment of an individual or a group. Others are based on mathematical approaches and formal reasoning. Here, we will be concerned with quantitative forecasting approaches based on a time-series representation of observations.

Representation of many real world phenomena in terms of a model is a very practical and useful approach for understanding and predicting system behavior. A model is constructed so as to reflect the way a system behaves over time due to changes in input to the system. Usually, modeling and associated analysis is considered to be an area of statistics, or statistical estimation theory. It is rich in the choice of models potentially offered the user, and for this reason, *modeling* is a particularly important component of a realistic systems analysis.

Statistical procedures useful for modeling software costs can vary from the drawing and assessment of a few simple graphs, with perhaps "eyeball" estimations of fit and average values, to very complex mathematical analysis that needs to be accomplished through use of very sophisticated computers. In any area that is appropriate for statistical analysis, there is an essential random nature to the observations that are taken. One purpose of a statistical analysis is the summarization, or standardized representation in terms of various norms, of data or information. There are a variety of ways in which this might be done. An idea of the "central value" of a random phenomenon can be obtained by using the average value of the observations. It turns out that there are a variety of measures of "average" such as mean, median, and mode of the observation. Another very important average measure of an observation concerns the variability of one piece of data from others. A frequently used measure of this "spread" is known as the *variance*. By definition, this is the ensemble or time average of the squared difference between the values of the observations and the average value. The average of the square of the observations is known as the *mean-square value*. It can be shown that the variance of an observation is the mean-square value of the observation minus the square of the mean of the observation. The square root of the variance is commonly known as the *standard deviation*. This is often a very useful measure of "spread" in a set of observations.

Regression techniques are used to obtain a mathematical model that specifies the relations between a set of variables. The input to the model is data that represents observations of those variables. Generally, a regression analysis equation describes the value of one variable, the dependent variable, as a function of other independent variables. Regression analysis equations may be helpful for interpolation or for extrapolation, or for forecasting events that are of interest. Alternately, they may be used as a part of a more complicated mathematical description of some problem. The result of a regression analysis may also be useful as evidence to support or reject hypothetical theories about the existence of relations between variables in a system.

Estimation theory, which is closely related to regression analysis, is concerned with the determination of those parameter values in a given equation, such that use of the equation results in the best possible fit to observed data. Regression analysis and estimation theory also include the search for an appropriate structural equation or, alternately, an input/output model that best replicates observed data. This aspect of regression analysis is rarely emphasized to the extent appropriate for identification of useful models.

The following activities are associated with the solution of a typical regression problem for model determination through parameter identification:

Determination of Candidate Variables and Data Collection   The dependent variables that need to be described as a function of other variables are defined. This is usually guided by experienced based intuition and existing theory and knowledge. Then, it should be ascertained that a sufficient number of joint observations of the values of all the variables considered is available. Usually, the number of data points should be not smaller than 10 times the number of variables. Often, it is not possible to directly observe the values of variables and, because of this, noise-corrupted observations must be made.

Postulation of a Mathematical Model or Structure   The form of the postulated equation may be linear, multiplicative, logarithmic, or exponential, for example. An initial postulate is made, and, when possible, transformations are generally performed such that a linear relationship between the transformed variables results. If, for example, the assumed model structure has the form

$$y = a\, x^b\, z^c \tag{10.1}$$

then the logarithm is taken on both sides to yield:

$$Y = \ln(y) = \ln(a) + b \ln(x) + c \ln(z) \tag{10.2}$$

or

$$Y = A + b X + c Z \tag{10.3}$$

where $A = \ln(a)$, $X = \ln(x)$, and $Z = \ln(z)$. It is important to note here that while the resulting equation [Equation (10.3)] is linear in the transformed variables X, Y, and Z, it is not linear in the original variables x, y, and z. It should be noted that even though the logarithm of all data is taken so that the postulated relationship between the transformed data becomes linear, the value of a, b, and c that best fit Equation (10.1) are not generally the values that best fit Equation (10.2) or (10.3).

Choice of Estimation and Selection Method   The most widely used estimation method is generally referred to as "least squares," to indicate that it determines those coefficient values that will yield the smallest possible value for the sum of the squares of the differences between observed values of the dependent variable and values computed from the estimated relationship. In mathematical notation, if the function $f(x)$ is to be determined such as to best express y as a function of the set of state variables $x = [x_1, x_2, ..., x_n]$, and we have N observed values of $y = [y_1, y_2, ..., y_N]$, then we determine the unspecified coefficients in $f(x)$ such that the sum from $i = 1$ to $i = N$ of the squared error expression $e^2 = [y - f(x)]^2$ is minimal. There are a number of generalizations on the basic least-squares estimation criterion, especially to include the dynamic evolution of observations over time and the notion of weights. These extensions render regression analysis and estimation theory problems virtually indistinguishable.

In regression analysis and estimation theory, one needs to determine which candidate independent variables need to be taken into account in order to obtain a good description of variations in the dependent variables. One approach to this calls for first taking all candidate variables into account and then estimating the associated coefficient values and their uncertainty. Then, through use of hypothesis testing techniques, it is determined which coefficients are most likely to represent no relation at all between the dependent and independent variables. The state variables corresponding to this are then dropped from further consideration in the analysis, and the process is repeated until the likelihood that any of the remaining coefficients actually represents no relation at all is smaller than some preset value or level of significance. The end result is the appropriate regression equation.

Another approach is based on a procedure that is inverse to the one just described. After all state variables to be considered have been included in the proposed regression equation, a ranking of the levels of significance of the respective coefficients in the regression equation is determined. Then, an equation is estimated using the most significant variables only. One state variable at a time is added to this regression equation, in decreasing order of initial significance, until it is observed that the addition of one more additional state variable does not lead to an "appreciable" improvement in the goodness of fit of the resulting regression equation.

Clearly, many variations of these basic approaches are possible and potentially desirable for many applications. These structural aspects of regression analysis, and systems engineering in general, are underexplored relative to areas more subject to completely analytical exploration. The success of a modeling effort is critically dependent, in most cases, on success in choosing an appropriate structural model.

Other activities in the regression modeling and analysis process include:

Determination of the Regression Curve   This step involves obtaining the needed data, and the use of a subportion of the regression analysis program in which algorithms for parameter estimation have been encoded.

Iteration and Sensitivity Analysis   Depending on the criticality of obtaining a good regression equation, various iterative and sensitivity forms of testing should be performed in which, for example, other structural models or different selection procedures are used.

Figure 10.2 illustrates the flow of these steps in regression analysis for software cost model determination.

In order to determine the completeness and usefulness of a regression analysis, it is important that the answers to the following questions be "yes:"

1. Have all the important explanatory variables been taken into account?
2. Do the obtained results make sense, and can this assertion be validated in some manner?
3. Are the results of the analysis useful in clarifying the structure of the problem and in leading to enhanced wisdom relative to its resolution?

The user of regression analysis and estimation theory techniques for software cost estimation and associated process management should be concerned with several observations that affect model validity:

1. The results of regression analysis and estimation theory will be unreliable if they are based on an insufficient number of observations.
2. Results that are obtained through use of these approaches in situations in which there exists little theoretical knowledge should be examined very carefully as there is no guarantee that a regression relation which displays an excellent fit to observed data will really have any predictive power at all. Causation is required here, and a good fit obtained using regression approaches only ensures high correlation. *In practice, this caveat seems often overlooked! This may well be a problem when correlated variables are treated, for software cost estimation, as if they were causally related.*
3. In a similar way, the results of a regression analysis do not necessarily provide evidence or proof of *causal* relations among events.

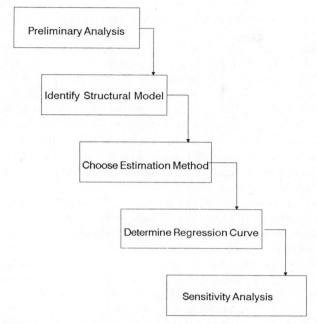

FIGURE 10.2 Steps in regression and estimation theory for software cost model building

4. Poor data quality may make even the optimum fit a very poor one. There is no automatic assurance that even the "*best*" data are necessarily very good.

5. The criteria for inclusion or exclusion of variables in an estimation or regression algorithm must necessarily be strongly dependent on the purpose to which the resulting model is ultimately to be used.

Ideally, a software cost estimation model should describe the relationships among the characteristics of the project so that we can determine the cost of the software from the relevant characteristics. These would usually be the system-level requirements specifications. However, the software-level requirements specifications would be essentially as satisfactory. If we had an automatic way of transitioning from system-level requirements to software requirements, and perhaps were able to solve the inverse problem as well, then knowledge of one would be equivalent to knowledge of the other.

The features useful as input to cost estimation models should include descriptions of not only the software to be developed but also the characteristics of the developing organization, such as personnel experience and capability levels, micro-level and macro-level software tools, and program management approaches.

This assumes a deterministic software production process, whereas there are a number of uncertain and imprecise matters associated with the project. A deterministic approach to a stochastic production process will not generally produce correct answers. The results thereby obtained will be precise; in reality, the results should be stochastic and imprecise. Hopefully, the deterministic estimates will provide a reasonable approximation of the realized cost. Let us now examine some of the cost models that have been proposed and then provide some commentary concerning their propriety.

Our efforts result in macro-cost models that are very similar to macro-economic models used to predict economic activity. Software cost models usually involve at least two types of estimates. These are *time* and *effort,* and these may be expressed according to the phases of the software lifecycle. Many existing software cost models estimate the number of weeks or months needed to produce a given software system. A time limit on system development is often identified by the client as one of the system-level requirements. This is generally assumed as a constraint in the transition of system-level requirements to software-level requirements and associated-effort requirements. For this reason, most cost models focus on effort requirements.

We will use effort estimates as input variables that result in the calculation of costs of development in terms of the human resources required to build the target system. Typically, this estimate is expressed in terms of the number of people needed integrated over the time to be spent, so that the measure of effort is person-months or person-years. The actual cost in dollars can be generated from an effort estimate by multiplying the effort by the average cost per unit time of software production. More sophisticated models may be based on the fact that the cost per person-hour of effort depends on the type of labor involved. A development effort that involves much use of systems engineering talent for technical direction and rapid prototyping would thus be costed at a higher amount than an effort that involves little of this effort and a great deal of routine coding.

Many simple software cost models describe the size of the software development program only in terms of the size of the software product produced in terms of *lines of code* delivered to the customer. Complexity figures, in terms of the number of programming operators and operands, and functionality measures are used in some models as we have noted. For example, Walston and Felix [1977] allow comments lines up to half of the delivered lines of code. Boehm [1981] does not allow the inclusion of comment lines at all. Bailey and Basili [1981] include the total number of lines of new code, including remarks, but only one-fifth of the total number of lines of reused code, including comments. There is no problem with any of these approaches, although it does make routine use of the same information on all models, as well as comparison of the various approaches, more difficult. The meaning of the expression "lines of code" must simply be interpreted for each model before use of the model.

10.3   WHOLISTIC EXPERT-JUDGMENT-BASED SOFTWARE COST MODELS

An *experiential model* uses expert-wholistic-based judgment as the primary input to the cost estimation or forecasting process. The accuracy of the prediction is a function of the experience and perception of the estimator.

In its simplest form, an estimate based on expert judgment involves one or more experts who make educated guesses about the effort that will be required for an entire software development program, or for a project thereof. The estimate may be derived from either a top-down or bottom-up analysis of the proposed system. Often, experts are asked to make three predictions in a DELPHI [Sage, 1977; Porter et al., 1980] approach to forecasting: an optimistic one, a pessimistic one, and a most likely prediction. If A represents the optimistic cost estimate, B the pessimistic one, and C the most likely cost estimate, the final estimate of cost or effort is presumed to be

$$\text{Cost} = \frac{A + 4C + B}{6}$$

This is simply a weighted average in which is it assumed that the weight of the most likely estimate has a worth of four times that of either the most optimistic or most pessimistic estimate. Alternately, the resulting estimate can be said to follow what is called a beta probability distribution. The Delphi technique can be used to generate A, B, and C as themselves averages of many individual responses. Of course, there is no scientific basis to support use of this cost relation. Many people would, in a judgmental situation such as this, simply provide optimistic and pessimistic estimates that are equally spaced about the most likely estimate

$$A = C + \delta \qquad B = C - \delta$$

such that the resulting estimate is Cost $= C$.

A number of other models add more structure to the expert judgment approach. Wolverton [1974] developed a software cost matrix approach in which matrix elements represent the cost per line of code as calibrated from historical data. The multipliers in a vector product equation represent a phase–activity distribution as derived from the judgments of experts. The choice of elements depends on expert judgment as to the type of software, novelty, and difficulty. Figure 10.3 represents a portion of the Wolverton model, which contains as many as 8 phases and 25 activities per lifecycle phase. Use of the

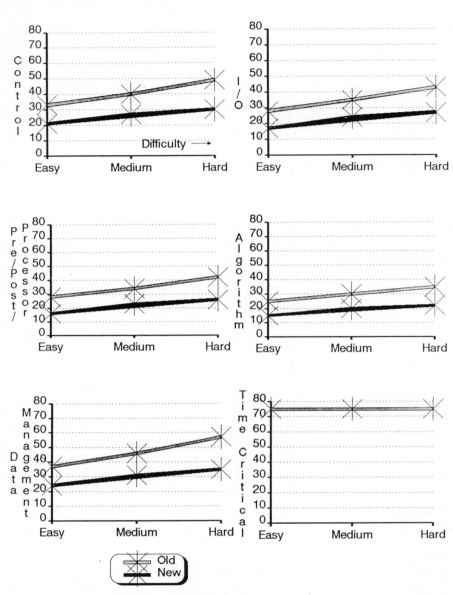

FIGURE 10.3   Wolverton cost attributes

model is generally predicated on breaking the software development into phases and estimating their costs individually. A software effort may represent a *new* or *old,* development effort depending on the familiarity of the software developer. Here, for example, a 2000-object instruction module of old autopilot flight control algorithm software of medium difficulty would be priced at $36 per instruction, excluding remarks, for a total of $72,000.

Wolverton's software cost–effort model is based on subjective estimates of software complexity. These estimates are made by considering the different types of software to be developed and the development difficulty expected. A software cost matrix can also be used, as an alternate to the graphical approach of Figure 10.3. For example, we have the data shown in Table 10.1.

In using this table, the costs are based on the type of software, represented by the row name, and the difficulty of developing such software, as represented by the several columns. The difficulty is determined by two factors: whether the problem is old (O) or new (N), and whether it is easy (E), moderate (M), or hard (H). The matrix elements are the cost per line of code as calibrated from historical data. To use the matrix, the software system under development may be partitioned into modules i for $i = 1, 2, ..., n$. An estimate is made of the size S_i of each module, as measured in the number of lines of developed uncommented code, for each of the n modules. If the kth module is of type $t(k)$ and difficulty $d(k)$, then the cost of developing each of the various-type components of the model is module is

$$C_t(k) = S_k \, C_{t(k)d(k)}$$

where $C_{t(k)d(k)}$ represents the cost per line of code for that particular type or category of software. This is given by the tdth entry in the preceeding matrix. To calculate the cost of the kth module, we multiply $C_t(k)$ by the appropriate matrix entry in Table 10.1. We then sum this over all k modules to obtain the total cost of producing the system.

This estimate does not consider software process variables, except to the extent that they influence either Figure 10.3 or Table 10.1. Fundamentally, the software cost estimate is a function only of product characteristics unless one is to have a different graph or table for each change in process, and management, characteristic. It is not even clear, for example, how questions of development approach, software development organization experience, availability of CASE tools, and other process-related factors affect the resulting cost estimates.

A *resource estimation model* has been proposed by Joe Fox [1985]. He identifies a total of 27 contributors to software development costs. The eight

Table 10.1   Software Cost Matrix for Wolverton Model

Type	Difficulty	OE	OM	OH	NE	NM	NH
Control		21	27	30	33	40	49
I/O		17	24	27	28	35	43
Pre-postprocessor		16	23	26	28	34	42
Algorithm		15	20	22	25	30	35
Data management		24	31	35	37	46	57
Time critical		75	75	75	75	75	75

major contributors to the cost of software development are identified in three major categories (function, use time environments, and development time factors) and assigned scale ranges as:

Function

1. *Scale* (1 to 8)—the amount of function to be developed
2. *Clarity* (1 to 10)—the degree to which functions developed are understood
3. *Logical complexity* (1 to 10)—the number of conditional branches per 100 instructions
5. The need for *user interaction with system* (1 to 5) and the intensity of this interaction

Use Time Environments

4. *Consequences of failure* (1 to 15)—the effort required to meet reliability and recovery requirements
6. *Real-time requirements* (1 to 5) in terms of how fast the various needed functions must be accomplished

Development Time Factors

7. *Stability of the software support tools* (1 to 10)
8. *Stability of the use phase computer hardware* (1 to 20)

Each of these factors is assumed to contribute to costs per line of delivered code. The code costs can vary up to $83.00 per line, as this is the sum of the largest numbers for each of these factors. Fox encourages use of a circle-like diagram on which is sketched the relative difficulty for each factor. Figure 10.4 illustrates a sample estimation exercise for a hypothetical software development effort.

Another important example of an expert-judgment-based approach is the Albrecht [1979] *function point model,* which, like the approach due to Fox, is based on an evaluation of several measures on which a software project is classified. Subjective assessments of the complexity of the software system are provided by expert judgment and incorporated into the parameters of the model.

To estimate the cost of a project, we begin by first completing two columns of Table 10.2, which is one possible form of a function point computation chart. To initiate the procedure, we first count each of the domain items specified in column 1, and then place that count in the corresponding row of column 2. The count is then multiplied by the appropriate weight from one of columns 3, 4 or 5, depending on a subjective estimate of the complexity of each of the five functions. This result is then placed in column 6.

The weight entries in Table 10.2 are generated by expert opinion and are

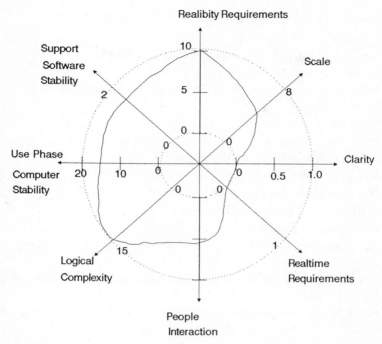

FIGURE 10.4   Estimation components for the Fox software cost model

Table 10.2   Function Point Computation Chart

Information	Count	Weight Simple	Average	Complex	Ω
Number of distinct input data items		3	4	6	
Number of types of on-line queries		3	4	6	
Number of files		7	10	15	
Number interfaces to other systems		5	7	10	
Number of output screens or reports		4	5	7	

based, therefore, on informed but subjective judgments. When the table is completed, the total of the sixth column, the number of unadjusted function points, is denoted Ω and saved in the upper right hand corner of the table for use in a subsequent step, after we have made some complexity adjustments. These complexity adjustments are next made, based on the answers to the following 14 questions [Arthur, 1985]:

1. Does the system require reliable backup and recovery?
2. Are data communications required?
3. Are there distributed processing functions?
4. Is the system performance critical?
5. Will the system run in an existing, heavily utilized operational environment?
6. Does the system require on-line data entry?
7. Does the on-line data entry require the input transaction to be built over multiple screens or operations?
8. Are the master files updated on-line?
9. Are the inputs, outputs, files, or inquiries complex?
10. Is the internal processing complex?
11. Is the code designed to be reusable?
12. Are conversion and installation requirements included in the design process?
13. Is the system designed for multiple installations in one or more different organizations?
14. Is the application designed to facilitate change over time and ease of use by the user?

A simple "yes" or "no" answer is insufficient here. What is desired is a set of complexity adjustments that go into the function point calculation. Each of the 14 complexity adjustment factors is rated on a scale from 0 to 5 in accordance with subjective feelings about the *influence* of these on software complexity. The unanchored scale used is:

0—no influence
1—incidental influence
2—moderate influence
3—average influence
4—significant influence
5—essential influence

To complete calculations using this model, the sum Σ of the 14 complexity adjustment values and the total Ω from Table 10.2 are used in a very simple computation to generate the function point value:

$$FP = \Omega * [0.65 + 0.01\Sigma]$$

where the constant values 0.65 and 0.01 are determined empirically, using an unspecified combination of expert judgment and curve matching.

Some variations on the function point exist. For example, Symons [1988] has developed an approach, called *Mark II,* in which a software system is viewed as consisting primarily of logical transaction types. Any object, real or abstract, about which the system provides information is a logical transaction type, according to this model. Rather than having the function points reflect functionality values of the system as delivered to the user, which is the general intent of software cost models as well as that of Albrecht in this particular case, Symons relates software system size to the effort that is required to analyze, design, and develop the system.

Symons also appends six questions to the 14 technical complexity adjustment questions noted before:

15. Is there a need to interface with other applications?
16. Is there a need for special computer software security features?
17. Is there a need for direct access for third parties?
18. Are there (extraordinary) documentation requirements?
19. Is there a requirement for special user training facilities, such as a training subsystem?
20. Is there a need to define, select, and install special hardware or software unique to this application?

Symons, in using these 20 factors for calibrating technical complexity adjustment, found that the coefficient of 0.01 in Albrecht's formula would be more accurate if readjusted to a value of 0.005 for some of the factors. A clear connotation from this suggestion is that function points, here or in Albrecht's model, are not at all independent of the structure of the model or the technology used for system development and implementation. This is very unlike the claim by Albrecht, who seems to suggest this independence. The seeming total lack of anchoring of the scales used would also seem to suggest a lack of independence, as well as to indicate potential difficulties in interpretation of the results obtained.

The function point approach is certainly based on the software requirements specification, as translated from the client's system level requirements. Given this, an estimate of costs can be made early in the software lifecycle. Much of the cost estimation is, however, based on very subjective, perhaps even mystical data. The empirical constants used are said to have been identified "*by debate and trial*" [Albrecht, 1983] in the business information system applications for which the function point approach has been used. The extent to which the model, especially with these constants, may be fully appropriate for diverse applications, such as real-time concurrent flight control systems or embedded command and control systems, seems very questionable. Since there is no implicit or explicit inclusion of information concerning the development language to be used, the software tools to be used, nor user or developer experience in using or producing software, we conclude that there are a number of important environmental and developmental factors that will influence cost but which do not seem to be incorporated in the model.

Another problem with function points relates to the calculating the unadjusted function points as needed in the first step of model usage. Many of the calculated function points will arise from the external processing requirements associated with inputs, outputs, interfaces, and queries. The internal processing requirements are reflected only in the number of logical file types, or as one of the general characteristics referred to by question 10. For programs involving highly complex algorithms, often occurring in autopilot and other physical system areas, neither program size nor complexity will be adequately captured by this model. Another more general complication may result from the three-level classification of all system modules as simple, average, or complex. It appears that this oversimplification could lead to a computation in which one component having a very large number of data elements cannot be assigned any more than twice the number of points that must be assigned to a component that contains only one data item.

There seems to be neither a direct physical meaning nor interpretation possible for the function point concept or how it really relates to software production effort. This seems to be supported by other research studies. For example, Albrecht and Gaffney [1983] made an effort to relate the computed function points to the number of lines of code. They experimented with COBOL, PL/1, and a fourth-generation data manipulation language and found that 110, 65, and 25 lines of code in these languages corresponded to one function point. In addition, the function point concept developed to date does not seem to allow for inclusion of the various macro-enhancement approaches that we have discussed.

Experiential, or expert-judgment-based, models are subject to all of the many illusions that have been reported to be associated with expert judgment [Sage, 1989]. The results of many studies illustrate that experts reach judgments, including cost judgments for software programs, by using analogous reasoning and other experientially based intuitive judgment modes. They follow the usually wise course of identifying projected cost in terms of known costs of previous efforts believed to be similar. However, programs that appear to be similar are often very different, in many ways. The differences are subtle and not always immediately apparent. This can lead to one of the stress based errors associated with the Janis–Mann model of judgment that we presented in our previous chapter. A 1978–1980 Yourdon survey, reported in DeMarco [1981], asked software project managers to estimate, on the basis of experience and without use of a formal model, the effort required to successfully complete software projects. He compared the program managers' estimated efforts to the actual effort required to produce the software product. The results of the study indicated that the managers were not very good at all in estimating such important variables as project costs. More often than not, cost estimates were in error by more than 100%.

10.4 HEURISTICS FOR SOFTWARE COST ESTIMATION

A more or less experiential approach to modeling software costs involves the use of time series like regression analysis. In this approach, a heuristic structural equation, with a number of unspecified parameters, is proposed. Regression analysis is then used, together with available data, to determine the unspecified parameters such that the model generates results as much like those obtained in actual practice as possible. Fundamentally, a linear estimation model is one represented by an equation of the form

$$C = \alpha + \Sigma \, \beta_i x_i$$

where each variable x_i represents a quantity or attribute of software cost that is believed to be important. The sum is presumed to be carried out over N terms. The parameters α and β_i are identified using data from past software projects.

There have been many studies using a linear model of this sort, including some software cost modeling studies. One of the earliest studies was due to Nelson [1966] at the System Development Corporation. In this study, 104 possible cost factors were identified in a study of 169 projects. Using the database of information for the 169 software projects, a least-squares curve fit was used to determine the coefficients of each attribute in the cost model. Ultimately, only the 14 most significant factors were retained in the final cost estimation model. The model obtained is described by Table 10.3. Unfor-

Table 10.3   Effort Attributes and Weights for the SDC Study

Attribute Number	Definition	Weight	Value Range
0	Constant value	−33.63	1
1	Lack of requirements	9.15	0–2
2	Design stability	10.73	0–3
3	Percentage math instructions	0.51	0–100
4	Percentage I/O instructions	0.46	0–100
5	Number of subprograms	0.40	number
6	Programming language complexity	7.28	0–1
7	Business application	−21.45	0–1
8	Stand-alone program	13.50	0–1
9	First program on computer	12.35	0–1
10	Connecticut hardware development	58.82	0–1
11	Random–access device used	30.61	0–1
12	Different host and target hardware	29.55	0–1
13	Number of personnel trips	0.54	number
14	Developed by the military	−25.20	0–1

tunately however, the errors in projecting costs are quite large [Conte et al., 1986], doubtlessly because the costs do not really increase linearly with the factors influencing costs.

In general, the simplest nonlinear models are of the form

$$C = \alpha + \Sigma \beta_i x_i^{\Gamma_i}$$

where each variable x_i represents a quantity or attribute measure of software cost that is believed to be important. The sum is presumed to be carried out over N terms. The parameters α, β_i, and Γ_i are identified using data from past software projects.

As in the linear model, the x_i values are presumed to be attribute measures or scores for specific projects, whereas the parameters α, β_i, and Γ_i are presumed to be constants, at least across software projects of a generic category, and are obtained from a database.

According to DeMarco [1982], uncontrollable factors in the development process will almost always result in 10 to 20% error in the accuracy of this type of estimate. Sadly, estimates using models of this sort are rarely this good!

One problem with the foregoing nonlinear equation is that it does not allow for multiplicative combinations of attribute scores. Most of the software cost models in use today identify *lines of code* as the *most important factor* influencing cost. A very simple nonlinear equation which will determine a *basic* cost, or effort, estimate as a function of lines of code is

$$B = a + b S^{\delta}$$

where S represents (thousands of) lines of code and δ is chosen in an appropriate manner that, somehow, represents reality. It turns out that this is the fundamental relation underlying essentially all of the software cost models in use today. This relation will be multiplied by a multiplier, which contains quantities other than lines of code, that influence cost and effort. The overall software cost estimate is then determined from

$$B = [a + b S^{\delta}]M(\mathbf{x})$$

where $\mathbf{x}$ is a vector of important cost factors, exclusive of lines of code. Table 10.4 presents this basic cost or effort estimator for some of these models. Immediately, we see that the parameters are fundamentally different. One explanation, but not an exclusive one, is that the definition of S is different across the several estimators. Generally, it is thousands of lines of source code and the estimate is in person-months of effort. The definition of a *line of code* varies from model to model, and we will indicate the one used in our specific discussions to follow. In a similar way, we need to know whether the

Table 10.4   Basic Estimate Relations for Various Software Cost Models

$C = 5.5 + 0.73\ S^{1.16}$	Bailey–Basili [1981]
$C = 2.4\ S^{1.05}$	Boehm—basic organic COCOMO [1981]
$C = 3.2\ S^{1.05}$	Boehm—intermediate organic COCOMO [1981]
$C = 3.0\ S^{1.12}$	Boehm—basic semidetached COCOMO [1981]
$C = 3.0\ S^{1.12}$	Boehm—intermediate semidetached COCOMO [1981]
$C = 3.6\ S^{1.20}$	Boehm—basic embedded COCOMO [1981]
$C = 2.8\ S^{1.20}$	Boehm—intermediate embedded COCOMO [1981]
$C = 5.29\ S^{1.047}$	Doty [Herd et al., 1977]
$C = 28\ S^{1.83}$	Schneider [1978]
$C = 5.25\ S^{0.91}$	Walston–Felix [1977]

effort and cost estimate is for production of code only, or whether it includes effort across all of the lifecycle phases, or something in between these.

We will now examine a number of costing or effort models to illustrate the similarities and differences among them.

10.4.1   The Bailey–Basili Model

The Bailey and Basili [1981] model was developed using data from a database of 18 large projects from the NASA Goddard Space Center. They make no claims that the model, based on empirical evidence from specific projects, applies to other than projects of the same general type. Most of the software in the NASA database used by Bailey and Basili was written in FORTRAN, and most of the applications they considered were scientific. Thus, the database is very homogeneous. The total number of lines of code is defined to be the total amount of new code written plus 20% of the old code that is reused. Comment lines of code are included in each.

The basic estimator equation that they used was

$$C = a + b\ S^{\delta}$$

and the model parameters were identified such as to minimize the *standard error estimate* (SEE), where

$$\text{SEE} = \sum_{i=1}^{N} \left[\frac{1 - (a + bS_i^{\delta})}{C_i} \right]^2$$

The sum is carried out over the projects in the database. The parameters that minimize SEE were such that the estimation equation was

$$B = 5.5 + 0.73S^{1.16}$$

and they obtain an SEE of 1.25. If we assume that the error distribution is Gaussian, this says that we can multiply and divide the actual estimate obtained by 1.25 in order to obtain the upper and lower error bounds for one standard deviation of error.

It turns out that this fit is a very good one for the 18 software projects used to determine the parameters for the cost estimator. Bailey and Basili attempt to improve on the estimator by calculating bounds based on software complexity factors, rather than just using the 1.25 factor. The actual modification relation used takes into account 21 other variables that may effect the software production person months. These are categorized as:

1. *Total method attributes* (METH) (which includes nine attribute measures)
   a. Chief programmer teams
   b. Code reading
   c. Design formulations
   d. Formal documentation
   e. Formal test plans
   f. Formal training
   g. Top-down design
   h. Tree charts
   i. Unit development factors
2. *Cumulative complexity attributes* (CPLX) (which includes seven attribute measures)
   a. Application complexity
   b. Customer initiated design changes
   c. Customer interface complexity
   d. Database complexity
   e. External communication complexity
   f. Internal communication complexity
   g. Program flow complexity
3. *Cumulative past experience attributes* (EXP) (which includes five attribute measures)
   a. Overall team experience
   b. Programmer application experience
   c. Programmer language experience
   d. Programmer machine experience
   e. Programmer qualifications

A least-squares error regression is used to calculate coefficients a, b, c, and d in

$$R_{adj} = a*METH + b*CPLX + c*EXP + d$$

and the adjustment factor is then used to modify the cost estimate up or down according to

$$C_{adj} = (1 + R_{adj})C$$

if it is believed that the complexity factors will increase costs and

$$C_{adj} = \frac{C}{1 + R_{adj}}$$

if it is believed that the complexity factors will decrease them. The person-months of effort obtained in this approach is assumed to be that for the total lifecycle development effort.

10.4.2 The Walston–Felix Model

The Walston–Felix [1977] model uses a size estimate adjusted by factors determined from the subjective answers to questions about 29 topics:

1. Customer interface complexity
2. User participation in the definition of requirements
3. Customer-originated program design changes
4. Customer experience with the application area of the project
5. Overall personnel experience and qualifications
6. Percentage of development programmers who participated in design of functional specifications
7. Previous experience with operational computer
8. Previous experience with programming languages
9. Previous experience with application of similar or greater size and complexity
10. Ratio of average staff size to project duration (people/months)
11. Hardware under concurrent development
12. Access to development computer open under special request
13. Access to development computer closed
14. Classified security environment for computer and at least 25% of programs and data
15. Use of structured programming
16. Use of design and code inspections
17. Use of top-down development
18. Use of chief programmer team
19. Overall complexity of code developed
20. Complexity of application processing
21. Complexity of program flow
22. Overall constraints on program design

23. Design constraints on program's main storage
24. Design constraints on program's timing
25. Code for real-time or interactive operation or executing under severe time constraint
26. Percentage of code for delivery
27. Code classified as nonmathematical application and I/O formatting programs
28. Number of classes of items in the database per 1000 lines of code delivered
29. Number of pages of delivered documentation per 1000 lines of delivered code

These process-related factors are quite specific. In the aggregate, they represent an attempt to measure understanding of the development environment, personnel qualifications, proposed hardware, and customer interface. Walston and Felix used these factors to supplement their basic equation with a productivity index. Using a large database of empirical values gathered from 60 projects in IBM's Federal Systems Division, they produced the foregoing list of 29 factors that can affect software productivity. Projects that were reviewed to determine parameters for the model varied from 4000 to 467,000 lines of code, were written in 28 different high-level languages on 66 computers, and represented from 12 to 11,758 person-months of effort. For each mean productivity value x_i calculated from the database, a composite productivity factor P was computed from

$$P = \sum_{i=1}^{29} w_i x_i$$

which is just a multiattribute utility theory (MAUT)-type calculation. The dimension associated with P is delivered source lines of code per program month. Here, the weights were set to reflect enhancing, inhibiting, or neutral support to productivity. The weight w_i is set equal to 1 if the variable x_i rating indicates increased productivity, 0 if the variable rating indicates nominal productivity, and -1 if the variable rating indicates decreased productivity. This productivity factor is used to modify the basic effort and schedule estimates. It is clear that the potentially large swings in productivity possible when weights swing from plus to minus one will make the resulting multipliers also change markedly.

The Walston–Felix [1977] model of software production effort that results is fundamentally based on the equation

$$C = 5.25 S^{0.91}$$

for effort, where S is the number of source lines of code, in thousands. Here, the lines of code variable S includes comments as long as they do not exceed 50% of the total lines in the program. At that point, no further lines of commentary are included in S. A similar equation is obtained for schedule, in terms of time to project completion

$$T = 2.47C^{0.35} = 4.1S^{0.35}$$

which is also obtained from a standard least-squares curve fit approach. The effort, or cost, C is estimated in person months of effort and the schedule in months. We note that this implicitly specifies the project workforce. Many of the models that we consider assume that there is a reasonable minimum development time and that it is very unwise to compress this. Other equations of interest in this model are

$$L = 0.54C^{0.06} = 0.96S^{0.055}$$

and

$$Z = 7.8C^{1.11} = 49S^{1.01}$$

where L and Z represent the staffing requirements in people and pages of documentation, respectively. The result that 49 pages of documentation, essentially, are required for every thousand lines of code is interesting.

We notice that the exponent for the term S in the Walston and Felix equation is less than 1. This implies economy of scale for software production and that the relative effort to produce a line of code will decrease as the number of lines of code increases. The notion of economies of scale for large projects is quite unsupported by available evidence, however. Just the opposite appears to be the case as large software projects increase the need for communications and interaction among the software team project members, and so effort and cost increase.

As an alternate to using all of these relations, the relations for project staffing, L and project duration, T may be estimated from a *historic baseline* using the productivity relation P and the 29 productivity factors noted at the beginning of this subsection. In terms of the nominal value of these and their deviation from smallest to largest values, these may be ordered as:

Factor Number	Nominal Value	Maximum Deviation
20	345	181
4	340	112
25	337	76
26	327	106
24	317	132
18	314	189

Factor Number	Nominal Value	Maximum Deviation
27	311	79
10	310	132
16	300	119
21	299	80
1	295	376
22	286	107
23	277	198
12	274	131
7	270	166
2	267	286
5	257	278
29	252	125
13	251	133
19	250	129
28	243	141
6	242	238
11	237	120
17	237	125
15	235	132
8	225	263
9	221	264
14	211	133
3	150	101

and so we see that the average or nominal productivity, in delivered source lines per person month, S/E is 7880. This is, of course, reflected in the equation for Z just noted.

10.4.3 The Putnam Resource Allocation Model

It is not unreasonable to postulate that development time will influence overall project effort and cost. Norden [1958] was perhaps the first to suggest a time sequencing of typical project effort. In investigating projects at IBM, he observed that the staffing of these research and development projects resembled a Rayleigh distribution, shown in Figure 10.5. Norden's observations were entirely empirical and it was only the shape of the Rayleigh curve that was of interest rather than any of its underlying theoretical and probabilistic constructs. The curves in Figure 10.5 are obtained from a Rayleigh differential equation for project *effort rate* $dy/dt = 2Kat \exp[-at^2]$. This is solved with the initial condition $y(0) = 0$ to obtain $y(t) = K(1 - \exp[-at^2])$. Here, it is presumed that $y(t)$ represents total person-months of effort.

Putnam [1978, 1980] uses Norden's observations for project effort expen-

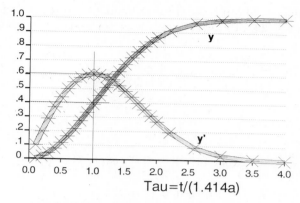

FIGURE 10.5   Rayleigh normalized solutions

ditures to develop a model of software costing. Putnam studied 50 projects from the Army Computer Systems Command and 150 other projects, thus developing one of the largest databases to support cost estimation. This *resource allocation* model includes several effort factors:

1. The volume of work
2. A difficulty gradient that measures complexity
3. A project technology factor that measures staff experience
4. Delivery time constraints

Putnam constructs a model for staffing that is based on:

1. Total cumulative staff
2. A project acceleration factor that measures how quickly the project can absorb new staff members
3. The number of 8-hour workdays in a project month

To derive the Putnam model, we use the Rayleigh differential equation and integrate it to yield $y(t)$ as the cumulative staff needed up to time t. If we set $dy^2(t)/dt^2 = 0$, and solve the resulting equation, we obtain values at which maximum effort rate occurs. In so doing, we easily obtain $a = 0.5\,t^{-2}$. At this value of time, which we may denote by $T = (2a)^{-0.5}$, the Rayleigh equation solution is the time where maximum project effort rate occurs. At this value, we obtain $y_{max}(t = T) = 0.3935K$. Each phase of development is assumed to have the general same type of curve with K different from phase to phase but with T representing the total project duration time.

Putnam is especially concerned with a *difficulty metric* defined by

$$D = K/T^2 = 2aK$$

that plays a major role in software development effort and cost. When we use the defined value of a, we obtain for the original Rayleigh equation

$$\frac{dy}{dt} = \left(\frac{K}{T^2}\right) t \exp\left[-0.5\left(\frac{t}{T}\right)^2\right] = Dt \exp\left[-0.5\left(\frac{t}{T}\right)^2\right]$$

and when we time scale by letting $\tau = t/T$, we obtain

$$\frac{dy}{d\tau} = K\tau \exp[-0.5\tau^2] = DT^2\tau \exp[-0.5\tau^2]$$

$$y(\tau) = K(1 - \exp[-0.5\tau^2]) = DT^2(1 - \exp[-0.5\tau^2])$$

From these relations, we see that we may now amplitude scale by letting $Y = Ky$. Then, the time and amplitude scaled functions expressing the proposed effort evolution over time

$$\frac{dY}{d\tau} = \tau \exp[-0.5\tau^2]$$

$$Y(\tau) = 1 - \exp[-0.5\tau^2]$$

are immutable over the many alterables that must surely be present in the milieu of activities associated with software development. We have illustrated these normalized values in Figure 10.5. We note that $Y_{max}(\tau) = 0.3945$ and $[dY(\tau)/d\tau]_{max} = 0.6065$ and that these occur at $\tau = 1$. There is, of course, some minor flexibility within the normalization of this in the sense that $y_{max}(t) = y(t = T) = KY(\tau = 1) = 0.3935DT^2$ and $[dy(t)/dt]_{max} = 0.6065DT$.

Rather than associating overall scope of a project with the value of $y(t)$ for very large time, which is $y(\infty) = DT^2$, it is not unreasonable to associate it with the ratio of the maximum effort rate to the time for peak effort rate. In a *simple scope* project, the peak effort rate is small and the time to peak can be large. For a *complex* or *large scope* project, the peak effort rate is large and the time allowed before the peak buildup occurs is small. However, $[dy(t)/dt]_{max} = 0.6065DT$ and thus we see that project complexity is directly proportional to D.

Putnam appears to use a rationale such as this and postulates that D is small for *easy* development systems. Likewise, for systems that are hard to develop, D is large.

There are other fundamentally useful relations. It is often stated that *the average software project productivity is defined to be the number of source lines of code per peak person month of overall effort for the entire project* or

$$P = \frac{S}{C}$$

and it is further postulated by Putnam that productivity is proportional to the difficulty metric

$$P = \phi \, D^{\mu} = \frac{S}{C}$$

Using nonlinear regression, Putnam determined from an analysis of 50 army projects that

$$P = \phi \, D^{-2/3}$$

where P is a measure of productivity. In general, this relationship may be written as

$$S = \phi \, K^{1/3} T^{4/3}$$

where S is measured in thousands of lines of code and ϕ is a technology factor reflecting hardware constraints, program complexity, personnel experience levels, and the programming environment extant.

Putnam calls ϕ a *technology factor*. He proposes 20 discrete values for ϕ, ranging from 610 to 57,314. In this model, K is expressed in programmer-years and T in years. Alternatively, the technology factor can be identified on the basis of historical data for a particular organization.

The name given by Putnam to the latter versions of this model is *Software LIfecycle Methodology* (SLIM). It, like the other models studied here, is basically a macro-level model that is based on a combination of expertise and statistical computations. The model is fundamentally, like the other models, a static model. The use of a differential equation for project life does allow computation of project life in terms of other variables, however, and in this very restricted sense it is a dynamic model.

This model could be used effectively for predictive purposes if we had a suitable algorithm that we might use to predict the value of ϕ for a software project. Unfortunately, such a relationship does not exist at this time. In addition, there appears no truly formal theory that suggests use of the Rayleigh differential equation as a model for project buildup and dimunition over time. As we have noted, there is very little freedom associated with the evolution over time of this relation. It seemingly does not allow, for example, much increased attention to be devoted during the requirements phase of a project in the hope that this would result in much lower costs during the operational implementation and maintenance phases of the project.

If we solve the foregoing equation for cumulative project effort, we obtain

$$K = \left(\frac{S}{\phi}\right)^{3} T^{-4}$$

which implies that *cumulative project effort varies inversely as the fourth power of time to peak project development* if we can somehow believe that the technology factor, ϕ varies linearly with the number of source lines of code. It is, of course, very reasonable to believe that significant compression of project schedules will bring about major problems.

A potential advantage to the Putnam model is that there is an explicit trade-off, in the form of the foregoing equation, between total development effort K and total development time T.

A number of potentially useful user-specified functions are provided in the SLIM model. These include *calibration*, to enable productivity measurements; *build*, to define a new software development effort; *estimate*, to identify minimal development time and costs for a development effort; *what if*, to specify development parameters for a fixed cost for development effort; *management constraints*, to enable trade-offs among costs and parameter changes; *implementation functions*, to define requirements and lifecycle staffing; *development program management parameters;* and *documentation*.

To accomplish all this, the SLIM model necessarily requires much input information. This is classified in three sections and includes:

Section I:

Calibration
> Development effort (worker-months)
> Development time (months)
> System name
> System size (source statements)

Section 2:

New System Information
> Fully burdened labor rate ($/worker-year)
> Function name for each module
> Inflation rate (decimal fraction)
> Largest possible number of source statements for each module
> Level of system
> Most likely number of source statements for each module
> Overall personnel skills
> Personnel experience with programming language(s)
> Personnel experience with system of similar size and application
> Primary development language
> Project start date
> Proportion of development computer capacity used for other production work
> Proportion of development computer dedicated to effort

Proportion of development in on-line, interactive mode

Proportion of memory of target machine utilized by the software system

Proportion of real-time code

Proportion of system coded in a higher-order language

Smallest possible number of source statements for each module

Standard deviation of the labor rate

System name

Technology factor

Type of system

Use of chief programmer teams (yes or no)

Use of design and code inspection (yes or no)

Use of structured programming (yes or no)

Use of top-down development (yes or no)

Section 3:

Constraints and Options

Criteria for optimization (e.g., design to cost)

Desired mean time to failure

Level of acceptable risk

Maximum allowable development cost (dollars)

Maximum development time (months)

Minimum and maximum number of people at peak staffing time

Output request (e.g., for graphic displays or Gantt charts)

Request for trade-off analysis

There are corresponding outputs. The model provides the calibration used, in terms of the technology factor, and the "*minimum time*" solution, resulting from some use of linear programming algorithms. Associated with this is an estimate of the standard deviation of each computer variable. There are a large number of output options, including Gantt charts, displays of major milestones, graphical displays of some aspects of the linear programming solutions, estimated code production per month, and outputs for other optimization criteria

An investigation of the accuracy of SLIM by the Purdue Software Metrics Research Group [Conte et al. 1986] indicates that the model exaggerates the effect of schedule compression on development. Another potential problem evolves from such heavy reliance on the project lines of code and development time characteristics. The value of ϕ should also reflect a great many other factors. To use the model, the software systems engineer must be able to supply or otherwise obtain a technology factor, ϕ, ranging from 0 to 22. The cumulative effort estimate is very sensitive to the choice of ϕ, especially since this term is cubed in the foregoing equation. A 25% error in ϕ will produce a 100% error in the estimate of K. This extreme sensitivity would seem quite bothersome. Kemerer [1987] has also performed an evaluation of the SLIM model, as well as several others.

Parr [1980] has suggested a variation of the SLIM model. It is based on the observation that, on many projects, the staff is already familiar with the project's tools, requirements, and methods and is ready to work. Thus, the work rate can begin at some positive point on the work axis, rather than at the origin as required through use of the Rayleigh equation. Both the Parr and Putnam models include maintenance, and other effort-consuming activities over the development lifecycle. In other words, they reflect staffing needs over the entire development lifecycle, as we have noted.

A potential need in Putnam's model is the ability to accommodate reusable code. Londeix [1987] proposes a modification to SLIM that will adjust for software reuse. He considers two cases:

1. Reuse without any change to the existing reused source code
2. Reuse involving change of this code

This model is quite new, and there is no empirical evidence to judge its validity, although there is every reason to expect that its performance should be similar to that of the basic Putnam model.

Jensen [1984] has proposed a variation to Putnam's SLIM model. Because the Putnam model is so sensitive to performance schedule compression, Jensen suggested a modification that uses an equation with an effective technology constant calculated differently from Putnam's original one. The suggested modification is the equation

$$S = \phi T K^{0.5}$$

where the constant ϕ is an effective technology factor that is similar to but calculated differently from Putnam's technology constant. Jensen described a basic technology factor, Φ, and 13 environmental adjustment factors, ϵ_i that modify this

$$\phi = \prod_{i=1}^{13} \epsilon_i$$

These environment adjustment factors are similar to those defined by Boehm for use in the COCOMO model that we shall soon discuss. The adjustment factors include aspects of the project involving project personnel, computers system used, and the nature of the using organization.

10.4.4 The Constructive Cost Model (COCOMO)

Barry Boehm [1981] of TRW has been intimately involved
software engineering, and especially involved in developing aₙₐ ⸱⸱
COnstructive COst MOdel (COCOMO) and associated database. The
model—actually models as there are three fundamental models involved—
was derived from a database of 63 projects that were active during the period
1964 to 1979. The database includes programs written in FORTRAN,
COBOL, PL/1, Jovial, and assembly language. They range in length from
2,000 to 1,000,000 lines of code, exclusive of comments). The COCOMO
database is more heterogeneous than most that have been used for software
cost projection, incorporating business, scientific, and supervisory control
software. In addition to estimating effort, COCOMO includes formulae for
predicting development time and schedule and a breakdown of effort by phase
and activity. This is a very extensive and thoroughly investigated model to
which much serious thought has been applied. Thus, it is appropriate for some
detailed comments.

There are three COCOMO levels, depending on the detail included in the
estimate: basic, intermediate, and detailed. As such, the COCOMO model
is a composite model that incorporates some wholistic expert judgment features and some heuristic rules, and also allows for some formal based
reasoning.

Each form of the COCOMO model uses a development effort estimate of
the form

$$C = a_i \, S^{\delta i} M(\mathbf{x})$$

where $M(\mathbf{x})$ represents an adjustment multiplier. It is a composite function
of 15 cost-drivers x_1 through x_{15}. The values a and δ *are not* obtained from
least-squares regression, as with many of the other cost estimation models.
Boehm incorporates his own experience, the subjective opinion of other software managers, the results from use of other cost estimation models, and
trial and error, in order to identify the structural relations as well as the
parameters within the structure. His initial parameters were fine-tuned using
the TRW database. Thus, COCOMO is a composite model, basically combining experiential observations and wisdom together with statistical rule-
based adjustments.

The parameters a and δ depend on what Boehm calls the *development
mode of a project.* He labels a project as belonging to an organic, embedded,
or semidetached mode, depending on the project's independence from other
systems:

1. The *organic mode* refers to the mode typically associated with relatively
   small programs that generally require relatively little innovation. They
   usually have relaxed delivery requirements and a stable in-house de-

velopment environment. The external environment is generally also stable. An organic software development program can often almost run by itself, and will never require extraordinary systems management and technical direction efforts.

2. An *embedded mode* program is relatively large and has substantial operating constraints. There is usually a high degree of complexity involved in the hardware to be used as well as in the customer interfaces whose requirements need to be incorporated into the software development program. Often, the requirements for the to-be-delivered *embedded software* are exacting, and there is generally a need for innovative design in typically one-of-a-kind programs that have not been done before and which will likely not be repeated.

3. A *semidetached program* has requirements and development characteristics that lie somewhere between organic and embedded.

The a and δ parameters for the basic and intermediate COCOMO model are presented in Table 10.5.

In the *basic COCOMO* model, the cost driver or adjustment multiplier, $M(\mathbf{x}) = 1$ for all x_i. For the *intermediate COCOMO*, the adjustment multiplier is calculated as the product of individual cost drivers:

$$M(\mathbf{x}) = \prod_{i=1}^{15} m(x_i)$$

The cost-drivers are grouped into four categories, as shown in Table 10.6.

Each of the 15 categories illustrated in Table 10.6 is associated with an appropriate multiplier factor $m(x_i)$. In the basic COCOMO, each cost factor $m(x_i)$ is assumed to be equal to 1; and so each of the adjustment multipliers are equal to 1. In the intermediate and detailed COCOMO models, the cost factors $m(x_i)$ vary as a function of the values for the various cost-drivers. For each category, a scale of five or six values is used to represent the possible choices for each category. For many of the cost-drivers, values were obtained for the COCOMO database using the classical Delphi technique. Reliability cost, for example, can be rated from very low to very high, as shown in Table 10.7. There is, in effect, a table like this for each of the 15 cost-drivers in the

Table 10.5 COCOMO Parameters for Basic and Intermediate Models

Mode	Basic		Intermediate	
	a	δ	a	δ
Organic	2.4	1.05	3.2	1.05
Semidetached	3.0	1.12	3.0	1.12
Embedded	3.6	1.20	2.8	1.20

Table 10.6   Intermediate-Level COCOMO Cost-Drivers

Product Attributes

CPLX	Complexity of the system
DATA	Size of the databases
RELY	Required software reliability

Computer Attributes

STOR	Storage constraints
TIME	Execution time constraints
TURN	Computer turnaround (response) time
VIRT	Virtual machine volatility

Personnel Attributes

ACAP	Capability of the analysts
AEXP	Applications experience
LEXP	Programming language experience
PCAP	Capability of the programmers
VEXP	Virtual machine experience

Project Attributes

MODP	Use of modern programming practices
SCED	Existence of required development schedule
TOOL	Use of software development tools

Table 10.7   Reliability Categories and Multipliers (RELY)

Tolerance	Effect	Multiplier
Very low	Slight inconvenience	0.75
Low	Losses easily recovered	0.88
Nominal	Moderate difficulty in recovery	1.00
High	High financial loss	1.15
Very high	Risk to human life	1.40

database. A complete list of the specific parameters associated with each of the normal 15 cost-driver factors is exhibited in Table 10.8.

There are actually two levels now in *intermediate COCOMO* as the result of a recent modification that allows one to consider *requirements volatility*, which is interpreted to mean the tendency for requirements to change after they have been initially identified and the software is in some phase of the development lifecycle.

The first *intermediate COCOMO 1* model or level is restricted to the cost-drivers listed in Table 10.8. *Intermediate COCOMO 2* includes an additional

Table 10.8   Cost-Drivers for COCOMO Function Multipliers

Cost-Driver	Very Low	Low	Nominal	High	Very High	Extrahigh
			Product			
CPLX	0.70	0.85	1.00	1.15	1.30	1.65
DATA		0.94	1.00	1.08	1.16	
RELY	0.75	0.88	1.00	1.15	1.40	
			Computer			
STOR			1.00	1.06	1.21	1.56
TIME			1.00	1.11	1.30	1.66
TURN		0.87	1.00	1.07	1.15	
VIRT		0.87	1.00	1.15	1.30	
			Personnel			
ACAP	1.46	1.19	1.00	0.86	0.71	
AEXP	1.29	1.13	1.00	0.91	0.82	
LEXP	1.14	1.07	1.00	0.95		
PCAP	1.42	1.17	1.00	0.86	0.70	
VEXP	1.21	1.10	1.00	0.90		
			Project			
MODP	1.24	1.10	1.00	0.91	0.82	
SCED	1.23	1.08	1.00	1.04	1.10	
TOOL	1.24	1.10	1.00	0.91	0.83	

driver for requirements volatility, with values ranging from a low of 0.91 to a high of 1.62. Table 10.9 presents the effort multipliers for requirements volatility.

While COCOMO does include many of the cost-drivers affecting software cost, effort, and productivity, not everything is included. Among these non-included factors are personnel continuity, management quality, customer interface quality, and documentation quality and quantity. This does not mean that these factors are necessarily neglected; only that they are assumed to be at some nominal values.

The *detailed COCOMO* model adds refinements not included in the basic or intermediate COCOMO model. Detailed COCOMO introduces two more components to the model. *Phase-sensitive effort multipliers* are included in order to reflect the fact that some phases of the software development lifecycle are more affected than others by the cost-driver factors. This phase distribution of effort augmentation is the primary change over intermediate CO-COMO. It provides a basis for detailed project planning in order to complete the software development program across all of the lifecycle phases.

In addition, a three-level product hierarchy is employed, so that cost-driver

Table 10.9   Effort Multipliers for Requirements Volatility (RQTV)

Tolerance	Effect	Multiplier
Low	Essentially none	0.91
Nominal	Small, noncritical redirection	1.00
High	Occasional, moderate redirection	1.19
Very high	Frequent moderate, or occasionally major redirections	1.38
Extrahigh	Frequent major redirection	1.62

ratings are supplied for modules, subsystems, and the entire system. These ratings are used at the level at which each attribute is most susceptible to variation.

To illustrate the phase sensitivity of detailed COCOMO, Boehm [1981] considered a hypothetical project whose cost-drivers were all chosen in order to provide the highest possible fraction of project effort in the system integration and testing phase of the lifecycle. We have:

ACAP	Capability of the analysts	Very low
AEXP	Applications experience	Very high
CPLX	Complexity of the system	Nominal
DATA	Size of the databases	Very high
LEXP	Programming language experience	Very low
MODP	Use of modern programming practices	Very low
PCAP	Capability of the programmers	Very low
RELY	Required software reliability	Very high
SCED	Existence of required development schedule	Very low
STOR	Storage constraints	Extrahigh
TIME	Execution time constraints	Extrahigh
TOOL	Use of software development tools	Very low
TURN	Computer turnaround (response) time	Very high
VEXP	Virtual machine experience	Very low
VIRT	Virtual machine volatility	Very high

Suppose that it turns out that the nominal distribution of 100% effort across four phases of development is:

Product design	18%
Detailed design	26%
Coding and unit testing	28%
Integrate and testing	28%

The cost-driver ratings can be used to modify the nominal efforts by incorporating the effect of these extreme ratings. Doing this results in:

Product design	2%

Detailed design		7%
Coding and unit testing		18%
Integrate and testing		73%

which indicates that much more effort is needed in the system integration and testing portions of the effort than in the nominal effort for development of software of the general class considered, as predicted by basic COCOMO.

It is interesting to obtain these results. From Table 10.8, we have for the various effort multipliers

ACAP	Very low	1.46
AEXP	Very high	0.82
CPLX	Nominal	1.00
DATA	Very high	1.16
LEXP	Very low	1.14
MODP	Very low	1.24
PCAP	Very low	1.42
RELY	Very high	1.40
SCED	Very low	1.23
STOR	Extrahigh	1.56
TIME	Extrahigh	1.66
TOOL	Very low	1.24
TURN	Very high	1.15
VEXP	Very low	1.21
VIRT	Very high	1.30

and we desire to use these to determine effort distribution across phases of the lifecycle. We will consider the utility of the COCOMO models in general, and will then return to this specific example, although we will not present all of the detailed matrices that will enable us to obtain the stated results.

Let us describe the use of the intermediate COCOMO model in some detail. The steps given here can be shortened such that they are applicable to the basic COCOMO model. Extension to the detailed COCOMO model will then be briefly described. The intermediate COCOMO model estimates the effort and cost of a proposed software development in the following manner:

1. A *nominal development effort* is estimated as a function of software product size S in thousands of delivered source lines of instructions. To make this calculation, we use the basic COCOMO effort determination equation $C = a^i S^{\delta}{}_i$ where a and δ are as given in Table 10.5.

2. A set of *effort multipliers* are determined from the rating of the software product on the set of 15 cost-driver attributes that we have described in Table 10.8. Each of the 15 cost-drivers have a rating scale and a set of effort multipliers that indicates the amount by which the nominal

estimate needs to be multiplied in order to accommodate the additional or reduced demands associated with these cost-drivers.

3. The *actual estimated development effort* is determined by multiplying the nominal development effort estimate by all of the software product effort multipliers. For a specific software development project, we compute the product of all the effort multipliers for the 15 cost-driver attributes. The resulting estimated effort for the entire project is the product of all of these terms times the nominal effort determined in step 1.

4. Additional factors are then used to obtain more disaggregate elements of interest from the development effort estimate, such as dollar costs, development schedule, phase and activity distribution, and annual maintenance costs. In addition to computing effort C in terms of person-months of effort, it is often desired to obtain the *development schedule* in months in terms of either the number of lines of code or the total person-months of effort. This turns out to be given by $T = b_i \, C^\epsilon$ where b and ϵ are also given numerical values, for the three software modes, as shown in Table 10.10.

The *detailed COCOMO model* also adjusts the estimate for software cost and effort when it is developed, in part, from existing code. The adjustment is made at the module level, and each module is evaluated to determine how much code will be used without modification and how much will be modified. If D is the percentage of the design to be modified, B the percentage of code to be modified, and I the percentage of code to be integrated without modification, then an adjustment factor F is calculated to be

$$F = 0.4D + 0.3C + 0.3I$$

The size of each module is adjusted according to the formula

$$S_i^a = \frac{S_i F}{100}$$

where the S_i represent the number of (thousands of) source lines of code for the ith module.

Table 10.10 COCOMO Effort and Schedule Parameters for the Intermediate Model

Mode	Parameter			
	b	ϵ	a	δ
Organic	2.5	0.38	3.2	1.05
Semidetached	2.5	0.35	3.0	1.12
Embedded	2.5	0.32	2.8	1.20

Multipliers have been developed that can be applied to the total project effort C and total project schedule completion time T in order to allocate effort and schedule components to each phase in the lifecycle of a software development program. There are assumed to be five distinct lifecycle phases, and the effort and schedule for each phase are assumed to be given in terms of the overall effort and schedule by

$$C_p = \mu_p C$$

$$T_p = \tau_p T$$

where μ_p and τ_p are as given in Table 10.11. There exist more sophisticated versions of this development that result in multipliers μ_p and τ_p that not only depend on the particular phase of the lifecycle and mode of operation of the software but also contain the correction terms for the 15 attributes shown in

Table 10.11   Effort and Schedule Fractions Occurring in Each Phase of the Lifecycle

Mode and Code Size	Plan and Requirements	Systems Design	Detail Design	Module Code and Test	Integrate and Test
		Lifecycle Phase Value of μ_p			
Organic small ($S \approx 2$)	0.06	0.16	0.26	0.42	0.16
Organic medium ($S \approx 32$)	0.06	0.16	0.24	0.38	0.22
Semidetached medium ($S \approx 32$)	0.07	0.17	0.25	0.33	0.25
Semidetached large ($S \approx 128$)	0.07	0.17	0.24	0.31	0.28
Embedded large ($S \approx 128$)	0.08	0.18	0.25	0.26	0.31
Embedded extralarge ($S \approx 320$)	0.08	0.18	0.24	0.24	0.34
		Lifecycle Phase Value of τ_p			
Organic small ($S \approx 2$)	0.10	0.19	0.24	0.39	0.18
Organic medium ($S \approx 32$)	0.12	0.19	0.21	0.34	0.26
Semidetached medium ($S \approx 32$)	0.20	0.26	0.21	0.27	0.26
Semidetached large ($S \approx 128$)	0.22	0.27	0.19	0.25	0.29
Embedded large ($S \approx 128$)	0.36	0.36	0.18	0.18	0.28
Embedded extralarge ($S \approx 320$)	0.40	0.38	0.16	0.16	0.30

Tables 10.6 and 10.7. In the example that we considered earlier, these multipliers would have to be used to obtain the final results shown for the example.

To obtain this, we need to take each of the 15 multipliers and disaggregate them by phase in the lifecycle and by their complexity rating. Boehm's text provides a detailed set of tables for this purpose. A new disaggregartion that results in module-level effort multipliers and subsystem-level effort multipliers is defined. The variables CPLX, PCAP, VEXP, and LEXP, from our present listing, constitute the module-level effort multipliers. The other 11 multipliers represent the subsystem-level effort multipliers. A lifecycle of four phases is used to define the matrix that is filled in to result in the various effort multipliers across phases. These are just the five phases used in Table 10.11:

1. Requirements and product design (RPD)
   a. Plans and requirements
   b. System design
2. Detailed design (DD)
   a. Detailed design
3. Code and unit test (CUT)
   a. Module code and test
4. Integrate and test (IT)
   a. Integrate and test

with the aggregation of the plans and requirements phase with the system design phase, the more conceptual portions of the lifecycle, into a single phase called *requirements and product design*. Figure 10.6 indicates how the multipliers for applications experience of the software team, AEXP, varies across the resulting four phases and as a result of the rating of this important factor. We need 15 curves of this sort, or equivalent tables, to convert this phase

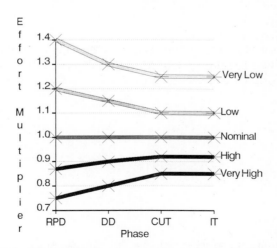

FIGURE 10.6   Effort multipliers across phases for applications experience

effort information for the detailed COCOMO model. This information may then be used to determine the results we indicated for our earlier prototypical example of use of the detailed COCOMO model.

10.4.5   Other Models

There are a number of other models of software development effort prediction. We will provide an overview of some of these.

Halstead [1977], known for his early research in measuring the characteristics of software, has developed a *software science* model. In particular, by counting the number of operators and operands in a module, Halstead proposes metrics to measure the complexity of the module. He extends this "software science" approach to effort estimation by postulating that the more complex a project, the more effort is needed. Unlike other models that describe the cost factors involved in the design, code, test, and delivery of a system, Halstead also includes the specifications of the system in his measurement.

Halstead makes two major assumptions regarding the software being developed: (1) there is a complete and unambiguous statement of the algorithm to be implemented in the module under consideration; and (2) the programmer assigned to write the code is fluent in the implementation language, will work alone, and will have a high degree of concentration (i.e., without interruptions). Clearly, many of Halstead's assumptions will often be violated, especially on large projects.

The basis of Halstead's model is as follows. We define n as the number of unique operators and operands in a module and N as the total number of operators and operands. The Halstead software science method begins by estimating the project size S. Then, N is calculated to be

$$N = k S$$

where k is a constant that signifies the average number of operators and operands per line of code for a particular language. For example, k is approximately 7 for FORTRAN and 5 for PL/1. Next, n is computed by using the formula

$$N = n \log_2\left(\frac{n}{2}\right)$$

and the effort projection is

$$C = 0.25 \; N^2 \log_2 n$$

Halstead's estimate of effort is entirely dependent on the size estimate and indirectly on the number of operators and operands in the software. One problem with an approach of this sort is that we seldom know the various terms needed in the effort projection equation until too late in the development of software. Nevertheless, this early work was very useful in introducing metrics into computer science and engineering.

Tausworthe [1979] has studied an interactive model, *Softcost*, which is a composite model that combines six productivity adjustment factors from a model developed by General Research Corporation [Carriere and Thibodeau, 1979], 29 factors from the Walston–Felix model, and a modified Rayleigh–Putnam curve. The resulting model contains 68 parameters that are generated from the answers to 47 questions posed to the user. Softcost is essentially a combination of estimators, and it is not clear how these models relate to one another to produce an effort estimate. At best, it seems unnecessarily complicated. Moreover, the technique of combining the three models or, more correctly, factors from three models does not take into account any overlap and lack of exclusivity in them. The possible redundancy among elements of the resulting model may require substantial calibration and adjustment effort.

Almost all software cost and effort estimation models use program size as the dominant driving factor that influences needed effort. Other factors are often used to *tune* the results of a basic computation that uses primarily program size in estimating effort. None of the approaches that we have examined thus far has included the size of the project team as a major component. A model that handles both program size and project team size factors must take into account not only the complexity of the software, in terms of the size estimate, but also the complexity of the interactions among the project team members.

The *cooperative programming model* (COPMO) [Thebaut and Shen, 1984] incorporates both software size and software development staff size by expressing effort in terms of team interactions. Effort is defined as

$$C = C_1(S) + C_2(W)$$

where C is overall effort, $C_1(S)$ is the effort required by one or more people working independently on module development who require no interaction with other modules, $C_2(W)$ is the effort required to coordinate the development process with other software development team members, and W is the average number of staff assigned to software program development.

Additional relations suggested by the modelers are

$$C_1(S) = a + b\,S$$

$$E_2(W) = c\,W^d$$

These equations are not especially different from the effort estimation equations used in the other models that we have studied. The value of d can be inferred to represent the amount of coordination, management, and communication needed on a project. Similarly, c is a measure of the weakness of the communication paths among the individuals working on the software effort.

COPMO is based on the mean values of measured project characteristics, so it may not be useful for projects whose complexity differ substantially from one another. Conte et al. [1986] have extended the COPMO model to a more generalized one that includes several effort complexity classes EC_i. These complexity classes can be determined in several ways. No matter which way is chosen, the classes have to be ordered, so that a project in EC_i will necessarily be of lower complexity than one in EC_{i+1}. One way to assign the classes is to categorize software projects in terms of productivity, assuming that the more complex a project is, the less productive is the staff working to develop it, according to the conventional definition of productivity. The Purdue Software Metrics Research Group [Conte et al., 1986] defined complexity classes in terms of the software productivity attributes enumerated in Boehm's COCOMO model. The group also suggested a method for estimating the average staffing W. This method is based on the fact that project maximum time duration is usually constrained by the customer, and bounded from below by the minimum time in which the project can be developed.

10.5 VALIDATION OF SOFTWARE EFFORT AND COST MODELS

The accuracy of the estimators generated by software effort and cost models can be considered a test of how well the models reflects the actual relationships among the cost and effort factors that effect development. We should be able to demonstrate that a proposed model of the software development process is valid, that is, that it accurately portrays the interactions among the components of the process. One way of doing this, perhaps the only scientific way, is to demonstrate that the metrics and the predicted results stemming from the model are valid. In particular, we validate an effort–cost model by comparing the estimated effort–cost predicted to occur with the actual cost, and examining and explaining the differences.

Validation of models is necessarily an empirical effort since a model is generally a hypothetical description of what is believed to be a real-world process. The creator of a process model usually begins with a theory of how the functional elements in the process relate to one another. This theoretical framework is used to express the relationships among the process elements in a formal way, usually as an equation, an algorithm, or a diagram of some kind. A verbal or semantic framework is acceptable for a model also. We may express ideas in terms of words, mathematics, and graphics; a model is just an *idea*.

Simulation and *modeling methods* are based on the conceptualization and use of an abstraction, one that hopefully behaves in a similar way as the real system or process. Impacts of policy alternatives are studied through use of the model, something that often cannot easily be done through experimentation with the real system. Models are, of necessity, dependent on the value system and the rationale for utilization of a model. We want to be able to determine the correctness of predictions based on usage of a model and thus be able to validate the model. Given the definition of a problem, a value system, and a set of proposed alternative courses of action we wish to be able to design a model consisting of relevant elements of these three sets and to determine the results of implementing proposed policies.

There are three essential steps in constructing a model, as we have previously noted:

1. Determine those issue formulation elements that are most relevant to a particular issue, problem, or need.
2. Determine the structural relationships among these elements.
3. Determine parametric coefficients within the structure.

We should interpret the word "model" here as an abstract generalization of an object or system. Any set of rules and relationships that describes something is a model, or *idea* of that thing.

When we model systems or processes, we enhance our abilities to comprehend their nuances, and to understand their interrelationships and our relationship to them. The engineering sciences have made contributions toward the improvement of clarity in modeling. A typical result of a systems engineering model is the opportunity to see a system from several viewpoints and perspectives such as economic, technical, political, and environmental. A system model may be viewed as a physical arrangement, as a causal flow diagram, and/or as a set of actions and consequences that can be depicted graphically through time, perhaps in a decision tree structure, as a simplified picture of reality. Developments and improvements in the methodology of modeling have become more important as systems have become more complex.

A model is generally based on both theory and data. Emphasis is placed on specification of structural relations, based upon software production theory, and the identification of unknown parameters, using available data, in the behavioral equations. Sadly, the state of the development of a theory of software productivity is not well advanced. The postulation of a model should always be followed by a collection of empirical evidence that might be used to demonstrate that the model is correct. Once the model is completely defined, additional statistics are generated from the database and used to compare predicted values with actual results.

If the statistics compare the *model generating database,* or database used to develop the model initially, with the model, the model is said to be undergoing *internal validation.* If the model is tested with data other than those from which the model was derived, we say that the model is undergoing *external validation.* In either case, the database used to test a model is called a *validating database.*

Most models can be expressed as a relationship between a dependent variable y and a corresponding set of independent variables. Often, this can be expressed as

$$y_1 = f_1(x_1, x_2, \ldots, x_k)$$
$$y_2 = f_2(x_1, x_2, \ldots, x_k)$$

.

.

.

$$y_k = f_k(x_1, x_2, \ldots, x_k)$$

or in equivalent state vector form

$$\mathbf{y} = \mathbf{f(x)}$$

for some k independent variables. Thus, the model acts as a predictor of $\mathbf{y}$ based on the values of $\mathbf{x}$. In an ideal situation, a metric is available for each independent variable, so that the value of each x_i can be determined. Unfortunately, quantitative objective metrics are not always available, and the values of the x_i will often have to depend on the subjective judgment of experts.

To model software systems program development cost, effort is the usual dependent variable. A determination of program cost is then obtained by the simple act of multiplying the predicted effort by the value of a unit of effort. For example, if effort is measured in person-months, then cost is the product of the number of person-months and the monthly salary of the average employee. In our discussion to follow, predicted effort will be denoted by $\hat{C}$, while actual effort will be denoted by C. The validating database may include historical data about n projects. Each project will have a predicted value of effort, $\hat{C}_i$, and an actual value, C_i, where i ranges from 1 to n.

Often, we want to test the degree to which the estimate and actual values are linearly related. The coefficient of multiple determination, which is also the square of the correlation coefficient, provides this and is defined by

$$R^2 = 1 - \frac{\sum_{i=1}^{n} (C_i - \hat{C}_i)^2}{\sum_{i=1}^{n} (C_i - \overline{C})^2}$$

where $\overline{C}$ is the mean of the values of C_i across the software projects of the particular type being considered:

$$\overline{C} = \frac{1}{n} \sum_{i=1}^{n} C_i$$

The coefficient of multiple determination must always be less than or equal to 1. If the estimated values are close to the actual values, the term resulting from the sum in the numerator will be small. For a perfect estimate, this term would be zero. When this term is very small, the estimator is quite accurate, and the value of R^2 is close to 1. When multiple regression analysis is used to determine the parameters, then it is possible to associate this coefficient of multiple determination with the percentage of the variance that is accounted for by the independent variables used for the analysis. A large value suggests that inclusion of additional structural parameters is unlikely to provide much improvement in model accuracy.

Another way to determine the validity of a model is to examine the *relative error* (RE) defined as

$$\text{RE} = \frac{C - \hat{C}T}{C}$$

For a set of n projects, the *average relative error* $(\overline{RE})$ is thus

$$\overline{\text{RE}} = \frac{1}{n} \sum_{i=1}^{n} \overline{\text{RE}}_i$$

If a model is a relatively good predictor of actual effort, the values of C and $\hat{C}$ for the specific software program undergoing analysis should be essentially the same. This will lead to a small relative error for the particular program in question, and a small average relative error for like programs when we average over an ensemble of them. However, the converse is not always true. A small average relative error may be the result of the canceling of large individual relative errors that are of different sign.

To make these measures more useful, we might consider the absolute value of the relative error, called the *magnitude of relative error* (MRE$_i$) for the ith project:

$$\text{MRE}_i = |\text{RE}_i| = \left| 1 - \frac{\hat{C}_i}{C_i} \right|$$

The MRE is an indicator of the quality of the prediction; a small MRE means the effort or cost prediction is good, while a large value of MRE means that the prediction is bad.

We can continue on with this. For example, we can calculate the *mean magnitude of relative error* (MMRE) for a set of n data points:

$$\overline{\mathrm{MRE}} = \frac{1}{n} \sum_{i=1}^{n} \mathrm{MRE}_i = \mathrm{MMRE}$$

A small MMRE indicates that, on the average, the model is a good predictor of the actual effort that resulted. In much work in this area, a model is considered to be acceptable if it has an MMRE of 0.25 or less.

Another figure of merit often calculated for software cost and effort models is an indicator of how many of the predicted values fall within a given range of the actual value. Suppose that the values of C_i and $\hat{C}_i$ are compared for each of n projects. If k of the n projects have a magnitude of relative error (MRE) of $j/100$ or less, then we write $\mathrm{PRED}(j) = k/n$. This means that k/n of the predicted effort values fall within j percent of their actual value. Often a software cost and effort model is considered to be acceptable if $\mathrm{PRED}(0.25) \geq 0.75$. In other words, we say that an estimate is reasonable if 75% of the predictions are within 25% of the actual value.

The validation of software cost models is difficult because the amount of data to be collected for a validating database is generally very large. To confirm that a model is applicable to a wide variety of situations, such a database must include measures from a large number of development environments. Even here, validation may overlook a fundamental difficulty. The usual situation is that we take an already completed project, determine the number of lines of delivered source code, and then apply the model to the number of lines of code, and other factors needed by the model. The major problem here is that we do not really know how many lines of code are needed in a to-be-developed project in order to complete the development. In using data from previous projects, we do know the number of lines of code that were needed to deliver the software product.

In general, none of these models assist in making an estimate of the number of delivered lines of source code. Usually, the correct *number of lines is used in the retrospective studies and evaluations that have been made.* A very significant question is: *What do we do if we need to estimate the number of lines of source code to be delivered,* as generally we always must, *and do not have a good way to do this.* Sadly, most contemporary software costing models are very silent on this point.

Even so, the statistics obtained for many of the models are disappointing even when there is no error in estimating the number of lines of code. However, it is important to remember the degree of subjectivity involved in each model and the extent to which this subjectivity can affect the validity of the estimate. In some cases, the inaccuracy of an estimate may be the result of requirements volatility and not an inadequate representation of relationships in the theoretical model. Thus, the improvement of a model may require not only a reexamination of the formula or algorithm but also a reevaluation of the way in which each independent variable is measured, the way in which lines of delivered code are estimated, and the very important influence of the volatility of the user environment and associated requirements.

Very significant changes in the structural models used for software cost estimation may be desired, as a result of this examination. *Perhaps, for example, lines of code should not be the central focal point for costing efforts!*

In concluding this discussion of validation, we remark that cost models hold potentially great promise, not only in providing accurate estimates of effort and cost but also in assisting us in identifying and understanding those factors that have the largest potential for improving software productivity. The fact that some existing models may yield disappointingly inaccurate predictions of effort and cost is only an indication of the need for higher-quality analytical, behavioral, and empirical research in this area.

10.7 SUMMARY

In this chapter, we have examined the costs and benefits of software. Most of our efforts concerned costing, although we did provide some comments concerning valuation. In this section, we will provide some summary guidelines for software valuation, including both costs and benefits. In the very early parts of this chapter, we noted that there are three fundamental ways in which we can go about determining the costs and the benefits of a product or service: wholistic, heuristic, and holistic. Further, we can take a structural, a functional, or a purposeful perspective relative to the way in which we go about gathering information for valuation. Obviously, there can be combinations of these.

Modeling and estimation of software effort and costs is a relatively new endeavor. Most are validated from databases of cost factors that reflect a particular user and developer organizations characteristics. Such models are useful when developer organizations are stable and continue to produce systems similar to those developed in the past for users who have similarly stable environments and needs. However, models have little utility if the mixture of personnel experience or expertise changes or if the development organization attempts to develop a new type of system or a user organization specifies a new system type.

It would be desirable to build models that are independent of either user or developer organization, so that the models can be transported to other development teams and user situations. This is clearly foolish, however, as it assumes context-free solutions to problems, and this is very unrealistic. *The major conclusion from this is that it is absolutely necessary to consider developer and user organization characteristics in the software cost estimation models that we build.*

A second problem is the use of cost influencing factors and the relationship expressed among them. It is not clear that the appropriate factors are identified; nor is it clear that they have been related correctly mathematically. Many of the cost models use adjustment multipliers in which the cost factors are summed or multiplied together. It is very well known in multiple attribute utility theory and in cost benefit analysis [Sage, 1983] that summations are justified only when the factors are *independent* of one another. However, it is clear that independence is usually not the case. In reality, there are a number of types of *independence*.

A third problem involves changes in technology, tools, and methods. The contribution made to cost by these three aspects of project development is not as well understood as it should be for high-quality valuation purposes. Consequently, the appropriate change required in the cost equation is not known when technology, tools, and methods differ from those in place when the supporting database for a model was generated. Many of the databases used for contemporary cost and effort models use decades old information, which is surely not reflective of current practices. Very few of the cost estimating models are able to incorporate the potential benefits (or disbenefits) brought out by the use (misuse) of CASE tools. Nor do they consider the macro-enhancement approaches of reusability, prototyping, and knowledge-based systems for software development.

The development process itself presents a fourth set of needs. Some models examine the *software product* rather than the *software development process* to obtain information about cost- and effort-influencing factors. An examination of only product-related variables will generally never provide sufficient information to allow us to estimate effort and cost. More work needs to be done to determine what aspects of the development process contribute most to software cost. The major improvements in software productivity will come about through better software development processes, and not at all through only implementing methods that ensure higher programmer productivity.

Most of the available methods select a single important deliverable, source lines of code, and use this variable as the core variable for estimation purposes. Various multipliers of this variable are proposed that presume to represent realities of conditions extant as contrasted with the nominal conditions under which the effort relationship to source lines of code was determined. While this is not necessarily an appropriate way to go, it might be more meaningful to develop a software program development plan in terms of client needs and then cost each of the phase distributed efforts of the plan.

It is vitally important to develop cost and effort estimation models that can be used very early in the software development process. The purpose of these models is to predict software development lifecycle costs and efforts as soon as possible, and to provide information as well about the costs and benefits of various approaches to the software development process and its management. This will allow us to develop accurate information about software development programs clients might wish to fund, and to allocate the appropriate resources to these developments. It will also result in feedback of important software development information that will predict how changes in user requirements, software specifications, design, maintenance, and other factors will affect cost, effort, performance, and reliability.

In summary, an appropriate and useful effort and cost estimation model is one that provides needed cost and effectiveness information that will enable pertinent and timely decisions to be made concerning software development programs and related projects. Above all else, this requires that software systems engineering efforts be involved not only with counting operands and estimating source lines of code (with or without comments) to a study of the software development process itself. Only in this way will we understand not only the technological complexity of a software system but also the relationship between that complexity and the cognitive, management, and organizational behavior needed to interact with it in an effective and efficient manner.

10.7 PROBLEMS

10.1. Using the basic COCOMO model, under all three operating modes, determine the performance relation for the ratio of delivered source code lines per person month of effort. Determine the reasonableness of this relation for several types of software projects.

10.2. The Doty model [Herd et. al., 1977] relates effort to source lines of code as a function of application according to the relation:

Application	Relation
All	$E = 5.258S^{1.057}$
Command and control	$E = 4.089S^{1.263}$
Scientific	$E = 7.054S^{1.019}$
Business	$E = 4.495S^{0.781}$
Utility	$E = 10.078S^{0.811}$

Prepare a brief study of this model using our discussion in this chapter as a basis. Do you agree with the basic equation form for each of the applications suggested?

10.3. A recent variation of COCOMO is called *Ada COCOMO* [Boehm, 1988]. It is very similar to the original COCOMO model with only a few differences. The nominal initial effort estimate is obtained from

$$C_n = 2.8S^{1.10 \, + \, w_1 \, + \, w_2 \, + \, w_3 \, + \, w_4}$$

in which the weights depend on characterization of the development process:

w_1 Experience with Ada process model
w_2 Design thoroughness at project design review level
w_3 Risks eliminated at project design review level
w_4 Requirements volatility during development

Each weight is assigned a value ranging from 0.00 to 0.04. One of the original cost-drivers (VIRT—volatility of the virtual machine) is eliminated and replaced by two others (VMVH—volatility of the host system; VMVT—volatility of the target system). Two additional cost drivers (SECU—development of a classified security application; RESU—a measurement of required reusability) are included. Please write a brief discussion of this model. Are there characteristics of Ada, as contrasted with FORTRAN, COBOL and other languages for which the original COCOMO was obtained that justify this change? What are they? What are the orders of the possible changes involved?

10.4. The effort distribution for a nominal 240 KDSL organic code software development project is: product design 12%, detailed design 24%, code and unit test 36%, integrate and test 28%. How would the following changes, from low to high, affect the phase distribution of effort and the total effort: analyst capability, use of modern programming practices, required reliability, requirements volatility?

10.5. Discuss the specific topic of software development for microprocessors as contrasted with software development for mainframes. Which of the cost models discussed here are able to account for any of these variations?

10.6. How would you go about including software development using rapid prototyping in the models for software costing discussed here?

10.7. Perform a sensitivity analysis of the intermediate COCOMO model. Which of the cost-drivers are the most significant? The least significant? Are your results intuitively reasonable?

10.8. The decision to *make* or *buy* software is often a very important one. For many potential software development programs, there are opportunities to purchase an already available package that will function as desired. Consider the following situations:

a. You are the manager of a software development organization. It costs your organization, on the average, $35 per line of code to develop software through all phases of the software development lifecycle. Your group estimates that a desired functional capability will require 10,000 lines of delivered source code. Someone notes that it is possible to buy a software package with the functional capability you desire for $20,000. Should you buy or build the software product? Why?

b. Further study indicates that 2000 lines of code will have to be written and added to the purchased software package to make it functionally useful. How does this alter the make or buy decision?

c. How do your responses to **a.** and **b.** change if you are the chief information officer (CIO) in a third firm that has the opportunity to purchase already developed software or to pay to have it developed specifically for your firm?

10.9. T. Capers Jones [1986] has identified 11 programming, or software, classes that may have significant impact on software development efforts:

a. Personal software developed for private use

b. Internal software developed for use within the same organization

c. Internal software developed for reuse

d. Internal software that is to be leased on time sharing networks

e. External software to be put into the public domain, often government-sponsored software development

f. External software to be leased for specified amounts per month

g. External software to be marketed to users

h. External software to be bundled with specific hardware purchases

i. External software produced under commercial contract for others

j. External software produced under government contract

k. External software procured under military contract

Prepare a paper concerning how you might do cost and benefit estimation under each of these classes. What modifications might be appropriate for the cost estimation models discussed in this chapter such that they are appropriate for each of these classes?

10.10. The following is proposed as a set of possible steps to evaluate whether to *make* or *buy* software:

a. Develop functional and purposeful specifications for the software in terms of user needs. Identify suitable metrics whenever possible.

b. Estimate the costs to accomplish a software development program.

c. Identify several alternative software packages that have already been developed and that meet all, or most of, the requirements specifications.

d. Identify costs to modify these software packages such that they meet these specifications.

e. Develop a *decision matrix* that presents a comparison of the costs and benefits of all of the available options, including the *make* option.

f. Interpret these impacts on the user needs, including expanded needs that consider software maintenance.

g. Conduct appropriate sensitivity studies.

h. Select the most preferred alternative.

Investigate this framework and potentially modify it to make it more appropriate. Integrate the resulting framework with your favorite cost estimating method as presented in this chapter.

10.11. Obtain software productivity data for two or three software development programs available to you. Use several of the cost estimating models discussed in this chapter. How do the results compare with actual project results?

10.12. How would you go about estimating source lines of code for a software development program? Write a brief paper outlining the method(s) that you identify.

10.13. From Jones [1986], prepare a brief paper outlining use of the *Software Productivity, Quality, and Reliability (SPQR) Model.*

10.14. How would you attempt to use one of the COCOMO models for cost estimation for a development that used reusable software? Please comment on the potential variation of cost if there are available *softproducts* or available *softprocesses.*

10.15. How would you attempt to use one of the COCOMO models for cost estimation for a development that used one of the three forms of prototyping software? Please comment on the potential variation of cost as the type of prototyping changes from structural to functional to purposeful.

Bibliography for Software Systems Engineering

There are a rather large number of references that could potentially be cited concerning the subject of this investigation. What follows is a selected list of recent references that are specifically germane to the subjects discussed here. For the most part, these are cited in the text. The code symbols used to provide at least a partial annotation are:

A. Systems engineering methodology and design
B. Software engineering lifecycle
C. Systems engineering for software productivity
D. Taxonomy of micro-enhancement aids
   1. Improved programming technology
      1.1. Error-prevention techniques
         1.1.1. Structured programming
         1.1.2. Composite design
         1.1.3. Hierarchical design
         1.1.4. Top-down design
      1.2. Error-removal techniques
         1.2.1. Design code inspection
         1.2.2. Structured walkthroughs
         1.2.3. Design reviews
      1.3. Direct aids to productivity
         1.3.1. High-level programming languages (e.g., Ada)
         1.3.2. On-line development tools
         1.3.3 Preprogrammed modules
   2. Nonprocedural techniques
      2.1. Query languages to update data and model bases
      2.2. Report generators to format and produce results

      2.3.   Graphic languages

      2.4.   Automatic program (applications) generators

      2.5.   Very-high-level programming languages (4GLs)

      2.6.   Parameterized or generic application software

E. Taxonomy of macro-enhancement approaches

    1. Software prototyping

    2. Reusable software

    3. Knowledge-based support for software production

F. Software assurance, reliability, quality control, and maintenance

G. Software metrics and evaluation (including cost analysis)

H. Software standards

I.   Software management

J. Cognitive science for software productivity

K. Information and requirements specifications

L. Software environments

M. Uncertainty and information imperfections

N. Case tools

There are many other references that could be cited—so many, in fact, that the reference list could easily become overwhelming. We have cited those references specifically cited in the text as well as a few other very notable works. We believe that the references cited here are especially important for a broad *Software Systems Engineering* emphasis.

If we had to select a subset of these for retrieval and study, we would first suggest some of the many *IEEE Computer Society Reprint Books* that we have cited. A major advantage to these is that they generally contain a large number of the now classic papers in this new field. To obtain these will minimize searching through a great many journals and proceedings volumes. Also, other recent textbooks in this area provide a good coverage of the material, generally from different and useful perspectives that are often associated with programmer productivity.

We would certainly not wish to make the claim that any reference on the following list is necessarily more important than a reference concerning a similar topic that is not on the list. Most of the items listed are the ones that we have found especially useful for our effort and we apologize to the authors of many fine papers that we have not included in our listing.

References

Adelman, L., *Evaluating Decision Support Systems,* QED Information Sciences, Wellesley, MA, 1989. [G]

Adrion, W. R., Bransted, M. A., and Cherniavsky, J. C., "Validation, Verification and Testing of Computer Software," *ACM Computing Surveys,* Vol. 14, No. 2, pp. 159–192, June 1982. [G]

Agresti, W. W. (Ed.), *New Paradigms for Software Development,* IEEE Computer Society Press, Silver Spring, MD, 1986. [C]

Alavi, M., "An Assessment of the Prototyping Approach to Information Systems Development," *Communications of the ACM,* Vol. 27, No. 6, pp. 556–563, June 1984. [E1]

Albrecht, A. J. "Measuring Application Development Productivity," *Proceedings of the IBM Application Development Symposium,* Monterey, CA, pp. 83–92, October 1979. [G]

Albrecht, A., and Gaffney, J., "Software Function, Source Lines of Code, and Development Effort Prediction: A Software Science Validation," *IEEE Transactions on Software Engineering,* Vol. SE9, No. 6, pp. 639–648. November 1983. [G]

Alford, M., "SREM at the Age of Eight: The Distributed Computing Design System," *IEEE Computer,* Vol. 18, No. 4, pp. 36–46, April 1985. [D2]

Alford, M. W., and Davis, C. G., "Experience with the Software Development System," in H. Hunke (Ed.), *Software Engineering Environments,* North Holland, Amsterdam, 1981. [N]

American National Standards Institute, "IEEE Guide to Software Requirements Specifications," 1984. [H,K]

Andriole, S. J., "Storyboard Prototyping for Requirements Verification," *Large Scale Systems,* Vol. 12, pp. 231–247, 1987. [E1]

Andriole, S. J., *Prototyping,* Petrocelli Books, Princeton NJ, 1989. [A,C]

Anthony, R. N., *Planning and Control Systems: A Framework for Analysis,* Harvard University Press, Cambridge MA, 1965. [I]

Applegate, L. M., Chen, T. T., Konsynski, B. R., and Nunamaker, J. F., "Knowledge Management in Organizational Planning," *Journal of Management Information Systems,* Vol. 3, No. 4, pp. 20–38, Spring 1987. [I,K]

Argyris, C., *Reasoning, Learning and Action: Individual and Organizational,* Jossey-Bass, San Francisco, 1982. [I,J]

Argyris, C., and Schon, D. A., *Theory in Practice: Increasing Professional Effectiveness,* Jossey-Bass, San Francisco, 1974. [I]

Argyris, C., and Schon, D. A., *Organizational Learning: A Theory of Action Perspective,* Addison-Wesley, Reading, MA, 1978. [I,J]

Arthur, L. J., *Measuring Programmer Productivity and Software Quality*, J. Wiley, New York, 1985. [F,I]

Arthur, L. J., *Software Evolution: The Software Maintenance Challenge*, J. Wiley, New York, 1988. [F]

Bailey, J. W., and V. R. Basili, "A Meta-model for Software Development Resource Expenditures," *Proceedings of the Fifth International Conference on Software Engineering*, pp. 107–116, 1981. [G]

Balzer, R., "Transformational Implementation: An Example," *IEEE Transactions on Software Engineering*, Vol. SE-7, No. 1, pp. 3–14, January 1981. [E1]

Balzer, R., "A 15 Year Perspective on Automatic Programming," *IEEE Transactions on Software Engineering*, Vol. SE-11, No. 11, pp. 1257–1268, November 1985. [D2.4]

Balzer, R. M., Goldman, N. M., and Wile, D. S., "Operational Specification as the Basis for Rapid Prototyping," *ACM Software Engineering Notes*, Vol. 7, No. 5, pp. 3–16, 1982. [E1]

Barnes, B., Durek, T., Gaffney, J., and Pyster, A., "A Framework and Economic Foundation for Software Reuse," *Software Productivity Consortium Technical Report, SPC-TN-87-011*, June 1987. [E2]

Basili, V. R., and Rombach, H. D., "Tailoring The Software Process to Project Goals and Environments," *Proceedings of the 9th International Conference on Software Engineering*, pp. 345–357, March 1987. [B,I]

Bass, B. M. (Ed.), *Stogdill's Handbook of Leadership*, Free Press, New York, 1981. [I]

Bauer, F. L., "From Specifications to Machine Code: Program Construction Through Formal Reasoning," *Proceedings, Sixth International Conference on Software Engineering*, pp. 84–91, 1982. [D2]

Beam, W. R., Palmer, J. D., and Sage, A. P., "Systems Engineering for Software Productivity," *IEEE Transactions on Systems, Man, and Cybernetics*, Vol. 17, No. 2, pp. 163—186, March/April 1987. [A,B,C]

Beizer, B., *Software Testing Techniques*, Van Nostrand Reinhold, New York, 1982. [G]

Beizer, B., *Software System Testing and Quality Assurance*, Van Nostrand Reinhold, New York, 1984. [G]

Belady, L., and Lehman, W., "A Model of Large Program Development," *IBM Systems Journal*, Vol. 15, No. 3, pp. 225–252, 1976. [I]

Bergland, G. D., and Gordon, R. D. (Eds.), *Software Design Strategies*, IEEE Computer Society Press, Silver Spring, MD, 1981. [C]

Biggs, C. L., Birks, E. G., and Atkins, W. A., *Managing the System Development Process*, Prentice-Hall, Englewood Cliffs, NJ, 1980. [A,B,I]

Boar, B. H., *Applications Prototyping: A Requirements Definition Strategy for the 80s*, Wiley, New York, 1984. [E1]

Boehm, B. W., "Software Engineering," *IEEE Transactions on Computers*, Vol. C-25, No. 12, pp. 1226–1241, December 1976. [B,G]

Boehm, B. W., *Software Engineering Economics*, Prentice-Hall, Englewood Cliffs, NJ, 1981. [B,G]

Boehm, B. W., "Verifying and Validating Software Requirements and Design Specifications," *IEEE Software,* Vol. 1, No. 1, pp. 75–88, January 1984. [F,G,I]

Boehm, B. W., "A Spiral Model of Software Development and Enhancement," *ACM SIGSOFT Software Engineering Notes,* Vol. 11, No. 4, pp. 14–24, August 1986. [B,G]

Boehm, B. W., "Improving Software Productivity," *IEEE Computer,* Vol. 20, No. 9, pp. 43–57, September 1987. [C,I]

Boehm, B. W., "Overview of Ada COCOMO," Slide Presentation, Fourth Annual COCOMO User Group Meeting, Pittsburgh, PA, 1988. [G]

Boehm, B. W., Brown, J. R., and Lipow, M., "Quantitative Evaluation of Software Quality," *Proceedings IEEE/ACM 2nd International Conference on Software Engineering,* October 1976. [F,G]

Boehm, B. W., Brown, J. R., Kaspar, H., Lipow, M., McLeod, G. J., and Merritt, M. J., *Characteristics of Software Quality,* North Holland, Amsterdam, 1978. [F,G,I]

Boehm, B. W., Gray, T. E., and Seewaldt, T., "Prototyping Versus Specifying: A Multiproject Experiment," *IEEE Transactions on Software Engineering,* Vol. 10, No. 3, pp. 290–303, May 1984. [C,E1]

Bohm, C., and Jacopini, G., "Flow Diagrams, Turing Machines and Languages with Only Two Formation Rules," *Communications of the ACM,* Vol. 9, No. 5, pp. 366–371, 1966. [D1]

Booch, G., "Object Oriented Development," *IEEE Transactions on Software Engineering,* Vol. 12, No. 2, pp. 211–221, February, 1986. [L]

Booch, G. M. *Software Engineering with Ada,* Benjamin Cummings, 1983, 1987. [D1.3.1]

Boorer, H. (Ed.), *People, Machines and Organizations; A MANPRINT Approach to Systems Integration,* Van Nostrand Reinhold, NY, 1990. [N]

Bratman, H., "The Software Factory," *IEEE Computer,* Vol. 8, No. 5, pp. 28–37, 1975. [C]

Brooks, F. P., Jr., *The Mythical Man Month,* Addison-Wesley, Reading, MA, 1975. [I,Historical]

Brooks, F. P., Jr., "No Silver Bullet: Essence and Accidents in Software Engineering," *Computer,* Vol. 20, No. 4, pp. 10–19, April 1987. [B,C,I]

Budde, R., Kuhlenkamp, K., Mathiassen, L., and Zullighoven, H., *Approaches to Prototyping: Proceedings of a Working Conference on Prototyping,* Springer-Verlag, New York, 1984. [D,E1]

Burton, B., Aragon, R. W., Bailey, S., Koehler, K., and Mayes, L., "The Reusable Software Library," *IEEE Software,* Vol. 4, No. 4, pp. 25–30, July 1987. [E2]

Cameron, J. R., "An Overview of JSD," *IEEE Transactions on Software Engineering,* Vol. SE 12, No. 2, pp. 222–240, February 1986. [D1]

Carey, T. T., and Mason, R. E., "Information System Prototyping: Techniques, Tools and Methodologies," *New Paradigms for Software Development,* W. W. Agresti (Ed.), IEEE Computer Society Press, Silver Spring MD, pp. 48–57, 1987. [E1]

Carriere, W. M., and Thibodeau, R., "Development of a Logistics Software Cost Estimating Technique for Foreign Military Sales," General Research Corporation Report CR-3-839, June 1979. [G]

Charette, R. N., *Software Engineering Environments: Concepts and Technology,* McGraw-Hill, New York, 1986. [A,B,I]

Cheatham, T. E., Jr., "Reusability through Program Transformation," *IEEE Transactions on Software Engineering,* Vol. 10, No. 9, pp. 589–594, September 1984. [E2,D]

Chen, P. P. S., "The Entity-Relationship Model—Towards a Unified View of Data," *ACM Transactions on Database Systems,* Vol. 1, No. 1, 1976. [D1.3.2]

Chow, T. S. (Ed.)., *Software Quality Assurance,* IEEE Computer Society Press, New York, 1985. [F]

Church, V. E., Card, D. N., Agresti, W. W., and Jordan, Q. L., "An Approach for Assessing Software Prototypes," *ACM Software Engineering Notes,* Vol. 11, No. 3, pp. 65–76, July 1986. [D,E1]

Churchill, W. S., *The Second World War, The Gathering Storm,* Houghton-Mifflin, Boston, 1951. [Historical]

Clark, S. J. and Schluter, R. G., *Software Cost-Estimating Guidebook,* McDonnell Douglas Astronautics Company, Huntington Beach, CA, February 1986. [G]

Cleaveland, J. C., and Kintala, C. M. R., "Tools for Building Application Generators," *AT&T Technical Journal,* Vol. 67, No. 4, pp. 46–58, July 1988. [D2.4]

Conte, S. D., Dunsmore, H. E., and Shen, V. Y., *Software Engineering Metrics and Models,* Benjamin Cummings, New York, 1986. [G]

Cook, M. L., "Software Metrics: An Introduction and Annotated Bibliography," *ACM SIGSOFT Software Engineering Notes,* Vol. 7, No. 2, pp. 41–60, April 1982. [G]

Cox, B. J., *Object Oriented Programming: An Evolutionary Approach,* Addison-Wesley, Reading, MA, 1986. [D1]

Curtis, B., Soloway, E. M., Brooks, R. E., Black, J. B., Ehrlich, K., and Ramsey, H. R., "Software Psychology: The Need for and Interdisciplinary Program," *Proceedings of the IEEE,* Vol. 74, No. 8, pp. 1092–1106, August 1986. [B,C,D,J]

Cyert, R. M., and March, J. G., *A Behavioral Theory of the Firm,* Prentice-Hall, Englewood Cliffs, NJ, 1963. [I]

Czarnik, M. R., "Software Engineering Challenges—CAMP," *Proceedings, 1st Software Productivity Workshop,* Herndon, VA, April 1987. [C]

Czuchry, A. J., Jr., and Harris, D. R., "KRBA: A New Paradigm for Requirements Engineering," *IEEE Expert,* Vol. 3, No. 4, pp. 21–35, Winter 1988. [K,L]

Daft, R. L., and Lengel, R. H., "Organizational Information Requirements, Media Richness, and Structural Design," *Management Science,* Vol. 32, No. 5, pp. 554–571, May 1986. [K]

Dart, S. A., Ellison, R. J., Feilter, P. H., and Habermann, A. N., "Software Development Environments," *COMPUTER,* Vol. 20, No. 11, pp. 18–28, November 1987. [L]

Davis, A. M., "A Taxonomy for the Early Stages of the Software Development Life Cycle," *Journal of Systems and Software,* Vol. 8, No. 4, pp. 297–311, September 1988. [B]

Davis, A. M., Bersoff, E. H., and Comer, E. R., "A Strategy for Comparing Alternative Life Cysle Models," *IEEE Transactions on Software Engineering,* Vol. 14, No. 10, pp. 1453–1461, October 1988. [B]

Davis, G. B., "Strategies for Information Requirements Determination," *IBM Systems Journal,* Vol. 21, No. 1, pp. 4–30, 1982. [K]

Dawes, R. M., "The Robust Beauty of Improper Linear Models in Decision Making," *American Psychologist,* Vol. 34, No. 7, pp. 571–582, July 1979. [J]

DeMarco, T., *Structured Analysis and System Specification,* Prentice-Hall, Englewood Cliffs, NJ, 1979. [B,D]

DeMarco, T., *Controlling Software Projects,* Yourdon Press, New York, 1981. [D1]

DeMarco, T., *Controlling Software Projects: Management, Measurement and Estimation,* Yourdon Press, New York, 1982. [D1]

Department of Defense, *Defense System Software Development—DoD-STD-2167,* June 1985. [H]

Department of Defense, *Defense Systems Management College, Systems Engineering Management Guide,* Ft. Belvoir, VA, 1986. [A]

Department of Defense, *Defense System Acquisition Management Software Quality Indicators,* AFSC Pamphlet 800-14, January 1987. [H]

Department of Defense, *Defense System Software Quality Program—DoD-STD-2168,* April 1987 [H].

Dijkstra, E. W., "Goto Statement Considered Harmful," *Communications of the ACM,* Vol. 11, No. 3, pp. 147–148, 1968. [Historical, D1.1]

Dreyfus, H. L., and Dreyfus, S. E., *Mind Over Machine: The Power of Human Intuition and Expertise in the Age of the Computer,* Free Press, New York, 1986. [I, J]

Dumas, J. S., *Designing User Interfaces for Software,* Prentice-Hall, Englewood Cliffs, NJ, 1988. [J]

Dunn, R. H., *Software Defect Removal,* McGraw-Hill, New York, 1984. [D1.2]

Dunn, R. H., and Ullman, R., *Quality Assurance for Computer Software,* McGraw-Hill, New York, 1982. [F]

Etzioni, A., *Modern Organizations,* Prentice-Hall, Englewood Cliffs, NJ, 1964. [I,J]

Fairley, R. E., *Software Engineering Concepts,* McGraw-Hill, New York, 1985. [D]

Fickas, S. F., "Automating the Transformational Development of Software," *IEEE Transactions on Software Engineering,* Vol. 11, No. 11, pp. 1268–1277, November 1985. [D]

Fitzsimmons, A., and Love, T., "A Review and Evaluation of Software Science," *Computing Surveys,* Vol. 10, No. 1, pp. 3–18, March 1978. [C, Historical]

Fox, J. M., *Software and Its Development,* Prentice-Hall, Englewood Cliffs, NJ, 1985. [C]

Freedman, D., and Weinburg, C., *Handbook of Walkthroughs, Inspections, and Technical Reviews,* Little Brown, Boston, 1982. [G]

Freeman, P., "Reusable Software Engineering: Concepts and Research Directions," *ITT Proceedings of the Workshop on Reusability in Programming,* 1983. [E2]

Freeman, P., *Software Perspectives: The System is the Message,* Addison-Wesley, Reading, MA, 1987a. [I]

Freeman, P., "A Conceptual Analysis of the Draco Approach to Constructing Software Systems," *IEEE Transactions on Software Engineering,* Vol. 13, No. 7, pp. 830–844, July, 1987b. [E.2]

Freeman, P. (Ed.), *Software Reusability*, IEEE Computer Society Press, 1987c. [E.2]

Freeman, P., and Wasserman, A. I. (Eds.), *Software Design Techniques*, IEEE Computer Society Press, Silver Spring, MD, 1983. [D]

Frenkel, K. A., "Towards Automating the Software Development Life Cycle," *Communications of the ACM*, Vol. 28, No. 6, pp. 578–589, June 1985. [E3]

Gargaro, A., and Pappas, F., "Reusability Issues and Ada," *IEEE Software*, Vol. 4, No. 4, pp. 43–51, July 1987. [E2]

Gehani, N., and McGettrick, A. D. (Eds.), *Software Specification Techniques*, Addison-Wesley, Reading, MA, 1986. [K]

Gilb, T., *Software Metrics*, Winthrop, Cambridge, MA, 1977. [G]

Gladden, G. R., "Stop the Life Cycle, I Want to Get Off," *ACM Software Engineering Notes*, Vol. 7, No. 2, pp. 35–39, 1982. [B]

Goetz, M. A., "Information Systems in the 1990's: Will the Chaos Continue," *Proceedings Technology Strategies '87*, ADPA, February 1987. [D2,L]

Goldberg, A., *Smalltalk: The Interactive Programming Environment*, Addison-Wesley, Reading, MA, 1984. [D1.3.2]

Goldberg, A., and Robson, D., *Smalltalk-80: The Language and Its Implementation*, Addison-Wesley, Reading, MA, 1983. [D1.3.2]

Gomaa, H., "A Software Design Method for Real Time Systems," *Communications of the ACM*, Vol. 27, No. 9, pp. 938–949, September 1984. [D1.3]

Gomaa, H., "Software Development of Real-Time Systems," *Communications of the ACM*, Vol. 29, pp. 657–668, July 1986. [D1.3]

Gomaa, H., "The Role of Prototyping in Large Scale Software System Development," *Large Scale Systems in Information and Decision Technologies*, Vol. 12, No. 3, pp. 217–229, 1987. [E1]

Gomaa, H., and Scott, D. B. H., "Prototyping as a Tool in the Specification of User Requirements," *Proceedings of the 5th International Conference on Software Engineering*, pp. 333–342, 1981. [E1]

Green, C., Luckham, D., Balzer, R., Cheatham, T., and Rich, C., "Report on a Knowledge Based Software Assistant," in *Readings in Artificial Intelligence and Software Engineering*, C. Rich and R. Waters (Eds.), Morgan Kaufman, Los Altos, CA, pp. 377–428, 1986. [E3]

Green, J., "Productivity in the Fourth Generation: Six Case Studies," *Journal of Management Information Systems*, Vol. 1, No. 3, pp. 49–63, Winter 1985. [D2]

Hall, A. D., *A Methodology for Systems Engineering*, Van Nostrand, New York, 1962. [A]

Hall, A. D., "A Three Dimensional Morphology of Systems Engineering," *IEEE Transactions on System Science and Cybernetics*, Vol. 5, No. 2, pp. 156–160. April 1969. [A]

Hall, R. H., *Organizations: Structure and Process*, Prentice-Hall, Englewood Cliffs, NJ, 1977. [I]

Halstead, M. H., *Elements of Software Science*, Elsevier, Amsterdam, 1977. [C]

Harrison, T. S., "Techniques and Issues in Rapid Prototyping," *Journal of Systems Management*, Vol. 36, No. 6, pp. 8–13, June 1985. [E1]

Hayre, J., "An Axiomatic Theory of Organizations," *Administrative Science Quarterly*, Vol. 10, No. 3, pp. 289–320, December 1965 [I]

Hekmatpour, S., "Experience with Evolutionary Prototyping in a Large Software Project," *ACM SIGSOFT Software Engineering Notes,* Vol. 12, No. 1, pp. 38–41, January 1987. [E1]

Heninger, K. L., "Specifying Software Requirements for Complex Systems," *IEEE Transactions on Software Engineering,* Vol. SE-6, No. 1, pp 2–13, January 1980. [K]

Heninger, K., "Specifying Software Requirements for Complex Systems: New Techniques and their Application," *IEEE Transactions on Software Engineering,* Vol. SE-9, No. 5, pp. 866–875, September 1982. [K]

Herd, J. R., Postak, J. N., Russell, W. E., and Stewart, K. R., *Software Cost Estimation Study—Study Results—Final Technical Report,* RADC-TR-77-220, Doty Associates, Inc., Rockville, MD, June 1977. [G]

IEEE Software Engineering Standards, IEEE ISBN: 471-63457-3, 1987. [H, a very complete collection of IEEE software standards]

Jackson, M., *Principles of Program Design,* Academic Press, Orlando, FL, 1975. [D1]

Jackson, M., *System Development,* Prentice-Hall, Englewood Cliffs, NJ, 1983. [D]

Janis, I. L., and Mann, L., *Decision Making: A Psychological Analysis of Conflict, Choice, and Commitment,* Free Press, New York, 1977. [J]

Jensen, R. W., "A Comparison of the Jensen and COCOMO Schedule and Cost Estimation Models," *Proceedings of the International Society of Parametric Analysis,* pp. 96–106, 1984. [G]

Jones, T. C., "Reusability in Programming: A Survey of the State of the Art," *IEEE Transactions on Software Engineering,* Vol. 10, No. 5, pp. 488–494, September 1984. [E2]

Jones, T. C., *Programming Productivity,* McGraw-Hill, New York, 1986. [D]

Kahneman, D., Slovic, P., and Tversky, A. (Eds.), *Judgments under Uncertainty: Heuristics and Biases,* Cambridge University Press, New York, 1982. [J]

Kaiser, G., and Garlan, D., "Melding Software Systems from Reusable Building Blocks," *IEEE Software,* Vol. 4, No. 4, pp. 17–24, July 1987. [E2]

Kant, E., and Barstow, D. R., "The Refinement Paradigm: The Interaction of Coding and Efficiency Knowledge in Programming Synthesis," *IEEE Transactions on Software Engineering,* Vol. SE-7, No. 5, pp. 458–471, September 1981. [D]

Keen, P. G. W., and Scott Morton, M. S., *Decision Support Systems: an Organizational Perspective,* Addison-Wesley, Reading, MA, 1978. [A,I]

Keeney, R. L., and Raiffa, H., *Decisions with Multiple Objectives: Preferences and Value Tradeoffs,* Wiley, New York, 1976. [A,J]

Kelly, J. C., "A Comparison of Four Methods for Real-Time Systems," *Proceedings of the 9th International Conference on Software Engineering,* pp. 238–252, March 1987. [C]

Kemerer, C. F., "An Empirical Validation of Software Cost Estimation Models," *Communications of the ACM,* Vol. 30, No. 5, pp. 416–429, May 1987. [G]

Kerschberg, L., and Weitzel, J. R., "Developing Knowledge-based Systems: Reorganizing the System Development Life Cycle," *Communications of the Association for Computing Machinery,* Vol. 32, No. 4, pp. 482–489, April 1989. [B]

Kraemer, K. L., and King, J. L., "Computer Based Systems for Cooperative Work and Group Decision Making," *AMC Computing Surveys,* Vol. 20, No. 2, pp. 115–146, June 1988. [A,J,L]

Lamb, D. A., *Software Engineering: Planning for Change,* Prentice-Hall, Englewood Cliffs, NJ, 1988. [C]

Lantz, K. E., *The Prototyping Methodology,* Prentice-Hall, Englewood Cliffs, NJ, 1986. [E1]

Ledgard, H., and Tauer, J., *Professional Software: Volume I—Software Engineering Concepts, Volume II—Programming Practice,* Addison-Wesley, Reading, MA, 1987. [C,D]

Lehman, M. M., and Belady, L. A. (Eds.), *Program Evolution: Processes of Software Change,* Academic Press, Orlando, FL, 1987. [C]

Lenz, M., Schmidt, H. A., and Wolf, P., "Software Reuse Through Building Blocks," *IEEE Software,* Vol. 4, No. 4, pp. 34–42, July 1987. [E2]

Lientz, B. P., and Swanson, E. B., *Software Maintenance Management,* Addison-Wesley, Reading, MA, 1981. [F,I]

Linger, R. C., Mills, H. D., and Witt, B. I., *Structured Programming—Theory and Practice,* Addison-Wesley, Reading, MA, 1979. [D1.1.1]

Londeix, B., *Cost Estimation for Software Development,* Addison-Wesley, Reading, MA, 1987. [G]

Mackenzie, R. A., "The Management Process in 3-D," *Harvard Business Review,* pp. 80–87, November 1969. [N]

Malone, T. W., Grant, K. R., Turbak, F. A., Brobst, S. A., and Cohen, M. D., "Intelligent Information Sharing Systems," *Communications of the ACM,* Vol. 30, No. 5, pp. 390–402, May 1987. [K]

March, J. G., and Simon, H. A., *Organizations,* Wiley, New York, 1958. [N]

Marshall, G. R., *Systems Analysis and Design: Alternative Structured Approaches,* Prentice-Hall, Englewood Cliffs, NJ, 1986. [D1]

Martin, J. *Fourth Generation Languages,* Prentice-Hall, Englewood Cliffs, NJ, 1985. [D2.5]

Martin, J., and McClure, C., *Software Maintenance: The Problem and Its Solution,* Prentice-Hall, Englewood Cliffs, NJ, 1984. [F]

Matsumoto, Y., "A Software Factory: An Overall Approach to Software Production," in *Software Reusability,* P. Freeman, (Ed.), IEEE Computer Society Press, New York, pp. 155–179, 1987. [E2]

McCabe, T. J., "A Complexity Measure," *IEEE Transactions on Software Engineering,* Vol. SE-2, No. 4, pp. 308–320, 1976. [G]

McCracken, D. D., and Jackson, M. A., "Life Cycle Concept Considered Harmful," *ACM Software Engineering Notes,* Vol. 7, No. 2, pp. 29–32, 1982. [B]

McDermid, J., and Ripkin, K., *Life Cycle Support in the Ada Environment,* Cambridge University Press, Cambridge, UK, 1984. [B,D1.3.1]

McIllroy, M. D., "Mass-Produced Software Components," in *Software Engineering Concepts and Techniques,* Buxton, J., and McIllroy, (Eds.), Petrocelli Brooks, Princeton, NJ, pp. 88–98, 1976. [Historical]

Meyer, B., "Reusability: the Case for Object-Oriented Design," *ACM SIGPLAN Notices,* Vol. 22, pp. 85–94, February 1987. [E2]

Mills, H. D., "On the Statistical Validation of Computer Programs," IBM Federal

Systems Division Report FSC-72-6015, Gaithersburg, MD, 1972. [Historical, F]

Mills, H. D., *Software Productivity,* Little, Brown, Boston, 1983. [C,D1]

Mintzberg, H., *The Nature of Managerial Work,* Harper and Row, New York, 1973. [I]

Myers, G. J., *The Cost of Software Testing,* Wiley, New York, 1984. [G]

Myers, G. J., *Software Reliability: Principles and Practice,* Wiley, New York, 1976. [F]

Myers, M., *A Knowledge-Based System for Managing Software Requirements Volatility, PhD Dissertation,* George Mason University, Fairfax, VA, 1988. [K,M]

Nadler, G., "Systems Methodology and Design," *IEEE Transactions on Systems, Man and Cybernetics,* Vol. 15, No. 6, pp. 685–697, November 1985. [A]

Nassi, I., and Schneiderman, B., "Flowchart Techniques for Structured Programming," *SIGPLAN Notices,* Vol. 8, No. 8, August 1973. [D1]

NASTEC Corp., "CASE 2000 Brochure," NASTEC Corp., Southfield, MI, 1987. [D1.3.2]

National Bureau of Standards, FIPS Pub. 38, *Guidelines for Documentation of Computer Programs and Automated Data Systems,* February 1976. [B,G,H]

National Bureau of Standards, FIPS Pub. 101, *Guideline for Lifecycle Validation, Verification and Testing of Computer Software,* June 1983. [B,G,H]

National Bureau of Standards, FIPS Pub. 106, *Guidance on Software Maintenance,* June 1984. [B,G,H]

National Bureau of Standards, *Validation, Verification and Testing of Computer Software,* NBS Special Pub. 500-25, 1986. [B,G,H]

Neighbors, J. M., "The Draco Approach to Constructing Software from Reusable Components," *IEEE Transactions on Software Engineering,* Vol. SE-10, No. 5, pp. 564–574, May 1984. [E2]

Nelson, E. A., *Management Handbook for the Estimation of Computer Programming Costs,* AD-A648750, System Development Corporation, Santa Monica, CA, October 31, 1966. [G]

Newell, A., and Simon, H. A., *Human Problem Solving,* Prentice-Hall, Englewood Cliffs, NJ, 1972. [J]

Nordby, K., "The Design Generator," Computer Science Corporation Report to RADC, July 1986. [N]

Norden, P. V., "Curve Fitting for a Model of Applied Research and Development Scheduling," *IBM Journal of Research and Development,* Vol. 2, No. 3, pp. , July 1958. [G]

Norden, P. V. "Useful Tools for Project Management," *Operations Research in Research and Development,* Wiley, New York, 1963. [G,L]

Norman, D. A., and Draper, S. W. (Eds.), *User Centered System Design: New Perspectives in Human–Computer Interaction,* Erlbaum, New York, 1986. [J]

Nunamaker, J. F., Applegate, L. M., and Konsynski, B. R., "Computer Aided Deliberation: Model Management and Group Decision Support," *Operations Research,* Vol. 36, No. 6, pp. 826–848, November 1988. [G,L,N]

Orr, K., *Structured System Development,* Yourdon Press, New York, 1977. [D1]

Page-Jones, M., *The Practical Guide to Structured Systems Design,* Yourdon Press, New York, 1980. [D1]

Palmer, J. D., and Myers, M., "Knowledge-Based Systems Application to Reduce Risk in Software Requirements," *Proceedings, Uncertainty and Intelligent Systems, 2nd International Conference on Information Processing and Management of Uncertainty in Knowledge-Based Systems,* Urbino, Italy, pp. 351–358, July 1988. [K,M]

Palmer, J. D., and Nguyen, T., "A Systems Approach to Reusable Software Products," *Proceedings IEEE Systems, Man and Cybernetics Conference,* pp. 1410–1419, October 1986. [E2]

Palmer, J. D., and Sage, A. P., "Cognitive Models of User Interfaces for an Advanced Software and Systems Engineering Development Environment," *Review Internationale de Systemique,* Paris, Vol. 2, No. 2, pp. 195–214, 1988. [I,L]

Parikh, G., *Techniques of Program and System Maintenance,* Little, Brown, New York, Boston, 1982. [F]

Parikh, G., *Handbook of Software Maintenance,* Wiley, New York, 1986. [F,L]

Parikh, G."The Several Worlds of Software Maintenance—A Proposed Software Maintenance Taxonomy," *ACM SIGSOFT Software Engineering Notes,* Vol. 12, pp. 51–53, April 1987. [F]

Parikh, G., and Zvegintzov, N. (Eds.), *Tutorial on Software Maintenance,* IEEE Computer Society Press, New York, 1983. [L]

Parnas, D. L., "A Technique for Software Module Specification with Examples," *Communications of the ACM,* Vol. 15, No. 5, pp. 330–336, May 1972. [D1]

Parr, F. N., "An Alternative to the Rayleigh Curve Model for Software Development," *IEEE Transactions on Software Engineering,* Vol. SE-6, No. 3, pp. 291–296, May 1980. [G]

Partsch, H., and Steinbruggen, R., "Program Transformation Systems," *ACM Computing Surveys,* Vol. 15, No. 3, pp. 199–236, September 1983. [E3]

Peters, L. J., "Software Representation and Composition Techniques," *Proceedings of the IEEE,* Vol. 68, No. 9, pp. 1085–1093, September 1980. [D1.1.2]

Peters, L. J., *Advanced Structured Analysis and Design,* Prentice-Hall, Englewood Cliffs, NJ, 1987. [D1.1]

Pfleeger, S. L., *Software Engineering,* Macmillan, New York, 1987. [C]

Polster, F. J., "Reuse of Software Through Generation of Partial Systems," *IEEE Transactions on Software Engineering,* Vol. SE-12, No. 3, pp. 402–416, March 1986. [E2]

Porter, A. L., Rossini, F. A., Carpenter, S. R., and Roper, A. T., *A Guidebook to Technology Assessment and Impact Analysis,* North Holland, New York, 1980. [A, G]

Pressman, R. S., *Software Engineering: A Practitioner's Approach,* 2nd ed., McGraw-Hill, New York, 1982, 1987. [D]

Pressman, R. S., *Making Software Engineering Happen,* Prentice-Hall, Englewood Cliffs, NJ, 1988. [I]

Prieto-Diaz, R., and Freeman, P., "Classifying Software for Reusability," *IEEE Software,* Vol. 4, No. 1, pp. 6–16, January 1987. [E2]

Prieto-Diaz, R. and Neighbors, J., "Module Interconnection Languages," *Journal of Systems and Software,* Vol. 6, No. 4, pp. 307–334, 1986. [E2]

Prywes, N., Shi, Y., Szmanski, B., and Tseng, J., "Supersystem Programming with

MODEL Equational Language," *IEEE Computer,* Vol. 19, No. 2, pp. 50–60, February 1986. [D2.5]

Putnam, L., "A General Empirical Solution to the Macro Software Sizing and Estimating Project," *IEEE Transactions on Software Engineering,* Vol. 4, No. 4, pp. 345–361, July 1978. [G]

Putnam, L. H., *Software Cost Estimating and Life-Cycle Control, Getting the Software Numbers,* IEEE Tutorial Catalog Number EHO-165-1, 1980. [G]

Putnam, L. H., and R. W. Wolverton, *Quantitative Management, Software Cost Estimating,* IEEE Tutorial Catalog Number EHO-129-7, November 1977. [G]

Putnam, L. H., Putnam, D. T., and Thayer, L. P., "Assessing the Proficiency of Software Developers," *Proceedings, 9th Annual Software Engineering Workshop,* pp. 264–298, November 1984. [G]

Rasmussen, J., *Information Processing and Human–Machine Interaction: An Approach to Coginitive Engineering,* North Holland/Elsevier, New York, 1986. [A,J]

Rich, C., and Waters, R. (Eds.), *Readings in Artificial Intelligence and Software Engineering,* Morgan Kaufman, Los Altos, CA, 1986. [E3]

Rich, C., and Waters, R., "The Programmer's Apprentice: A Research Overview," *Computer,* Vol. 21, No. 11, pp. 10–25, November 1988. [E3]

Riddle, W., E., "An Assessment of Dream," in H. Hunke (Ed.), *Software Engineering Environments,* North Holland, Amsterdam, 1981. [L]

Riddle, W., and Williams, L. G., "Software Environments Workshop Report," *ACM SIGSOFT Software Engineering Notes,* Vol. 11, No. 1, pp. 73–102, 1986. [L]

Robertson, L. B., and Secor, G. A., "Effective Management of Software Development," *AT&T Technical Journal,* Vol. 65, No. 2, pp. 94–101, March 1986. [C]

Roman, G. C., "A Taxonomy of Current Issues in Requirements Engineering," *IEEE Computer,* Vol. 18, No. 4, pp. 14–23, 1985. [K]

Ross, D. T., "Applications and Extensions of SADT," *IEEE Computer,* Vol. 18, No. 4, pp. 25–34, 1985. [D]

Ross, D. T., and Shoman, K. E., Jr., "Structured Analysis for Requirements Definition," *IEEE Transactions on Software Engineering,* Vol. SE-3, No. 1, pp. 69–84, January 1977. [D1.3.2]

Royce, W. W., "Managing the Development of Large Software Systems: Concepts and Techniques," *Proceedings WESCON,* pp. 1–9, 1970. [B]

Rzepka, W. E., "A Requirements Engineering Testbed: Concept, Status and First Results," *Rome Air Developement Center,* Griffis Air Force Base, NY, 1988. [K]

Sage, A. P., *Methodology for Large Scale Systems,* McGraw-Hill, New York, 1977. [A]

Sage, A. P., "Behavioral and Organizational Considerations in the Design of Information Systems and Processes for Decision Support," *IEEE Transactions on Systems Man and Cybernetics,* Vol. 11, No. 9, pp. 640–678, September 1981a. [A,J]

Sage, A. P., "A Methodological Framework for Systemic Design and Evaluation of Computer Aids for Planning and Decision Support," *Computers and Electrical Engineering,* Vol. 8, No. 2, pp. 87–102, 1981b. [A,G]

Sage, A. P., "Methodological Considerations in the Design of Large Scale Systems Engineering Processes," in Y. Y. Haimes, (Ed.), *Large Scale Systems,* North Holland, Amsterdam, pp. 99–141, 1982. [A]

Sage, A. P., *Economic Systems Analysis: Microeconomics for Systems Engineering, Engineering Management, and Project Selection,* North Holland, New York, Amstderdam, 1983. [A,G]

Sage, A. P. (Ed.), *System Design for Human Interaction,* IEEE Press, New York 1987a. [A,C,J]

Sage, A. P., "Knowledge Transfer: An Innovative Role for Information Engineering Education," *IEEE Transactions on Systems, Man and Cybernetics,* Vol. 17, No. 5, pp. 725–728, September 1987b. [A]

Sage, A. P. (Ed.), *Concise Encyclopedia of Information Processing in Systems and Organizations,* Pergamon Press, Oxford, UK, 1989. [J]

Sage, A. P., and Melsa, J. L., *System Identification,* Academic Press, New York, 1971. [G]

Sage, A. P., Galing, B., and Lagomasino, A., "Methodologies for the Determination of Information Requirements for Decision Support Systems," *Large Scale Systems,* Vol. 5, No. 2, 1983, pp. 131–167, 1983. [A,K]

Schneider, R. J., "Prediction of Software Effort and Project Duration: Four New Formulas," *ACM SIGPLAN* Notes, pp. 49–59, July 1978. [G]

Schneider, R. J., "Prototyping Toolsets and Methodologies: User/Developer Sociology," *Proceedings of the 1987 IEEE International Conference on Systems Man and Cybernetics,* pp. 208–216, 1987. [E1]

Schneiderman, B., *Software Psychology: Human Factors in Computer and Information Systems,* Winthrop, Cambridge, MA, 1980. [J]

Schneiderman, B., *Designing the User Interface: Strategies for Effective Human–Computer Interaction,* Addison-Wesley, Reading, MA, 1987. [J]

Shere, K. D., *Software Engineering and Management,* Prentice-Hall, Englewood Cliffs, NJ, 1987. [C,I]

Shooman, M. L., *Software Engineering,* McGraw-Hill, New York, 1983. [C]

Simon, H. A., "From Substantive to Procedural Rationality," in *Method and Appraisal in Economics,* Spiro J. Latsis (Ed.), Cambridge University Press, New York, pp. 129–148, 1976. [J]

Smith, D., Klotik, G., and Westfold, S., "Research on Knowledge-based Software Environments at Kestrel Institute," *IEEE Transactions on Software Engineering,* Vol. 2, No. 2, pp. 1278–1295, November 1985. [L]

Smoliar, S. W., "Operational Requirements Accommodation in Distributed System Design," *IEEE Transactions on Software Engineering,* Vol. SE-7, No. 6, pp. 531–537, November 1981. [D2,K]

Software Products and Services, Inc., "EPOS Overview," Software Products and Services, NY, 1986. [L,N]

Sommerville, I., *Software Engineering,* 2nd ed., Addison-Wesley, Reading, MA, 1989. [D,C]

Sommerville, I. (Ed.), *Software Engineering Environments,* IEE Computing Series Vol. 7, Peter Peregrinus, UK, 1986. [L]

Stefik, M., Foster, G., Bobrow, D. G., Kahn, K., Lanning, S., and Suchman, L., "Beyond the Chalkboard: Computer Support for Collaboration and Problem Solving in Meetings," *Communications of the ACM,* Vol. 30, No. 1, pp. 32–47, January 1987. [I,K]

Stenning, V., "On The Role of An Environment," *Proceedings of the 9th International Conference on Software Engineering,* pp. 30–34, March 1987. [L]

Strelich, T., "The Software Life Cycle Support Environment (SLCSE): A Computer Based Framework for Developing Software Systems," in *Proceedings of the ACM SIGSOFT/SIGPLAN Software Engineering Symposium on Practical Software Development Environments,* P. Henderson (Ed.), Software Engineering Notes, Vol. 13, No. 5, November 1988. [B,L]

Swartout, W., and Balzer, R., "On the Inevitable Intertwining of Specification and Implementation," *Communications of the ACM,* Vol. 25, No. 7, pp. 438–440, July 1982. [B,K]

Symons, C. R., "Function Point Analysis, Difficulties and Improvements," *IEEE Transactions on Software Engineering,* Vol. SE-14, No. 1, pp. 2–10, January 1988. [G]

Taggart, W. M., and Tharp, M. O., "A Survey of Information Requirements Analysis Techniques," *Computing Surveys,* Vol. 9, No. 4, pp. 273–290, 1977. [K]

Tausworthe, R. C., *Standardized Development of Computer Software,* Prentice-Hall, Englewood Cliffs, NJ, 1979. [C]

Taylor, T., and Standish, T., "Initial Thoughts on Rapid Prototyping Techniques," *ACM SIGSOFT Software Engineering Notes,* Vol. 7, No. 5, pp. 160–166, December 1982. [E1]

Teichroew, D., "A Survey of Languages for Stating Requirements for Computer Based Information Systems," *Proceedings AFIPS National Computer Conference,* Vol. 41, pp. 1203–1224, 1972. [K]

Teichroew, D., and Hershey, E. A., PSL/PSA: "A Computer Aided Technique for Structured Documentation and Analysis of Information Processing Systems," *IEEE Transactions on Software Engineering,* Vol. SE-3, No. 1, pp. 41–48, January 1977. [D1.3]

Teledyne Brown Engineering, "TAGS Overview," *Teledyne Brown Engineering,* Huntsville, AL, 1987. [N]

Thayer, R. H. (Ed.), *Software Engineering Project Management,* IEEE Computer Society Press, Silver Spring, MD, 1987. [I]

Thebaut, S. M., and Shen, V. Y., "An Analytic Resource Model for Large-scale Software Development," *Information Processing and Management,* Vol. 20, No. 1–2, pp. 293–315, 1984. [G,I]

Tracz, W. (Ed.), "Special Issue on Reuaability," *IEEE Software,* Vol. 4, No. 4, July 1987. [E2]

Tracz, W., "Software Reuse Myths," *ACM SIGSOFT, Software Engineering Notes,* January 1988. [E2]

Van Leer, P., "Top Down Development Using a Program Design Language," *IBM Systems Journal,* Vol. 15, No. 2, pp. 155–170, 1976. [D.1]

von Neuman, J., and Morgenstern, O., *Theory of Games and Economic Behavior,* Princeton University Press, Princeton, NJ, 1953. [Historical, M]

von Winterfeldt, D., and Edwards, W., *Decision Analysis and Behavioral Research,* Cambridge University Press, Cambridge, 1986. [G]

Wallace, D. R., and Fujii, R. U., "Planning for Software Verification and Validation," *ACM SIGSOFT Software Engineering Notes,* Vol. 12, p. 37, April 1987. [G]

Wallace, R. H., Stockenberg, J. E., and Charette, R. N., *A Unified Methodology for Developing Systems,* McGraw-Hill, New York, 1987. [I]

Walston, C., and Felix, C., "A Method of Programming Measurement and Estimation," *IBM Systems Journal,* Vol. 10, No. 1, 1977. [G]

Warnier, J. D., *Logical Construction of Programs,* Van Nostrand, New York, 1977. [D1.3]

Wasserman, A. I. (Ed.), *Software Development Environments,* IEEE Computer Society Press, Silver Spring, MD, 1986. [B,I,L]

Wasserman, A. I., and Pircher, P. A., "A Graphical, Extensible Integrated Environment for Software Development," *ACM Sigplan Notices,* Vol. 22, No. 1, pp. 131–142 January 1987. [L]

Wasserman, A. I., Pircher, P. A., Shewmake, D. T., and Kersten, M. L., "Developing Interactive Information Systems with the User Software Engineering Methodology," *IEEE Transactions on Software Engineering,* Vol. SE-12, No. 2, pp. 326–345, 1986. [C]

Waters, R. C., "The Programmer's Apprentice: A Session with KBEmacs," *IEEE Transactions on Software Engineering,* Vol. 11, No. 11, pp. 1296–1320, November 1985. [E3]

Weick, K. E., *The Social Psychology of Organizing,* Addison-Wesley, Reading, MA, 1979. [I]

Weiderman, N. "Evaluating Software Development Environments," *Proceedings of the 9th International Conference on Software Engineering,* pp. 292–293, March 1987. [L]

Wile, D. S., "Program Developments: Formal Explanation of Implementations," *Communications of the ACM,* Vol. 26, No. 11, pp. 902–911, November 1983. [D2]

Wirth, N., "Program Development by Stepwise Refinement," *Communications of the ACM,* Vol. 14, No. 4, pp. 221–227, 1971. [A]

Wirth, N., *Algorithms + Data Structures = Programs,* Prentice-Hall, Englewood Cliffs, NJ, 1976. [C,D]

Wolverton, R. W., "The Cost of Developing Large-scale Software," *IEEE Transactions on Computers,* Vol. C-23, No. 6, pp. 615–636, 1974. [G]

Yadav, B. B., "Determining an Organizations Information Requirements: A State of the Art Survey," *Database,* pp. 3–20, Spring 1983. [K]

Yau, S. S., and Tsai, J. J. P., "A Survey of Software Design Techniques," *IEEE Transactions on Software Engineering,* Vol. 12, No. 6, pp. 713–721, June 1986. [D]

Yeh, R. T., "Requirements Analysis—A Management Perspective," *Proceedings COMSPAC '82,* pp. 410–416, 1982. [K]

Yeh, R., "Software Engineering," *IEEE Spectrum,* Vol. 21, No. 11, pp. 91–94, November 1983. [D]

Yeh, R. T., and Zave, P., "Specifying Software Requirements," *Proceedings of the IEEE,* Vol. 68, No. 9, pp. 1077–1085, September 1980. [K]

Yourdon, E., *Techniques of Program Structure and Design,* Prentice-Hall, Englewood Cliffs, NJ, 1975. [1.1.1]

Yourdon, E. N., *Managing the System Life Cycle: A Software Development Methodology Overview,* Yourdon Press, New York, 1982, 2nd ed., 1988. [C,B,D]

Zave, P. "An Operational Approach to Requirements Specification for Embedded Systems," *IEEE Transactions on Software Engineering,* Vol. SE-8, No. 3, pp. 250–269, May 1982. [K]

Zave, P., "The Operational Versus the Conventional Approach to Software Development," Communications of the ACM, Vol. 27, No. 2, pp. 104–118, February 1984. [A,B,C]

Zave, P., and Schell, W., "Salient Features of an Executable Specification Language and Its Environment," *IEEE Transactions on Software Engineering,* Vol. 12, No. 2, pp. 312–325, February 1986. [D]

Zelkowitz, M. V., "Perspectives on Software Engineering," *ACM Computing Surveys,* Vol. 10, No. 2, pp. 197–216, 1987a. [A]

Zelkowitz, M. V., *Selected Reprints in Software,* IEEE Computer Society Press, Silver Spring, MD, 1987b. [C]

Zvegintzov, Nicholas, "Tools for Software Maintenance," *Proceedings of the Software Maintenance Workshop,* IEEE Computer Society Press, Silver Spring, MD, pp. 66–70, 1984. [F]

Index

This is combined author and subject index. Only the first page for subject entries appears, regardless of whether the associated discussion is completed on that page. We do not list page numbers for author entries that are in the bibliography since it is a simple matter to find author listings there.